I0622898

STATE INCOME TAXATION

Clara Penniman is Oscar Rennebohm Professor of Public Administration at the Center for the Study of Public Policy and Administration, University of Wisconsin, Madison. With Walter W. Heller, she is co-author of *State Income Tax Administration* (1959), one of the first books on the subject.

Clara Penniman

STATE INCOME TAXATION

THE JOHNS HOPKINS UNIVERSITY PRESS

Baltimore and London

 Printed in the United States of America.

The Johns Hopkins University Press, Baltimore, Maryland 21218
The Johns Hopkins Press Ltd., London
Library of Congress Catalog Card Number 79-20081
ISBN 0-8018-2290-4

Library of Congress Cataloging in Publication data will be found on the last printed page of this book.

Contents

Tables

Charts

Foreword

With this study, Clara Penniman in a sense completes a research Odyssey that began forty years ago. In 1939-40, as a Social Science Research Fellow —"using a suitcase and a 1937 Plymouth as primary research equipment," as the late Harold Groves put it—I conducted field studies of some thirty-three state and provincial income taxes and based my Ph.D. disseration on them in 1941. Sate income taxation was already forty years old by then, but still a sapling in the state tax forest. It accounted for only 9% of state tax revenues.

By the mid-fifties, when Clara Penniman, to my delight, turned her interests and keen research hand to the same field, the income tax was coming up in the state tax world. The Public Administration Service saw fit to publish our joint effort as *State Income Tax Administration.* When that volume appeared in 1959, the state income tax was producing 18% of total state tax revenues.

And now the state income tax has really come of age. Forty-five states are raising 35% of their tax revenues from this source. With rate structures that are generally more sharply progressive than the federal income tax, states have found that inflation, coupled with economic growth, has turned the *individual* income tax into a money machine. Thus, in addition to its traditional attraction as the fairest tax, the income tax has also assumed the role of potent state revenue producer.

All the more reason, then, that states should look to their income tax laurels, both in structure and in administration. Resources devoted to improving the income tax and its administration will yield a high rate of return, a high benefit-to-cost ratio.

In this undertaking, Professor Penniman's book can show the way. Going beyond the broad purpose of providing an informed and analytical view of the state income tax movement, Clara Penniman has provided an invaluable guidebook for those who would improve and strengthen state income taxes and their administration. It will lead, in short, not just to a better understanding of state income taxes in today's world, but to better state income taxes in tomorrow's.

Walter W. Heller

Preface

In 1959 the Public Administration Service published the predecessor to this volume under the title *State Income Tax Administration* with the present author and Walter W. Heller as coauthors. The present volume draws heavily on that earlier book for the history of state income taxes and their administration; but like state income taxes and their administration in the subsequent years, it expands into areas judged nonexistent or insignificant earlier.

State income taxes took root in a dozen states before and during the World War I years. An additional dozen and a half states enacted state individual and corporation income taxes in 1929 and through the years of the Great Depression. By the end of World War II, twenty-nine states had both individual and corporation income taxes, Delaware had an individual income tax only, and three other states had corporation income taxes only. Fewer than ten states raised 30% or more of their state revenues from individual and corporation income taxes in 1959. The authors in the preface to *State Income Tax Administration,* however, anticipated growth: "Given the push of higher spending and the pull of its star performance as a growth tax, the state income tax has entered what appears to be a new phase of vigorous expansion." Growth has indeed been a major characteristic of state income taxes in the intervening years. Today forty-five states have either a broad-based individual income tax or a corporation income tax or both. In fiscal 1978, not only did combined corporate and individual income taxes rank number one among state taxes as revenue producers, but thirty states raised 30% or more of their state revenues in this fashion.

Implementation, administration, enforcement, execution—either as synonyms for the same activity or as slightly different elements in the function of carrying out the intent of the legislative body—remain key issues in state income taxation. Economists, lawyers, accountants, and policy-makers generally devise more and more sophisticated model income tax statutes to meet the demands of individuals or groups. Legislative bodies pass some version of the model proposed. And the assumption follows that such policies, placed on the statute books, will be carried out. *Unfortunately, collecting the taxes in accordance with existing statutory provisions remains today, as in 1959 and in 1911, when the first modern state income tax statute was passed, the difficult practical application of the theories embodied in the laws.* Administration, like medical practice, continues to be in large part an art. Every income tax state today collects substantial revenue under its statute, yet every income tax state could collect more revenue and thereby provide more equity than it does.

The states differ in the degree to which administration is an institutionally limiting factor in the equitable enforcement of their income tax laws. The present volume attempts to point up some of these differences and especially some of the standards for grading state efforts. It does not rank the states on a scale of full and equitable income tax collection, nor does it fully separate administrative flaws, reflecting statutory complexity and legislative unwillingness to provide sufficient resources, from tax department and legislative ineptitude. Nevertheless, these issues are touched upon and the book should provide a foundation for subsequent investigation by interested scholars.

The book begins with a history of the development, expansion, and productivity of income taxes among the states. Chapter 2 looks generally at the major policy characteristics of income tax statutes and at the legal administrative tools provided. Chapter 3 examines patterns of administrative organization and chapter 4 considers management resources for enforcement. The next four chapters (5, 6, 7, 8) describe steps in processing returns, collecting taxes, and auditing and examining individual and corporation returns. Chapter 9 takes up the very important topic of intergovernmental relations and income tax administration—both federal-state relations and interstate relations that aid enforcement or make it more difficult. Along with computers and payroll withholding, intergovernmental relations has been an area of great development in the last two decades. Finally, in chapter 10, the author attempts to tie some of the threads together from the preceding chapters and to look into the future.

It is hoped that these ten chapters will provide economists, political scientists, and all others interested in tax policies some understanding of income tax administration. It is also hoped that experienced and inexperienced tax administrators as well as lawmakers will find here a ready reference on administrative issues in the income tax field.

The author's debts are numerous. The Oscar Rennebohm Foundation (Madison) fully supported the author's time and resource needs throughout the writing of this book. State tax administrators whom the author visited gave generously of their time not only once but, in the case of California, New York, and Wisconsin, on repeated visits. Hence Martin Huff, William Craven, Daniel Smith, and others in their agencies deserve special thanks.

Many administrators answered detailed letter inquiries from time to time. Every one of the forty-five income tax states' administrators answered the author's lengthy questionnaire. Both Charles Conlon and Leon Rothenberg at the Federation of Tax Administrators gave advice and encouragement over the period of research and writing. Three graduate research assistants helped collect the enormous amount of detail needed for the study: Jerome Johnson, Dennis Affholter, and Richard Kester. Several colleagues at the University of Wisconsin, especially Willim H. Young, have added advice and encouragement over the years. Without the 1959 study and all the support for the writing of a follow-up volume, the present book would not have materialized. Appreciation is extended to all.

Finally, I am indebted to Marilyn Henry for her excellent typing of the manuscript.

For any errors, I must bear the blame.

STATE INCOME TAXATION

Chapter One

The Income Tax in the State Setting

State income taxes occupy an extraordinarily different space in the state tax picture today than they did two decades ago. In 1958, thirty-one states had a broad-based individual income tax, two had limited individual income taxes, and thirty-five had a corporate income tax.[1] Today forty-one states have a broad-based individual income tax, three have a limited individual income tax, and forty-four have a corporation income tax (table 1). Only five states have neither an individual nor a corporate income tax. In 1958, none of the states in the industrial belt—Pennsylvania, Ohio, Indiana, Michigan, and Illinois—had an individual income tax, and only Pennsylvania had a corporate income tax. In less than fifteen years thereafter, all of these industrial states had adopted individual and corporation income or franchise (measured by income) taxes, although Michigan repealed its corporation income tax in 1975 when it combined all its business taxes in a value-added tax it designated "a single business tax."

In 1958, state income taxes (individual and corporate combined) raised $2.5 billion, or 17.5% of total state tax revenue. In 1978, state income taxes produced $39.8 billion in state tax revenue, or 35.2% of total tax receipts, almost sixteen times as much money and more than double the percentage of twenty years earlier (table 2). State income taxes—in their individual and corporate forms—have been the number one source of state tax revenue in each of the last five years.[2] Whether individual and corporation income taxes will maintain their present first-place ranking depends both on the economy and on future state tax policies. Certainly the combined effects of more income tax states, more individuals in the labor market,

[1]Included in the thirty-one broad-based individual income tax states are Alaska and Hawaii, which were not yet states in 1958. The District of Columbia also had, and has, an individual and corporation income tax. New Hampshire and Tennessee taxed (and still tax) only interest and dividends.

[2]The number one ranking of individual and corporation income taxes combined separates gross receipts and excise taxes, a "goulash," from the readily identifiable general sales tax.

TABLE 1
State Individual and Corporate Income Taxes
in Effect December 31, 1978, by Type and Date of Adoption

State	*Individual income tax*	*Corporation income taxes*	
		Net income tax	*Excise or franchise*
Alabama	1933	1933	
Alaska[a]	1959	1959	
Arizona	1933	1933	
Arkansas	1929	1929	
California	1935	1937	1929
Colorado	1937	1937	
Connecticut	1969[b]		1915
Delaware	1917	1957	
D.C.	1939		1939
		(Also taxes unincorporated businesses)	
Florida	None		1971
Georgia	1929	1929	
Hawaii[a]	1959	1959	
Idaho	1931	1931	—[c]
Illinois	1969	1969	
Indiana	1963[d]	1963	
Iowa	1934	1934	
Kansas	1933	1933	
Kentucky	1936	1936	
Louisiana	1934	1934	
Maine	1969	1969	
Maryland	1937	1937	
Massachusetts	1916[e]		1919
Michigan	1967	(1967 corporate income tax repealed in 1975)	
Minnesota	1933	1933	1933
Mississippi	1912	1921	
Missouri	1917	1917	
Montana	1933	—[f]	1917
Nebraska	1967	1967	1967
Nevada	None	None	None
New Hampshire	1923[g]	1970	
New Jersey	1976		1958
New Mexico	1933	1933	
New York	1919		1917
		(Also taxes unincorporated businesses)	
North Carolina	1921	1921	
North Dakota	1919	1919	
Ohio	1971		1971
Oklahoma	1915	1931	
Oregon	1930	1955	1929
Pennsylvania	1971[d]	1951	1935
Rhode Island	1971	1947	
South Carolina	1922	1922	
South Dakota	(Depression income taxes repealed within a few years)		
Tennessee	1931[g]	1923	
Texas	None	None	None
Utah	1931	—[f]	1931
Vermont	1931	1931	
Virginia	1961	1915	

TABLE 1—*Continued*

State	*Individual income tax*	*Corporation income taxes* — *Net income tax*	*Corporation income taxes* — *Excise or franchise*
Washington	None	None	None
West Virginia	1961	1967 (Depression income taxes repealed shortly thereafter and after a lapse reenacted)	
Wisconsin	1911	1911	1965
Wyoming	None	None	None

Source: U.S., Advisory Commission on Intergovernmental Relations, *Federal-State-Local Finances: Significant Features of Fiscal Federalism, 1976-77,* vol. 2, *Revenue and Debt* (Washington, D.C.: Government Printing Office, March, 1977), table 66, pp. 99-100.

[a]Both Alaska and Hawaii had individual and corporate income taxes when they were admitted to the Union in 1959.

[b]Taxes only capital gains and dividends.

[c]Franchise tax later added to corporate net income tax.

[d]Flat-rate income tax.

[e]Classified income tax.

[f]Net income tax later added to corporate franchise tax measured by income.

[g]Taxes only interest and dividends.

increasing wages and salaries, economic growth, and inflation have wrought near miracles in the productivity of state income taxes in the 1970s.[3]

Improved administration has further contributed to productivity. Every income tax state except North Dakota utilizes general payroll withholding, which brings in most taxes due on wages and salaries.[4] The Internal Revenue Service (IRS) has extended its cooperation to all the states and has made many more services available than existed in 1958. About half of the states with a corporation income tax have joined the Multistate Tax Commission in order to obtain corporation income (and sales) tax auditing on a joint basis. Many states have found the computer an enormous aid in matching returns with the state's own master list and with the IRS master list, in arithmetic verification, and in audit selection, billing, etc.

The number one national revenue ranking of individual and corporation income taxes reflects the position of these taxes in many but not all of the states. Wisconsin and a few other states that adopted income taxes before the Great Depression gave income taxes first place among their state revenues early. Yet in a majority of the states, it took decades to win acceptance of the income tax as a policy choice and to develop individual and corporate income taxes somewhat near their potential for raising revenue.

[3]The very success of the income tax in bringing increased collections may, however, have encouraged erosion of the tax base by leading to legislative acceptance of numerous claims to exempt income or to increase the number of deductions (see chapter 2).

[4]Connecticut, New Hampshire, and Tennessee, which do not tax wage and salary income, have no withholding.

TABLE 2
Productivity of Individual and Corporation Income Taxes and General Sales Taxes for Selected Years

Year	(1) Total state tax revenue (million $)	(2) Individual income taxes (million $)	(3) Corporation income taxes (million $)	(4) Total income taxes (million $)	(5) Ratio of income to total state taxes (%)	(6) General sales taxes (million $)	(7) Ratio of general sales to total (%)
1922[a]	947	43	58	101	10.7	—	—
1927[a]	1,608	70	92	162	10.1	—	—
1932[a]	1,890	74	79	153	8.1	7	0.4
1936[a]	2,618	153	113	266	10.2	364	13.9
1942[a]	3,903	249	269	518	13.3	632	16.2
1946[a]	4,937	389	442	831	16.8	899	18.2
1952[a]	9,857	913	838	1,851	18.8	2,229	22.6
1957[a]	14,531	1,563	984	2,547	17.5	3,373	23.2
1962[a]	20,561	2,728	1,308	4,036	19.6	5,111	24.9
1967[a]	31,926	4,909	2,227	7,136	22.4	8,923	28.0
1970[a]	47,962	9,183	3,738	12,921	26.9	14,177	29.6
1971[b]	51,541	10,153	3,424	13,577	26.3	15,473	30.0
1972[b]	59,870	12,996	4,416	17,412	29.1	17,619	29.4
1973[b]	68,069	15,587	5,425	21,012	30.9	19,793	29.1
1974[b]	74,207	17,078	6,015	23,093	31.1	22,612	30.5
1975[b]	80,155	18,819	6,642	25,461	31.8	24,780	30.9
1976[b]	89,256	21,448	7,273	28,721	32.2	27,333	30.6
1977[c]	101,026	25,453	9,187	34,640	34.3	30,870	30.6
1978[d]	113,142	29,088	10,717	39,805	35.2	35,229	31.1

[a]Columns 1, 2, 3, and 6, for the years indicated, from U.S., Department of Commerce, Bureau of the Census, *Historical Statistics of the United States, Colonial Times to 1970,* bicentennial ed., pt. 2 (Washington, D.C.: Government Printing Office, 1975), p. 1129.

[b]Columns 1, 2, 3, and 6 from U.S., Department of Commerce, Bureau of the Census, *State Government Finances in 1971* (Washington, D.C.: Government Printing Office, 1972), table 7; see also the same report for the years 1972, 1973, 1974, 1975, and 1976.

[c]Columns 1, 2, 3, and 6 from U.S., Department of Commerce, Bureau of the Census, *Tax Collections in 1977,* "Government Finances," no. 1 (Washington, D.C.: Government Printing Office, 1978), table 3.

[d]U.S., Department of Commerce, Bureau of the Census, *State Government Tax Collections in 1978,* ser. GF-78, no. 1 (Washington, D.C.: Government Printing Office, 1978), table A, p. 1.

CHART 1
State Tax Revenue and State Income Tax Revenue (Corporation and Individual)—Graph for Selected Years

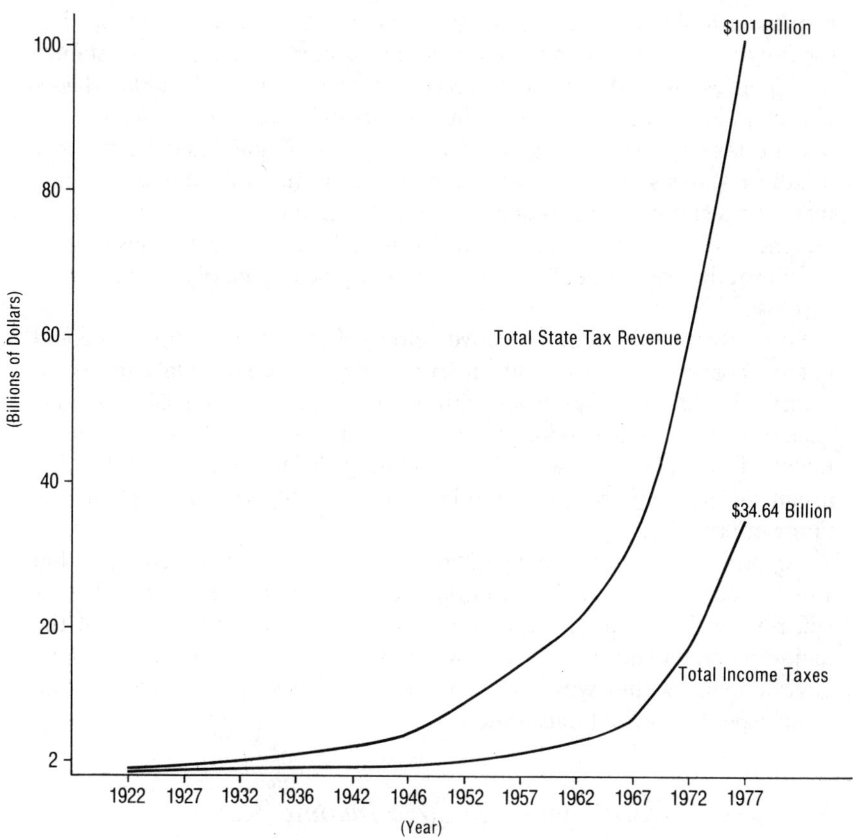

The current productivity of income taxes follows more than a half-century of rising state expenditures and attempts to meet growing budgets with a variety of sales taxes, other taxes, and state lotteries. At the beginning of the twentieth century, states were just starting to take on the manifold responsibilities that would require more and higher taxes to raise the necessary revenues. Automobiles required more and better highways. An industrial economy necessitated more educated workers as well as numerous social services to assist citizens in the impersonal urban setting. The possibility of widespread economic hardship required increasing governmental services, as later population growth and affluence brought demands for greater volume and improved quality of public services.

In 1900, Progressives, Populists, Socialists, and other "liberal" political activists looked at American society and saw vast and increasing wealth, great disparities in its distribution, and many unmet public needs that only active state governments with greater revenues could meet. Many of these reformers hesitated to advocate state income taxes because of the historically poor record of income tax administration by a number of states.[5] Tax policies, like other policies, require implementation. In 1900, Massachusetts still had its old law providing for "ability" taxes—a precursor of the income tax—as part of its general property tax. Virginia and a few other Southern states still collected some revenue on the basis of decentralized income tax statutes with colonial or confederate roots.[6] None of these state income taxes produced significant revenue, however. In the absence of administrative tools for collection, the philosophical value of taxing incomes was lost.

Formerly tolerable administrative defects of older income tax laws could not be borne by America's twentieth-century economy. Only under an agrarian-based economy—where citizen administrators and neighbors knew each other well enough to judge income—could collections have reasonably matched taxes legally owed. In a rapidly growing, complex, industrial-urban society, more sophisticated income tax legislation and implementation were required.

To provide a fuller understanding of the general state setting within which income tax administration operates, the remainder of this chapter will review the adoption of state income taxes, summarize some of the major characteristics of present laws, consider the political and economic environments within which state income tax laws operate, and outline some aspects of tax administration.

Development of State Income Taxes

CHRONOLOGY

Adoption

Wisconsin. Before the Sixteenth Amendment to the U.S. Constitution cleared sufficient state legislatures to permit twentieth-century adoption of a national income tax, Wisconsin, at the height of its political progressivism, enacted the first modern state income tax in 1911. This 1911 statute included

[5]For a brief account of the fascinating attempt of the national government in 1798 to levy a property tax on a progressive basis, see Lee Soltow, "America's First Progressive Tax," *National Tax Journal* 30 (March, 1977): 53-58.

[6]For the pre-1911 history of the income tax, see the first chapter of Clara Penniman and Walter W. Heller, *State Income Tax Administration* (Chicago: Public Administration Service, 1959).

three critical provisions that were not in earlier state laws: (1) business could deduct payroll costs as expenses *only if information returns* for each individual worker were filed (and the same applied to deductions for dividends, interest payments, etc.); (2) employees of county tax offices would be hired through *a state merit system;* (3) *the state,* not the counties, *controlled and directed* the county tax offices. If we add the provisions for withholding or "pay as you go" that would result from the experience of the national government in World War II, we have identified four of the major administrative provisions of any income tax statute down to the present time. Without centralized control, competent personnel, and a means to compel information returns from payers, plus current payments from income earners when taxes are high, no income tax could succeed today. These provisions alone do not guarantee success, but no income tax statute will be effectively administered without them. They dramatize the role of imaginative and knowledgeable individuals who are conscious of practical roadblocks to successful policy implementation.[7]

Other Early Income Tax States. Before 1920 New York and Massachusetts, together with several states of less wealth and industry, enacted tax laws based on the incomes of individuals and corporations (see table 1). Both Massachusetts and New York enacted corporation franchise taxes based on net income rather than a corporation net income tax like Wisconsin's. In the area of personal income taxation, these two states appear more responsible than Wisconsin for the subsequent general pattern of state income tax organization. They used the raw materials that Wisconsin had proved were essential to administrative success, but they recast them into a more centralized mold. Massachusetts at first followed Wisconsin's system of administering the personal income tax through district offices, but it abandoned this method shortly in favor of centralization of all returns and authority in Boston, combined with decentralization of services through ten branch offices. When New York copied the revised Massachusetts system in 1919, the pattern for most states was set: centralized files, auditing activities, and control; decentralized services to the extent that administrative funds would allow. Not until the 1960s did Wisconsin centralize to this extent, although it long before consolidated its county offices into four district offices.

By 1930, a total of eighteen states had adopted corporate or individual income taxes. The expenditure burdens of the Depression forced many other states to add new state taxes. In those difficult years, fifteen of the states and the District of Columbia chose either the individual or corpora-

[7]In Wisconsin, economics professors John R. Commons and Henry C. Adams played major roles in securing passage of the 1911 law with its critical administrative provisions. In 1943, Beardsley Ruml led the successful effort to achieve pay-as-you-go or payroll withholding for the federal income tax.

tion income tax (usually both). Although Illinois, Indiana, Michigan, Ohio, Washington, and Wyoming voted to adopt only sales taxes during the Depression, the other fifteen states that adopted sales taxes in those years either already had income taxes, adopted them with the sales tax, or added them during a subsequent legislative session.[8] For many states, dire fiscal straits required more revenue at almost any cost. Adoption of income *and* sales taxes represented both political and fiscal expediency. By the year 1939, less than half (fourteen) of the thirty-three income tax states had weathered the Depression without adopting a sales tax.

The Post-World War II Period. The prosperity of the forties and fifties slowed the growth of additional taxes as current tax systems in many states generated revenue to meet increasing expenditures. Three states—Delaware (1957), New Jersey (1958), and Rhode Island (1947)—added corporation income taxes. In the sixties and seventies expenditure demands surpassed the productivity of most state tax systems. Six more states (plus Alaska and Hawaii, which had come into the Union with both personal and corporation income taxes) adopted individual and corporation income taxes. West Virginia readopted personal and corporation income taxes after a lapse of twenty years. New Jersey, Pennsylvania, and Rhode Island added personal income taxes to their older corporate ones. And New Hampshire (1970) and Florida (1971) adopted corporation, but not individual, income taxes.

Just as sales tax states adopted income taxes, so hitherto stalwart income tax states such as Massachusetts, Minnesota, New York, and Wisconsin adopted sales taxes in the sixties and seventies.[9] The earlier, sharper division between sales and income tax states blurred as only Alaska, Delaware, Montana, New Hampshire, and Oregon continued to avoid a general sales tax. In the Midwest, Indiana adopted income taxes in 1963; Michigan adopted them in 1967 (but repealed the corporation income tax in 1975) after having depended heavily on sales taxes since 1933; Illinois, which had also had a sales tax since 1933, adopted income taxes in 1969; and in 1971

[8]This figure excludes South Dakota and West Virginia, which added both sales and income taxes but after a few years repealed their income taxes (and were not counted in the fifteen new income tax states). West Virginia returned to income taxes in the 1960s, but without repealing its sales tax. South Dakota has a minor "corporation" income tax that applies only to banks.

[9]John Kenneth Galbraith's popular book, *The Affluent Society* (Boston: Houghton Mifflin, 1958), helped convince many liberals to accept the less philosophically congenial sales tax as the price of higher public expenditures. The rising incomes of liberal intellectuals may also have eased this transformation of support from increasing income taxes to accepting sales taxes. In any event, despite the increase in the number of states using income taxes, the overall pattern of regressivity in state and local taxes in 1950 has changed little. See Joseph A. Pechman and Benjamin A. Okner, *Who Bears the Tax Burden?* (Washington, D.C.: The Brookings Institution, 1974). The "new" theories of property tax incidence may reduce the subsequent regressivity findings without bringing about any actual changes in state-local tax patterns.

Ohio added income taxes to its older 1934 sales tax. Indiana, Illinois, and Michigan chose low-rate, proportional individual income taxes. Pennsylvania, bordering the Midwest and part of the belt of industrial states, also added a flat-rate personal income tax to its older corporation income tax.

Non-Income Tax States

In 1979 six states still lacked corporate income taxes (whether net income, franchise, or excise) and six states lacked any individual income taxes, with or without progressive rate structures.[10] Constitutional barriers explain only partially the absence of income taxes in these states.[11]

The hard core of the non-income tax states includes Nevada, South Dakota, Texas, Washington, and Wyoming, which have neither an individual nor a corporate income tax. Apart from the fact that all these states are west of the Mississippi, no easily discernible measures of wealth, industry, degree of urbanization, or political competition differentiate them from other states east and west of the Mississippi that have both individual and corporation income taxes. Whatever might be considered different in Nevada's combination of characteristics is not widely shared by any of the other non-income tax states. Adding on to the list the other states that either lack a broad individual income tax or a corporation income tax—five states east of the Mississippi—only confounds any possible geographic explanation. And designation of the non-income tax states as more politically conservative than any of the income tax states can be justified only if conservatism is defined as the absence of an income tax and greater dependence on a sales tax!

IMPORTANCE OF REVENUE

Not only has the entrance of new income tax states increased the proportion of revenues raised by income taxes, but both general income growth and inflation have raised the base of taxable incomes. Table 2 provides a summary of the amount of taxes raised by the states, the amount

[10]The six states without corporation income taxes in 1979 were Michigan, Nevada, South Dakota, Texas, Washington, and Wyoming. The six states without individual income taxes were Florida, Nevada, South Dakota (which did have both a corporation and individual income tax for a few years in the 1930s), Texas, Washington, and Wyoming. As I have already noted, Connecticut, New Hampshire, and Tennessee levy an individual income tax on only a few types of income.

[11]An analysis, now almost fifteen years old, found no barriers in the constitutions of South Dakota or Texas to either individual or corporation income taxes. Neither is there a barrier to a corporation income tax in Michigan, which had one from 1965 until 1975. Florida and Tennessee do bar general income taxes on individuals; and Nevada, Washington, and Wyoming appear to prohibit progressive individual income taxes. See U.S. Advisory Commission on Intergovernmental Relations, *Federal-State Coordination of Personal Income Taxes* (Washington, D.C.: Government Printing Office, 1965).

of income taxes collected, and the growth of these taxes as a ratio of total state taxes for selected years. The table shows the relatively low role of income taxes prior to World War II and the slow growth even afterward, until the sixties. By the seventies the tax had reached its number one standing among taxes levied by the fifty states.

Growth Trend

The gain in stature of the income tax in state revenue systems cannot be ascribed wholly to active policy decisions. Revenues from progressive income taxes automatically grow with growth in national income. On the one hand, the tax base responds directly to the growth in income. On the other hand, the aggregate effective ratio of total tax liabilities to total net income automatically increases more rapidly than income as income levels rise above exemption levels and push into higher tax brackets.[12] Wisconsin, in a much earlier period, provided a striking illustration of the increased revenue productivity of a progressive income tax in good times with essentially no rate changes:

> During the trend cyclical period from 1933 to 1951, tax returns increased 10 times; income assessed and tax yields increased 20 times; while state income payments increased only 5 times and the state population increase was relatively negligible.[13]

Continued growth and inflation have permitted half of the states with an income tax at the end of World War II to leave their tax rate structures essentially untouched and still enjoy the bounty of increasing revenues. When one considers that the legislators in most of these states have in the same years increased the available itemized deductions, income exclusions, and tax credits or rebates, the increased productivity of the income tax would truly amaze any earlier observer.

Several income tax states additionally have made a number of changes in rates, income brackets, and individual exemptions in the last several decades. California, New York, and Virginia, among others, have utilized the income tax as a budget-balancing mechanism by granting adjustments

[12]Whereas the elasticity of the sales tax to income growth has recently been estimated at 1.00 or less, the elasticity of the individual income tax is usually estimated at 1.7 or even higher. The corporate income tax has shown an elasticity of about 1.00 or slightly higher. See U.S., Advisory Commission on Intergovernmental Relations, *Federal-State-Local Finances: Significant Features of Fiscal Federalism, 1976-77,* vol. 2, *Revenue and Debt* (Washington, D.C.: Government Printing Office, March, 1977), table 139, p. 254.

[13]Lee Soltow, "The Historic Rise in the Number of Taxpayers in a State with Constant Tax Law," *National Tax Journal* 8 (December, 1955): 379. Mr. Soltow prefaced the above statement as follows: "From 1933 to 1951 [Wisconsin's] exemption and rate schedules remained the same, a situation made possible by achieving flexibility through the use of surtaxes. The definition of taxable income remained essentially the same." This older citation illustrates the point well. There have been so many subsequent changes in Wisconsin law, as well as in the laws of other states, that a new calculation would involve great complexity without providing any greater confirmation.

or credits or by raising or lowering rates in successive legislative sessions to match anticipated tax yields with appropriations.

Stability

The graduated rate net income tax produces magnificently under conditions of economic growth and inflation, but it can fall rapidly during recession. Both its growth and its fall exceed that of the general sales tax or of a flat-rate income tax. Such is its nature, and all means to reduce swings—apart from maintaining a steady economy—reduce its progressivity and the presumed reason for its adoption. Since World War II, only a few years of recession have marred the general growth pattern in the country as a whole. With inflation added, the income tax has starred.

National Setting of State Income Taxes

National constitutional provisions, congressional legislation, and presidential and administrative policies provide the setting within which state income tax legislation must conform to overall national legal constraints and policies.[14] The U.S. Supreme Court determines the taxing jurisdiction of the states under the national constitution and congressional statutes. The 1970s are witnessing tension over national government "intrusion" into the state tax field. The expansion of multinational corporations has brought an increasing number of treaties and executive agreements that may more and more "interfere" with state corporation taxing powers. Congressional definitions of "privacy" could restrict state access to federal returns and records for enforcement purposes and even limit or eliminate state requirements that taxpayers attach copies of their federal income tax returns. Chapter 9 considers these issues.

The greatest single fact of political and economic consequence limiting reliance on state income taxes continues to be the commanding position of the federal government's income tax levels. Income tax opponents in every state have found the high federal exactions a rallying ground for opposition to state adoption of an income tax or to more steeply graduated state rates of an existing tax. Opponents may then turn around and push federal definitions, exclusions, or exemptions for state adoption when the federal law appears particularly advantageous to them.

But the barrier to the states of high federal progressive income taxes can be overdrawn. The deductibility of state taxes under the federal law insures against a confiscatory combination of federal and state income taxes, reduces the specter of interstate competition for the income tax states, and

[14]Discussion of cooperation and coordination between the IRS and state tax agencies will be postponed until chapter 9.

provides a type of subsidy or "general revenue sharing" for the states that choose to use income taxes. (The subsidy or "revenue sharing" is, of course, greater in the income tax states that do not provide a reciprocal deductibility for federal income taxes.)

INTERSTATE COMPETITION

Issues

Most states wish to maintain and possibly increase their relative position in terms of business activity. Few state tax studies omit emphasis on the relationship of the tax structure to the state's attractiveness for industry, even though most economic analyses and careful surveys regularly cast doubt on the priority given to taxes by business in decisions to locate or to remove plants.[15] Both New York and Ohio had severe economic problems in 1976. New York usually ranks first in state and local tax burdens, whereas Ohio is regularly in the lower forties in tax burden! Something other than taxes had been at work!

Taxes are without doubt important at the margins, but most business decisions appear to be made on the basis of other differences among the states that outweigh taxes. Moreover, federal deductibility of state income taxes sharply limits the net impact of either state corporation or individual income taxes. Whatever the facts, the fear of driving industry and wealth out of a state haunts legislators and voters. This fear frequently enables active business lobbyists to gain concessions from one state legislature by citing the positive advantage of being lowest, and then from another state legislature by emphasizing the advantages present in the first state over the second. Even the existence of income taxes in all but five of the states has not produced a moratorium on such pressures. Michigan in 1975 repealed its business taxes, including a corporation income tax, and substituted its single business tax—a form of value-added tax.[16] This action set off tremors in neighboring states, although the Michigan act was directly tailored to benefit its automobile industry, which is not a major enterprise elsewhere.

Jurisdiction

Individuals. State jurisdiction to tax individual incomes is fairly clear. The state in which an individual resides or maintains a domicile may tax his entire income, wherever in the country it is earned; the state of origin of

[15]For the latest study that indicates doubt as to the priority of taxes on residence or business location, see District of Columbia, Tax Revision Commission, *Financing an Urban Government* (Washington, D.C.: University of the District of Columbia, 1978), pp. 18, 19, and 47-51.

[16]For a description of Michigan's single business tax, see U.S., Advisory Commission on Intergovernmental Relations, *The Michigan Single Business Tax: A Different Approach to State Business Taxation* (Washington, D.C.: Government Printing Office, March, 1978).

incomes from unincorporated business, property, municipal bonds, and personal services may tax such incomes, regardless of location of the recipients. Within this jurisdictional framework, what incomes have states chosen to tax? The majority have taxed as fully as the courts allow, i.e., they tax residents on their entire net income from all sources and nonresidents on all income earned within the state. For example, New York, with its substantial commuting population from New Jersey and Connecticut, has sought a broad tax base that would include all income earned in the state. Thus, all income from New York sources (whether from personal services, property, or business) accruing to residents and nonresidents alike, plus income earned outside New York State by New York residents, is brought into the state's income tax base.

A few states still stop short of their legal potential by failing to tax nonresidents for at least some types of income earned in the state or by failing to tax residents on income from particular sources earned outside the state. It is still possible for a Minnesota resident to earn income from property located outside the state and be exempt from including such income in his state return to either state. Even if the state where such property is located has an income tax, such income might be exempt to a nonresident. The taxpayer could thus avoid paying taxes to either state on this property income. The same rules sometimes apply to businesses outside Minnesota. The state always taxes residents' income from intangibles and wages, wherever earned, as well as the property and business income of nonresidents earned in Minnesota. The possibility of arranging reporting and even withholding on residents' out-of-state personal service income, plus the ability to cross-check residents' federal returns, now aids each state in verifying the reporting of out-of-state income by its residents. Earlier administrative difficulties no longer need bar a state from its wider taxing range for residents.

State laws recognize hardships to taxpayers who have income from sources in more than one income tax state. States also recognize the opportunities for avoidance and evasion by citizens when one state has no income tax and another has a top rate of 15% or higher. Uniform adoption of the Minnesota taxing principle would reduce, if not eliminate, multiple state taxation but would leave room for avoidance.[17] New York's definition of tax jurisdiction reduces avoidance possibilities but requires tax crediting and reciprocity arrangements if serious multiple taxation is to be avoided.

[17] "Elimination" of multiple state taxation is too strong a term. Not only must the general definition of income tax jurisdiction be the same but subsidiary terms such as "residence" and "domicile" must have the same legal meaning in all states. Reciprocity and credit provisions thus continue to be significant. Chapter 9, which deals with interstate cooperation and coordination as administrative matters, will consider reciprocity in more detail.

So long as neither Connecticut nor New Jersey had an income tax, there was no problem. New York's general liberalness in crediting taxes paid to other states by residents and nonresidents alike took care of possible injustices elsewhere. However, when New Jersey adopted a commuter tax in 1961 that was aimed at New York residents earning income in New Jersey and New Jersey residents earning income in New York, New York, retaliated by allowing credits for income taxes paid to other states *only* to New York residents.[18]

Corporations. States are legally empowered to tax the entire income of resident corporations and the in-state income of nonresident corporations doing business within the state. In practice, however, no distinction is ordinarily made between resident and nonresident corporations; states limit their taxes to that part of the in-state corporation's net income which is "earned within the state." In other words, states do not interpret their effective jurisdiction to tax—in the light of political, economic, and administrative limitations and equity considerations—to be as broad as their constitutional jurisdiction.

Apportionment of income for the interstate corporation remains a vexing problem. Some forms of income (e.g., rents and dividends) are directly allocable to states according to the origin of the income or the domicile of the corporation. In some cases, separate accounting by states is possible. But the unitary nature of much interstate business creates a vast no man's land where apportionment is possible only by formula. The multiplication of business mergers and multinational organizations has magnified the problem. (Chapter 8 considers further the problem of taxing multistate and multinational corporations.)

DIFFERING STATE TAX ENVIRONMENTS

Economic Interests

Beyond the common legal, political, and other bonds of the nation within which each state makes decisions, the interaction of the state's own political, economic, and social environment and traditions affects its tax policies. Michigan restructured its business taxes in 1975 and eliminated its infant corporation income tax in response to the recession in its automobile industry. North Carolina has never found it desirable to tax tobacco heavily, nor has Wisconsin overtaxed its beer industry. California has repeatedly demonstrated sympathy for the movie industry when it has set tax policies. New York's omission of individual brokers or unincorporated brokerage firms under its unincorporated business tax provides still another example of favoring local economic activity.

The state's economic characteristics reinforce, or are reinforced by, its

[18]Again, see chapter 9 for a discussion of such laws.

political characteristics: the degree of party competition, the strength of the office of governor, the strength of legislative institutions, the traditions of clean government, or its opposite. All these—plus such characteristics as the level of education and its distribution, the distribution of income and wealth, and ethnic distribution—may influence tax politics and tax policies. Implementation of an income tax takes place within each state's environment and within the context of the political decisions that have emerged from these environments.

In this and the next chapter we will examine some of the *formal political decisions to enact an income tax,* as well as *the policies and administrative tools provided.* Then, after describing tax administration in the states in the succeeding chapters, we will attempt to relate the character of these political policy and implementation decisions to administrative processes.

Political Decisions

When legislatures adopt income taxes, they make a number of political decisions, and over the subsequent years they make many more that modify, strengthen, revise, or reverse their original decisions. All these decisions, as well as the politics of the decisions, may have a positive or negative effect on administrative achievement. In table 3 the states are rated on their "devotion" to the income tax in terms of early adoption, dependency or role of income taxes in the state tax picture, highest personal income tax rate, and date of adoption of a general sales tax (and the current rate), the other broad-based tax that often has competed with the income tax for initial adoption or as an alternative to higher rates and greater dependence on the income tax.[19] In table 4 the states are rated on their actions regarding the role of federal income taxes. State legislatures that adopted income taxes *before* adopting a general sales tax, and have continued to emphasize the former, express political preference for taxes based on the ability to pay. Subsequently we will consider, at least sketchily, the extent of statutory erosion over the decades.

In cases where a state legislature adopted the income tax shortly after a campaign for the appropriate constitutional amendment, or after a political campaign that centered on adoption of the income tax, or in a referendum after legislative adoption, we have evidence of the extent of general citizen support. In all adoptions we know the *formal vote* of the legislative houses and the attitude of the *governor.* The stronger the support shown by these indicators, the more we would expect a progressive, productive income tax with adequate administrative provisions.

Constitutional Provisions. The original thirteen state constitutions generally included broad authority for legislative action in levying taxes, and

[19]By 1960, only a few states, e.g., Nebraska and New Jersey, still used the property tax as a significant tax source for state government. By the 1970s, no states drew importantly on the property tax.

TABLE 3
State Ratings for Policy Decisions Indicating Support of Income Tax

State	Adoption of income tax (individual)[a]	Dependence on income tax (individual and corporation)[b]	Top income tax rate 1978 (individual)[c]	Sales tax		Total score
				Adoption[d]	Rate (1978)[e]	
Alaska	1	1	1	0	0	3
Alabama	2	5	3	4 (1936)	2	16
Arizona	2	5	3	4 (1933)	2	16
Arkansas	1	5	3	4 (1935)	1	14
California	2	3	2	4 (1933)	2	13
Colorado	2	4	3	4 (1935)	1	14
Connecticut	5	6	5	3 (1947)	4	23
Delaware	1	1	1	0	0	3
Florida	5	6	5	3 (1949)	2	21
Georgia	1	5	3	3 (1951)	1	13
Hawaii	1	5	2	4 (1935)	2	14
Idaho	2	2	3	2 (1965)	1	10
Illinois	3	5	4	4 (1933)	2	18
Indiana	3	5	4	4 (1933)	2	18
Iowa	2	4	3	4 (1933)	1	14
Kansas	2	4	3	4 (1937)	1	14
Kentucky	2	4	3	3 (1960)	3	15
Louisiana	2	5	3	4 (1938)	1	15
Maine	3	5	3	3 (1951)	3	17
Maryland	2	1	3	3 (1947)	3	12
Massachusetts	1	1	3	2 (1966)	3	10
Michigan	3	3	4	4 (1933)	2	16
Minnesota	2	1	1	2 (1967)	2	8
Mississippi	1	5	4	4 (1932)	3	17
Missouri	1	5	3	4 (1934)	2	15
Montana	2	2	2	0	0	6
Nebraska	3	5	3 (% of fed.)	2 (1967)	3	16

New Hampshire	5	6	5	0	0	16
New Jersey	4	5	4	2 (1966)	4	19
New Mexico	2	5	3	4 (1933)	2	16
New York	1	1	1	2 (1965)	2	7
North Carolina	1	1	3	4 (1933)	1	10
North Dakota	1	5	2	4 (1935)	1	13
Ohio	4	5	4	4 (1934)	2	19
Oklahoma	1	4	3	4 (1933)	1	13
Oregon	2	1	2	0	0	5
Pennsylvania	4	4	4	3 (1953)	4	19
Rhode Island	4	4	3 (% of fed.)	3 (1947)	4	18
South Carolina	1	5	3	3 (1951)	2	14
Tennessee	5	6	5	3 (1947)	2	21
Utah	2	5	3	4 (1933)	2	16
Vermont	2	2	3 (% of fed.)	2 (1969)	2	11
Virginia	1	1	3	2 (1966)	1	8
West Virginia	3	5	3	4 (1933)	2	17
Wisconsin	1	1	2	2 (1961)	2	8

[a]See table 1, pp. 0-0, for dates of adoption of the income tax.

Scoring: If broad individual income tax adopted by 1930, 1; if between 1930 and 1950, 2; if between 1950 and 1970, 3; if after 1970, 4; and if no individual income tax, 5.

[b]See table 4, pp. 00-00 for taxes raised by income and sales taxes for selected years.

Scoring: 1, where income tax productivity has consistently surpassed the general sales tax, if any, *and* income tax productivity (% of state tax revenues) has been in the upper quartile of the states in at least 3 of the 4 decennial years of 1947, 1957, 1967, 1977; 2, in at least 2 of the 4 decennial years; 3, where income tax productivity has surpassed the general sales tax at least since 1972 and state has been in the upper quartile of income tax states in at least 1 or 2 of the decennial years; 4, where income tax overtook the general sales tax in productivity by fiscal year 1978; 5, states with individual and corporation income taxes, but in which general sales tax has regularly been number one in productivity; 6, states with either a broad individual income tax or corporation income tax, but not both, and in which general sales tax has been number one in productivity (New Hampshire is an exception here, in that it has neither a broad-based individual income tax nor a sales tax).

[c]*Scoring:* 1, highest income tax rate is 14% or over; 2, highest income tax rate is between 10% and 14%; 3, highest income tax rate is between 5% and 10%; 4, highest rate is below 5%; 5, no broad-based personal income tax.

[d]*Scoring:* 4, sales tax adopted between 1930 and 1945; 3, adopted between 1946 and 1960; 2, adopted between 1961 and 1970; 1, adopted since 1970; 0, no sales tax.

[e]*Scoring:* 1, sales tax rate is less than 4%; 2, sales tax rate is 4% or 4.5%; 3, sales tax rate is 5% or 5.5%; 4, sales tax rate is 6% or above; 0, no sales tax.

TABLE 4
State Ratings on Policy Actions for Income Tax and the National Government

State	*Action on sixteenth amendment*[a]		*Sought constitutional convention to limit top national income tax rate to 25%*[b]		*Sought constitutional convention (or congressional) action to limit federal deficit spending (1970s)*[c]		*Total score*
Alabama	Approved	1	Yes*	2	Yes	3	6
Alaska	Not a state	1	No	1	No	1	3
Arizona	Approved	1	No	1	Yes	3	5
Arkansas	Approved	1	Yes*	2	No	1	4
California	Approved	1	No	1	Yes	3	5
Colorado	Approved	1	No	1	Yes	3	5
Connecticut	Rejected	4	No	1	No	1	6
Delaware	Approved	1	Yes	3	Yes	3	7
Florida	Rejected	4	Yes	3	Yes	3	10
Georgia	Approved	1	Yes	3	Yes	3	7
Hawaii	Not a state	1	No	1	No	1	3
Idaho	Approved	1	No	1	Yes	3	5
Illinois	Approved	1	Yes*	2	No	1	4
Indiana	Approved	1	Yes	3	Yes	3	7
Iowa	Approved	1	Yes*	2	No	1	4
Kansas	Approved	1	Yes	3	Yes	3	7
Kentucky	Approved	1	Yes*	2	Yes	3	6
Louisiana	Approved	1	Yes*	2	Yes	3	6
Maine	Approved	1	Yes*	2	No	1	4
Maryland	Approved	1	Yes	3	Yes	3	7
Massachusetts	Late approval	2	Yes*	2	No	1	5
Michigan	Approved	1	Yes	3	No	1	5
Minnesota	Approved	1	No	1	No	1	3
Mississippi	Approved	1	Yes	3	Yes	3	7
Missouri	Approved	1	No	1	No	1	3
Montana	Approved	1	No	1	No	1	3
Nebraska	Approved	1	Yes*	2	Yes	3	6
New Hampshire	Late approval	2	Yes	3	Yes	3	8
New Jersey	Approved	1	Yes*	2	No	3	6
New Mexico	Approved	1	Yes	3	Yes	3	7
New York	Approved	1	No	1	No	1	3
North Carolina	Approved	1	No	1	Yes	3	5
North Dakota	Approved	1	No	1	Yes	3	5
Ohio	Approved	1	No	1	No	1	3
Oklahoma	Approved	1	Yes	3	Yes	3	7
Oregon	Approved	1	No	1	Yes	3	5
Pennsylvania	Never acted	3	Yes	3	Yes	3	9
Rhode Island	Rejected	4	Yes*	2	No	1	7
South Carolina	Approved	1	No	1	Yes	3	5
Tennessee	Approved	1	Yes	3	Yes	3	7
Utah	Rejected	4	Yes	3	No	1	8
Vermont	Late approval	2	No	1	No	1	4
Virginia	Never acted	3	Yes	3	Yes	3	9
West Virginia	Approved	1	No	1	No	1	3
Wisconsin	Approved	1	Yes*	2	No	1	4

those Eastern states that entered the twentieth century with their old constitutions have generally not had to go through the lengthy process of amendment in order to adopt an income tax. Similarly, the constitutions of states that came into the Union in the twentieth century often provided for legislative enactment of income taxes (Arizona, 1912; Alaska, 1959; Hawaii, 1959; New Mexico, 1912; and Oklahoma, 1907). Territorial legislatures in both Alaska and Hawaii enacted income taxes before statehood, so inclusion in their new state constitutions was assured. In contrast, states that wrote their constitutions in the nineteenth century (especially in the middle years of that century) usually found it necessary to amend the typically restricted tax authorization to permit legislative enactment of an income tax. Whereas Rhode Island's constitution of 1843 (copied from the constitution of its Revolutionary period) read simply that the legislature "may provide for valuation of property and assessment of taxes," the 1870 Illinois constitution provided for taxes "proportional to value," and only the revised, 1966 Illinois constitution permitted income taxes.

At the beginning of the twentieth century, Populist-Progressive political philosophy captured the enthusiasm of enough voters and legislators in some of the states to secure enactment of a state income tax as well as approval by three-fourths of the states for the Sixteenth Amendment to the U.S. Constitution. Massachusetts (1916), New York (1919), and Wisconsin (1911) were early successes for Progressives seeking ability-to-pay taxation. Some states were brushed by the Progressive tax philosophy without adopting income tax legislation in those years. California made provision in a new constitution adopted in 1879, but waited until 1935 to enact individual income tax legislation (a corporation franchise tax had passed in 1929). In Ohio, voters approved a constitutional amendment in 1912 that permitted

TABLE 4—*Continued*

[a]State approval of the Sixteenth Amendment to the U.S. Constitution to permit levying of a national income tax taken from Roy G. Blakey and Gladys C. Blakey, *The Federal Income Tax* (New York: Longmans, Green, 1940), table 6, p. 69.

Scoring: 1, within the first 36 states to approve; 2, approved later; 3, never acted; 4, rejected.

[b]Between 1939 and 1959 the 27 states listed as "Yes" here and Wyoming passed resolutions (not always in identical form) seeking a constitutional convention to limit the national income tax rate to 25%. This so-called liberty amendment was subsequently rescinded by 12 states (those with asterisks). Information supplied by David C. Huckabee of the American National Government Division, Library of Congress, with a copy of the committee print of the Committee on the Judiciary, House of Representatives, January 30, 1959, *State Applications Asking Congress to Call a Federal Constitutional Convention.*

Scoring: 1, state never passed "Liberty Amendment,"; 2, passed, but later rescinded; 3, passed.

[c]During the 1970s, the National Taxpayers Union has sponsored a campaign for state legislatures either to request a constitutional convention to limit national deficit spending or to memorialize Congress to limit deficit spending. In one form or another, 28 states, the ones listed as "Yes" here plus Texas, Nevada, and Wyoming, have cleared such petitions. Apparently none has so far rescinded such action. Information supplied by David C. Huckabee, American National Government Division, Library of Congress, as of August 21, 1978, through a paper entitled "Constitutional Convention Applications: Addressing the Controversy of Counting State Applications Relating to a Deficit Spending Amendment."

Scoring: 3, state passed such a resolution; 1, did not.

adoption of income taxes, but the Ohio legislature failed to enact income taxes until 1971!

Case Studies. The following case studies add detail in political decision-making in terms of timing, substance, support, and emphasis on the income tax in Wisconsin and Ohio.

I. After *Wisconsin* voters approved the income tax amendment in 1908 by a vote of 85,696 to 37,729, the 1911 legislature passed an income tax statute by a vote of 54 to 25 in the House and by 20 to 6 in the Senate. Progressive-Republican Governor McGovern quickly signed it. The voters indulged in no political reprisals. Both the governor and most legislators were reelected in 1912.

Review of the legislative history and the earlier political campaigning for the amendment in Wisconsin established the clear intent of the electorate and the state's progressive political leaders. The state needed a new revenue source if it was to decrease its dependence on the general property tax and eliminate the tax on intangibles. Progressive leaders urged a shift to an ability-to-pay tax.[20] Not only did Wisconsin indicate a preference for a graduated-rate income tax, but the legislative act showed particularly strong commitments to the ability-to-pay concept. All income not barred by the national constitution (as then interpreted) came into the base, as did the estimated rental value of owner-occupied housing and the estimated value of farm produce consumed by the household. Differentiation among income recipients permitted deductions for business costs and property taxes and a minimum income exemption. Further, personal exemptions for the taxpayer and his dependents were in the form of tax credits that meant equal value for all taxpayers regardless of income. Wisconsin citizens, legislators, and the governor wanted to replace the intangibles tax with the income tax as not only a more equitable tax but as one that was more feasible to administer.

The law laid a responsibility on every citizen with taxable income to report: it provided the administrative agency with significant tools in information returns; centralized control of personnel; a merit system; subpoena power for both records and taxpayers; jeopardy assessment power; and power to file judgment, attach property, and, if necessary, to sell for taxes due. The state then and subsequently provided reasonably good budget resources and positions for carrying out administration.

[20]The author believes this is a more accurate statement of the times than the reference in the Advisory Commission on Intergovernmental Relations' *Federal-State Coordination of Personal Income Taxes* (p. 52) to a single article by Kossuth Kent Keenan ("The Wisconsin Tax," *Quarterly Journal of Economics* 26 [November, 1912]: 171) that discounts the search for progressivity and merely stresses the demand to replace the intangible personal property tax. Replacement of the intangibles tax was part of the reason for the income tax in Wisconsin; almost every state taxed intangibles at that time, but most did not adopt an income tax then.

The income tax so met the expectations of its supporters and later generations of voters that Wisconsin added only one other major state tax, the excise on gasoline imposed in 1925, during the next half-century. In those fifty years, the productivity of the income tax met the state's relatively high expenditure decisions. Not until 1961, when Wisconsin adopted a general sales tax, did its politicians waiver from their exclusive allegiance to the income tax. It is entirely possible the sales tax then would have failed to win approval in a popular referendum.[21]

II. *Ohio* Progressives made the income tax an issue in the state in the first years of the twentieth century up to World War I. They secured voter approval of a constitutional amendment that permitted the legislature to adopt a graduated-rate income tax by a popular vote of 296,635 to 214,829. But the income tax opponents prevented adoption in the next legislatures. And by World War I, the state's flirtation with Progressive reform had faded. When Ohio required a broad-based tax during the Depression, it chose the general sales tax, in 1934. Only when the state sales tax reached a rate of 4%, in the late sixties, did the income tax again become a salient issue in Ohio politics.

"In December, 1971, a reluctant, agonized, and bitterly divided Ohio General Assembly enacted that state's first state taxes on personal and corporate income."[22] The state's delay in adopting income taxes had permitted municipal income taxes to spring up in many communities (some 300 municipalities) in the 1950s and 1960s and there to attain "a fiscal prominence matched in few other states." Ohio had managed well for some years following World War II, living off the sales tax and the war-engendered surplus, but increasingly in the fifties and subsequent years Ohio budgets were tight and counties and municipalities especially hard-pressed. Yet the ability of a long line of governors and legislators to avoid any state tax increases was so much a part of the political climate that it took ten years from the first introduction of an income tax in the Ohio General Assembly in 1961 to actual passage of income taxes in 1971. By 1970, the fiscal problems of the state had reached such an impasse that both Democratic and Republican gubernatorial candidates emphasized that they would bring in a tax reform program that would include an income tax.

The positions of interest groups in support and opposition to an income

[21]See Leon D. Epstein's analysis of the issue of the sales tax in the 1962 election for governor, *Voters and Taxes* (Madison: University of Wisconsin Press, 1964).

[22]Frederick D. Stocker, "The Rough Road to Tax Reform: The Ohio Experience," Working Papers in Public Policy, no. 1 (reproduced by the College of Administrative Science, The Ohio State University, March, 1972; originally prepared for the Advisory Commission on Intergovernmental Relations as part of the commission's presentation to the President's Commission on School Finance). The author has used this paper as the basis of this abbreviated case study of Ohio's uphill struggle to get an income tax.

tax in Ohio reflected some of the same shifts from earlier decades that had been identified in Michigan and Illinois. Labor's traditional support of state personal income taxes has lagged as wages have grown higher and higher. Usually, official labor bodies continue to work for income taxes as the most equitable form of taxation, but rank-and-file union members do not always follow the leadership. In Ohio in the late sixties, the AFL-CIO (and the UAW) argued that the state's tax system so much favored business that new taxes must be levied on business. Labor's own tax change program was one that would have raised additional revenues only from business taxes. Without opposing personal income taxes, this program included none. During the 1971 legislative struggle, only the UAW actively supported the bill.

By 1971, business groups also had shifted positions somewhat. Only the Ohio Manufacturers Association consistently opposed the income tax program. The Chamber of Commerce, unwilling to support an income tax, was also unwilling to oppose passage of the income tax program in 1971. The State Council of Retail Merchants accepted the income tax program and reduction of personal property taxes as a reasonable compromise over its preferred extension of the general sales tax to services.

Active lobbying for the income tax came from such groups as the Ohio Citizens Council for Health and Welfare and the Cleveland Welfare Federation, which sought increased program support, and from such "public interest groups" as the League of Women Voters and the Ohio Council of Churches. Then, on February 15, 1971, a report from Governor Gilligan's "Citizens Task Force on Tax Reform" recommended adoption of a graduated-rate personal income tax and a corporation net income tax by a vote of 30 to 4. Even these efforts might have failed had not both houses of the Republican-controlled legislature found that current state revenues would not balance the most minimal budget they could pass. (Democratic Governor Gilligan was defeated in 1974.)

Effective January 1, 1972, many Ohioans were liable for personal income taxes, and corporations doing business in Ohio became liable for corporation income taxes. The action by the Ohio General Assembly could be considered great fiscal reform only in the context of the state's sixty-year refusal to adopt any income tax. The law's progressive rate structure and administrative tools were modest in comparison with those of the leading states in the field. Rates began at 0.5% for net income (after personal deduction) up to $5,000 and increased to 3.5% for net income of $40,000 or more.

Provisions of the 1971 legislation which had direct administrative effects included use of the federal tax base, agreements for federal-state cooperative use of tax returns, and withholding. Federal income taxes are not deductible, which both reduces the need to check and improves the progressivity of the tax. The Advisory Commission on Intergovernmental Relations judged the Ohio personal income tax in "moderate conformance" with the federal personal income tax base.[23]

Role of the Income Tax

The political decision to adopt an income tax may or may not be followed by political decisions to emphasize the income tax above other general revenue state taxes. Where the income tax *is* emphasized in the state's tax structure, higher, more progressive rates may be required. Table 5 provides some historical data to identify those states that over the decades made the income tax their number one revenue source; table 6 lists the current top rate that would normally be the historically highest rate in force for the individual income tax.

The shift to dependence on the income tax grew more and showed a much earlier first-place trend in several states than was true in the majority of states. In 1939 only five states realized more than 15% of their state tax revenues from income taxes. By 1947, eight states raised more than 25% of their tax revenues from income taxes. In 1957, five states raised more than a third of their taxes from this source. Ten years later six states raised more than 40% from income taxes. By 1977, five states raised more than 50% of their state tax revenues from income taxes (Delaware, Massachusetts, New York, Oregon, and Wisconsin). Outstanding in their reliance on income taxation are New York, Oregon, and Wisconsin, which have raised more than 40% of their state taxes from this source almost every year since 1939. In 1978 their ratios were 53.5%, 70.0%, and 52.1%, respectively.

A comparison of data in tables 1 and 5 indicates that often the older the income tax, the stronger the political support for an income tax; and the younger the sales tax in a given state, the more likely it is that the income tax will have achieved its number one standing early and sustained it. And, of course, it is in these states that one tends to find the highest, most progressive rate structures. A more important finding may be the close association of these findings with the statutory provision of administrative tools shown in tables 10 and 11 (see chapter 2).

Administration as a Continuing Challenge

No tax is self-administering. Administrative officials must locate and appraise the subject of the tax, identify the taxpayer, collect the tax, and solve the numerous questions of equity among taxpayers in different

[23]See U.S., Advisory Commission on Intergovernmental Relations, *Federal-State-Local Finances: Significant Features of Fiscal Federalism, 1976-77,* vol. 2, *Revenue and Debt* (Washington, D.C.: Government Printing Office, March, 1977), table 110.

TABLE 5

Relative Dependence of States on Individual and Corporation Income Taxes and on General Sales Taxes in Selected Years

State	Ratio of individual and corporation income taxes to total state taxes				Ratio of general sales taxes to total state taxes			
	1947[a]	*1957*[b]	*1967*[c]	*1977*[d]	*1947*[a]	*1957*[b]	*1967*[c]	*1977*[d]
Alabama	8.8	13.7	18.2	24.1	26.9	32.4	35.4	32.4
Alaska	—	—	44.9	31.8	—	—	—	—
Arizona	13.8	14.1	13.7	20.9	37.5	33.0	34.9	43.4
Arkansas	8.1	12.1	19.8	28.8	25.8	28.6	31.2	34.2
California	18.9	19.0	27.3	41.8	41.4	36.9	30.5	34.3
Colorado	14.1	18.0	31.0	39.0	34.6	27.5	29.4	33.4
Connecticut	14.4	13.1	17.1	17.9	—	34.8	31.1	40.0
Delaware	12.5	32.4	47.8	50.4	—	—	—	—
Florida	—	—	—	5.9	—	26.9	34.3	42.7
Georgia	22.0	15.2	24.7	35.0	—	39.5	36.2	36.1
Hawaii	—	—	33.6	33.6	—	—	47.4	49.7
Idaho	27.0	28.0	31.7	39.0	—	—	25.5	28.2
Illinois	—	—	—	33.8	44.8	42.9	49.2	34.6
Indiana	—	—	22.4	26.2	39.6	41.5	39.1	48.3
Iowa	11.6	13.1	26.1	41.7	39.1	35.0	25.1	26.8
Kansas	12.3	11.3	26.7	34.3	38.3	32.4	33.3	33.7
Kentucky	14.8	31.2	26.0	30.1	—	—	29.1	29.7
Louisiana	10.0	7.8	10.2	13.4	13.1	21.7	21.2	28.1
Maine	—	—	—	23.5	—	24.3	41.3	36.2
Maryland	22.3	28.3	33.9	43.3	—	18.3	21.2	21.9
Massachusetts	26.0	34.3	34.0	54.1	—	—	13.4	15.1
Michigan	—	—	—	46.6	54.3	42.6	44.4	29.0
Minnesota	27.1	29.4	48.1	48.9	—	—	—	18.8
Mississippi	12.3	12.4	8.9	18.3	29.2	34.6	41.8	49.1
Missouri	8.8	14.1	18.0	31.0	47.9	37.7	41.6	37.3

Montana	18.3	18.8	34.3	43.8	—	—	—	—
Nebraska	—	—	—	35.9	—	—	—	32.6
Nevada	—	—	—	—	—	28.1	26.8	35.2
New Hampshire	3.7	4.6	4.1	19.8	—	—	—	—
New Jersey	—	—	7.1	33.6	—	—	25.0	29.4
New Mexico	5.0	5.3	8.8	9.4	36.9	36.3	33.0	43.0
New York	39.5	50.5	48.6	54.2	—	—	14.9	20.6
North Carolina	30.8	26.6	34.1	41.4	20.0	19.9	24.0	21.4
North Dakota	12.4	8.9	16.6	26.0	32.6	27.5	27.4	37.2
Ohio	—	—	—	26.0	34.3	34.7	31.7	31.8
Oklahoma	12.2	9.8	13.4	25.2	25.1	21.1	18.9	18.0
Oregon	46.5	58.2	57.5	67.1	—	—	—	—
Pennsylvania	16.6	16.7	13.8	33.0	—	19.3	36.0	27.3
Rhode Island	1.2	12.6	12.2	32.9	—	24.1	34.1	32.3
South Carolina	27.0	18.3	26.8	33.5	—	29.0	28.8	35.0
South Dakota	0.8	0.4	0.7	1.3	3.8	30.5	37.0	50.5
Tennessee	8.1	9.0	10.2	11.7	—	34.4	36.6	48.0
Texas	—	—	—	—	—	14.0	19.4	35.7
Utah	15.5	23.9	29.0	34.5	36.9	30.5	31.8	42.7
Vermont	13.7	32.7	38.1	38.0	—	—	—	14.1
Virginia	20.5	42.3	38.1	42.5	—	—	13.7	20.8
Washington	—	—	—	—	59.2	54.2	54.9	55.8
West Virginia	—	—	9.6	20.8	60.1	51.1	45.2	46.6
Wisconsin	41.3	46.6	51.2	51.1	—	—	10.6	24.4
Wyoming	—	—	—	—	33.6	28.9	32.0	40.5
All states	15.05	17.5	22.3	34.3	20.4	23.2	27.9	30.6

[a]U.S., Department of Commerce, Bureau of the Census, *Compendium of Government Finances in 1947: State Finances, 1947*, no. 2 (Washington, D.C.: Government Printing Office, 1948), table 6.

[b]U.S., Department of Commerce, Bureau of the Census, *Compendium of Government Finances in 1957: State Finances, 1957*, no. 2 (Washington, D.C.: Government Printing Office, 1958), table 5.

[c]U.S., Department of Commerce, Bureau of the Census, *State Government Finances in 1967*, no. 1 (Washington, D.C.: Government Printing Office, 1968), table 7.

[d]U.S., Department of Commerce, Bureau of the Census, *State Tax Collections in 1977*, no. 1 (Washington, D.C.: Government Printing Office, 1978), table 2.

TABLE 6
State Personal Income Taxes as of January 1, 1979

State or other jurisdiction	Rate range[a] (%)	Income Bracket: Lowest: ends with ($)	Income Bracket: Highest: over ($)	Personal exemptions: Single ($)	Personal exemptions: Married ($)	Personal exemptions: Dependents ($)
Alabama	1.5-5.0(4)	1,000	5,000	1,500	3,000	300
Alaska	3.0-14.5(24)	2,000[b]	200,000[b]	750[c]	1,500[c]	750[c]
Arizona[d]	2.0-8.0(7)	1,000[c]	6,000[e]	1,000	2,000	600
Arkansas	1.0-7.0(6)[f]	3,000	25,000	17.50[g]	35[g]	6[g]
California[h]	1.0-11.0(11)	2,000[i]	15,500[i]	100[g]	200[g]	8[g]
Colorado[h]	3.0-8.0(11)[j]	1,000	10,000	850	1,700	850
D.C.	2.0-11.0(10)	1,000	25,000	750	1,500	750
Delaware	1.6-19.8(15)	1,000	100,000	600	1,200	600
Georgia	1.0-6.0(6)	750[k]	7,000[k]	1,500[l]	3,000[l]	700
Hawaii	2.25-11.0(11)[m]	500	30,000[k]	750	1,500	750
Idaho	2.0-7.5(6)[n]	1,000	5,000	750[n,c]	1,500[n,c]	750[n,c]
Illinois	2.5	Flat rate		1,000	2,000	1,000
Indiana	2.0	Flat rate		1,000	2,000[o]	500
Iowa	0.5-13.0(13)[p]	1,000	75,000	15[g]	30[g]	10[g]
Kansas	2.0-9.0(8)	2,000	25,000	750	1,500	750
Kentucky	2.0-6.0(5)	3,000	8,000	20[g]	40[g]	20[g]
Louisiana	2.0-6.0(3)[q]	10,000	50,000	2,500	5,000	400
Maine[d]	1.0-10.0(8)	2,000	25,000	1,000	2,000	1,000
Maryland	2.0-5.0(4)	1,000	3,000	800	1,600	800
Massachusetts	5.375[r]	Flat rate		2,000	2,600[s]	600
Michigan	4.6	Flat rate		1,500	3,000	1,500
Minnesota	1.6-17.0(13)	500	40,000	40[g]	80[g]	40[g]
Mississippi	3.0-4.0(2)	5,000	5,000	4,500	6,500	750
Missouri	1.5-6.0(10)	1,000	9,000	1,200	2,400	400
Montana	2.0-11.0(10)[t]	1,000	35,000	650	1,300	650
Nebraska	16% of U.S. tax[u]	—[v]	—[v]	—[v]	—[v]	—[v]
New Jersey	2.0-2.5(2)[w]	20,000	20,000	1,000	2,000	1,000
New Mexico	0.8-9.0(19)[x]	500	100,000	750[c]	1,500[c]	750[c]

Ohio	0.5-3.5(6)	5,000	40,000	650	1,300	650
Oklahoma	0.5-6.0(7)[aa]	1,000	7,500	750	1,500	750
Oregon	4.0-10.0(7)	500	5,000	750[c]	1,500[c]	750[c]
Pennsylvania	2.2	Flat rate		No personal exemptions		
Rhode Island	19% of U.S. tax	—[v]	—[v]	—[v]	—[v]	—[v]
South Carolina	2.0-7.0(6)	2,000	10,000	800	1,600	800
Utah	2.25-7.75(7)[bb]	750	4,500	750[c]	1,500[c]	750[c]
Vermont	25% of U.S. tax[cc]		—[v]	—[v]	—[v]	—[v]
Virginia	2.0-5.75(4)	3,000	12,000	600	1,200	600
West Virginia	2.1-9.6(24)[dd]	2,000	200,000[dd]	600	1,200	600
Wisconsin	3.1-11.4(15)	1,000	14,000	20[g]	40[g]	20[g]

Sources: Table of "State Individual Income Taxes," *The Book of the States, 1978-1979* (Lexington, Ky.: The Council of State Governments, 1978), pp. 310-11. The 1978 information was supplemented by current data supplied to the author by the Federation of Tax Administrators.

[a]Figures in parentheses indicate the number of steps from lowest to highest tax rate.

[b]The range reported is for single persons. For joint returns, the same rates are applied to brackets ranging from $4,000 to $400,000. For heads of households, the brackets range from $2,000 to $300,000.

[c]These states by definition allow personal exemptions provided in the IRS Code. Under existing law, Idaho follows the federal code as of January 1, 1977; North Dakota, as of December 31, 1976; and Utah (for purposes of personal exemptions), as of December 31, 1974. Alaska, New Mexico, and Oregon automatically accept amendments to the federal code.

[d]Arizona and Maine provided changes for the tax year 1978 only. Thus the rates shown here were true for 1977 income and will be true for 1979 income unless the legislatures act. For 1978 in Arizona, the amount of the personal exemption (and several other items not included in the table) was adjusted to reflect the difference between the state consumer price index for the second quarter of 1978 and the second quarter of 1977. For 1978 in Maine, the personal exemptions were $1,200, $2,400, $1,200, provided that certain revenue expectations are met.

[e]For joint returns, the tax is twice the tax imposed on half the income.

[f]Provides for the exemption of, or the imposition of lower rates on, taxpayers with incomes below certain levels.

[g]Tax credits.

[h]Both California and Colorado in 1978 provided an inflation adjustment factor in their tax calculations.

[i]The range reported is for single persons. For married persons, the tax is twice the tax imposed on half the income. For heads of households, brackets range from $4,000 to $18,000.

[j]Imposes a surtax of 2% on gross income from intangibles which exceeds $5,000. A credit allowed on taxable income up to $9,000 is computed by dividing taxable income by 200.

[k]The range reported is for single persons. For joint returns and heads of households, the same rates are applied to income brackets ranging from $1,000 to $10,000. For married persons filing separately, the income brackets range from $500 to $5,000.

[l]In addition, low-income taxpayers are allowed a tax credit up to $15 for single persons and $30 for heads of households or married persons filing jointly.

[m]The range reported is for single persons. For joint returns, the tax is twice the tax imposed on half the income. Different rates and brackets apply to heads of households.

[n]In the case of joint returns, the tax is twice the tax imposed on half the income. A filing fee of $10 is imposed on each return. A credit of $15 is allowed for each personal exemption.

[o]Allows $1,000 for individual taxpayers and $500 for dependents. On joint returns, each spouse may subtract the lesser of $1,000 or adjusted gross income;

situations and of effectiveness in the application of administrative resources in the collection of the tax. As initially a self-assessed tax, the income tax requires a base of fundamental honesty among taxpayers, a generally literate society, an economy of largely money-exchange transactions, and an enforcement organization which has both the legal means and the fiscal and personnel resources to reinforce the taxpayer's honesty. In turn, taxpayer honesty or morale is in large measure a function of public conviction that the tax is fair and the tax agency is diligent, not only in checking and apprehending the deliberately dishonest but also in aiding the honest or the careless in the necessary intricacies of the tax to assure that no more and no fewer taxes are collected than are due. Neither income tax nor any other tax administrators meet these goals perfectly, but the degree to which the goals are met will add to or subtract from the degree of popular acceptance of the tax and the level of voluntary compliance by the taxpayer.

In seeking these goals, income tax administrators are faced with the following tasks: (1) to educate and assist taxpayers in income tax compliance through publicity, by furnishing filing forms, and through direct assistance in filling out tax return forms; (2) to build up adequate coverage of taxpayers

---

TABLE 6—*Continued*

the minimum exemption is $500 for each spouse.

[p]No tax is imposed on persons whose net income does not exceed $4,000.

[q]These are the official rates and exemptions mandated by state constitution. The actual tax is found by referring to a table that relates federal tax liability, exemptions, and filing status to amount of state tax.

[r]A 10.75% rate is applied to interest and dividends (other than from savings deposits) and on net capital gains. The 5.375% rate applies to all other income, including earned income and interest and dividends from savings deposits. These rates include a 7.5% surtax.

[s]Minimum allowance; permits exemption of a spouse's earnings up to $2,000.

[t]In addition, a permanent 10% surcharge is imposed.

[u]The rate is determined annually by the state's Board of Equalization and Assessment.

[v]By providing that the state income tax is a percentage of the federal tax liability, these states have in effect adopted the personal exemptions of the IRS Code.

[w]A separate tax is levied on New York-New Jersey commuters. Taxpayers are liable only for the larger of the applicable taxes.

[x]The rate range reported is for single persons; for joint returns and heads of households, tax rates range from 0.8% on income not over $2,000 to 9.0% on income over $200,000. Different rates apply to married persons filing separately.

[y]New York's highest tax bracket will be lowered to $23,000 beginning with tax years ending in 1979. Each personal exemption will be $700 in 1979, $750 in 1980 and thereafter.

[z]Also, a 1% tax is imposed on net incomes over $2,000 derived from a business, trade, or profession other than as an employee.

[aa]The rate range shown is for single persons. For joint returns, and surviving spouses, tax rates range from 0.5% on the first $2,000 to 6.0% on amounts over $15,000. For heads of households, tax rates range from 0.5% on the first $1,500 to 6.0% on amounts over $11,250.

[bb]The rate range reported is for single persons. For joint returns, rates range from 2.75% on income up to $1,500 to 7.75% on amounts over $7,500. Different rates and brackets apply to married persons filing separately.

[cc]If Vermont tax liability for any taxable year exceeds Vermont tax liability determinable under federal law in effect January 1, 1967, the taxpayer is entitled to a credit equal to the excess plus 6% of that amount.

[dd]The range reported is for single persons and heads of households. For joint returns, the same rates are applied to brackets ranging from $4,000 to $400,000.

and income by exploiting all available sources of information, and especially to utilize available IRS services; (3) to check returns for arithmetical accuracy and for fidelity of reporting by office and field auditors; (4) to dispose of protests and taxpayer disputes over tax determinations by providing for informal and formal conferences and hearings; and (5) to collect current and delinquent taxes by providing channels for convenient payment and by using legal means for enforcement when needed.

The operating tasks of income tax administration require general and technical staff services. Organizational structures can either facilitate or impede the translation of legislative policy into administrative fact. Budget and personnel staffs make or fail to make efficient use of appropriated moneys and provide competent personnel for income tax enforcement. Planning and research staffs are needed to analyze deficiencies in income tax administration as well as to make revenue estimates and assist in translating policy and administrative recommendations into proposals for legislative action where that is needed.

Under the triple pressure of population increase, rapid economic growth, and inflation, the number of taxpayers has sometimes doubled and trebled in a decade or two. At the same time, more and more provisions have been put into the income tax laws to refine the definition of income, block avenues of tax escape, and provide a variety of tax relief measures or tax credits on humanitarian grounds or preferential treatment as an economic incentive. In fact, the states—often urged on by the U.S. Advisory Commission on Intergovernmental Relations—have recently exhibited a veritable passion for decreasing the presumed regressivity or inequities of other taxes by adopting provisions for deductions, tax credits, or tax rebates under the income tax. Meanwhile the taxpayer and his accountants and attorneys are engaged in a never-ending game of devising new and involved financial arrangements to provide "tax-sheltered investments."

All the foregoing woes are shared with federal income tax officials, and *properly used,* the generous array of federal facilities available to the states can ease many of these problems. But quite apart from some differences in exemption levels and definitions of income, state administrators face difficulties to which the federal agency is largely immune. State boundary lines create innumerable problems of determining situs of income, the legal domicile of the recipient, and the proper allocation of interstate income. In the individual income tax, the problems associated with geographical limits include much more than allocation: large sums may be earned by nonresidents within a state or by residents outside the state; taxpayers moving out of a state may leave unpaid tax bills behind; interstate movements of income may result in avoidance of taxes or in double taxation in the absence of adequate crediting arrangements.

In short, though he may have proportionately far fewer resources at his command than has the director of the IRS, the state administrator faces tasks that are in important respects more difficult than those of federal income tax administrators. Yet at least a few states appear to administer the individual income tax nearly as well as does the IRS, and a number of states show competent administration by this author's measures of effectiveness.

Conclusion

Nineteenth-century philosophical support for state income taxes faltered under the evidence of administrative failures. Wisconsin's demonstration that its 1911 law contained tools that made the income tax an administrable revenue-raiser converted many economists and reformers to the practicality of such a tax and to its merits in raising state revenues in accord with ability to pay.

Within the framework set by federal taxes, our federal system, state political and economic environments, and state laws, the equitable application of the state income tax is squarely the responsibility of state tax administrators. The law can be tailored—by adjustment of personal exemptions, rate schedules, and definitions of income—to suit the fiscal characteristics of each state tolerably well and to reduce unnecessary diversity between federal and state income tax structures. Administration alone cannot guarantee the fiscal success or political sense of equity of a state income tax, but good administration is a condition precedent to successful adjustment of the income tax law to a state's fiscal capacities and needs.

In 1959, Walter W. Heller and I attempted to describe the structures, personnel, techniques, problems, and promising developments observed in state income tax administration and to identify administrative issues that might contribute to the growth of the tax and broaden its horizons. In the present study, I hope to provide a description and analysis based on the seventies. As part of the focus for that description, I will examine the relationship between quality, timing, and revenue dependence in the political decision to adopt or amend an income tax, as well as the statutory provisions for implementation as they relate to organizational structure, enforcement tools, professional personnel and budget resources, *and* effective administration as indicated by both the descriptive evidence of administrative activities and the available measures of achievement.

Chapter Two

Statutory Policy and Administrative Provisions

States normally have adopted individual income taxes to provide the progressive or ability-to-pay element in their revenue systems. Whatever the intent, the impact of the particular income tax adopted has not always been progressive. Sometimes the initial policy as modified through governors' messages, legislative committee recommendations, legislative enactments, the law signed by the governor, and the interpretations by administrative agencies and the courts has resulted in tax burdens that reflect little of the claimed ability-to-pay value.[1] Where the progressive intent held up well through early political processes, decades of successive amendments to increase income exclusions or income exemptions, or to increase the number of itemized deductions (always, of course, in the name of "greater equity"), may have eroded the progressivity despite the progressive rate structure.[2] According to a recent state report from New York, which had one of the earliest progressive income taxes, "Our fairest tax, the personal income tax, is at best a proportional tax."[3]

Policy and administration interact, and each is dependent on the other. Policy provisions may simplify or increase the complexity of the law and make enforcement easier or more difficult. A property tax rebate or credit may be desirable public policy, but its existence adds to the administrator's task of reviewing returns and to the cost of administration, as do all the other deductions and credits. Adoption of progressive income taxes was

[1]In some states the original concept of ability to pay was not widely or deeply held but represented more of a slogan, so the final statute was "symbolic" rather than meaningful. See Murray Edelman, *The Symbolic Uses of Politics* (Urbana: University of Illinois Press, 1967).

[2]Joseph A. Pechman has long called attention to the erosion of the federal income tax. See, e.g., his "Erosion of the Individual Income Tax," *National Tax Journal* (10 March, 1957): 1-25. See also Clara Penniman and H. Rupert Theobald, "The Wisconsin Income Tax and Erosion," *National Tax Journal* 15 (December, 1962): 413-22, for an early analysis of the erosion of the Wisconsin income tax.

[3]New York, Department of Taxation and Finance, *Annual Report, 1975/76* (Albany, 1977), p. 4.

delayed because of the inability to enforce the earlier laws. Only after Wisconsin provided for improved administration through information returns, central state control, and quality personnel did economists and reform politicians accept the individual income tax as a practical ability-to-pay policy. Withholding and quarterly estimates and payments have become minimal additional features in today's economy. Not all provisions that might aid the administrator meet public policy tests, but excessively complex policies or insufficient administrative tools make a mockery of equity.

This chapter will examine a few of the major public policy decisions of present state individual income tax laws, their administrative implications, and some of the significant statutory administrative tools of the states for individual income taxes.[4] The two succeeding chapters will consider some of the organization, budget, personnel, and other resources made available to tax agencies and administrators for carrying out income tax policies. Later chapters will take up ways in which the states utilize their statutory tools and resources in the areas of auditing and compliance.[5]

Major Policy Characteristics of Individual Income Taxes

GENERAL STRUCTURE

Statutory Rates

Tables 6 and 7 provide information on the income tax laws administrators are called upon to implement. Of the forty-four states with individual income taxes, thirty-six states apply graduated rates to net income. Massachusetts classifies income and varies its tax rates according to source rather than according to total income. Illinois, Michigan, and Pennsylvania apply a single rate to the net income figure established by the taxpayer. Indiana applies a single rate to "adjusted gross income" rather than to net income. Colorado imposes a 2% tax on income from intangibles *in addition to* its general rate structure for net income. Connecticut, New Hampshire, and Tennessee levy flat-rate taxes on a few selected income sources. The classification of these three states as having personal net income taxes

[4]The author has not attempted to make a detailed analysis of corporation income tax policies and specific statutory tools for corporation income tax enforcement in the states. In a very general way, there have been parallel developments (some erosion of the tax base, similar administrative tools in any given state). See also chapter 8 of this study. See also U.S., Advisory Commission on Intergovernmental Relations, "Uniform Personal Income Tax Statute," *State-Local Finances and Suggested Legislation, 1971* (Washington, D.C.: Government Printing Office, December, 1972), pp. 218-64.

[5]For a good discussion of the issues that are covered in capsule form in the following pages, see Joseph A. Pechman, ed., *Comprehensive Income Taxation* (Washington, D.C. The Brookings Institution, 1977). Although the book focuses on the federal income tax, many of the issues are similar for the state income tax.

involves considerable overstatement since these taxes are neither very personal nor very net.[6]

State rates have varied only slightly over the years. Increased tax productivity reflects the state of the economy, which through growth and inflation has pushed incomes substantially above the median of two decades ago. Income tax states with a rich tax base also show increased income tax collections.

Until recently state income taxes have amounted to only a small percentage of federal income taxes. In 1957, state personal income taxes produced receipts of about 5% of federal individual income taxes; but twenty years later state personal income taxes had climbed to almost 17% of federal individual income taxes. The heavy emphasis of the states on taxing median and below-median incomes, together with changes in the federal structure which deemphasize taxes on lower incomes and levy a nearly proportional rate in the median income ranges, has produced a parallel to the relationships before World War II. The income tax states in those earlier years tended to occupy income levels that went largely untouched by the national government. The federal tax, after substantial income exemptions, picked up and added its progressive rates to incomes far above the average.[7]

None of the state rates approach the height of the federal individual income tax rates, but the state rates frequently rise more steeply in the lower and middle brackets. No two states have currently elected identical rate structures. Table 6 demonstrates that the states, individually and collectively, do not exhibit a soak-the-rich attitude. Sixteen states apply their highest rate on incomes (after exemptions and deductions) of $5,000, $6,000, $7,500, or $10,000. With today's incomes, these states tend to have tax structures only slightly different in impact than the states with a flat-rate income tax. This is surely true for Maryland, with its 2% rate on the first $1,000, 3% on the next $1,000, 4% on the following $1,000, and a top rate of 5% for all imcome of $3,000 or above (table 6).

The New Jersey personal income tax, first enacted in 1976, was set at 2% on net income of $20,000 or less and 2.5% on net income over $25,000. New York's highest tax bracket was "over $30,000" for a couple of years but dropped down to $23,000 for 1979 income. Arkansas and the District of Columbia have the same top bracket, $25,000. Only ten states (Alaska,

[6]Nevertheless, the basic Bureau of the Census state finance tables from which almost all studies are derived classify these states as having individual income taxes; to avoid problems of comparison, this book follows the pattern, although it omits the tiny "corporate income" tax levied by South Dakota only on banks.

[7]During World War II, the national government drastically changed its income tax rate structure to leave few working citizens untaxed, and the general pattern remained until the seventies. The addition of such rich tax-base states as Illinois, Michigan, Ohio, and Pennsylvania also accounts for the increased state ratio.

Delaware, Hawaii, Iowa, Louisiana, Minnesota, Montana, New Mexico, Ohio, and West Virginia) have rate brackets that distinguish income above that level. Although Ohio's top rate is only 3.5% at the $40,000 level, Alaska's is 14.5% at the over $200,000 level, and Delaware's is 19.8% at the $100,000 level. Nebraska, Rhode Island, and Vermont utilize the federal income brackets since the state tax in these cases is a percentage of the taxpayer's federal tax.

Effective Rates

Studying the schedule of statutory rates is only the first step in determining comparative rates among the income tax states. To translate statutory rates into effective rates, one needs to take into account personal exemptions, differences in exempt income and deductions, and whether or not federal income taxes are a deductible item. All states that allow the taxpayer the deductions claimed on his federal return *without adjustment* automatically permit deduction of the state income tax against itself. Minnesota permits deduction of federal income tax payments and differs in exempt income and deductions from the IRS Code. Its 1977 statutory rate of 15% on net income of $50,000 became an effective rate of 7.7% for a married couple with two dependents. New York's 15% rate, with no deduction for federal income taxes and some other differences, became an effective rate of 8.5% for such a family in 1977.[8]

Personal Exemptions or Credits

State personal exemptions, except some of those for dependents, usually equal or exceed federal exemptions, but laws differ substantially. Exemptions for single individuals in 1978 varied from $600 in several states to $4,500 in Mississippi, and for married couples or heads-of-family from $1,200 to $6,500. Again, several states had $1,200 and Mississippi alone had $6,500. As in the case of rates and rate brackets, Nebraska, Rhode Island, and Vermont have no separate exemption schedules since their taxes are a percentage of the federal tax liability. Six states (Arkansas, California, Iowa, Kentucky, Minnesota, and Wisconsin) provide for a personal tax credit instead of an income exemption to assure that the exemption comes off the lowest tax rate for all. Louisiana does not use a tax credit but achieves the same result by providing that the exempt income come from the lowest tax bracket. Under the tax credit system, gross tax liability is

[8]See U.S., Advisory Commission on Intergovernmental Relations, *Federal-State-Local Finances: Significant Features of Fiscal Federalism, 1976-77*, vol. 2, *Revenue and Debt* (Washington, D.C.: Government Printing Office, March, 1977), table 104. The table takes into account whether or not federal income taxes are deductible but does not consider all other differences in the tax laws of the states.

computed directly from net income, and then tax credits are deducted to give the net tax liability.[9] From an administrative point of view, exemptions are important not only in defining tax liability but also in affecting the state's filing requirements (table 6).

Income Exemptions and Exclusions

The "fastest growing sector" of state income tax law in the last decade or so has been the statutory provisions for income exemptions and exclusions plus deductions (considered in the next section) (table 7). Whether responding to inflation, to the generally bountiful state treasuries, or simply to pressure-group demands for particular "equities" and to similar changes in the federal code, legislators have recognized the claims of one special interest group after another. The elderly, the married, the unmarried, parents with natural children, parents with adopted children, the blind, and many others have laid claim to special consideration under the income tax law.

Exempt or excluded income reduces the progressivity and the productivity of the income tax. Wisconsin recently estimated (table 8) that exclusions from gross income, plus adjustments under the IRS Code, cost the state a total of $222.5 million. Its own further modifications cost an additional $12.6 million in revenue. The latter figure includes $7 million as a result of the presumed constitutional bar to taxing interest on U.S. obligations. Wisconsin, unlike thirty-eight other income tax states, does tax the interest paid to holders of its own bonds (table 8).

One of the large revenue losses shown in table 8 is $25 million for imputed net rent (the text of the Wisconsin report states that the figure may actually be nearer $35 million). Early Wisconsin law recognized that sometimes expenditures produce noncash income for the same individual. The homeowner has an investment on which he pays out property taxes that he claims as deductible expenditures, but the home also produces shelter for him which has an imputed rental value that represents income to him. Another example is the farmer, whose operating costs are deductible, but some of these costs go into producing meat and other foods from the farm for his own table. Their value represents part of his income as much as the cash he receives for milk or corn. (The state's estimated revenue loss here is $10 million.) Wisconsin's income tax law in earlier years recognized the legitimacy of the expenditures involved in the earning

[9]President Carter at one time in 1977 suggested a tax credit system instead of the present income exemption for the national government. Seemingly no national news commentator knew that the proposal had been in effect in some states since their adoption of the income tax.

TABLE 7

Selected Policy Characteristics of State Individual Income Taxes, 1978

State	Degree of conformity with IRS code	Special exemptions		Low-income homestead credit/circuit-breaker rebate	Sales tax credit	Deductions for	
		Age ($)	Blind ($)			Federal income taxes	State income taxes
Alabama	Nonconformance	—	—	—	—	Yes	—
Alaska	Substantial	—	—	—	—	—	—
Arizona	Nonconformance	1,000	500	Yes	—	Yes	Yes
Arkansas	Nonconformance	17.50 (credit)	17.50 (credit)	Yes	—	—	—
California	Nonconformance		8 (credit)	Yes	—	—	—
Colorado	Moderate	750	750	Yes	Yes	Yes	—
Connecticut							
Delaware	Moderate	600	600	—	—	Limited	—
Georgia	Moderate	700	700	—	—	—	—
Hawaii	Substantial	750	5,000	—	Yes	—	—
Idaho	Substantial	750	750	—	Yes	—	—
Illinois	Moderate	1,000	1,000	—	—	—	—
Indiana	Moderate	500	500	Yes	—	—	—
Iowa	Moderate	15	15	Yes	—	Yes	—
Kansas	Moderate	600	600	—	—	Limited	—
Kentucky	Moderate	20	20	Yes	—	Limited	—
Louisiana	Moderate	Fed.	Fed.	—	—	Yes	—
Maine	Moderate	1,000	1,000	Yes	—	—	—
Maryland	Moderate	800	800	Yes	—	—	—

Massachusetts	Moderate	600	2,000	—	Yes	—	—
Michigan	Moderate	1,500	1,500	Yes	—	—	—
Minnesota	Moderate	20	20 (credit)	Yes	—	Yes	—
Mississippi	Nonconformance	750	750	—	—	—	—
Missouri	Moderate	—	—	Yes	—	Yes	—
Montana	Moderate	650	650	—	—	Yes	—
Nebraska	Virtual compliance	Follows federal			—	—	—
New Hampsire		—	—	—	—	—	—
New Jersey	Nonconformance	1,000	1,000	Yes	—	—	—
New Mexico	Substantial	750	750	Yes	Yes	—	Limited
New York	Moderate	650	650	Yes	—	—	—
North Carolina	Nonconformance	1,000	1,000	—	—	—	—
North Dakota	Substantial	750	750	Yes	—	Yes	—
Ohio	Moderate	—	—	Yes	—	—	—
Oklahoma	Substantial	750	750	Yes	—	Limited	Yes
Oregon	Substantial	675	675	Yes	—	Yes	—
Pennsylvania	Nonconformance	—	—	Yes	—	—	—
Rhode Island	Virtual compliance	Follows federal		Yes	—	—	—
South Carolina	Nonconformance	800	800	—	—	Limited	—
Tennessee	No broad-based income tax	—	—	—	—	—	—
Utah	Substantial			Yes	—	Yes	—
Vermont	Virtual compliance	Follows federal		Yes	Yes	—	Yes
Virginia	Moderate	1,000	600	—	—	—	—
West Virginia	Moderate	600	600	—	—	—	—
Wisconsin	Moderate	5		Yes	—	—	Yes

Sources: Updated from U.S., Advisory Commission on Intergovernmental Relations, *Federal-State-Local Finances: Significant Features of Fiscal Federalism, 1976-77,* vol. 2, *Revenue and Debt* (Washington, D.C.: Government Printing Office, 1977), tables 107, 110, and 111.

TABLE 8
List of Exclusions, Adjustments, and Modifications to Individual Gross Income—Wisconsin, 1976

Exclusions, adjustments, and modifications	*1975/76 fiscal effect ($)*
Exclusions from Gross Income	
Dividends—first $100	2,000,000
Gains from sale or exchange of residence	10,000,000
Gains from sale or exchange of residence for the elderly	700,000
Social Security benefits	30,000,000
Unemployment compensation	25,000,000
Railroad unemployment benefits	400,000
Railroad retirement annuities and pensions	2,300,000
Public assistance	5,000,000
Imputed net rent	25,000,000
Cash value of crops for home consumption	10,000,000
Sickness and injury benefits	*
Group term life insurance purchased for employees	6,000,000
Death benefits	15,000,000
Meals and lodging to employees	2,000,000
Scholarships and fellowships	1,600,000
Awards and prizes	Minimal
Rental value of parsonages	500,000
Reduced armed forces retirement pay	NA
Armed forces combat pay	Minimal
Mustering-out pay for members of the armed forces	None
Miscellaneous armed forces exclusions	6,000,000
Life insurance dividends	10,000,000
Cancellation of business property indebtedness	NA
Income from debt cancellation through bankruptcy	NA
Interest from public housing authorized bonds issued by Wisconsin municipalities	1,000,000
Appreciation of property held at the time of death	70,000,000
Campaign contributions received by a candidate	Minimal
Total exclusions	222,500,000
Adjustments to Gross Income	
Capital losses	*
Losses from the sale or exchange of business property	800,000
Expenses related to rent and royalty income	40,000,000
Pension, profit-sharing, annuity and bond purchase plans of self-employed individuals	3,000,000
Individual retirement accounts	4,000,000
Lump-sum distributions from pension plans	500,000
Moving expenses	1,000,000
Trade and business expenses	13,000,000
Employee's trade and business expenses	20,000,000
Total adjustments	82,300,000
Modifications to Federal Adjusted Gross Income	
Interest on U.S. obligations	7,000,000
Military pay	2,000,000
Net long-term capital losses	1,000,000
Retirement benefits	2,000,000

TABLE 8—*Continued*

Exclusions, adjustments, and modifications	*1975/76 fiscal effect ($)*
Income or losses from small business corporations	*
Distributive share of estates and trusts	*
Distributive share of partnership modifications	*
Wisconsin net operating loss carry-over	500,000
Constant-basis assets	100,000
Adjusted basis of assets acquired after January 1, 1965	Minimal
Interest on earnings for prisoners of war	Minimal
Total modifications	12,600,000

Source: Wisconsin, Department of Revenue, *Tax Exemption Devices, 1977* (Madison), pp. 8 and 9.
Note: Asterisk indicates complexity; fiscal effect is discussed in the report, but an estimate is not provided.

of such income but also required reporting for the taxing of imputed income.[10]

A high proportion of employees today have employer-paid health insurance, sick leave, and other fringe benefits that constitute deductible expenditures for the employer without necessarily becoming income for tax purposes to the recipient.[11] Benefits from health insurance and health insurance paid by the employer are specifically exempt under the IRS Code. For a period the code went further and exempted sick leave pay when the illness extended over a specific period. Some of the states have continued to make this provision. Employer child-care facilities constitute income to employees that is specifically exempt. The commissioner of the IRS was reported in July, 1977, and again in May, 1978, to have insisted that many economic benefits as a result of employment are taxable and should be reported, such as price discounts, free college tuition for faculty families, free airplane rides for personal convenience by an executive on a company plane, or free airplane rides by airline company employees and their families. Expense-account living and employee fringe benefits remain large untaxed income sources for enough taxpayers to represent a formidable lobby if anyone had the temerity to suggest their inclusion in

[10]Chapter 374 of Wisconsin's *Laws of 1917* eliminated the imputed rental value of a home from income, but did not change the provision for reporting the value of farm products consumed. From 1945 through 1958, the state's tax department disallowed the costs of raising food and other products consumed by the farmer from his expense schedule instead of adding an estimate to his income. Legislative action in 1959 voided this administrative procedure.

[11]*U.S. News and World Report,* May 8, 1978, pp. 76-77, listed forty "income sources" not now taxed that Commissioner Kurtz believes should be taxed under present law. The states generally follow the IRS in excluding these items.

calculations of net taxable income. Some states go further than these examples to exempt state teachers' retirement income, all state retirement income plus military pensions, all or part of the pay of members of the U.S. armed forces, or to omit capital gains (Pennsylvania).

Highly inclusive definitions of income can pose implementation problems: imputed home rental value, farm produce estimates, employer gifts of small value, etc. Imputed income may be difficult to calculate, adequately report, and enforce, but other exclusions pose no such problems. Health insurance payments by employers could easily be identified and included. Their omission stems from a decision in World War II when general wages and salaries were frozen and such fringe benefits provided some flexibility for the government in handling labor-management problems. Untaxed fringe benefits continue to represent important gains to unions in contract bargaining.

Deductions

Standard Deductions. Legislative decisions as to what is and what is not deductible are as much a part of policy making as the initial decisions defining income to be reported. Until 1944, all deductions claimed on both federal and state income tax returns had to be itemized. With the growth in numbers of taxpayers during the war, the growth in personal incomes, and the national government's lowering of exemptions, Congress detemined that "lower" income taxpayers, if they wished, could utilize a standard deduction in lieu of itemizing deductions.[12] Over the succeeding years, the states too have adopted legislation to permit taxpayers to use a standard deduction rather than itemize deductions.

Low-Income Allowance. Whether considered as an addition to personal exemptions or as a type of deduction, Congress has adopted a so-called low-income allowance that requires no income tax payments from individuals whose incomes are beneath a "tax poverty" line. Several states, including California, New York, and Wisconsin, have developed similar provisions. States such as Mississippi, with its unusually high personal exemptions, have provided a kind of allowance for everyone (without special benefit for the poor) since average incomes climbed to $10,000 or more.

Itemized Deductions. If the concept were accepted that deductions are simply the opposite of income and that everyone's deductions should appear in someone's income, legislators would have far less difficulty in determining policy. No income tax statute meets that standard today.

[12] Although the use of the standard deduction appeals more to individuals in lower income brackets than to those in middle or higher brackets, the choice between standard deduction and itemization depends in part on the type of income involved, the amount of the deductions, and the taxpayer's sophistication.

Deductions for one taxpayer may never become income for another. Justice demanded by one group after another has produced an ever-growing list of deductions. Wisconsin's list (table 9) shows a total loss of income taxes due to deductions of $246.95 million in 1975/76, plus $82 million for personal exemption credits and $49.75 million for homestead credits. A few of the numerous deductions in the Wisconsin (or other state) statutes are discussed below.

1. From 1917 to 1979 Wisconsin taxpayers deducted the property taxes paid for their home or homes. When Wisconsin taxed imputed income from owner-occupied homes, the deduction of property taxes logically followed, but when the legislature removed imputed rent as an income item, it did not follow its logic and remove property taxes as a deduction.[13] Neither the national government in its 1913 statute nor any other state ever used the imputed rent income concept, but all provided for property taxes as an itemized deduction.

2. Until 1979 Wisconsin permitted deductions for Wisconsin sales and gasoline taxes, state income taxes, but not federal income taxes. States generally permit such tax deductions, and a number still permit the deduction of the federal income tax (table 7). Either the national government or the states must permit deduction of the other's income tax to avoid the possibility of the two exceeding 100%. The national government has always permitted deduction of state income taxes, and the early income tax states normally provided for deduction of the federal income tax. As federal taxes climbed with World War II, many of the states eliminated the provision and most of the newer income tax states made no such provision. Federal income tax deductibility significantly reduces the productivity of the state income tax without changing the individual income taxpayer's total tax burden appreciably. In other words, the income tax states, and especially those with no deductibility for the federal income tax, gained a federal revenue-sharing provision years ago. In its model uniform tax law, the Advisory Commission on Intergovernmental Relations does not provide for deductibility of the federal income tax. Neither does it provide for deductibility of the state income tax against itself as did the Wisconsin law.

3. Beginning in 1963, Wisconsin legislators adopted the rebate/credit concept for property taxes for the low-income elderly and later for low-income individuals without regard to age. The concept was then extended to renters in these classes. State legislators in state after state have eagerly embraced the popular idea of a credit, rebate or other adjustment for the

[13]Property taxes for rental property or for business property would be deductible in arriving at net income. At issue here are the strictly owner-occupied home or homes, owner-used recreation lands, etc. As of January 1, 1979, Wisconsin no longer permits the property tax deduction. Instead the state has substituted a *limited tax credit* for nonbusiness property taxes.

TABLE 9
List of Deductions from Individual Adjusted Gross Income, Wisconsin, 1976

Deductions and tax credits	*1975/76 fiscal effect ($)*
Deductions	
Medical expenses	11,000,000
Taxes	102,000,000
Interest	62,000,000
Charitable contributions	27,000,000
Casualty and theft losses	700,000
Political contributions	150,000
Expenses for care of dependents	1,000,000
Alimony	1,000,000
Production of income	1,000,000
Dues and membership fees	3,000,000
Gambling losses	NA
Educational expenses	NA
Tax return preparation, refunds, and audits	1,000,000
Uniform and work clothes expenses	4,000,000
Employment agency fees	NA
Entertainment expenses	1,000,000
Business gifts	2,000,000
Optional standard deduction	30,000,000
Splitting itemized deductions between spouses	NA
Doubling-up deductions	100,000
Effect of eliminating deductions	*
Total deductions	246,950,000
Tax Credits (in lieu of deductions)	
Personal exemption credit	82,000,000
Homestead credit	49,750,000
Income taxes paid to other states/Minnesota reciprocity	*
Total tax credits	131,750,000

Source: Wisconsin, Department of Revenue, *Tax Exemption Devices, 1977* (Madison), p. 9
Note: Asterisk indicates complexity; fiscal effect is discussed in the Report, but estimate is not provided.

property taxes paid by the elderly (sometimes with a means test, sometimes not) and by low-income taxpayers. Several of the states also make similar provisions for renters (see table 7).[14]

Once the credit/rebate concept for property taxes cleared a number of

[14]Especially in the case of the property tax credit/rebate, advocates have ignored the fact that some state income taxes are based on a flat rate rather than a progressive rate structure. In either a flat rate or very low, graduated rate structure, the tax burden may be regressive if exempt income, deductions, and actual administration are considered. Not only is there division among economists as to whether the burden of property taxes is or is not regressive; in addition, the general deductibility of home property taxes under a graduated income tax adds a regressive element to the property tax. Moreover, most of the assumptions of property tax regressivity rest on issues of exempt property and inept administration; exemptions under either the income or the sales tax or the actual quality of administration of these taxes is not taken into account. In other words, as in the case of

state legislatures, legislative actions were taken to provide tax credits/rebates on sales taxes paid by all or selected groups of taxpayers. The Advisory Commission on Intergovernmental Relations has supported income tax credits and rebates for both the property tax and the sales tax paid by low-income heads-of-households regardless of age (table 7).

4. And so the deduction lists grew to reach Wisconsin's twenty-two categories and the many more categories (at even higher costs) adopted by some other states. A number of states have added political contributions, the personal political campaign expenditures of a candidate (Minnesota), at least a part of the premiums paid for an endowment or life insurance policy (New York), expenses incurred in adopting children (Arizona, California, etc.), housing insulation, solar energy for heating and cooling (at least fifteen states) and social security taxes (Alabama). Wisconsin and all other states permit a deduction for mortgage interest and interest paid on personal loans for almost any objective, including loans for investment purposes. These deductions, of course, follow federal practice. California and Minnesota have even reversed the deduction trend by disallowing the usual business deductions from a real estate owner's gross income if the housing is judged substandard!

Once made, policy decisions to exempt income or to authorize deductions live on. President Carter's campaign proposal to withdraw the deductibility of property taxes and interest payments for mortgages (a logical alternative to the practice of excluding imputed rental value) for nonbusiness property—whether one or more homes, recreation property, or some other—was shot down in the press immediately.

CONFORMITY OF STATE WITH FEDERAL INCOME TAXES

A majority of the states today begin with federal adjusted gross income as the initial information required of the taxpayer for calculating his income tax. A few states use federal net income and a few others use the federal tax as a base for the state income tax (see table 7). The Advisory Commission on Intergovernmental Relations has repeatedly supported state income tax conformity with the IRS Code.[15] Its uniform state income tax law (1971) uses the adjusted gross income on the federal return and repeatedly refers

---

many other deductions, a good economic and policy argument can be made for the other side. There are innumerable studies on the question of deducting property taxes generally and on the special tax credit/rebate. Two recent good ones that are not highly technical are Diane Paul, *The Politics of the Property Tax* (Lexington, Mass.: D. C. Heath, Lexington Books, 1975); and U.S., Department of Housing and Urban Development, Office of Policy Research and Planning, *Property Tax Relief Programs for the Elderly: An Evaluation,* prepared by Abt Associates, Inc., Cambridge, Mass., May, 1976; see especially chap. 3, pp. 42-63.

[15]The Advisory Commission has pushed the states toward conformity with the IRS and supported the 1972 and 1976 "piggy-back" provisions of the IRS Code. See chapter 9 for discussion of these provisions.

to the federal code for refining definitions throughout its model law. The recommendation emphasizes simplification of the taxpayer's burden through agreement. This objective supersedes any policy concern that the congressional income tax statute may represent the decision of a majority of the senators and representatives of the fifty states but probably not the policy preferences of the legislators and citizens of any one state.

Pressure on the states to conform to the IRS Code has gradually won converts since World War II. "Large" taxpayers, attorneys, accountants, and other taxpayer representatives either find direct benefits thereby for themselves or find it simpler to maintain books and reports in similar fashion for both federal and state tax agencies. Correspondence between federal and state law, or "tax simplification," as its supporters prefer to title it, has less impact on taxpayers who report largely wage income and use the standard deduction.

POLICY AND ADMINISTRATION

Brief attention has been given to some policy issues involved in the number of *income exemptions* and *exclusions* and to the varied types of *deductions* simply to provide a background to the administrative considerations posed by these legislative decisions. Too often the affirmative legislative response to pressures to adopt "good ideas" does not attend to whether these measures will make administration easier or more difficult, less costly or more costly, or whether the adoption of particular proposals will likely shift the present tax burden as a result of better or worse enforcement. Administrative issues alone should not determine policy, but failure to consider administration may produce unanticipated and undesired policy impacts.

Close agreement with the IRS Code tends to ease the state administrator's problems (table 7). Taxpayers show less confusion over differences in requirements under the two sets of statutes. The state tax agency can more easily verify that taxpayers report consistently to both the IRS and the state revenue department. Federal compliance and audit efforts can be added to state efforts with fewer adjustment checks. Whatever the administrative gains in state conformity with national income tax legislation, greater administrative gains and simplification could be achieved if both national and state governments reduced exceptions to the form of income exemptions and exclusions or reduced the number of deductions. These exceptions, and the rules and regulations that are used to interpret them, continually add to the complexity of the income tax codes for the taxpayer and to the number of checking points required by computers and auditors.[16]

[16]Three former commissioners of the IRS testified before the Joint Congressional Committee on Taxation on July 12, 1977, to plead for simplification of the national income tax. Donald C. Alexander stated: "Making our system simple and understandable is more important than trying to attain every social and economic objective perceived at the time

Extensive income exemptions and exclusions may lead the taxpayer intentionally or accidentally to forget other income that should be reported. Exempt income adds to the complexity of any aggregate analysis that attempts to establish whether most income has, in fact, been reported to the IRS and to the state. Exempt income also makes more difficult the enforcement effort, which depends to a substantial extent on awareness of a taxpayer's living style and the income he/she reports for tax purposes. Whether a sense of injustice by taxpayers without such income exemptions may encourage incomplete reporting has never been fully tested.

As in the case of income exemptions and inclusions, administrative pragmatism would argue for adoption of the federal code concerning permissible *deductions.* Only the states that tax on the basis of federal net income or as a proportion of the federal tax fully follow the IRS Code. Other states adopt a significant number of federal deductions, but as we have seen, add others of their own or sometimes subtract a few. If taxpayer returns are to be reasonably reviewed, some verification is needed for deductions; and each additional legislative deduction adds to the administrative load.

The provision for property tax credits/rebates for the elderly or for all taxpayers in lower income brackets has added to the work load in every income tax office in states that have legislated such provisions. Wisconsin in the mid-1970s estimated processing costs at about $3.00 per return in fiscal years 1973 and 1974, and that cost included little audit time. Some of the states did not provide administrative funds for handling these claims, and the agencies usually absorbed the extra work by reducing the quality of income tax administration in other ways. Other states made little effort to advise taxpayers of their rights under the credit/rebate provisions or to assist them in filing.

Apart from general rules that relate income, employment, family status, etc., to deduction probabilities (or comparison with federal returns), few immediate office verifications are practical. Only inquiries to churches, insurance companies, local tax offices, etc., or field investigations can provide proof of each claimed deduction. And when tax administrators —as in California and Minnesota, for example—have the added burden of disallowing the business expenses of owners of substandard rental housing, they must either rely exclusively on the decisions of others officially relayed to them or face an impossible burden.

Even a policy of low rates may undermine administrative efforts (table 6). Legislators generally fail to recognize that very low tax rates, especially

to be worthwhile." Mortimer Caplin argued that Congress should be willing to "accept some tax leakage as the price of a workable tax system" and added: "When I hear of a proposed insulation credit, I just shudder as a former tax administrator. I see a proliferation of attic playrooms in the name of insulation." Quoted in an Associated Press story in the *Wisconsin State Journal* (Madison) on July 14, 1977.

if combined with overly generous income exclusions and expenditure deductions, discourage energetic administrative effort. No tax agency has unlimited resources, and a normal part of administrative judgment (auditor and even clerical judgment) concerns whether the question that arises in review is "serious" enough to be given time and attention. Translate "serious" as tax productive. State statutes may provide explicitly that refunds or collections involving a dollar or less (or even five dollars or less) shall not be made. Whether or not specific legal provision exists, tax agencies normally employ some cutoff figure even on office-identified arithmetic errors in seeking additional collections. Few tax officials check out questions with a taxpayer that would produce only small amounts of further revenue if the official's suspicions were confirmed. And there is always the possibility that the taxpayer's report is fully accurate as filed.

Unusually low tax rates, then, invite administrative neglect. Payroll withholding produces the bulk of the taxes collected. If other taxpayers incompletely report income, or even on occasion neglect to file, the agency may make little or no effort to follow up. Neither office nor field investigation costs would warrant the probable tax yield from a fully accurate return.[17] More than one tax administrator in states with very low rates told the author that *at their rates* even routine investigations were not worthwhile. Marginal considerations will not disappear in any tax agency, but the lower the tax rates, and the higher the number of income exclusions and expenditure deductions, the greater the probability that the income tax will become largely a payroll withholding tax. In terms of equity, employees who are subject to payroll withholding and who take the standard deduction lose out increasingly to the limited or even negative marginal return on office or field auditing of taxpayers who itemize deductions and whose income is not exclusively or substantially subject to payroll withholding.

Administrative Tools in State Statutes

Tax policies may add or detract from administrative effectiveness, but without adequate tools administrators cannot carry out even the most equitable tax. Legislators may give a tax agency a full arsenal of aids or they may provide an agency with antique weapons to carry out a modern responsibility among taxpayers equipped with the latest weapons. The model uniform tax law of the Advisory Commission on Intergovernmental Relations appears to assume both a single centralized state tax agency and

[17]The author's discussions with tax administrators suggest that this problem also exists fairly widely in the area of property tax rebates or credits, where most returns are accepted as filed.

a merit system for personnel selection. Detailed provisions specify payroll withholding, information returns, and numerous other means for enforcing the income tax. Tables 10 and 11 identify the major administrative tools provided by the Uniform Personal Income Tax Statute and those provided by individual state statutes.

TAX LIABILITY

Information Returns

Wisconsin's provision for information returns assures the state a means of verifying the taxpayer's statement of income and thereby assures general reporting by all taxpayers. The more comprehensive a state tax department's information return system and the more usable the data, the better equipped the department is for enforcement. The Advisory Commission's Uniform Personal Income Tax Statute does not specify information return requirements, but does authorize the tax commissioner to require such returns when needed, "showing to whom dividends, interests, rents, salaries, wages, premiums, annuities, compensations, remunerations, emoluments or other fixed or determinable gains, profits, or income, except interest coupons payable to bearer" are paid.[18] Under the model law, the monkey is on the administrator's back to issue the proper regulations and to enforce them in securing the returns, and then to make use of them in the subsequent verification and audit procedures. Currently, only twenty-six states specifically require information returns on dividends, interest, rents, royalties, etc., over a specified amount. In several other states revenue commissions may make such demands (table 10).

Withholding

The annual withholding statement may be substituted for an information return on wages and salaries under payroll deduction. Without withholding, no government could collect annually a relatively high amount of taxes from many taxpayers (see chapter 6). Setting aside large sums of money each week or month to pay taxes at some future time does not fit the habits of most individuals. A low-rate tax on average or above-average incomes can be collected annually, as the pre-World War II record in this country demonstrates; but high tax rates, or even low tax rates on increasing incomes, place impractical budget burdens on taxpayers. Pay-as-you-go through payroll withholding and quarterly estimates and prepayment for other income keeps taxpayers more honest and yields the needed taxes on a continuing basis.

Although Oregon adopted payroll withholding in 1948 (Alaska, not yet a

[18] *Uniform Personal Income Tax Statute,* sec. 60, p. 241.

TABLE 10

Administrative Tools: State Individual Income Tax and Information-Return Filing Requirements

State	Minimum income filing requirements: Tax returns[a] — Net income: Single ($)	Net income: Married ($)	Gross income: Single ($)	Gross income: Married ($)	Information returns by payers for non-wage and salary income[b]: Dividends ($)	Interest ($)	Rents and royalties ($)	Other
Uniform Personal Income Tax Statute	—	—	600	1,200	10	10	600	$600
Alabama	1,500	3,000	—	—	1,500	1,500	1,500	$1,500, including foreign items
Alaska	Federal requirements				10	10	600[d]	Annuities, pensions, and other gains, $600[d] Foreign items, $600
Arizona	1,000	2,000	5,000	5,000	300	300	300	Patronage dividends, $100
Arkansas	1,500	3,000	—	—	100	100	2,500	$2,500, including foreign items
California	Single: if AGI over $3,250 or total income over $7,000 Married: $6,500, $7,000				10	10	1,000[d,e]	Annuities, pensions, profit sharing, $1,000[d,e] Foreign items, $1,500 Patronage dividends, rebates, refunds, $100
Colorado	—	—	1,750	2,500				
Connecticut	No broad-based income tax							
Delaware	Federal requirements		1,600	1,200	10	10	10[d]	Salaries, pensions, and fees not subject to withholding, $600[d]
D.C.					600[d]	600[d]	600[d]	All other taxable income, $600

Florida	No personal income tax							
Georgia	Federal requirements				100	1,000[d]	1,000[d]	$1,000[d]
Hawaii	—	—	750	750	10	600[d]	600[d]	Foreign items, annuities, and pensions, $600[d]; Patronage dividends, $10
Idaho	Federal requirements				10	10	600	Board and lodging furnished and other fixed income, $600
Illinois	Federal requirements or $1,000 × no. of exemptions							Annuities and pensions, $600
Indiana					600	600[f]	600	Salaries, wages, fees, commissions, prizes, awards, $100
Iowa	$2,000 or federal requirements				100	1,000[d]	1,000[d]	Compensation, remuneration, and other payments over $1,000
Kansas					600[d]	600[d]	600[d]	Wages, premiums, annuities, $600
Kentucky					—	—	—	—
Louisiana	If tax owed or		6,000	6,000	May be requested by Secretary of Taxation[g]			
Maine	Federal requirements or $1,000 × no. of dependents				May be required			
Maryland	—	—	2,450	3,600	Not required to the extent reports are made under federal law			
Massachusetts	—	—	2,000	2,000	10	10[f]	600[d]	Taxable annuities, $10
Michigan	—	—	1,500	3,000	—	—	—	—
Minnesota	—	—	1,000	1,800	10.01	10	600.01	Savings, building and loan associations distributions, $10.01; Other income, $600.01
Mississippi	—	—	4,500	6,500 plus personal exemptions	600	600	600	Premiums and annuities, $600
Missouri	Federal requirements or 600				Not required	Not required	1,200	f,h
Montana	—	—	720	1,445	10	10.01	600.01	All other taxable income, $600

TABLE 10—*Continued*

State	Tax returns[a]: Net income, Single ($)	Net income, Married ($)	Gross income, Single ($)	Gross income, Married ($)	Information returns by payers for non-wage and salary income[b]: Dividends ($)	Interest ($)	Rents and royalties ($)	Other
Nebraska	Federal requirements				—[i]	—	—	—
New Hampshire	—	—	$600 interest or dividends		—	—	—	—
New Jersey					1,000	1,000	1,000	All other taxable income, $600.01
New Mexico	If required to file federal return				—	—	—	—
New York	Federal requirements or plus $650 × personal exemptions		2,500	5,000	Not required	600[f]	600[d]	Annuities, prizes, awards, $600[d]
North Carolina	—	—	1,000	2,000	100	100	600	Pensions and annuities, $100[k]
North Dakota	—	—	2,450	3,600	10[h]	10[h]	600[d]	$600[d]
Ohio	If subject to income tax				—	—	—	—
Oklahoma					100	100	750	Premiums, annuities, oil and gas bonuses, rents and royalties, $750[d]
Oregon	—	—	1,800	2,550	10[k]	10	600	Travel expenses, car allowances, lease deposits, bonuses, etc., $0.01 Annuities, fixed income, $600

Pennsylvania	If have income subject to tax				—	—	—	—
Rhode Island	Rederal requirements or income in excess of federal personal exemptions				100	100	100	Premiums and annuities, $100
South Carolina	—	—	800		200	200	800	$800[d]
Tennessee	25	50			—	—	—	—
Utah					—	—	—	—
Vermont	Federal requirements				—[i]	—	—	—
Virginia	—	—	1,900	2,500	—	—	—	—
West Virginia	Federal requirements or if income in excess of West Virginia personal exemptions					Not required for current year		
Wisconsin	—	—	1,950	2,600	100	100	100	All patronage dividend transfers of capital stock by residents

Sources: Compilation for columns 1, 2, 3, and 4 from individual state forms and instructions for 1976 and 1977 filing. Compilation for columns 5, 6, 7, and 8 based on Commerce Clearing House, *State Tax Handbook, 1978* (Chicago: Commerce Clearing House, October, 1978).

[a]These columns show the normal filing requirements. There may be exceptions, e.g., filing requirements for taxpayers over 65 are higher in most states. Returns must also be filed to claim any refunds due to overwithholding.

[b]Not required in Colorado, Illinois, Kentucky, Michigan, Nebraska, New Mexico, Ohio, Pennsylvania, Vermont, or Virginia.

[c]Provisions included by the Advisory Commission on Intergovernmental Relations for its recommended uniform statute. U.S., Advisory Commission on Intergovernmental Relations, *State-Local Finances, 1971 Edition* (Washington, D.C.: Government Printing Office, December, 1970), pp. 220-64.

[d]Aggregate of several types of income.

[e]Although the law requires information returns on payments of $1,000 or more, the Franchise Tax Board has ruled that payments of less than $1,500 to single persons or less than $3,000 to married persons need not be reported.

[f]Other than certain municipal bonds in Indiana and interest coupons payable to bearer in Massachusetts and New York.

[g]When required by the collector, persons and firms making payments of $1,000 or more per year must file an information return by June 1 of the following year.

[h]If an information return for such amount is required for federal purposes.

[i]Since state tax is a percentage of federal tax, columns on information return could be considered irrelevant.

[j]Other compensation, including pensions, not reported on Form IT-2102.

[k]Patronage dividends, rebates, and refunds, $100.

TABLE 11
Additional Statutory Administrative Tools for Individual Income Taxes

State	Subpoena power for: Taxpayer (1)	Subpoena power for: Records (2)	Jeopardy assessment authority (3)	Net worth, doomage assessment authority (4)	Conviction for fraud penalty[a] (5)	Taxpayer required to report changes made by IRS (6)	Years normal statute of limitations[b] (7)	Authority to use refunds/overpayments to offset income, other tax, other debts to state (8)	Late payment interest rate (%) (9)
Uniform Personal Income Tax Statute[c]	Yes	Yes	Yes	Yes	Felony	Yes	3	Taxes only	6[d]
Alabama	Yes	Yes	Yes	Yes	Felony	No	3	Income tax only	6
Alaska	Yes	Yes	Yes	Yes	Felony	Yes	3	All state debts	8
Arizona	Yes	Yes	Yes	Yes	Felony	Yes	4	Income tax only	6
Arkansas	Yes	Yes	Yes	Yes	Misdemeanor	Yes	3	Income tax only	6
California	Yes	Yes	Yes	Yes	Felony	Yes	4	All state debts	6
Colorado	Yes	Yes	Yes	No	Felony	Yes	4	Taxes only	6
Connecticut	No broad-based income tax for individuals					—			
Delaware	Yes	Yes	Yes	No	Misdemeanor	Yes	3	Taxes only	12
Florida	No individual income tax					—			
Georgia	Yes	Yes	Yes	Yes	Felony	Yes	3	Income taxes only	9
Hawaii	Yes	Yes	Yes	Yes	Misdemeanor	Yes	3	Taxes only	8
Idaho	Yes	Yes	Yes	Yes	Felony	Yes	3	Taxes only	8
Illinois	Yes	Yes	Yes	No	Misdemeanor	Yes	3	Any debt due state	9
Indiana	Yes	Yes	Yes	Yes	Felony	No	3	All state debts	6
Iowa	Yes	Yes	Yes	Yes	Felony	No	3	Income or excise taxes only	9
Kansas	Yes	Yes	Yes	Yes	Felony	Yes	4	Past due taxes	12
Kentucky	Yes	Yes	Yes	Yes	Felony	Yes	4	All state debts	8
Louisiana	Yes	Yes	Yes	Yes	Felony	Yes	3	Taxes only	12
Maine	Yes	Yes	Yes	Yes	Misdemeanor	Yes	3	Taxes only	6
Maryland	Yes	Yes	Yes	Yes	Misdemeanor	Yes	3	All state debts	9
Massachusetts	Yes	Yes	Yes	Yes	Misdemeanor	Yes	3	Taxes only	8
Michigan	Yes	Yes	Yes	Yes	Misdemeanor	Yes	3	All state debts	9

Minnesota	Yes	Yes	Yes	Yes	Felony	Yes	3½	Taxes only	8
Mississippi	Yes	Yes	Yes	Yes	Misdemeanor	Yes	3	Income taxes only	6
Missouri	Yes	Yes	Yes	Yes	Felony	Yes	3	Taxes only	6
Montana	Yes	Yes	Yes	Yes	Misdemeanor	Yes	5	All state debts	9
Nebraska	Yes	Yes	Yes	Yes	Felony	Yes	3	All state debts	6
New Hampshire	No broad-based income tax					—	—	—	—
New Jersey	Yes	Yes	Yes	Yes	Misdemeanor	Limited	3	Taxes only	9
New Mexico	Yes	Yes	Yes	Yes	Felony	Yes	3	Taxes only	6
New York	Yes	Yes	Yes	Yes	Misdemeanor	Yes	3	Taxes only	12
North Carolina	Yes	Yes	Yes	Yes	Misdemeanor	Yes	3	Income and some other taxes only	6
North Dakota	Yes	Yes	No	Yes	Misdemeanor	Yes	3	Income taxes only	12
Ohio	Yes	Yes	Yes	Yes		Yes	3	Taxes only	6
Oklahoma	Yes	Yes	Yes	No	Felony	Yes	3	Taxes only	6
Oregon	Yes	Yes	Yes	Yes	Misdemeanor	Yes	3	Income taxes and debts due state	12
Pennsylvania	Yes	Yes	Yes	Yes	Misdemeanor	No	3	Income taxes only	6
Rhode Island	Yes	Yes	No	Yes	Misdemeanor	Yes	3	Taxes only	8
South Carolina	Yes	Yes	Yes	Yes	Felony	No	3	Income taxes only	6
Tennessee	No broad-based income tax					—			
Utah	No	No	Yes	No	Misdemeanor	No	3	Income taxes only	8
Vermont	Yes	Yes	Yes	Yes	Felony	Yes	3	Taxes only	12
Virginia	Yes	Yes	Yes	Yes	Felony	Yes	3	Income taxes only	7
West Virginia	Yes	Yes	Yes	Yes	Misdemeanor	Yes	3	None	6
Wisconsin	Yes	Yes	Yes	Yes	Felony	Yes	4	Taxes only	18

Sources: Except for columns 6 and 9, data supplied to author by state tax departments on questionnaire of August, 1978. Column 6 from Commerce Clearing House, *State Tax Handbook, 1978* (Chicago: Commerce Clearing House, October, 1978), p. 657. Column 9 from *Tax Administrators News* 40, no. 5 (May, 1976): 49.

[a] Statutes that make "fraud" a felony usually also provide for a misdemeanor for lesser counts. Dollar penalties plus interest may also be provided.

[b] Whatever the number of years for the "normal statute of limitations," many states as well as the "Uniform Personal Income Tax Statute" provide a 6-year statute of limitations if more than 25% of taxable income has been omitted and no statute of limitations if the taxpayer (1) fails to file; (2) files a fraudulent return; or (3) fails to notify the state tax department of changes made by the IRS.

[c] Provisions included by the Advisory Commission on Intergovernmental Relations for their recommended uniform statute. U.S., Advisory Commission on Intergovernmental Relations, *State-Local Finances*, 1971 (Washington, D.C.: Government Printing Office, December, 1970), pp. 220-64.

[d] Plus monetary penalties in certain cases.

state, in 1949), and Vermont followed in 1951, fewer than half of the income tax states had adopted withholding by 1959. Subsequently, all income tax states except North Dakota have amended their statutes to provide for withholding or have included it in their new statutes. In 1964, Alan P. Murray estimated that collections in the states increased from 10% to 25% in the years immediately following adoption of withholding.[19] Withholding has proved so acceptable and so administratively desirable that the authorized tables tend to lead to overwithholding, the rationale being that refunds are easier to process than collections. Taxpayers not only accept the overwithholding but some understate personal exemptions in order to earn larger refunds!

Payroll withholding and quarterly estimates with prepayment by individuals and corporations were not always accepted simultaneously. Oregon adopted withholding for payrolls in 1948 but failed to adopt quarterly estimates and prepayment by corporations until 1974 (when it set a 50% current payment requirement) *and still has not required such from individuals.* Oregon further favors nonpayroll income by permitting such taxpayers to pay these taxes in two installments the following year! A few other states have adopted wage and salary withholding without quarterly reports and current tax payments on nonwage income. Some states with the statutes enforce them only casually.[20]

Although payroll withholding eases the taxpayer's payments and increases the state's collections, it entails administrative costs both for the employer and for the tax department. Receipt of employer reports and payments requires checking and matching the payments and reports as well as some cross-verification with withholding statements attached to returns. (Again, see the discussion of these issues in chapter 6.)

Filing Requirements

Any self-assessed income tax law requires individuals to file returns and to pay any remaining tax balance. Some statutes rather casually allow the taxpayer to determine whether or not there is a tax due (e.g., Ohio) and therefore whether or not he has an obligation to file a return. The model uniform income tax law, which gives the individual an income exemption of $600 and the couple an income exemption of $1,200, requires the single taxpayer with a gross income of $600 to file a return and the couple to file if their gross income exceeds $1,200.

[19] Alan P. Murray, "Wage-Withholding and State Income Taxes," *National Tax Journal* 17 (December, 1964): 405-17.

[20] As of 1976, Alabama, Arizona, Idaho, Iowa, Mississippi, Montana, North Dakota, Ohio, and Utah did not require current payment of corporation income taxes. Several states permit corporations to pay part of their taxes in the succeeding year: Connecticut (30%), Maryland (50%), New Jersey (40%), Oregon (50%), and Pennsylvania (10%). *Tax Administrators News* 40 (May, 1976): 49, 50.

Although any tax agency would like to receive only returns that show a tax due, administrators prefer the no-tax return to engaging in Sherlock Holmes operations to uncover the taxpayer whose self-interpretation of exempt income and allowable deductions had disadvantaged the state coffers. More rather than fewer filing requirements will produce revenue. Table 10 lists the filing requirements of the income tax states.

STATUTORY COMPLIANCE AIDS

Our income tax laws are generally respected, and most taxpayers, whether from choice or fear of discovery, file and report honestly. But always a minority of taxpayers—through ignorance, negligence, or intent —(1) fail to file, (2) file but fail to report all income, (3) file but exaggerate exemptions or deductions, or (4) file but fail to pay taxes due. Tax departments must review and audit returns in the interests of the honest taxpayer and encourage both the honest and the tempted taxpayer to file fully and accurately. Information returns and filing requirements help the department to get returns and the information with which to verify returns. Withholding and quarterly estimates aid in the collection of taxes due. But other statutory provisions also assist in enforcement. Even comparatively simple provisions may be valuable, such as the provision that a taxpayer is required to report any changes as a result of IRS action (table 11). If he fails to make such a report, the statute of limitations (discussed below) does not run. Although the department normally receives such information directly from the IRS, enforcement is simplified if the taxpayer also advises the department of the change.

Not all state statutes permit a tax department to apply a refund due to an overpayment through withholding or otherwise to pay other income or taxes due the department. Tax collection for unpaid accounts can be difficult and time-consuming. Where a taxpayer has overpaid one tax and underpaid another, it can be in the interest of the taxpayer and the department to allow the refund to offset the debt. Several states go even further and permit other agencies of the state to collect accounts owed by taxpayers through tax refunds due (see table 11 and chapter 6).

Statutes of Limitations

A tax department needs time in which to review or audit tax returns, and the ordinary taxpayer needs to know at some point that his return has been accepted as filed. Both the Uniform Personal Income Tax Statute and most state laws provide such statutes of limitations. Three- or four-year statutes are most common. A four-year statute of limitations gives a state tax department an opportunity to incorporate any IRS audit findings with any changes indicated by its own auditors, since the IRS has a three-year statute of limitations. A one- or two-year statute of limitations almost guarantees that a state tax department will audit few returns; a three-year statute limits use of IRS audit findings; and a period longer than four years would give the taxpayer reason to complain about having to retain records. Negligence, in a legal sense, may extend the statute of limitations, and the national government and most states give tax agencies an indefinite period for investigation and prosecution if a taxpayer fails to file or is guilty of fraud in his tax return. Table 11 lists the basic time periods allowed under the various state statutes.

Access to Taxpayer Records

To carry out a field audit, the state tax department's auditor must have access to the taxpayer and to his records. Most taxpayers accept the legal right of an auditor to examine his books and to review issues with him, but an uncooperative taxpayer may be subpoenaed with his books and records to appear in the office of a tax auditor. Only with such clear statutory authority will some taxpayers respect the enforcement rights of the state tax department.[21]

ASSESSMENTS

Filing tax returns and paying taxes are considered voluntary actions by the taxpayer. If, when carrying out its responsibilities, the tax department determines that the taxpayer owes additional taxes, it levies some type of assessment which it can then collect from the taxpayer directly or enforce through court judgments by attaching property owned by the taxpayer or by garnisheeing his wages or salary. The exact provisions in state laws in these matters vary and sometimes depend on general statutory provisions rather than on the tax statute.

Deficiency Assessment

Whether a taxpayer makes an arithmetic error, claims a deduction he is not entitled to, files an incomplete or inaccurate return, etc., the tax administrator may make an additional or deficiency assessment. States generally provide for adjustment of arithmetic errors without recourse by the taxpayer. In other deficiency assessments, the taxpayer is given a period of time in which to defend his earlier return and to contest the legitimacy of the department's action. All state statutes provide for deficiency assessments.

[21]The subpoena powers of tax departments may exceed those of other state officials, e.g., the attorney general. On occasion, these officials may seek to get a tax department to use its subpoena power in a case of more interest to the other officials than to the tax agency. Tax departments normally, and the author believes rightly, refuse. Again, table 11 lists the statutory provisions of the states.

Jeopardy Assessment

Most state statutes recognize occasions when the state's interest can be served only by immediate action by the tax department. Whenever the tax department believes collection of the income tax is in jeopardy due to the apparent conditions of the taxpayer's finances, the possibility that the taxpayer will move his assets out of state, or to the failure of a taxpayer to respond to departmental inquiries, a jeopardy assessment may be issued. Jeopardy assessments also often serve tax collection interests in the case of probable illegal income from drugs or crime or gambling. If the police pick up a suspect, e.g., a suspected drug peddler with an unusual amount of money on him, they may call the state tax department to permit an official to file a jeopardy assessment and attach the funds. Cooperation here depends on the tax statute and the relations department personnel have established with the police.

Any jeopardy assessment is another form of deficiency assessment. Its advantage for the tax agency is the ability to ignore normal statutory waiting periods for taxpayer replies and to attach property immediately. Depending on state law, the taxpayer will have a chance to be heard by the tax department and possibly by a court before the attached property can be used to pay taxes held to be owed.[22]

Net Worth Assessment

To provide equitable enforcement of income tax laws, the government must have the option of estimating assessments in order to secure taxes due. For the taxpayer who refuses or fails to file, the Uniform Personal Income Tax Statute, the IRS, and most states authorize the department to estimate income, expenditures, and the amount of taxable income (table 11).

Uncooperative taxpayers who fail to file a return, fail to produce records, or otherwise impede investigation may find auditors reconstructing their accounts based on whatever evidence they find. Such audit actions might follow where the taxpayer's mode of living or apparent assets appear to require filing a return or reporting more income than that shown on the return filed. Once the tax department has determined its estimate of net worth and the resulting taxes due, it may levy an assessment. (Whether this would be a jeopardy assessment would depend on departmental practices and the circumstances of the case.) The burden of proof, then, is on the taxpayer to establish that his taxable income in one or more years is less

[22]For a discussion of the use of jeopardy assessments by the IRS, see U.S., Department of the Treasury, Comptroller General, *Use of Jeopardy and Termination Assessment by the IRS, Department of the Treasury: Report to the Joint Committee on Internal Revenue Taxation, Congress of the United States, GGD-76-14* (Washington, D.C.: General Accounting Office, July 16, 1976).

than the department asserts. Although the net worth technique can be abused, it is probably used less often than would be legitimate under those statutes that provide for it. A net worth assessment that will hold up in court requires many audit hours to produce an appropriate reconstruction of income and expenditures.

Conclusion

This chapter has summarized some of the major tax policies that make the tax administrator's lot easier or more difficult. The more complex the law, the more difficult it is for the taxpayer to comply fully, and the more difficult it is for the department to have the resources to review or audit all the items on every return. Citizens and groups often seek special tax provisions in the name of "equity," but simpler (grosser?) tax laws may promote equity through better and more equitable administration.

Whatever the tax policies chosen by legislators, administrators can enforce them only if they have appropriate statutory tools. Departments need (1) information returns on all sources of taxpayer income; (2) tax withholding and quarterly estimates and payments; (3) filing requirements that make all citizens who may owe a tax submit a return; (4) time in which to make reasonable reviews or audits of returns; (5) power to make deficiency, jeopardy, and net worth assessments; and (6) other authority that will assure fair enforcement. Such tools do not guarantee enforcement but they are a necessary foundation.

Chapter Three

Patterns of Administrative Organization

A sound organizational structure facilitates efficient administration of the income tax. The well-designed organization canalizes administrative efforts to allow their free flow to tax policy objectives. Faulty organization may force an administrator to dissipate energy in unproductive activities, cut down the productivity of the investment in tax administration, and jeopardize the interests of all taxpayers. But no fixed formula of organization has proved most appropriate under all conditions. Tradition often determines the structure in a particular state, since change may require statutory revision and affect the status of individuals. And tradition may have embedded so much institutional memory of "how things should be done" that a seemingly incongruous organizational structure works well, if not optimally. Optimal organizations still differ, depending on such variables as number of taxpayers, geographic size of the state, urban-rural mix, current degree of automation, or whether all parts of the organization are physically close or separated by blocks or miles.

The organizational patterns of state tax departments and the disposition of the income tax function differ in five major respects: (1) the degree of consolidation, i.e., the extent to which other taxes and fiscal functions are included with income tax administration; (2) direction of the tax agency by a single executive/administrator or a commission; (3) the degree of integration, i.e., the extent to which the administrative functions for different taxes are interwoven; (4) the role of field offices or the territorial distribution of administrative authority and services; and (5) the arrangements for administrative handling of disputes and appeals.

This chapter will examine organizational patterns for income taxation under the above five headings. We cannot measure quantitatively the effect of different organizational patterns on income tax administration. The discussion will, however, suggest likely favorable and unfavorable elements of differing organizational structures.

Consolidation versus Multiple Tax Agencies

The expansion of state government activities has encouraged governors and legislators to seek reorganizations that would reduce the number of agency heads reporting to them and presumably increase the effectiveness of governmental actions by reducing the number of departmental jurisdictional boundaries. Probably no state tax agency has remained untouched organizationally since 1965. Both the functional consolidation trend and the trend toward more cabinet-like state governments have affected tax agencies as well as others.[1] Thirty-one of the forty-five states (plus the District of Columbia) with a corporation or individual income tax in 1978 had one agency that collected all taxes or all except motor vehicle taxes.[2] (See table 12.) California, with four separate tax agencies, is the only state where sales and income taxes are collected by different agencies.[3]

Advocates of consolidation into a single tax department emphasize (1) the possible savings or greater efficiency in use of appropriations and personnel that can be realized through integration of staff functions, (2) easier exchange of information, (3) better division of labor, and (4) development of broader perspectives. Particularly in less populous states, bringing several taxes together into one agency may be the only way to effect economies of scale in the collections function, computer processing, and such staff activities as budgeting, personnel, internal accounting, planning, statistical analysis, and other research. Less tangible benefits might also accrue in the form of better taxpayer relations since taxpayers would have to deal with only one agency.

A few states have extended consolidation concepts to include more general revenue collection and treasury functions within a single agency. Michigan, New York, and New Jersey follow this pattern, although neither New York nor New Jersey includes motor vehicle licenses within the

[1]George A. Bell, "State Administrative Organization Activities, 1974-75," *The Book of the States, 1976-1977* (Lexington, Ky.: The Council of State Government, 1976), p. 105, reported that nineteen states (eighteen had either a corporation or an individual income tax) comprehensively restructured their executive systems between 1965 and 1975: Arkansas, California, Colorado, Delaware, Florida, Idaho, Georgia, Kentucky, Louisiana, Maine, Maryland, Massachusetts, Michigan, Missouri, Montana, North Carolina, South Dakota, Virginia, and Wisconsin.

[2]The majority of these states assigned collection of taxes on motor vehicle licenses, driver's licenses, etc., to a separate department which had other highway responsibilities.

[3]California established the Franchise Tax Commission in 1929 to collect the corporation franchise tax. The older Board of Equalization, with responsibility for the property tax, took on sales tax administration in 1933. When the personal income tax was adopted by the state in 1935, the Franchise Tax Commission was assigned this responsibility. Only a detailed history of California in these years would fully explain the diverse assignments that have remained frozen in succeeding decades. In 1950, slight changes were made in California's statutes to replace the Franchise Tax Commission with the Franchise Tax Board and to establish the executive officer as the administrative head of the agency. Today the Franchise Tax Board is an agency within the Department of State and Consumer Services. The Board of Equalization remains apart.

TABLE 12
State Assignment of Tax Administration to Income Tax Agency

State	*Income tax agency*	*Responsibilities*[a]
Alabama	Department of Revenue	Taxes: income, sales, gasoline, motor vehicle, tobacco, death
Alaska[b,c]	Department of Revenue	Taxes: income, gasoline, tobacco, death, alcoholic beverage Other: payment of warrants
Arizona	Department of Revenue	Taxes: income, sales, tobacco, death, alcoholic beverage
Arkansas[b]	Department of Finance and Administration	Taxes: income, sales, gasoline, motor vehicle, tobacco, death, alcoholic beverage Budget, accounting, preaudit, etc.
California	Franchise Tax Board[d]	Taxes: income Audit responsibility for state campaign expenditures
Colorado[b]	Department of Revenue	Taxes: income, sales, gasoline, motor vehicle, tobacco, death, alcoholic beverage
Connecticut[b]	Tax Department	Taxes: income, sales, gasoline, tobacco, death, alcoholic beverage
Delaware[b,c]	Division of Revenue, Department of Finance	Taxes: income, tobacco, death, alcoholic beverage Other: budget and accounting controls, preaudit, warrant issuance
Florida	Department of Revenue	Taxes: income, sales, gasoline, death
Georgia[b]	Department of Revenue	Taxes: income, sales, gasoline, motor vehicle, tobacco, death, alcoholic beverage
Hawaii[b]	Department of Taxation	Taxes: income, sales, gasoline, tobacco, death, alcoholic beverage
Idaho[b]	Department of Revenue and Taxation	Taxes: income, sales, gasoline, tobacco, death, alcoholic beverage
Illinois	Department of Revenue	Taxes: income, sales, gasoline, tobacco, alcoholic beverage
Indiana[b]	Department of Revenue	Taxes: income, sales, gasoline, tobacco, death, alcoholic beverage
Iowa[b]	Department of Revenue	Taxes: income, sales, gasoline, tobacco, death, alcoholic beverage
Kansas[b]	Department of Revenue	Taxes: income, sales, gasoline, motor vehicle, tobacco, death, alcoholic beverage
Kentucky[b]	Department of Revenue	Taxes: income, sales, gasoline, tobacco, death, alcoholic beverage
Louisiana[b]	Department of Revenue and Taxation	Taxes: income, sales, gasoline, motor vehicle, tobacco, death, alcoholic beverage
Maine	Bureau of Taxation	Taxes: income, sales, gasoline, tobacco, death
Maryland	Comptroller	Taxes: income, sales, gasoline, tobacco, alcoholic beverage Other: determination of accounting system, preaudit, warrant issuance
Massachusetts[b,e]	Executive Office for Administration and Finance (Department of Revenue)	Taxes: income, sales, gasoline, tobacco, death, alcoholic beverage

TABLE 12—*Continued*

State	*Income tax agency*	*Responsibilities*[a]
Michigan	Department of the Treasury	Taxes: income, sales, gasoline, tobacco, death Other: usual treasury functions, including investment of state funds and payment of warrants
Minnesota[b]	Department of Revenue	Taxes: income, sales, gasoline, tobacco, death, alcoholic beverage
Mississippi[b]	Tax Commission	Taxes: income, sales, tobacco, death, alcoholic beverage
Missouri[b]	Department of Revenue	Taxes: income, sales, gasoline, motor vehicle, tobacco, death, alcoholic beverage
Montana[b,c]	Department of Revenue	Taxes: income, gasoline, tobacco, death, alcoholic beverage
Nebraska	Department of Revenue	Taxes: income, sales, gasoline, tobacco, death
New Hampshire[c]	Department of Revenue Administration	Taxes: income, tobacco, death
New Jersey[b]	Department of Treasury	Taxes: income, sales, gasoline, tobacco, death, alcoholic beverage Other: usual treasury functions, including investment of state funds, state budget and accounting, preaudit, issuance and payment of warrants, separate Division of Tax Appeals
New Mexico[b]	Department of Taxation and Revenue	Taxes: income, sales, gasoline, tobacco, death, alcoholic beverage
New York[b]	Department of Taxation and Finance	Taxes: income, sales, gasoline, tobacco, death, alcoholic beverage Other: usual treasury functions
North Carolina[b]	Department of Revenue	Taxes: income, sales, gasoline, tobacco, death, alcoholic beverage
North Dakota	Tax Commissioner	Taxes: income, sales, gasoline, tobacco, death
Ohio[b]	Department of Taxation	Taxes: income, sales, gasoline, tobacco, death, alcoholic beverage
Oklahoma[b]	Tax Commission	Taxes: income, sales, gasoline, tobacco, death, alcoholic beverage, motor vehicle
Oregon	Department of Revenue	Taxes: income, tobacco, death
Pennsylvania[b]	Department of Revenue	Taxes: income, sales, gasoline, tobacco, death, alcoholic beverage
Rhode Island[b]	Department of Administration	Taxes: income, sales, gasoline, tobacco, death, alcoholic beverage Other: state budget, accounting, preaudit, warrant issuance
South Carolina[b]	Tax Commission	Taxes: income, sales, gasoline, tobacco, death, alcoholic beverage
Tennessee[b]	Department of Revenue	Taxes: income, sales, gasoline, tobacco, death, alcoholic beverage
Utah[b]	Tax Commission	Taxes: income, sales, gasoline, motor vehicle, tobacco, death, alcoholic beverage

TABLE 12—*Continued*

State	*Income tax agency*	*Responsibilities*[a]
Vermont[b]	Commissioner of Taxes	Taxes: income, sales, gasoline, tobacco, death, alcoholic beverage
Virginia	Department of Taxation	Taxes: income, sales, tobacco, death, alcoholic beverage
West Virginia	Tax Department	Taxes: income, sales, gasoline, tobacco, death
Wisconsin[b]	Department of Revenue	Taxes: income, sales, gasoline, tobacco, death, alcoholic beverage

Source: *The Book of the States, 1978-1979* (Lexington, Ky.: The Council of State Governments), pp. 138, 139. Massachusetts organization represents later change as department advised author September, 1978.

[a]Only major taxes listed for each state; most state tax agencies also have some supervisory responsibility for local property taxes.

[b]The Franchise Tax Board is technically part of the Department of State and Consumer Services.

[c]Collects all taxes or all taxes except motor vehicle.

[d]These five states have no sales tax.

[e]With summer, 1978, reorganization, the Department of Corporations and Taxation became the Department of Revenue within the Executive Office for Administration and Finance. The overall agency has responsibility for budgeting, personnel, and general central administration, as well as for the Department of Revenue's tax administration functions.

combined agency, and Michigan excludes both motor vehicle licenses and alcoholic beverage taxes. Arkansas, Missouri, and, most recently, Massachusetts have adopted a different pattern by placing tax administration in a general fiscal/administrative agency which controls the budgetary and other service functions for all state agencies. Arkansas's Division of Revenue is part of the larger Department of Finance and Administration.

The advantages of broad consolidation into a treasury or general department of administration sometimes have at least partially offsetting disadvantages. A large, diversified agency must either establish substantial control and develop layers of hierarchy or maintain loose control, a somewhat reduced number of layers, and a number of separate units reporting to the top. In either type of agency, but more so in the layered one, activities that would be the focus of attention in smaller, more specialized organizations must bid for consideration in this larger structure.[4]

In Michigan, with its consolidated Department of the Treasury, the revenue commissioner (despite the title) is generally subordinate to the treasurer, the deputy treasurer, and their staffs (see chart 2). It is they who

[4]Legislative bodies and chief executives frequently wish to reduce the number of individuals and agencies seeking their attention, yet they may not want to delegate authority broadly. This inherent contradiction may not surface in calls for reorganization, but may come up later in criticism of the policy-making in the consolidated agency when governors or legislators complain, "*that* should have come to the elected representatives."

most often interact with the governor and legislature.[5] The "revenue voice" is heard within the department, and perhaps occasionally at the request of legislators; but the concern with tax administration is only one of the several line responsibilities of the agency. The immediate income tax responsibility is some five levels below the appointed state treasurer (chart 3).

We have insufficient data with which to measure the effects on tax administration of varying degrees of administrative consolidation. Judgment and common sense condemn multiple, small organizations that duplicate services which experience elsewhere shows may easily be consolidated —e.g., mailing services or computers. Yet an agency that is too large and diverse may permit less attention to tax enforcement needs and a lower level of effectiveness of tax administration. It could be readily assumed that the attention of the appointed treasurer in Michigan is less focused on tax administration than is the attention of an appointed secretary of revenue in a number of states where tax administration is the primary reason for the agency's existence. Placing tax administration in a central administration department—as in Arkansas, Missouri, or Massachusetts—may mean less attention to tax enforcement than would be paid in a strictly tax-oriented agency or even a treasury department, but it may also mean more generous budgets. At least some evidence suggests that central departments of administration share disproportionately in state budgets. Can this be substantiated over time among the states? Would it be as true for the tax function? A detailed study of tax budgeting in Massachusetts since its 1978 attachment to the Massachusetts Executive Office for Administration and Finance might provide some tentative evidence.

Advocates of any proposed reorganization that would consolidate a state's tax administration further should consider questions that focus on effectiveness issues as well as possible economies. Will the reorganization (1) assure at least the present quality of administration and withstand the inevitable turmoil among affected employees; (2) assist or maintain the present beneficial political relations with the legislature; (3) provide at least the current general level of budget support? Lacking better evidence in general, these are the questions that should concern any state considering more and more consolidations.

Even multiple tax agencies within a state do not necessarily illustrate ineffective tax administration, nor do their costs always run higher. California's iconoclastic tax organization structure has not resulted in poor

[5]The fact that the revenue commissioner had Democratic Party associations, while the governors and treasurers since reorganization have been Republican (with the legislature controlled by the Democrats), may also have affected the influence of Treasury individuals and the former revenue commissioner. The income tax was adopted in Michigan about the same time as reorganization, but its administrative location was not thought to be as important as that of the (older) sales tax. Even in the case of the sales tax, however, the line administrative level is five steps below the appointed state treasurer.

CHART 2
Michigan Department of the Treasury

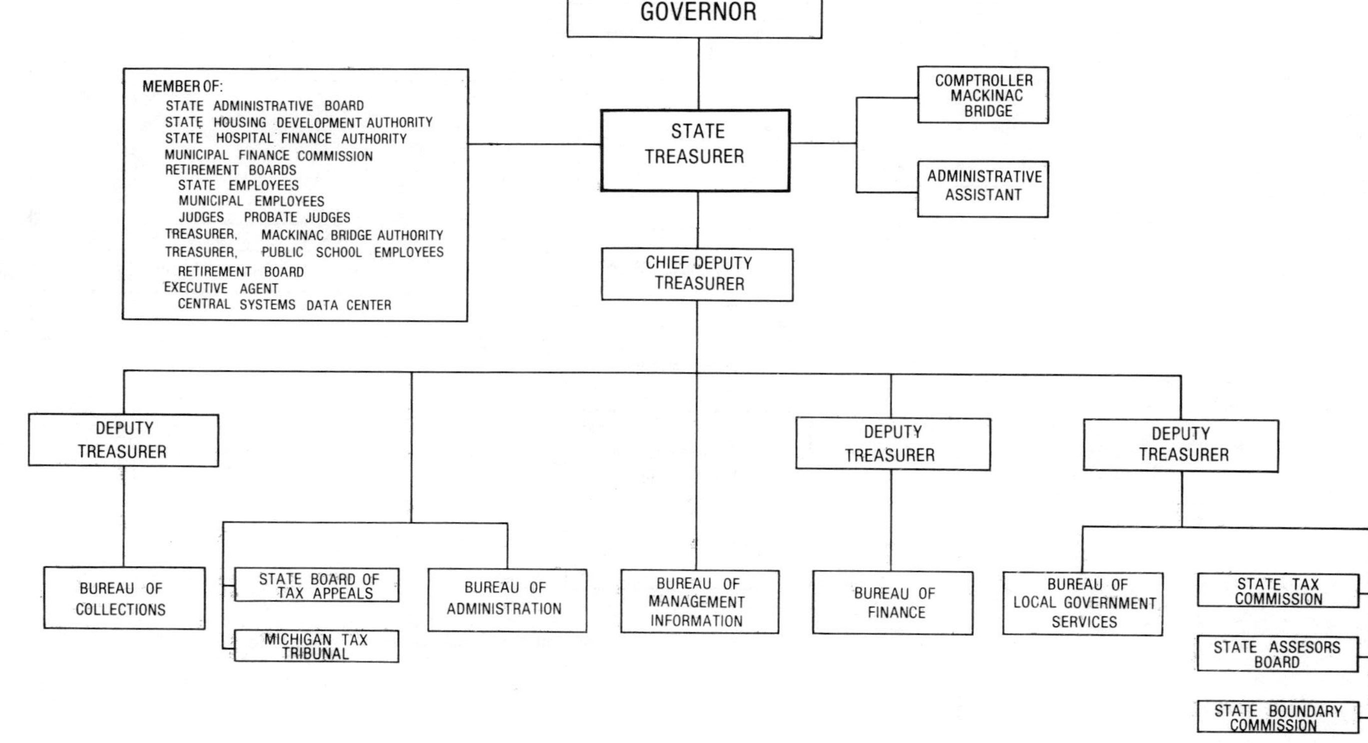

CHART 3
Michigan Department of the Treasury—Bureau of Collections

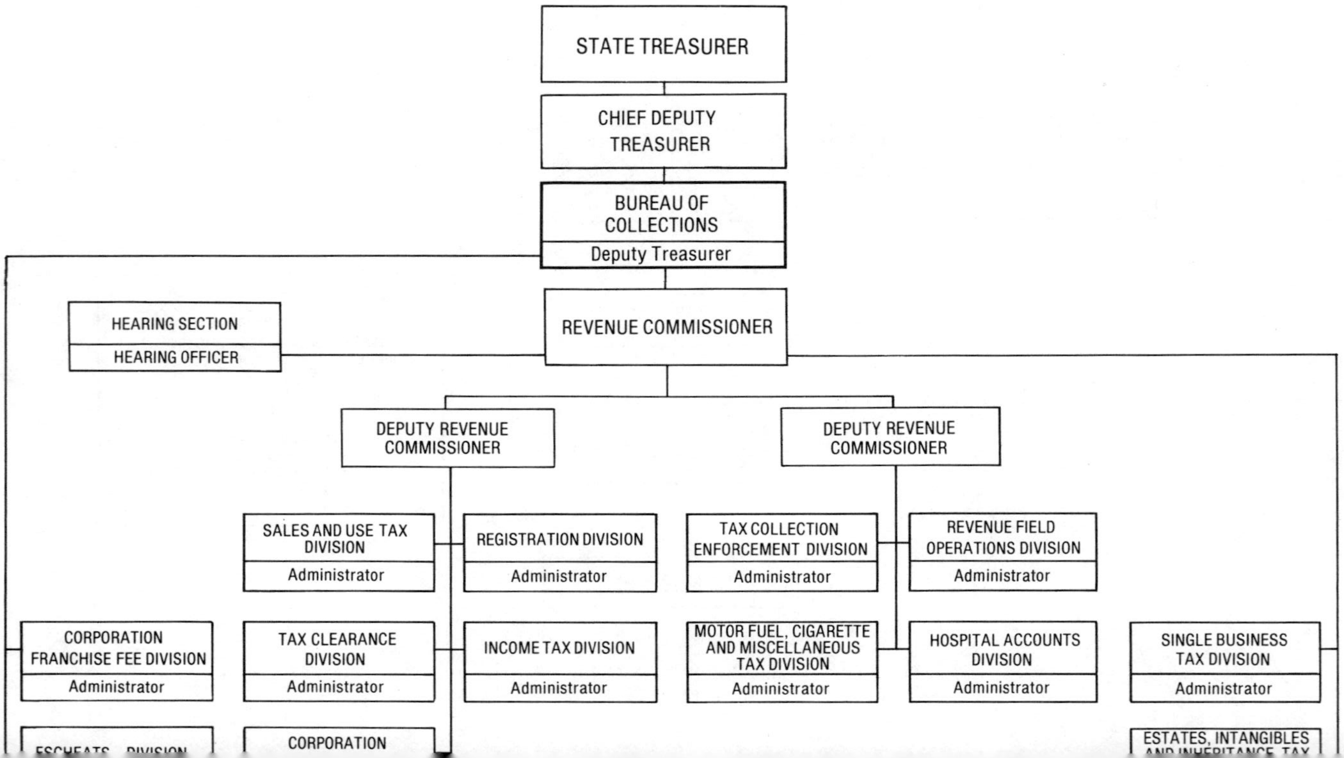

administration (charts 4 and 5). The state has large income and sales tax work loads, and hence their separation may have little effect on cost and no effect on enforcement quality. Both the Franchise Tax Board, which administers the income tax, and the Board of Equalization, which administers the sales tax, have long had reputations for successful administration. Older institutional arrangements, political decisions, and personalities have played roles in the state's unusual division of tax collecting responsibilities. The direct election of members of the Board of Equalization and the *ex officio* membership of the Franchise Tax Board also continue to stand in the way of consolidation.

Single Tax Administrator versus the Tax Board

The trend toward tax departments headed by one executive has frequently coincided with the consolidation movement.[6] As several tax agencies may operate to fragment the total tax administrative effort, so an executive board fragments administrative effort and diffuses responsibility within a particular department. Today thirty-eight of the forty-five income tax states have a single departmental administrator.

Only California, Idaho, Mississippi, New York, Oklahoma, South Carolina, and Utah retain the tax board or commission. Even here there are wide variations. In establishing a three-member commission with administrative responsibilities centered in one member, Massachusetts in 1953 generally copied New York's organization, although the New York chairman is more nearly the sole administrative head than was true in Massachusetts.[7] Mississippi makes the chairman of its tax commission *the* administrative officer, but the chairman delegates some administrative responsibility to other members. Idaho, Oklahoma, and Utah follow the older pattern of dividing administrative responsibilities among members of the commission (Idaho, charts 6 and 7). California has a three-member *ex officio* board that appoints the executive officer and provides general administrative oversight.[8] The tax commission serves as the only appeals body other than the courts in Mississippi, New York, Oklahoma, and South Carolina. California, Idaho, and Massachusetts have another administrative appeals body between the commission and the courts.

[6]This discussion refers only to tax departments having income tax divisions.

[7]As noted earlier, reorganization of the Massachusetts tax department in July, 1978, eliminated the board and established a single commissioner of revenue.

[8]California's Franchise Tax Board has three members: the chairman of the Board of Equalization (the property, sales, etc., tax administrative agency), to which appeals go from the Franchise Tax Board; the elected state controller; and the director of finance appointed by the governor. Legislation in 1979 changed this.

CHART 4
California State Government—the Executive Branch, 1978

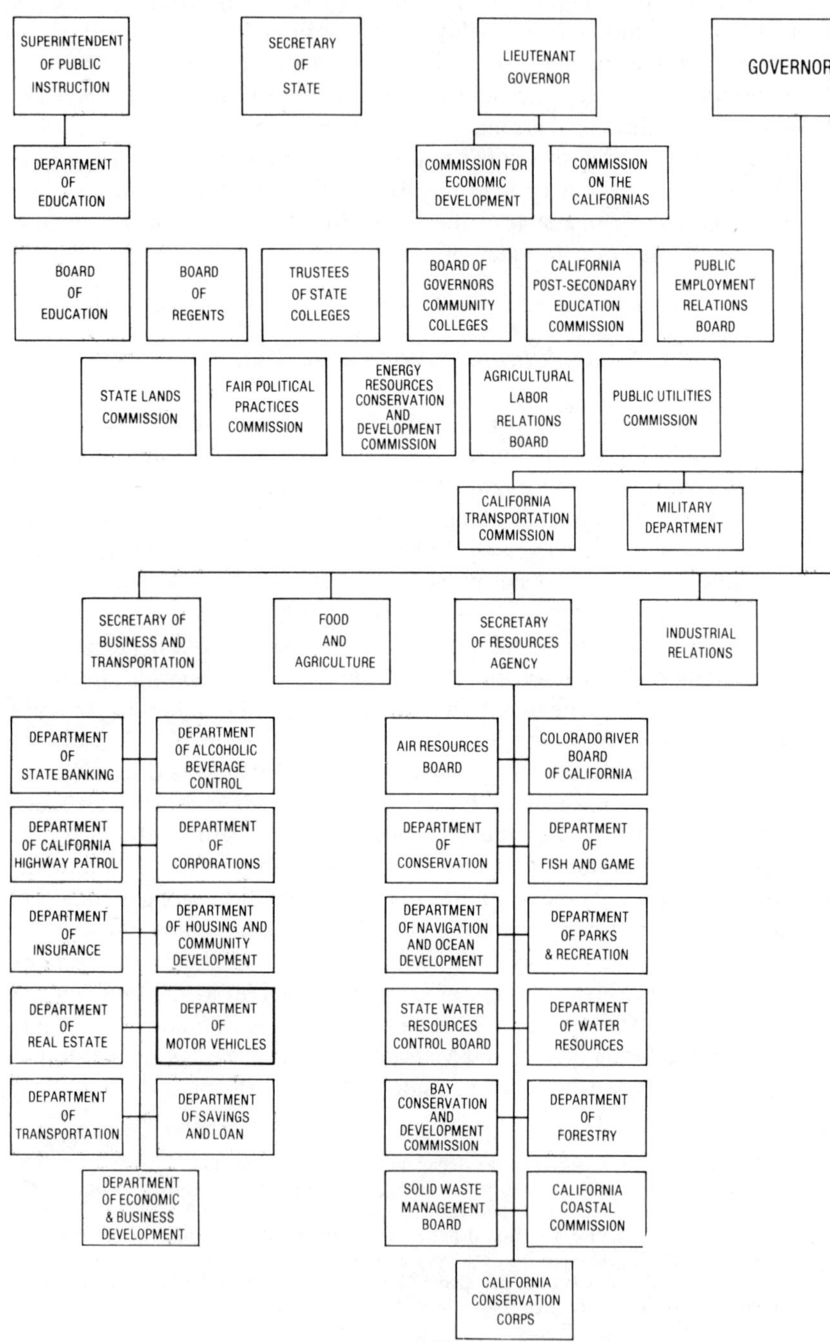

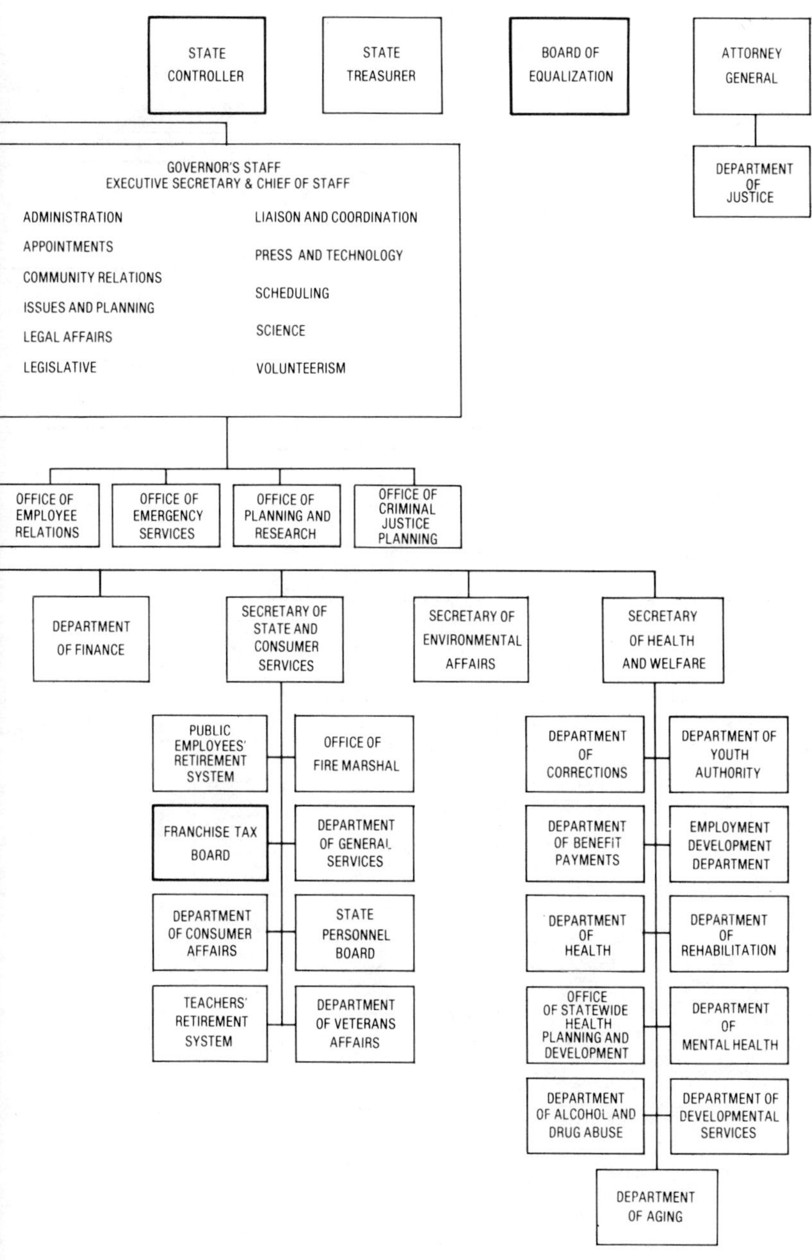

STATE CONTROLLER
STATE TREASURER
BOARD OF EQUALIZATION
ATTORNEY GENERAL
DEPARTMENT OF JUSTICE
GOVERNOR'S STAFF
EXECUTIVE SECRETARY & CHIEF OF STAFF
ADMINISTRATION
APPOINTMENTS
COMMUNITY RELATIONS
ISSUES AND PLANNING
LEGAL AFFAIRS
LEGISLATIVE
LIAISON AND COORDINATION
PRESS AND TECHNOLOGY
SCHEDULING
SCIENCE
VOLUNTEERISM
OFFICE OF EMPLOYEE RELATIONS
OFFICE OF EMERGENCY SERVICES
OFFICE OF PLANNING AND RESEARCH
OFFICE OF CRIMINAL JUSTICE PLANNING
DEPARTMENT OF FINANCE
SECRETARY OF STATE AND CONSUMER SERVICES
SECRETARY OF ENVIRONMENTAL AFFAIRS
SECRETARY OF HEALTH AND WELFARE
PUBLIC EMPLOYEES' RETIREMENT SYSTEM
OFFICE OF FIRE MARSHAL
FRANCHISE TAX BOARD
DEPARTMENT OF GENERAL SERVICES
DEPARTMENT OF CONSUMER AFFAIRS
STATE PERSONNEL BOARD
TEACHERS' RETIREMENT SYSTEM
DEPARTMENT OF VETERANS AFFAIRS
DEPARTMENT OF CORRECTIONS
DEPARTMENT OF YOUTH AUTHORITY
DEPARTMENT OF BENEFIT PAYMENTS
EMPLOYMENT DEVELOPMENT DEPARTMENT
DEPARTMENT OF HEALTH
DEPARTMENT OF REHABILITATION
OFFICE OF STATEWIDE HEALTH PLANNING AND DEVELOPMENT
DEPARTMENT OF MENTAL HEALTH
DEPARTMENT OF ALCOHOL AND DRUG ABUSE
DEPARTMENT OF DEVELOPMENTAL SERVICES
DEPARTMENT OF AGING

CHART 5
California Franchise Tax Board

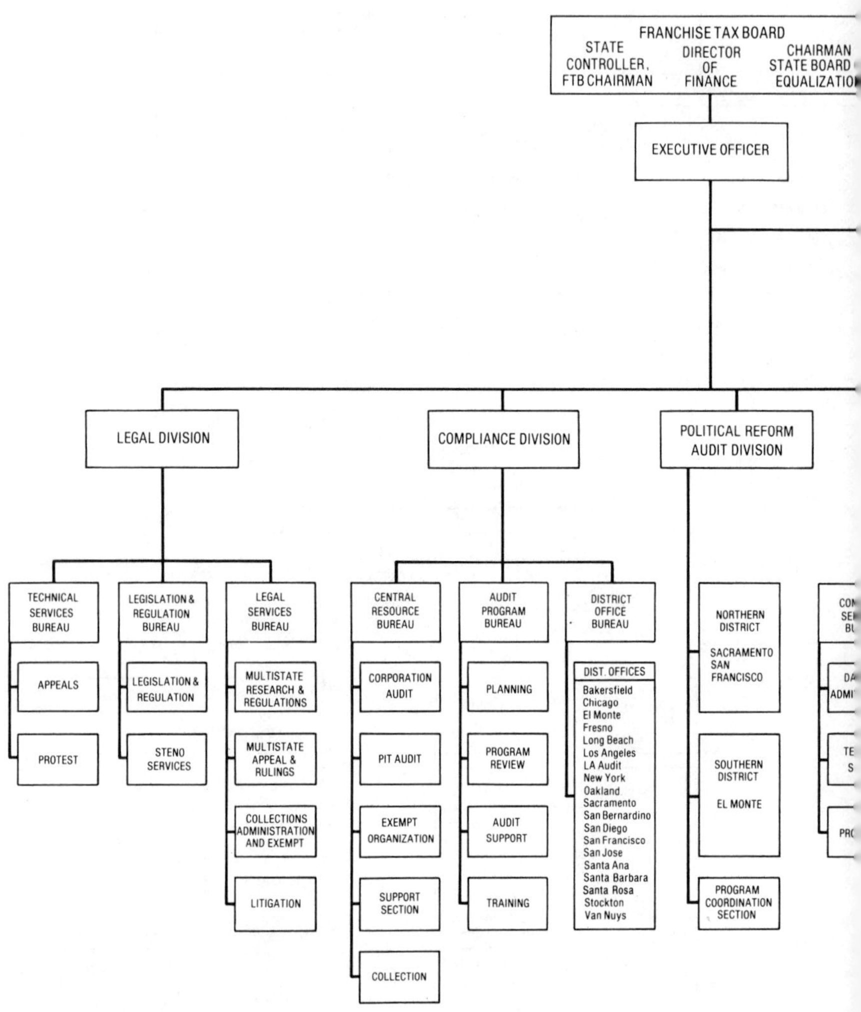

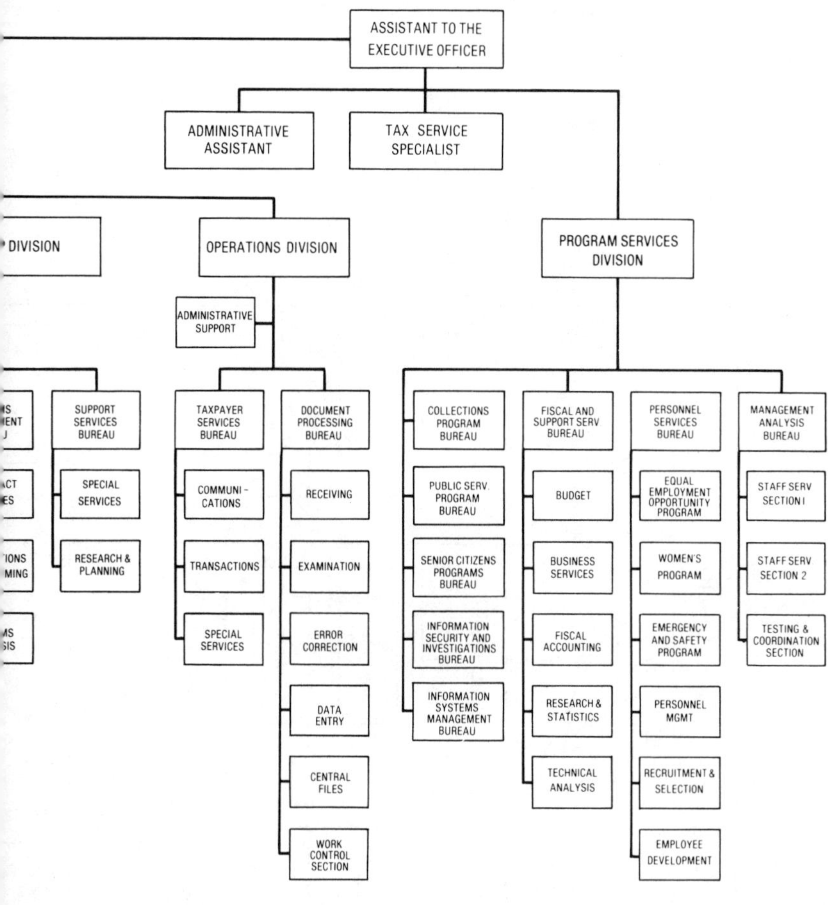

ASSISTANT TO THE EXECUTIVE OFFICER
ADMINISTRATIVE ASSISTANT
TAX SERVICE SPECIALIST
DIVISION
OPERATIONS DIVISION
PROGRAM SERVICES DIVISION
ADMINISTRATIVE SUPPORT
SUPPORT SERVICES BUREAU
SPECIAL SERVICES
RESEARCH & PLANNING
TAXPAYER SERVICES BUREAU
COMMUNI - CATIONS
TRANSACTIONS
SPECIAL SERVICES
DOCUMENT PROCESSING BUREAU
RECEIVING
EXAMINATION
ERROR CORRECTION
DATA ENTRY
CENTRAL FILES
WORK CONTROL SECTION
COLLECTIONS PROGRAM BUREAU
PUBLIC SERV. PROGRAM BUREAU
SENIOR CITIZENS PROGRAMS BUREAU
INFORMATION SECURITY AND INVESTIGATIONS BUREAU
INFORMATION SYSTEMS MANAGEMENT BUREAU
FISCAL AND SUPPORT SERV. BUREAU
BUDGET
BUSINESS SERVICES
FISCAL ACCOUNTING
RESEARCH & STATISTICS
TECHNICAL ANALYSIS
PERSONNEL SERVICES BUREAU
EQUAL EMPLOYMENT OPPORTUNITY PROGRAM
WOMEN'S PROGRAM
EMERGENCY AND SAFETY PROGRAM
PERSONNEL MGMT
RECRUITMENT & SELECTION
EMPLOYEE DEVELOPMENT
MANAGEMENT ANALYSIS BUREAU
STAFF SERV SECTION I
STAFF SERV SECTION 2
TESTING & COORDINATION SECTION

CHART 6
Idaho Department of Revenue and Taxation

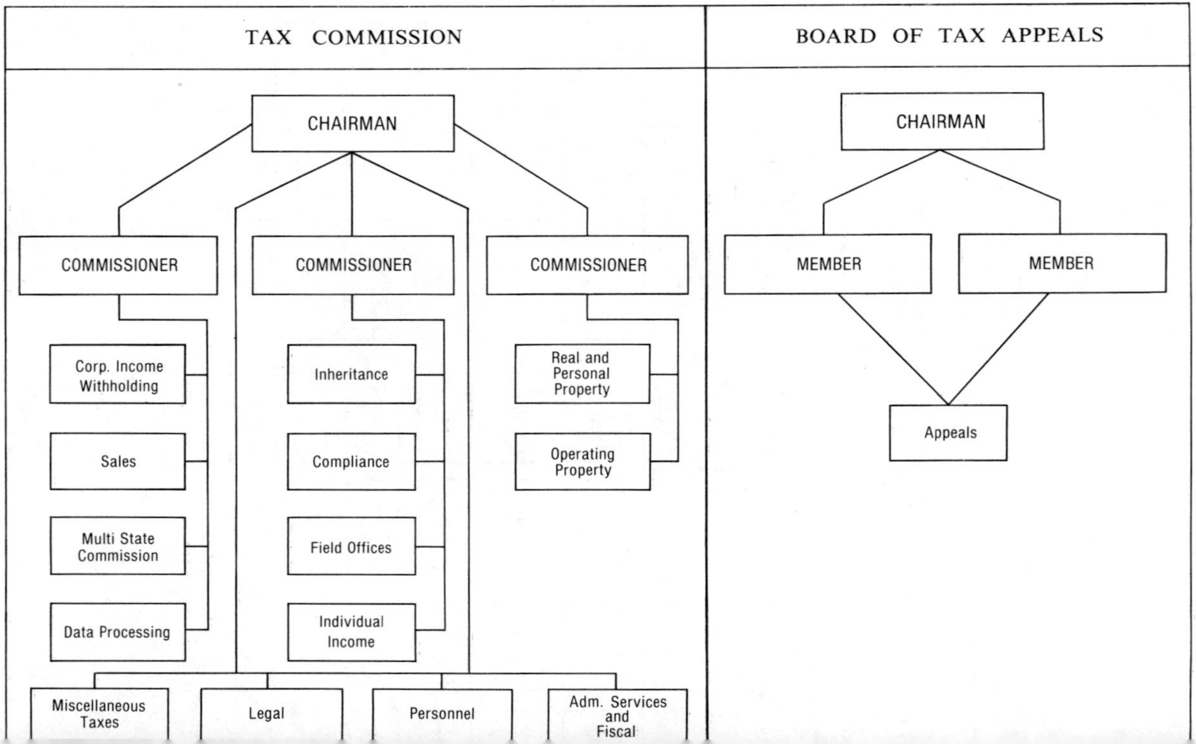

TAX COMMISSION

CHAIRMAN

COMMISSIONER
Corp. Income Withholding
Sales
Multi State Commission
Data Processing

COMMISSIONER
Inheritance
Compliance
Field Offices
Individual Income

COMMISSIONER
Real and Personal Property
Operating Property

Miscellaneous Taxes
Legal
Personnel
Adm. Services and Fiscal

BOARD OF TAX APPEALS

CHAIRMAN

MEMBER
MEMBER

Appeals

Idaho State Tax Commission

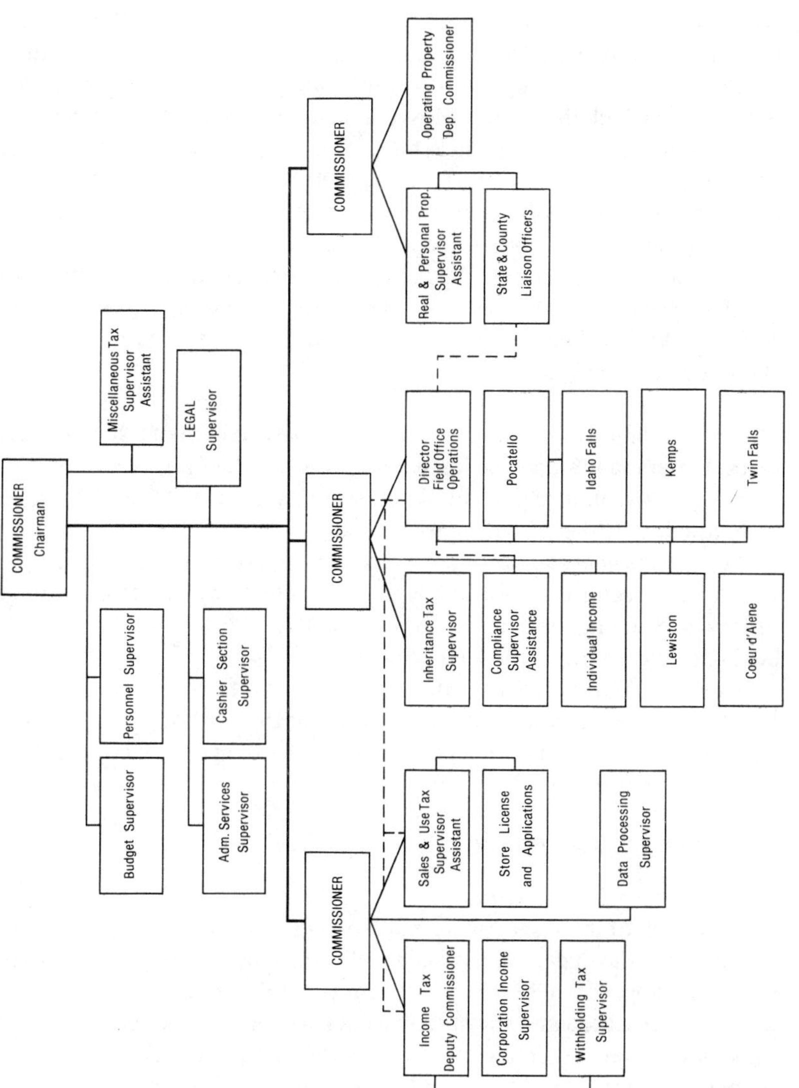

Integrated versus Tax-by-Tax Structure

Consolidation of the administration of different taxes into one or two agencies prepares the way for integration of activities common to more than one tax. Yet "consolidation" does not automatically produce either complete or partial "integration." Consolidation may go no further than housing a number of taxes under a single administrative roof. In an integrated structure, functions of a feather are grouped together regardless of the tax to which they apply. Most consolidated organizations do integrate major staff services: personnel, budgeting, purchases, accounting, data processing, statistical and research activities, and legal services. Many administrators have moved to integrate sales and income tax audit and collection activities in both the central office and the field. Integration may offer automatic or freer exchange of information, elimination of duplication of effort, greater possibilities of functional specialization, the creation of a sufficient work volume to permit computerization of more processes, etc. But integration may detract from full, rounded attention to one or another tax.

State legislatures determine the extent of consolidation of a state's several taxes, but in many states the legislature gives the chief tax administrator(s) authority to structure the divisions, sections, and units, and to assign responsibility as the administrator(s) find(s) most appropriate. According to the 1976 *Annual Report* of the Colorado Department of Revenue, "The Executive Director is authorized by statute to create within the Department of Revenue such departments, divisions, and sections as are necessary for efficient functioning of the Department."

If most of our states' tax administrators have flexibility in organizing their departments, how much integration do they choose? Why do they choose varying patterns of integration? What are the possible consequences of the different patterns?

INTEGRATION PATTERNS

Staff Service Integration

Regardless of the size of an agency, somehow the functions of personnel recruitment, classification, payrolling, etc., must be accomplished. Into the same category of necessity fall such general services as purchasing, budgeting, research and statistics, legal advice, and public relations. Commonly the revenue secretary or commissioner finds it convenient to attach such units to his own office, or at least to separate divisions apart from the line responsibilities for the several taxes. In unusually large agencies, some of these functions may reappear in attenuated form at the division level.

Most tax departments today also integrate such functions as receiving and sending mail, opening mail, depositing and accounting for revenues received, and data processing. These facilitating services are common to all taxes and present few planning or other difficulties among the taxes for which the department is responsible. Charts 8 and 9 illustrate the integration of both staff and facilitating services within the tax departments of North Carolina and South Carolina, but note that both states have retained separate tax-by-tax structures in other ways.

Line Integration

Tax departments exist to collect taxes, which in an immediate sense they do by receiving and processing returns received, auditing the returns received, checking for returns due but not received, and collecting taxes either not initially received with returns or due as a result of assessments. For purposes of discussion here, these are the line functions. Any tax statutorially assigned to a revenue department involves these line responsibilities, which require direct contact with a few or many taxpayers. Is the critical organizing focus, then, the tax or the function or process? If it is the tax, the department organization chart will show a series of divisions labeled with the name of the particular tax[9] (see chart 8, North Carolina). If it is not the tax, the organizational chart will likely reflect the functional divisions of compliance, auditing, collection, and field operation (see charts 10 and 11, New York and Wisconsin).

The general argument for the tax-by-tax structure asserts that the department is responsible for the collection of each tax specified by statute, and accountability and evaluation follow best from such a program organization focus. The argument for the process organizational principle developed as more and more states adopted both income and sales taxes and it rests frequently on the grounds that there is (1) a large overlap of taxpayer clientele and (2) a large overlap in the records that constitute the basic audit information.[10] The argument goes on to assert that auditing is auditing, collecting is collecting, without regard to the particular tax.

The several changes in organization of tax administration that have occurred in Minnesota exhibit the prototype metamorphosis of tax agencies among the states with the spread of income and sales taxes (as seen in charts 12, 13, and 14, dates and details will vary). When Minnesota adopted the income tax, the legislature assigned its collection and enforcement to the existing three-man tax commission. In 1939, the commission was abolished and a department with a single commissioner, appointed by the

[9]Although the organization of North Carolina's tax department suggests that it is one of the least process- or function-oriented structures among state agencies, even here the field division acts for all the tax divisions. The chart for South Carolina shows separate field sections for the income and sales tax divisions.

[10]The overlap in taxpayer clientele is in business, whether incorporated or unincorporated. The proportion of taxpayers who do not own a business or are not in a profession has grown over the years.

CHART 8
North Carolina Department of Revenue

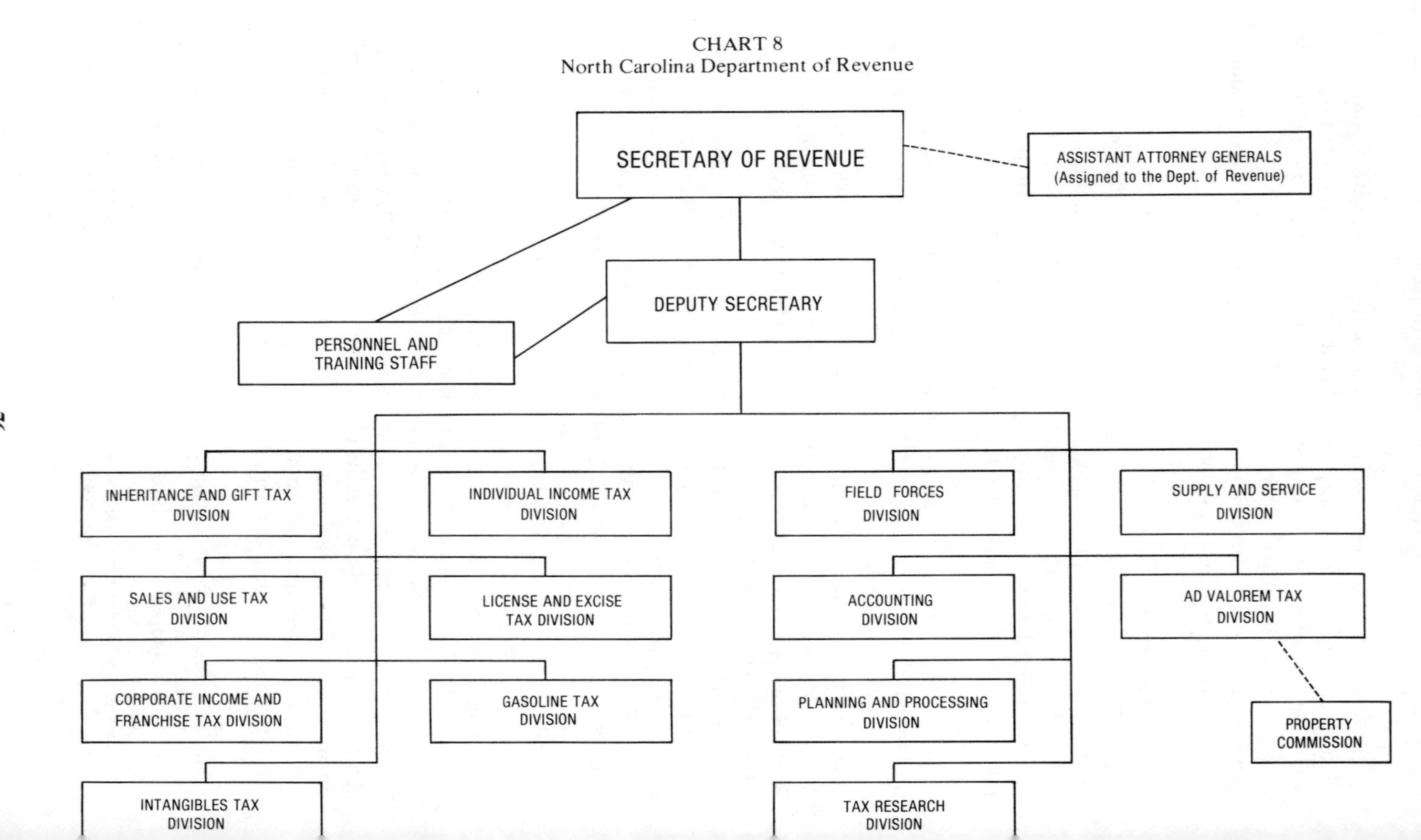

CHART 9
South Carolina Tax Commission

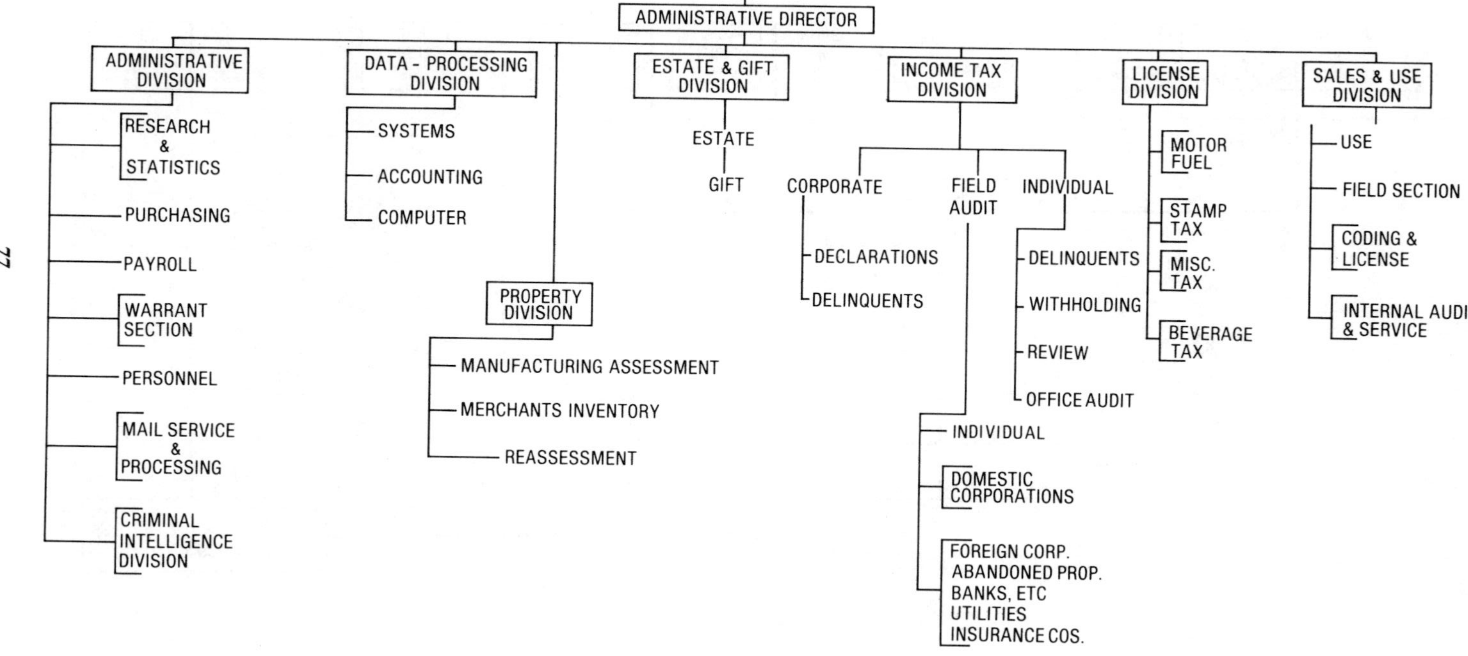

CHART 10
New York Department of Taxation and Finance

STATE TAX COMMISSION
President
Commissioner Commissioner

COMMISSIONER OF TAXATION AND FINANCE and President of the State Tax Commission

SPECIAL ASSISTANT

PUBLIC RELATIONS OFFICE

SPECIAL COUNSEL

DEPUTY COMMISSIONER and COUNSEL

EXECUTIVE DEPUTY COMMISSIONER

DEPUTY COMMISSIONER and TREASURER

DIVISION OF THE LOTTERY

SECRETARY TO THE COMMISSION

OFFICE OF THE ADMINISTRATIVE DIRECTOR

TAX APPEALS BUREAU

SPECIAL INVESTIGATIONS BUREAU

AUDIT DIVISION

TAXPAYER SERVICES DIVISION

TAX COMPLIANCE BUREAU

PROCESSING DIVISION

OFFICE OF TAX SYSTEMS

BUSINESS ADMIN-ISTRATION BUREAU

OFFICE OF MANPOWER MANAGEMENT

CORPORATION TAX BUREAU

INCOME TAX BUREAU

DISTRICT OFFICES (12)

MISCELLANEOUS TAX BUREAU

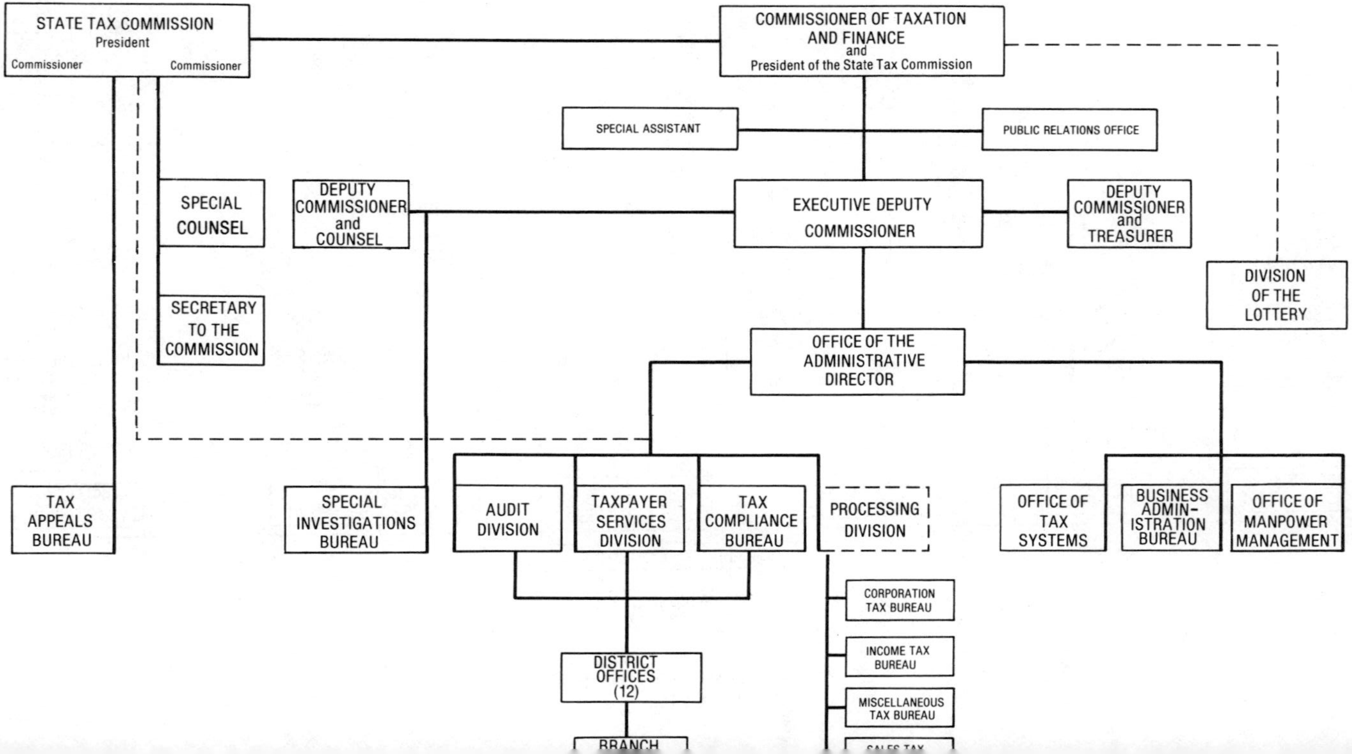

CHART 11
Wisconsin Department of Revenue, 1978

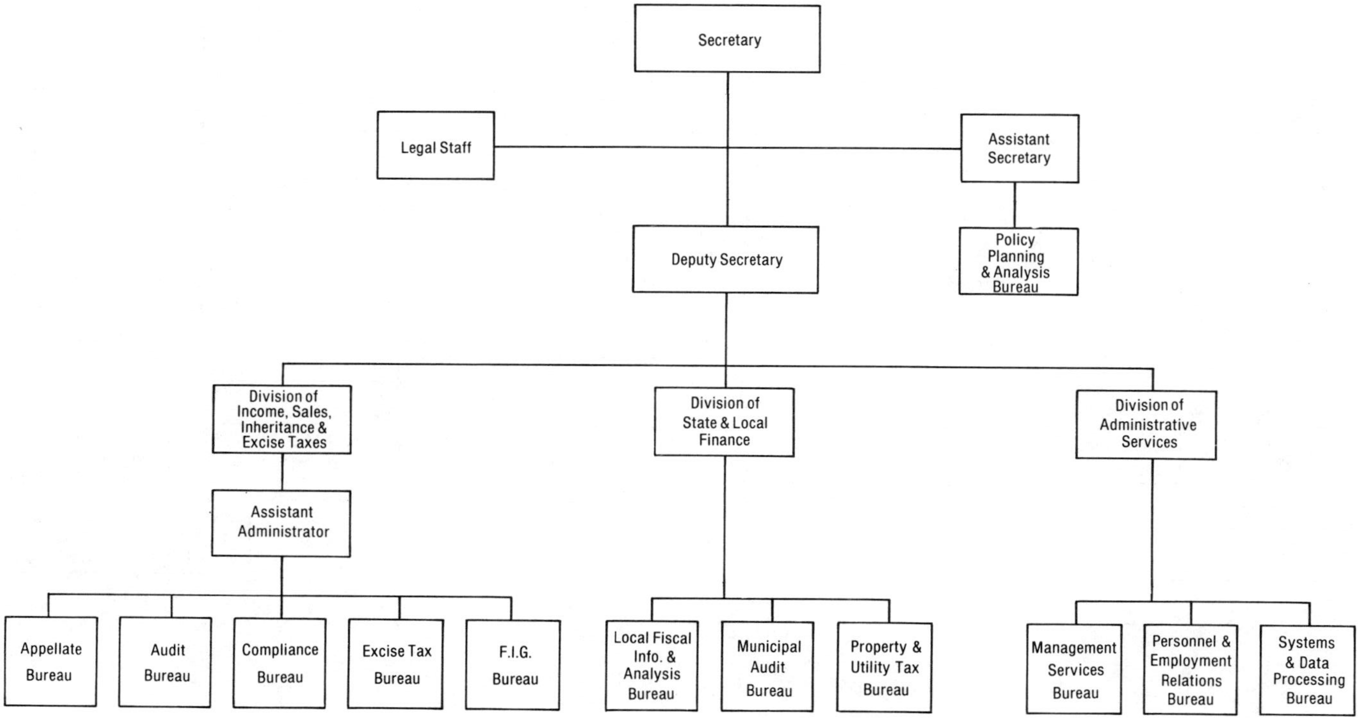

Secretary

Legal Staff

Assistant Secretary

Policy Planning & Analysis Bureau

Deputy Secretary

Division of Income, Sales, Inheritance & Excise Taxes

Assistant Administrator

Appellate Bureau

Audit Bureau

Compliance Bureau

Excise Tax Bureau

F.I.G. Bureau

Division of State & Local Finance

Local Fiscal Info. & Analysis Bureau

Municipal Audit Bureau

Property & Utility Tax Bureau

Division of Administrative Services

Management Services Bureau

Personnel & Employment Relations Bureau

Systems & Data Processing Bureau

CHART 12
Minnesota Department of Taxation, 1958

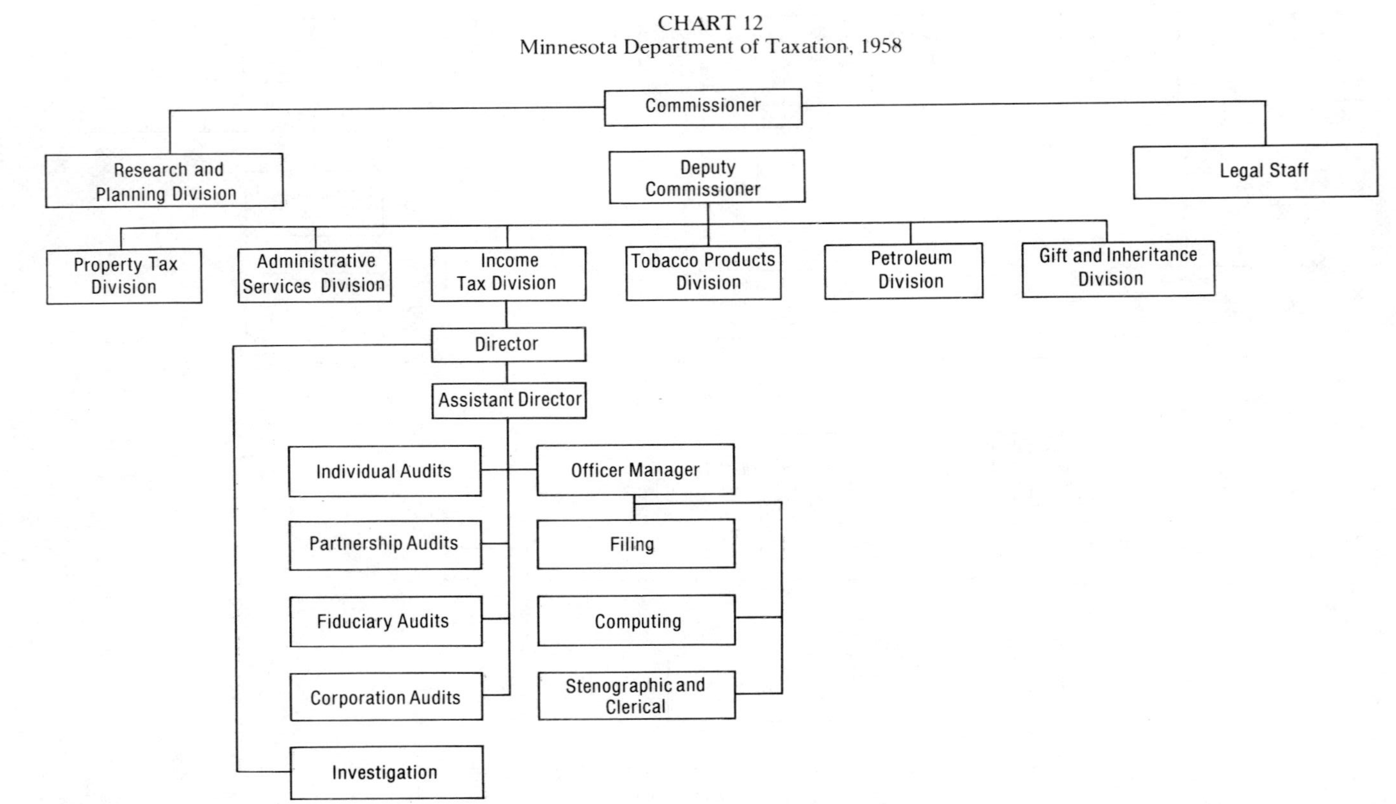

CHART 13
Minnesota Department of Taxation, 1966

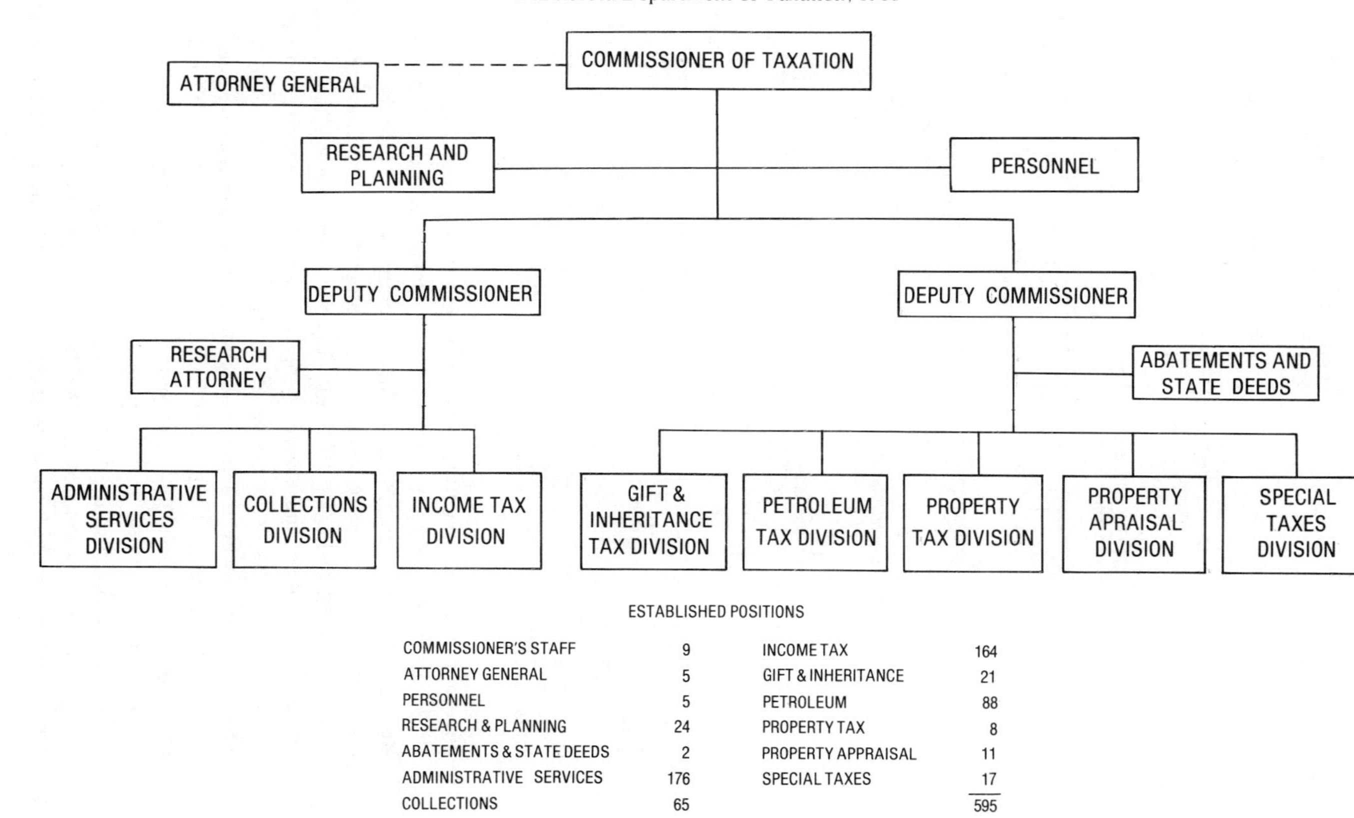

ESTABLISHED POSITIONS

COMMISSIONER'S STAFF	9	INCOME TAX	164
ATTORNEY GENERAL	5	GIFT & INHERITANCE	21
PERSONNEL	5	PETROLEUM	88
RESEARCH & PLANNING	24	PROPERTY TAX	8
ABATEMENTS & STATE DEEDS	2	PROPERTY APPRAISAL	11
ADMINISTRATIVE SERVICES	176	SPECIAL TAXES	17
COLLECTIONS	65		595

CHART 14
Minnesota Department of Revenue, 1978

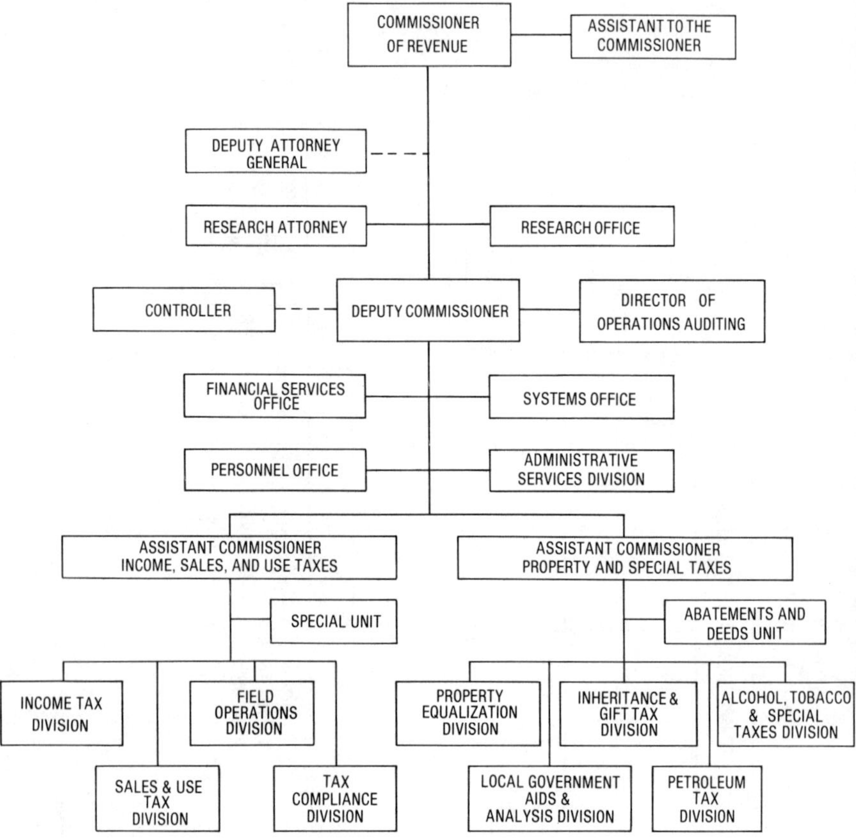

governor and reporting to the governor, was established. Subsequently, in 1973, the legislature rechristened the Tax Department the Department of Revenue. In 1967, Minnesota adopted a general sales tax. In the early days of its administration, there was little or no integration of common processing or enforcement tasks. By 1978, the revenue commissioner had gradually made a series of organizational changes designed to integrate most of the common processes or functions of income and sales tax administration. There remain, however, separate income tax and sales tax divisions largely responsible for audits. Field auditing of individual returns (largely individual businesses) is consolidated with sales tax field auditing. Office and field auditing of corporation income remain separated.

Throughout most of the first forty years of existence of income taxes in Oregon, administration was handled by a separate division of the Oregon Tax Commission. With the exception of general supervision and appeals, most administrative income tax responsibilities were assigned to this division. In 1969, the legislature replaced the commission with the Department of Revenue and provided for the appointment of its director by the governor. Although the new department responded to outside recommendations that a process or functional organization be adopted to replace the tax-by-tax structure, the change has made only slight differences to income tax administration. The audit division has responsibility for individual and corporate income taxes. Oregon has no sales tax, and the income tax remains its largest tax source. A general administrative service division has responsibility for receiving, processing, handling computer operations, and filing for all taxes. A collections division has responsibility for collecting income tax assessments and all other taxes (chart 15).

Massachusetts and New York retained separate income and sales tax bureaus until 1977. Both states further divided individual and corporation income taxes into separate bureaus. Both states had long emphasized income taxes in their revenue systems. When their legislatures enacted sales taxes in the 1960s, each provided a specific budget for the new sales tax to assure administrative attention.

EXPLANATIONS AND IMPACTS OF DIFFERENT INTEGRATION PATTERNS

Organization and reorganization at the general state level have never proceeded at an identical pace across the nation, although there have been periods of "reform" when a significant number of state governors or legislatures have established committees or commissions to recommend broad structural changes. Always a few states take the lead in adopting these changes, some follow, while others completely ignore the latest fashions in organization.[11]

Frequently, as broader changes occur, there is encouragement for internal departmental reorganization. In the seventies, several governors (including those of Minnesota, North Carolina, and Oregon) accepted the services of business executives to examine both the state's general structural arrangements and to look at individual departments and make recommendations for change. Some reorganization followed. Individual tax administrators found the advent of a new tax or adoption of a major technological change—e.g., computerization—an occasion for internal change. Actions of other state tax administrators influenced some administrators. Whether a tax administrator accepts the going organization or chooses to reorganize,

[11] It should be emphasized and reemphasized that "reform" or "reorganization" normally involves preferences, values, and judgments of what can or ought to be achieved. Some organizational changes will bring about the stated goals, particularly if the change is small and the goal limited, but other changes may bring unexpressed or unanticipated results. "Reorganization" and "reform" are *good* only if what results reflects the preferences of the onlooker, whether administrator, legislator, or taxpayer.

CHART 15
Oregon Department of Revenue, 1978

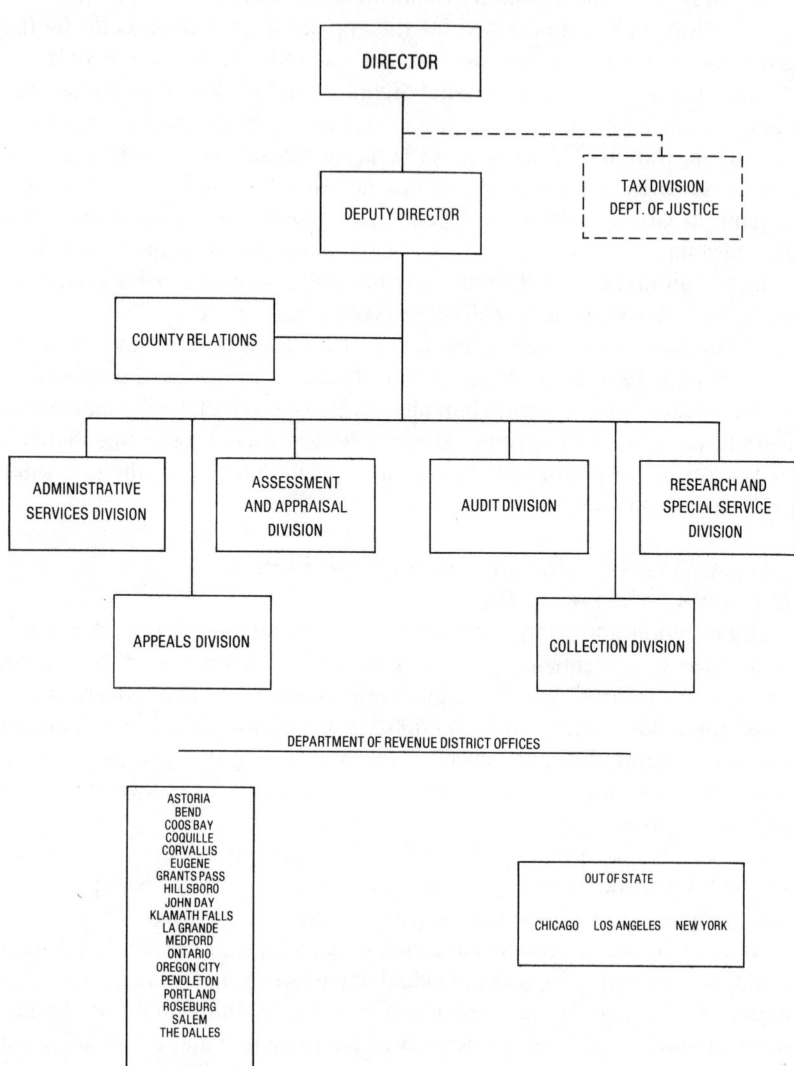

he makes a judgment as to the economy and effectiveness of the present organization and the possible achievements in economy, taxpayer services, effective collection, etc., a structural change might bring.[12]

By the late 1970s, tax administrators generally had accepted the rationale for combined staff and facilitative services. Where these services are not

[12]Most administrators would put an "adjustment" cost into any equation of the benefits of reorganization. Most employees do not normally embrace change.

fully integrated within a tax department, investigation will frequently disclose substantial physical distance between some of the tax programs. In Ohio and Pennsylvania, the individual income tax came into existence long after the sales tax. The large space requirement of the individual income tax—accommodation for its millions of returns for processing and auditing—could not be met in any available space adjacent to the sales tax operation in either Columbus or Harrisburg (charts 16 and 17). Placing the income tax operation several miles away from the central office required duplication of some of the staff and facilitative services that might otherwise have been expanded and consolidated for common use.

Differences in organizational perspectives in tax departments often center on auditing and possibly other elements of compliance, collection, and field operations. The fully tax-by-tax organization, such as exists in Idaho, North Carolina, and South Carolina, is less common now than it was twenty years ago. A large number of separate tax divisions may serve (1) the need to divide tax programs among commissioners in multiheaded departments; (2) the desirability of more patronage positions with titles; or (3) management's unwillingness to go through the hassle of change. Given the differences in work loads required by individual taxes, some consolidation of line responsibilities would probably bring economies.[13] Any internal tax enforcement consolidation, however, might reduce the attention each separate tax would have received at the top of the departmental hierarchy. It is this possibility and its implications that must be offset against potential savings.

As noted earlier, state adoption of both income and sales taxes tended to generate movements for line integration. Since these two taxes normally account for the larger part of state revenues, administrative consolidation may have substantial implications. Difficulties follow if integration removes (1) everyone who might give a whole, yet reasonably intimate, overview of income tax policy in terms of strengths and weaknesses of its administration; and (2) everyone who has developed specialized knowledge of the specific links in income tax administration which may or may not relate to sales tax administration. If merger is undertaken simply to economize, it may prove false. Too thin a cloak of combined auditing will no more impress businessmen than will separate auditing without sufficient coverage.

[13]Wherever a state tax department has a large number of divisions, bureaus, or whatever the designation only one remove from the secretary, internal consolidation could probably achieve some economies. Not only may there be an unnecessary load on the secretary's deputies, but consolidation is likely to prove economical *if* (1) every division director has the same classification and thus requires the same or similar salary; (2) each division director, regardless of the size of the work load, maintains an administrative distance that does not permit sharing of tasks; (3) division directors insist on questions and information going up vertically rather than being shared horizontally by auditors and other professionals in an easy exchange across division lines.

CHART 16
Ohio Department of Taxation

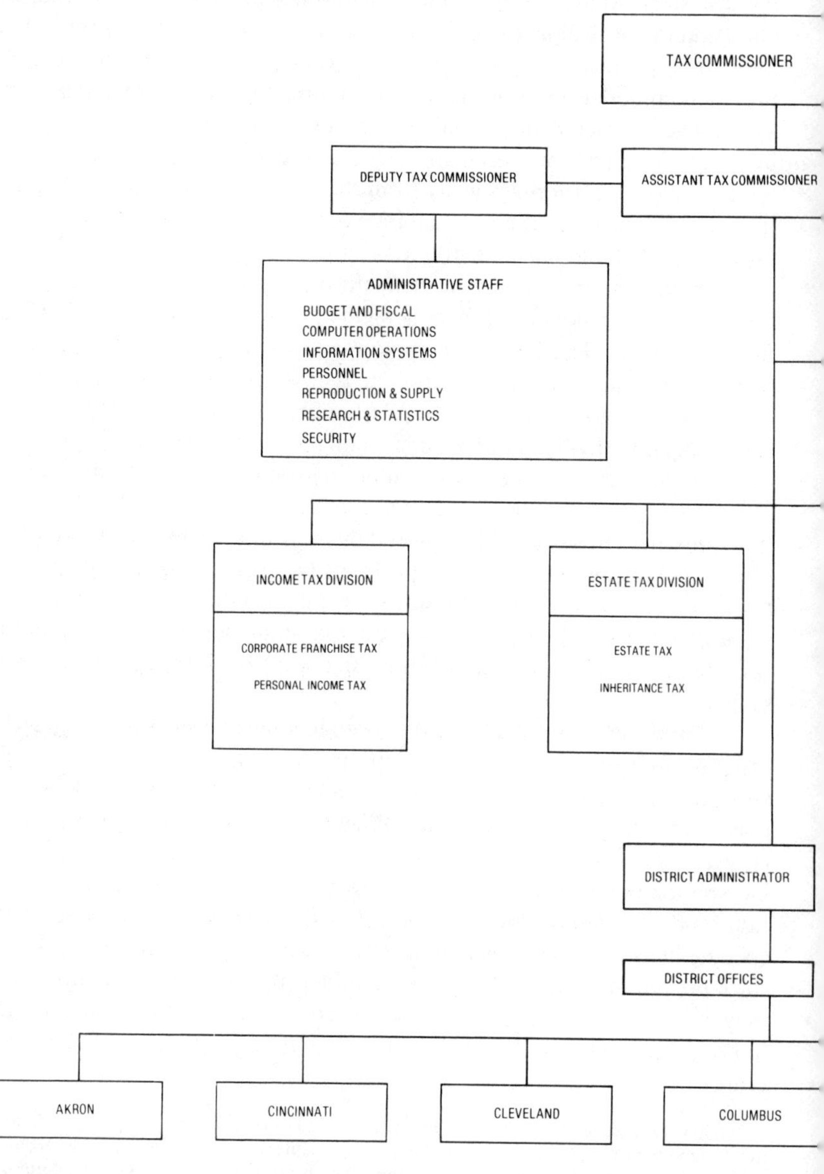

Line integration does not always mean what the term appears to imply. In several states—e.g., Georgia—the integrated audit division has developed and expected specialization among auditors, much as in a combined individual and corporation audit unit. Georgia auditors examining business accounts in the field found that the natural calendar for income and sales

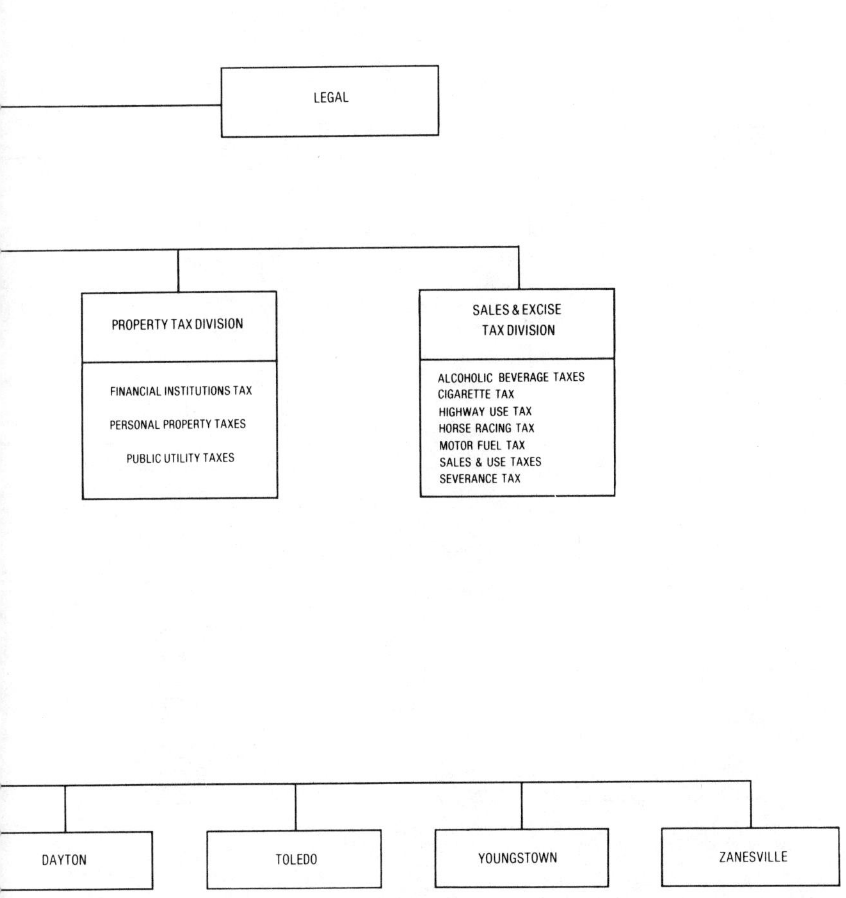

taxes did not agree, or the revenue agent found auditing needs for one tax far in excess of those of the other in particular periods or for particular businesses. Even during orientation and training, the beginning auditor learns first to do office reviews of individual income tax returns and only gradually moves on possibly to sales tax reports. The most highly trained

CHART 17
Pennsylvania Department of Revenue

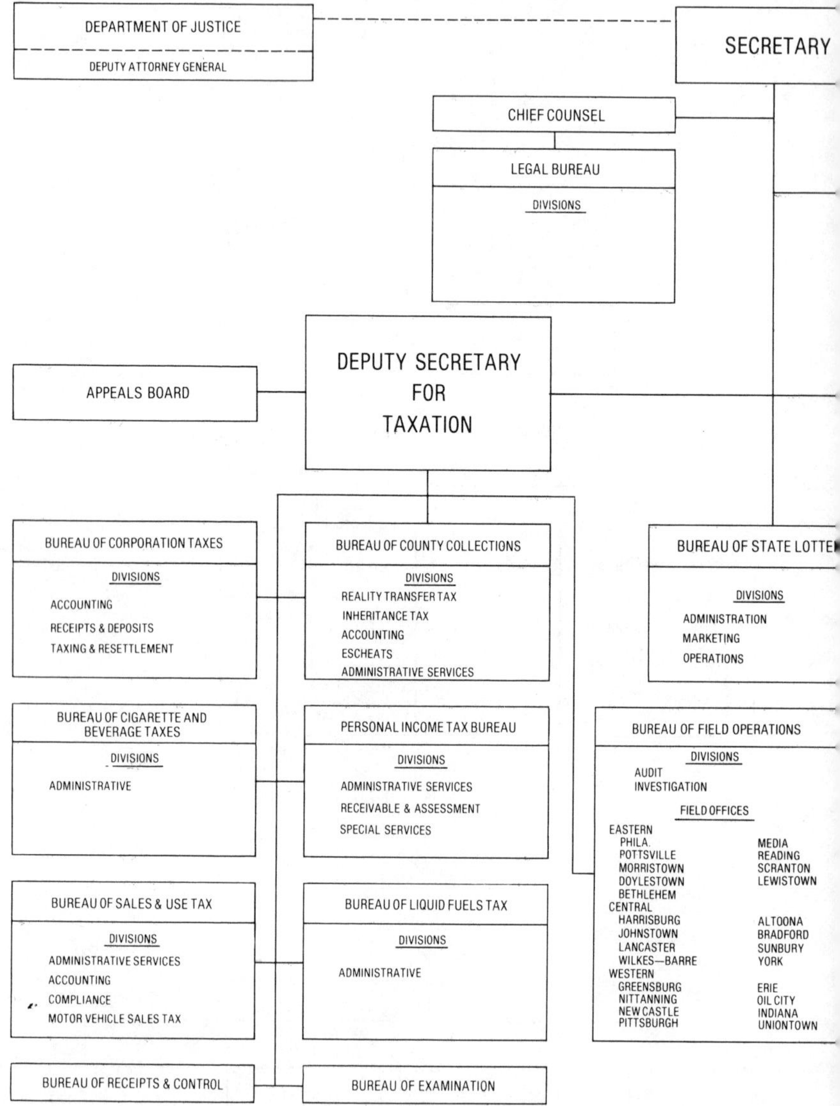

auditors in states such as Minnesota and Wisconsin spend almost all their time on corporation income tax audits.[14]

[14]Most auditors and administrators with whom the author spoke clearly considered the corporation income tax audit (especially the field audit of a large corporation) to be much more complex than the sales tax audit of the same firm. Michigan auditors strongly dissented from this view. The difference in opinion may be due to the peculiarities of Michigan tax laws or to the general priority given by Michigan auditors to the sales tax.

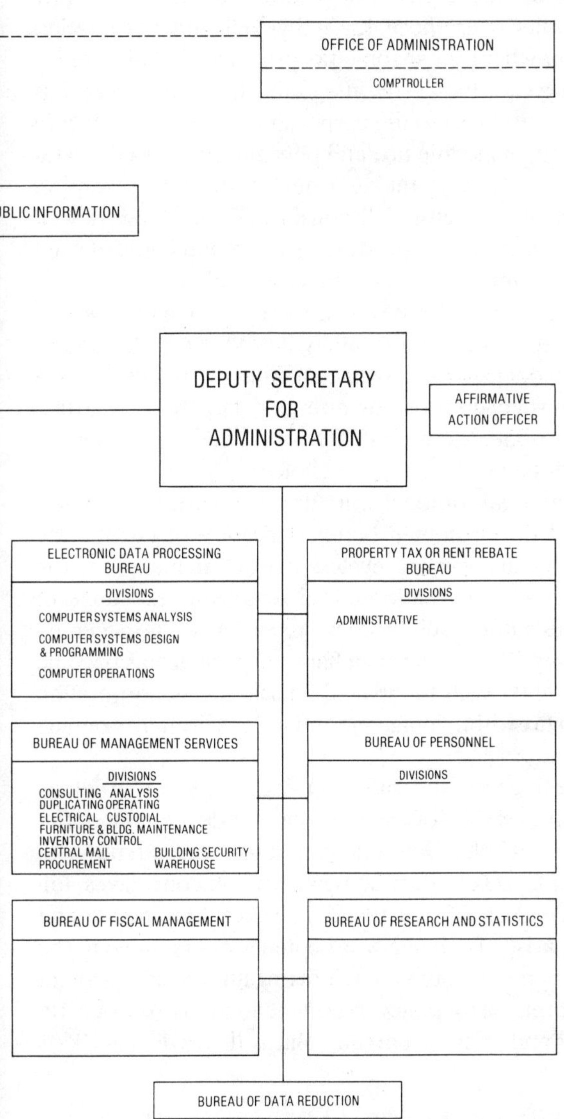

The apparently integrated audit bureau sometimes focuses attention on one or another tax and thereby permits the specialization that many auditors prefer. A field auditor can choose to make only a quick check of the corporation records on withholding accounts and either the sales or income tax, and devote most of his time to producing a quality audit for the other tax. Under the goad of central office mandates, the auditor might occasionally reverse priorities but then slip back to his preferred ways.

In Michigan, where the sales tax was already thirty-two years old when the income tax was adopted, the integrated field audit staff has consistently emphasized sales tax audits over those for individual and corporation income taxes.[15] Wisconsin, where the income tax predated the sales tax by fifty years, showed the reverse bias. The integrated field audit staff has traditionally given primary attention to the corporation income tax, then to withholding and the individual income tax, and only after these to the sales tax. Some change in emphasis was taking place in the late seventies. According to the state's tax director, Wisconsin auditors long viewed corporation income tax auditing as the prestige specialty and concentrated on that in spite of directions for more even-handed attention.[16]

The above observations in several states do not prove that an integrated "process" organization in the audit area is fatally flawed. They do suggest that an "integrated audit operation" may mean different things—a thin cloak, individual auditor specialization, or attention largely to one tax. Where serious auditing is done, the probability is that auditors specialize either by administrative design or by auditor's choice.

Supporters of functional organizational structures emphasize the professional talents needed and the presumed better utilization of talents; the greater ease of dovetailing the varying cycles of work demand for the different taxes; and the more automatic and advantageous exchange of information across tax lines within each process. According to the accepted wisdom, "auditing is auditing," and rather than have different agents become a plague through multiple audit visits in the field for sales taxes, corporation income taxes, and income tax withholding, one auditor can usefully examine all the taxes of a taxpayer.

Supporters of separate income and sales tax organizational structure emphasize the need for an overview of each tax and the dovetailing of the administrative parts to that whole. How else can you assure attention to policy issues in a particular tax unless somewhere someone gives full attention to the implementation of that tax and the resulting policy and administrative issues that arise. Technically, of course, it is possible in the process organizational scheme to reunify each tax again for management planning, revenue estimating, and policy recommendations through research or policy planning and analysis bureaus. But is the review as likely

[15] Michigan, Department of the Treasury, *Annual Report of the Commissioner of Revenue* (Lansing). The lack of devotion to the corporation income tax was apparent in the department's central office staffing as well as in its field audit priorities and may have been a factor in the state's replacing the corporation income tax (and other business taxes) with the 1975 single business tax, which is a "kissing cousin" to the value-added tax.

[16] Although John F. Due, in *State and Local Sales Taxation* (Chicago: Public Administration Service, 1971), rated Wisconsin's sales tax administration high on many points, he found no field auditing in the late sixties or early seventies and thus left Wisconsin off the list of states with effective sales tax administration. Without commenting on this judgment, this author agrees with Due on the past diversity of attention to income and sales tax auditing by Michigan and Wisconsin.

to be done thoroughly in the process organization as in the tax program organization? In summary, this author agrees with John F. Due but, of course, would substitute *income* for *sales:* "The experience with integrated audit has been by no means universally satisfactory, and serious question can therefore be raised about functional organization, with the inevitable loss of centralization of responsibility for sales [read *income*] tax administration."[17]

FIELD OFFICES

The nineteenth-century assumption of decentralized income tax administration has disappeared. Only Virginia relies on local officials for any part of the administrative responsibility. States do differ in the use of field offices for enforcement and taxpayer services and in the number of permanent and temporary offices spread over the state. States also differ in the establishment of out-of-state audit offices (see discussion in chapter 8).

Whatever the old arguments for decentralization, important phases of modern income tax administration adapt better to a centralized operation. A great many sources of information on income and its recipients exist only in the state capital. Withholding and the information-at-source dragnet are more effective when applied to the state as a unit. Centralization of many of the activities connected with processing returns and office auditing may require as a minimum the whole volume of state records in order (1) to allow routine tasks to be standardized, (2) to utilize mechanical equipment efficiently, and (3) to generate a continual flow of technical problems and thereby facilitate specialization and technical expertise.

Computer processing of returns, computer arithmetic verification of returns, and identification of returns for audit have made earlier functions of field offices obsolete. Even taxpayer assistance has increasingly become a central office function with toll-free numbers provided for taxpayers anywhere in the state (see chapter 5). In these instances there is little conflict between taxpayer convenience and operating efficiency—the general standards for centralization or decentralization.

Taxpayers do need some types of assistance that even sophisticated telephone service or television instructions cannot provide. As more and more elderly taxpayers must file, as must taxpayers with limited literacy, departments find it necessary to provide field services in established and temporary offices. The income tax agency must make citizens aware that it is alive and active. Field offices maintained on a permanent or occcasional basis serve both goals of assistance and enforcement.[18] Assistance to

[17]Ibid., p. 105.

[18]In states where political patronage remains significant, numerous field offices offer an opportunity not only for appointments but also for maintaining contact with voters. Where states have an unusually large number of field offices (disproportionate to state population and size) and also have a lax merit system (or none at all), the explanation may lie in political opportunism as much as in a desire for widespread taxpayer service and tax enforcement.

taxpayers, field auditing, collection of taxes from recalcitrant taxpayers, and coverage work that relies on local sources of information require face-to-face relations between the tax agency and the citizen. Depending on population, area, and perhaps regional economic peculiarities, states will differ on the use of "flying squadrons" or permanent field offices for these purposes.

States with major cities other than the capital will almost always provide for special administrative activities in these populous areas. Oregon's Portland office, California's San Francisco and Los Angeles offices, and New York's New York City office are all assigned important office and field audit functions. New York's special investigations section operates out of New York City. For years California designated Los Angeles and San Francisco "regional offices." Even in the recent move toward greater centalization, these offices retained special responsibilities.

Appellate Organization

No clear, fixed line exists between administrative and judicial functions. And in income taxation, the essentially "judicial" nature of the central "administrative" function—the determination of taxable income—almost obliterates any distinction. Legislated rules cannot (and ought not attempt to) provide a label of "taxable" or "nontaxable" for every conceivable item of income in every conceivable combination of circumstances. Tax liabilities, especially in the area of business and professional income, capital gains and losses, and rental income, depend in considerable part on administrative interpretation, and administrators necessarily become "judges" in their day-to-day actions. But in practice, their actions are not labeled "judicial" until a dispute arises.

The organization for hearing appeals in a tax agency is frequently similar for all types of taxes the department administers. The income, sales, utility, or other tax divisions handle initial discussions and conferences; appeals from divisional determinations go to the department administrator or commission and thence in some states to separate boards or commissions before moving into the courts.

APPELLATE PROCEDURE

Informal Conference

Since many disputes between taxpayers and the tax agency reflect misunderstanding or a communication failure, the states provide for taxpayers to come into the department and discuss differences with qualified staff members. A number of states designate staff members to whom all taxpayers are directed for discussion of differences. Such an arrangement permits specialization and reduces the probability that the original examining auditor will attain a vested interest in his initial decision. These selected auditors, sometimes called "conferee examiners," discuss the original grievance with the taxpayer and, if the case is appealed, follow it through to the tax director and possibly to the board of appeals, if such exists.

If informal conferences fail to satisfy a taxpayer, he normally may secure a hearing before the income tax director or selected technical personnel. In California and New York, members of conference staffs hold this hearing. Wisconsin has established an especially formal appellate system within its tax department. A system of careful departmental appeals is likely to reduce appeals outside the department to a handful of taxpayers who differ on significant statutory interpretations by agency personnel. Reducing the number of appeals serves the interests of the department, taxpayer, and general public insofar as a reduction is not brought about at the expense of applying the law equitably to all taxpayers.

Further Administrative Appeals

The income tax states exhibit four appellate patterns for the taxpayer who is still dissatisfied after the hearing held within the income tax division or its equivalent. (See table 13 for the appellate routes followed in each state.) The most familiar pattern assigns the final administrative determination to the tax director and permits appeal of his decision directly to the regular state courts. Eighteen states follow this appellate pattern: Alabama, Alaska, Arkansas, Colorado, Connecticut, Florida, Georgia, Illinois, Indiana, Maine, Nebraska, New Hampshire, New Mexico, North Dakota, Rhode Island, Vermont, Virginia, and West Virginia. In each case, the tax director's ruling is binding on the income tax division and may be appealed to the lower courts only by the taxpayer. The courts usually review both the facts and the law unless the facts are stipulated by agreement between the taxpayer and the tax director.

A second group of state tax departments, organized under a commission or board instead of a single director, follows the traditional commission-court appeals route. The final administrative appeal is to the Tax Commission, and the first court appeal is either to a subordinate court or to the state supreme court. Seven states follow this pattern: Mississippi, Missouri, New York, Oklahoma, South Carolina, Tennessee, and Utah. The first judicial appeal in Oklahoma and Utah is to the highest state court.

The third appellate pattern places review in the tax agency but provides for appeal to an independent board or commission and then to the courts. Usually the taxpayer may not appeal to the courts until he has appealed to

TABLE 13
Taxpayer Appellate Opportunities

State	*Administrative agency*	*Appellate Route*[a]
Alabama	Department of Revenue	Commissioner; taxpayer may appeal to courts (1)
Alaska	Department of Revenue	Commissioner; taxpayer may appeal to courts (1)
Arizona	Department of Revenue	Director; taxpayer may appeal to Board of Tax Appeals; department or taxpayer may appeal to courts (3)
Arkansas	Department of Finance and Administration	Director; taxpayer may appeal to courts (1)
California	Franchise Tax Board	Executive officer; Board of Equalization; taxpayer may go on to sue for recovery of tax payment in courts (3)
Colorado	Department of Revenue	Executive director; taxpayer may appeal to courts (1)
Connecticut	Tax Department	Commissioner; taxpayer may appeal to courts (1)
Delaware	Division of Revenue, Department of Finance	Director or secretary; Tax Appeal Board; either department or taxpayer may appeal to courts (3)
Florida	Department of Revenue	Executive director; taxpayer may appeal to courts (1)
Georgia	Department of Revenue	Commissioner; taxpayer may appeal to courts (1)
Hawaii	Department of Taxation	Director; Tax Appeal Court; state supreme court (3)
Idaho	Department of Revenue/ Taxation	Commissioner; Board of Tax Appeals; taxpayer may appeal to courts (3)
Illinois	Department of Revenue	Director; taxpayer may appeal to courts (1)
Indiana	Department of Revenue	Director; taxpayer may appeal to courts (1)
Iowa	Department of Revenue	Director; Board of Tax Review; taxpayer may appeal to Board of Tax Appeals, then to courts (3)
Kansas	Department of Revenue	Secretary; taxpayer may appeal to Board of Tax Appeals and then to courts (3)
Kentucky	Department of Revenue	Commissioner; taxpayer may appeal to Board of Tax Appeals and either party may appeal to courts (3)
Louisiana	Department of Revenue and Taxation	Secretary; taxpayer may appeal to Board of Tax Appeals and either may appeal to courts (3)
Maine	Bureau of Taxation	Assessor; taxpayer may appeal to the courts (1)
Maryland	Comptroller	Comptroller; taxpayer may appeal to Tax Court; either may appeal to state's circuit court (3)
Massachusetts	Department of Revenue (Executive Office for Administration and Finance)	Commissioner; taxpayer may appeal to Tax Commission; decision may be appealed to the Appellate Tax Board (3)

TABLE 13—*Continued*

State	*Administrative agency*	*Appellate Route*[a]
Michigan	Department of the Treasury	Department; taxpayer may appeal to Tax Tribunal (or court of claims if tax paid) (3)
Minnesota	Department of Revenue	Commissioner; taxpayer may appeal to Tax Court; either may appeal to state supreme court (4)
Mississippi	Tax Commission	Commission; the courts (2)
Missouri	Department of Revenue	Director, Tax Commission; taxpayer or director may appeal to courts (2)
Montana	Department of Revenue	Director; Tax Appeal Board; taxpayer may appeal to courts (3)
Nebraska	Department of Revenue	Tax commissioner; taxpayer may appeal to courts (1)
New Hampshire	Department of Revenue/ Administration	Tax commissioner; Division of Taxes; taxpayer may appeal to Board of Taxation or courts (1)
New Jersey	Department of Treasury, Division of Taxation	Director; Division of Taxes (taxpayer may appeal to Division of Tax Appeals); taxpayer or director may appeal to courts (3)
New Mexico	Bureau of Revenue	Commissioner; taxpayer may appeal to courts (1)
New York	Department of Taxation and Finance	Tax Commission; taxpayer may appeal to courts (2)
North Carolina	Department of Revenue	Commissioner; Tax Review Board; taxpayer or commissioner may appeal to courts (3)
North Dakota	Tax Commissioner	Tax commissioner; taxpayer may appeal to courts (1)
Ohio	Department of Taxation	Tax commissioner; taxpayer may appeal to Board of Tax Appeals; commissioner or taxpayer may appeal to courts (3)
Oklahoma	Tax Commission	Tax Commission; taxpayer may appeal to state supreme court or pay tax and sue in district court (2)
Oregon	Department of Revenue	Director; taxing authority or taxpayer may appeal to Tax Court; either may appeal to state supreme court[b] (4)
Pennsylvania	Department of Revenue	Director; taxpayer may appeal to Board of Finance and Revenue; director or taxpayer may appeal to commonwealth court (3)
Rhode Island	Department of Administration	Tax administrator; taxpayer may appeal to courts (1)
South Carolina	Tax Commission	Tax Commission; taxpayer may appeal to courts (2)
Tennessee	Department of Revenue	Commissioner; taxpayer may appeal to courts (2)
Utah	Tax Commission	Tax Commission; taxpayer may appeal to state supreme court (2)
Vermont	Commissioner of Taxes	Commissioner; taxpayer may appeal to courts (1)

TABLE 13—*Continued*

State	*Administrative agency*	*Appellate Route*[a]
Virginia	Department of Taxation	Local commissioner of revenue; taxpayer may appeal from state commissioner to courts (1)
West Virginia	Tax Department	Commissioner; taxpayer may apply to courts (1)
Wisconsin	Department of Revenue	Commissioner; taxpayer may appeal to Tax Appeals Commission; either party may appeal to circuit court (3)

Source: Data drawn from departmental annual reports and *Tax Administration News* 42 (August, 1978): 85.

[a]The numbers in parentheses indicate the appeals group pattern of each state.

[b]Where appeal is for $250 or less, case goes to the Small Claims Division of the Tax Court and its decision is final.

this special tax review board.[19] Since the appellate unit is independent of the tax agency, most states (except California) with separate appellate bodies permit either the taxpayer or the tax department to appeal to the courts. Presently, nineteen states authorize appeals from the tax agency to an independent administrative review board: Arizona, California, Delaware, Hawaii, Idaho, Iowa, Kansas, Kentucky, Louisiana, Maryland, Massachusetts, Michigan, Minnesota, Montana, New Jersey, North Carolina, Ohio, Pennsylvania, and Wisconsin. Hawaii and Minnesota permit appeals only to the top state court.[20]

Oregon's appellate procedure could be categorized under group one since there is no administrative appeal beyond the department, yet its separate tax court is also a judicial variant of the administrative review board of group three. In 1961 Oregon established the "first true state tax court." The court not only has a regular division for hearing appeals but also has a small claims division to which taxpayers may appeal tax assessments of $250.00 or less. There is no appeal from a decision of the small claims division. Appeals by either the tax department or the taxpayer from the regular division go to the state supreme court. These provisions parallel

[19]Taxpayers do have a further alternative, whether the administrative appeal is to the review board or to a separate tax court. They can pay the tax and sue for recovery through the regular courts. Not all taxpayers wish to make an appeal before a specialized tax body but prefer to take their chances in the courts after paying the tax. In both the national government and in states like Minnesota, Oregon, Oklahoma, and Utah, which limit the taxpayer's appeal in the general courts to the highest court of the state, recovery suits often provide varied outcomes since different courts in the several districts hear the cases. Unless all differing judgments are taken to the supreme court, they remain to confuse the tax department, taxpayers, and the public.

[20]Hawaii and Minnesota use the term "tax courts," but these are not separate, specialized branches of the judiciary as they are in Oregon.

national practice whereby either the IRS or the taxpayer may appeal decisions of the U.S. Tax Court to the U.S. Supreme Court.

POLICY

States copy other states in organizational and policy matters just as many people copy clothes fashions. And in both instances there appear to be cycles. In the nineteenth century, the states gradually established tax commissions or boards to act as appellate bodies for review and equalization of local property taxes. When twentieth-century state governments began to raise more and more of their own taxes directly rather than through levies on property, they usually assigned administration of some or all of the new taxes to existing tax commissions. The review and appellate bodies for local property assessments thereby acquired administrative as well as quasi-judicial responsibilities. And then a new reform movement stressed control of tax agencies by one director rather than commission- or board-directed departments. States that accepted this reform pattern and eliminated the older tax commission or board sometimes sought to reproduce the commission in a multimember administrative appeals forum for taxpayers to utilize before seeking formal judicial remedies. Hence were born the tax appeals boards that currently exist in nineteen states.

The tax appeals board separated administrative functions from quasi-judicial responsibilities and thus met the criticism that experts may acquire a vested interest in the outcome of a particular case, whatever the merits of technical expertise.[21] Little or no empirical attention was directed at the actual practices of specific state tax departments. Public and judicial debates and decisions about the desirability of separating immediate enforcement and appeals have influenced administrators. Several tax administrators stressed to me their practice of not discussing cases with staff members before the taxpayer has had a hearing. Although the administrative appeal for New York taxpayers is to the commission that heads the department, two of the three commission members have essentially no concern for income tax administration. Even the chairman never goes into detail. Growing work volumes in New York and elsewhere have forced agency heads (whether commission or single individual) to delegate responsibilities and have reduced the opportunities to follow individual cases.

More and more the purpose of tax appeals boards—to ensure separation of enforcement and review—is being accomplished within the agencies

[21] As has often been true, national events affected the direction state legislators took. *The Report of the President's Commission on Administrative Management* (Washington, D.C.: Government Printing Office, 1937), as well as subsequent national organizational commissions, emphasized the need for direct accountability to the elected chief executive. Hence single administrators often replaced tax commissions. Some of the organizational reformers also accepted the need to separate "judicial" and "administrative" functions, and the Administrative Procedures Act of 1941 further reinforced such a philosophy.

whether or not there is a separate appeals board. Do these tax boards, then, represent an unnecessary extra step in the review process? How many formal appellate opportunities are needed to ensure justice? A number sufficient to promote justice and yet not so many as to defeat justice is a good standard, but it offers little guidance as to specifics. Few would advocate leaving the final decision to the top administrator alone or even to a single court. Yet several stages of appeal may mean undue delay in settlement and excessive costs for both the taxpayer and the state. Too many opportunities to appeal in tax cases, as in automobile accident cases, may chiefly benefit the party with a poor case. Wisconsin, for example, permits the taxpayer to discuss his differences with auditors and with a special internal conference panel. If disagreement remains, the taxpayer may appeal to the secretary of the Department of Revenue and from there to the Board of Tax Appeals. Even if he loses each of these appeals, the taxpayer need not surrender. He can still go to the circuit court, appeals court, possibly the state supreme court, and perhaps the U.S. Supreme Court. It is at least proper to inquire whether elimination of the appeal either to the Board of Tax Appeals or to the circuit court would impair justice or overburden the state appeals court. If it would not, the advantages of lower costs, greater speed, and discouragement of "bad cases" call for shortening the appellate ladder.

A few years after Oregon had established its Tax Court, a committee of the American Bar Association reviewed the state's experience and recommended general adoption of tax courts by other states in preference to separate quasi-administrative/judicial review bodies.[22] In its *Model Tax Court Act,* the Bar Association has further provided for appeal only to the state's highest court. Not only did Oregon pioneer among the states in establishing the first state tax court in the nation, but its small claims division was the first judicial, small claim type remedy, state or federal, in the United States. The American Bar Association's model court also includes a small claims division.

The locus of the right of appeal is also a vital part of the appellate picture. Until cases have reached the courts or an independent board of tax appeals, the income tax states traditionally limit the right of appeal to

[22]The American Bar Association recommended the establishment of "a fully judicial tax court in the judicial branch of government with plenary, general jurisdiction. Its proceedings should be *de novo* and without a jury. . . . The goal of tax litigation procedure should be to provide the taxpayer with a determination of his tax liability at the least cost to the taxpayer and the state by a tribunal which not only is, but which the taxpayer believes is, completely impartial." *1968 Report of the Subcommittee on State Tax Courts of the Committee on State and Local Taxes of the Section of Taxation of the American Bar Association.* The Model Tax Court Act, part of the committee's report, follows Oregon law in providing that the court have both a regular and a small claims division with appeal only to the state's highest court. The fact that establishment of a tax court would require a constitutional amendment in most states may explain why other states have not followed Oregon.

the taxpayer. The income tax division is not ordinarily considered an entity apart from the tax director or commission and is therefore not permitted to appeal. To protect the public interest in case tax administrators or commissions prove to be "taxpayer-minded," it may be desirable to provide for appeals by some other agent of the state. Minnesota's *Statutes,* for example, permit the attorney general or any citizen taxpayer to appeal decisions of the tax commissioner. Whether such a "public interest advocate" can serve a useful purpose, given the secrecy surrounding most income tax cases while they remain within the department, is questionable.[23] On the other hand, the failure of the California *Statutes* to permit the Franchise Tax Board as well as the taxpayer to appeal to the courts from a decision of the Board of Equalization appears undesirable in the extreme.

The appellate organization for tax disputes should be devised to promote equity and justice for all of a state's taxpayers within the framework of the tax law and with the least delay and at the lowest cost possible. The solution adopted by Minnesota, Oklahoma, Oregon, and Utah presumably reduces time and cost for both taxpayers and the state by limiting judicial review. An appraisal of the value of separate boards would be facilitated by an analysis both of the number of board reversals of departmental findings and of the action of the courts in upholding the department or board upon appeal. A historical study along such lines to compare the number of appeals, number of reversals, and, it is hoped, some measurements of elapsed time in Oregon would have particular value.

Conclusion

By the late seventies, the income tax states had moved far to provide a structural framework for centralized administration. The states had increasingly consolidated the administration of all taxes in one or two agencies. Even in the majority of states that still had more than one tax department, income tax administration was in the same department with sales, death, and other taxes most closely related administratively to the income tax. Only California was an exception in this respect. A handful of states continued to have multiheaded state tax agencies, but some of these assigned day-to-day administration to a single official. Hearings and appeals from administrative determinations within the departments were more and more being separated from administration. Nineteen states had developed fully separate appellate bodies apart from the courts to give the public and taxpayers the combined value of specialized knowledge and greater judicial safeguards.

[23]Such a provision may be more feasible for property or estate tax cases.

Consolidation has permitted substantial integration of housekeeping and staff functions common to the several taxes administered. New York, the first state to achieve consolidation of tax administration, originally integrated important staff and housekeeping functions. Not until 1977 did it integrate office and field auditing, collection, and other line functions. Integration rather than separate tax bureaus or units especially for income and sales taxes has become the fashionable organizational pattern. The case for line function integration appears less compelling than that for staff and facilitating services. Overintegration may defeat the values of specialized experience and knowledge that can produce a needed overall view of administration and policy for the income, sales, or other tax as a unit.

Differences among the states in field operations occasionally reflect traditions, as do Virginia's decentralization and North Carolina's numerous field offices. States generally establish and revise their field arrangements every few years to take account of shifting loads and the geographic size of the state. Technological changes—e.g., the increased use of telephones for taxpayer assistance as the cost of statewide telephone use has decreased, or on-line computer operations that permit the field man in collections to verify the current standing of an account—also affect field organization.

The Oregon Tax Court represents the one significant structural change in appellate organization among the states. Although the court is almost twenty years old, no other state has established a specialized tax court within its judicial system. Internally, many of the states have made their taxpayer conferences more formal and more independent of the auditors who made the original tax decisions.

Chapter Four

Management Resources

A tax department with an excellent organizational structure and a fine, workable income tax statute that includes optimal administrative tools cannot carry out its responsibilities equitably without sufficient resources. State appropriations must fund adequate housing, personnel, travel, computer and other technology, and such further needs as are appropriate to the accomplishment of the objectives sought. Appropriations are in part a response to the quality of staff services in each department, staff services that aid the operating activities of income tax administrators. (1) Through the budget function, the administrators make an evaluation of the financial needs, seek suitable appropriations, and apportion the funds received. (2) Recruitment, classification/promotion, termination, and a miscellany of other personnel activities—including affirmative action, collective bargaining, salary determination, payrolling, and fringe benefits—require a professional staff to serve the mutual interests of the agency and its employees. (3) Research and statistical services gather and analyze data on actual operations for management analysis and for developing information on the revenue, economic, and equity aspects of the several taxes as a basis for tax policy decisions. (4) Computer services in today's tax agency permit and promote expeditious processing and review of returns beyond the comprehension of an earlier generation. This chapter considers housing, budgeting, personnel, and research and statistical services. Chapter 5 includes a discussion of computer services.

Physical Setting

The fifty states have spent billions of dollars in building additional state office space in the last two decades to keep pace with the escalating growth of state governments. Parkinson's Law is continually fulfilled as each building fills and the need remains to lease, buy, or build more space. Political observers often say, "If you want to understand this state's politics, study its building and real estate operations!" Extravagance, favoritism, inefficiency, poor planning, outright corruption, as well as careful, expert planning with open bidding could be documented by any analysis of the extensive building that has taken place in each of the states in the last two decades.[1]

Depending on the size of the state and its capital city, state office buildings may be within easy walking distance of the capitol or miles away. New York built a state office campus in the post-World War II years (extending into the 1960s) on the eastern edge of Albany, several miles from the capitol building. Then in the late sixties and seventies, the state, under Governor Rockefeller, built a billion-dollar state office mall immediately south of the capitol and overlooking the Hudson River.[2] Most state building additions in Massachusetts are part of Boston's urban renewal program and are close to the old capitol and downtown. Of Wisconsin's half a dozen state office buildings, several are clustered near the capitol, while the others are located more than five miles away. Oregon's state office buildings surround its capitol.

State tax departments usually occupy part of the general complex of state office buildings and share the same advantages and disadvantages of their general appearance, parklike or crowded urban setting, good or no public transportation arrangements, presence or absence of nearby eating facilities, etc. Only infrequently is a tax department (or any state office) located in a building of unusual architectural design. New Mexico is an exception. The new building into which its Bureau of Revenue and Department of Motor Vehicles moved in the mid-seventies is an adobe structure.

> The final expression, in warm-tone concrete with the natural Santa Fe gravel exposed for warm tone and its textural quality, gives the appearance of a crack-free stucco building. . . .
>
> The contemporary expression of the traditional slit windows and the use of corner windows were basically drawn from some of the older pueblos in the state. The battered walls express the weathered characteristics of older adobe walls. The symmetry of the building was dictated by multiple use of the forms, an economy measure. The influence of old space finishes on contemporary design was expressed by interior latilla panels, a major recall of old latilla ceilings. This use of wood

[1]Urban politics, too, are often tied to real estate, whether by means of city purchases, building, or zoning. Just think of Chicago, or almost any city, for example. Lincoln Steffens came to believe in the honesty of Wisconsin government under Robert M. LaFollette and the Progressive Republicans in the first decade of this century because of the absence of discernible corruption in the rebuilding of the state capitol. Lincoln Steffens, *The Autobiography of Lincoln Steffens* (New York: Harcourt Brace, 1931), chap. 14.

[2]At the urging of Governor Alfred E. Smith, New York State purchased a substantial tract of land east of Albany fifty years ago. Over a thirty-year period this land provided the setting for both a dozen state office buildings and the campus of the State University of New York at Albany. Whether later generations will view Governor Rockefeller's mall as favorably as they do Governor Smith's land purchase remains an open question. But in all this development, political decisions were repeatedly made. See Neal R. Peirce, *The Megastates of America* (New York: W. W. Norton, 1972), pp. 34, 35.

added a warm and aesthetic touch that is in keeping with the main character of the building.[3]

Since a modern income tax administration office, with its processing, filing, and computer needs, requires substantial space, it is physically close to the general tax department only if the whole department secured its space after development of its income tax administration. Ohio's income tax administration (late in coming to the state) is located in a separate building at some distance from the capitol and the office building that houses the tax department in downtown Columbus. Pennsylvania's corporation income tax administration has been physically located within the state-office-building complex not far from the capitol, but the much newer individual income tax administration is located several miles away across the Susquehanna River. Both Ohio and Pennsylvania leased the additional space until building appropriations would permit a regathering of all tax department functions.[4]

Even where tax department operations are wholly within state office buildings, they may still be separated. The large space requirements for computers and for receiving, processing, and auditing returns may have a lower claim for central space than agencies having heavy client traffic. Wisconsin's secretary of revenue, division directors, and some other staff members work in a downtown state office building in Madison; but receiving, processing, filing, and auditing-income and sales tax functions are carried on in another state office building some five miles away. California's Franchise Tax Board has a few offices in downtown Sacramento within a few blocks of the capitol, but the bulk of the department's activities are carried on in space leased from Aero-Jet twenty miles away. The board's executive officer commutes between the two locations.[5]

The appearance of most income tax departments improved between the 1950s and the 1970s. New buildings, greater space, and some general upgrading of furniture and equipment enhanced the physical appearance of many departments. The design of many of the newer buildings may be spartan, but it gives the impression of clean, uncluttered work space.[6] The

[3]See New Mexico, Bureau of Revenue, *Annual Report, 1975/76* (Santa Fe), pp. 9, 10, for further descrptions of the architecture and the flexibility of the interior of the Manuel Lujan, Sr., Building. The name of New Mexico's tax department is now Department of Taxation and Revenue.

[4]Pennsylvania expects to locate all its revenue department operations in a new downtown state office by 1980 or so.

[5]When it became known that the Franchise Tax Board's operations would be moved out to Aero-Jet, office morale hit a new low. According to the executive officer, only an intensive effort to develop home-to-office automobile pool service for employees who did not own a car or did not normally use a car for work saved the situation. Six years later, the problem had disappeared. Parking is ample at Aero-Jet. The open space of the building made the installation of computers and the arrangement of appropriate space for all income tax functions relatively easy.

[6]Departments still located in older buildings often have not shared in this general upgrading. "Dinky" and "crowded" may be appropriate adjectives for them.

newer buildings often permit ready changes of walls without the need of masons, carpenters, and electricians. The Michigan Treasury offices, for example, permit most walls to be moved along ceiling grooves to fit any number of patterns that changes in personnel and organizational structure might require.

The IRS has upgraded its physical surroundings more than the states have. The Saint Paul IRS office, for example, provides attractive, movable screens that give privacy to groups of auditors without involving fixed walls. Carpeting on the floors and accoustical tile ceilings reduce noise. The result is an appearance that is pleasant for the employee and pleasing without appearing sumptuous to the outsider. Does the taxpayer see such surroundings as "a waste of *his* money," as one state tax official asserted, or is an attractive taxpayer conference room a necessity when tax department lawyers and auditors confer with large corporation tax representatives?

The number of private offices has diminished everywhere. Division directors, executive officers, and lawyers are among the few likely to have offices behind closed doors. Martin Huff (California) proclaims the desirability of completely open space. Other tax department officials in the country appear to share the view—though not all of them personally practice the style. From Massachusetts to California and from Wisconsin or Maine southward, most auditors, collectors, other professionals, and clerical personnel work in large open areas. Yet it was noticeable to the author that individuals in great open areas often attempted to set up barriers around their desks or to arrange files or other substantial furniture to subdivide unusually large areas. (Massachusetts uses color coding—not a physical barrier but still a means of identifying different functions.) Our mass society may make a degree of individual privacy desirable at work.

One recent study suggests that "the organization discharging an undesirable output will manipulate symbols in such a way as to encourage client acceptance of the output. . . . Acceptance-inducing symbols operate by impressing the client with the agency's legal and political legitimacy."[7] Such symbols may be flags, emblem or seal, certificate, citation or diploma, photograph of governor (or president), "no entry" or "employee only" signs. Other authority symbols include extent of barrier between receptionist and client, uniform, or formal or informal civilian clothing. Without compiling any detailed catalog of symbols used by tax department offices, the author did note that tax department personnel recognize the need to induce acceptance of a tax duty by most adult citizens. National and state flags fly over most buildings whether or not they are present in the reception office, agency heads often have pictures of the current state governor as

[7] Charles T. Goodsell, "Bureaucratic Manipulation of Physical Symbols: An Empirical Study," *American Journal of Political Science* (February, 1977): 80ff. On p. 84, Goodsell lists the variety of symbols that might be tallied.

well as professional citations or certificates in their offices.[8] Given the statutory emphasis on the confidentiality of income tax returns, it should not surprise anyone that every state tax department has doors or areas marked "no entry" or "employees only." The extent of the barrier in front or behind a receptionist varies with the degree to which taxpayers in general might be expected to come in for assistance or be called in for audit review.[9]

State Income Tax Budgeting

In state government, budget preparation offers an opportunity for reevaluation of the road traveled in the past and the choice of roads for the future. Implicit in every budget decision is competition among alternative uses for a limited quantity of resources. A rational allocation plan must be based on some concept of the relative return per resource unit (expressed in dollars of cost) that can be realized in the several possible uses. In principle, an optimal allocation is achieved when the marginal yield per budget dollar is equal for all competing uses. In practice, it is impossible to quantify, measure, and match marginal returns. This difficulty has defeated the attainment of the goals proclaimed for a series of attempted budget reforms in the national and state governments in the last two decades. The budget process has grown more sophisticated, but we must resort to a combination of qualitative and quantitative analyses to approximate ideal budget decisions. Most often we utilize a qualitative analysis plus the available data to justify a rough incrementalism.[10]

Incrementalism is the general rule of budgeting, although exceptions abound. In either new programs or major revision of existing programs,

[8] A governor's picture may serve as a symbol of authority, but this author would also suggest that the frequency of gubernatorial pictures has political, including political patronage, connotations. The infrequency of governors' pictures in some state tax departments may symbolize the relative absence of politics in tax administration.

[9] Most tax officials were gracious to the author and assumed her scholarly interests would not involve use of confidential information. They provided escorts through the frequently enormous spaces of the departments. Oregon officials were the most literal about their rules and though hospitable, did not offer a tour of their tax operation.

[10] The literature on budgeting has become so voluminous in the last decade that a footnote cannot possibly do it justice, but see especially Robert T. Golembiewski and Jack Rabin, eds., *Public Budgeting and Finance: Readings in Theory and Practice,* 2nd ed. (Itasca, Ill.: Peacock, 1975); S. Kenneth Howard, *Changing State Budgeting* (Lexington, Ky.: The Council of State Governments, 1973); Robert D. Lee, Jr., and Ronald W. Johnson, *Public Budgeting Systems* (Baltimore: University Park Press, 1973); Frederick B. Mosher and John E. Harr, *Programming Systems and Foreign Affairs Leadership: An Attempted Innovation* (New York: Oxford University Press, 1970); Peter A. Phyrr, *Zero-Base Budgeting* (New York: Wiley, 1973); Allen Schick, *Budget Innovation in the States* (Washington, D.C.: The Brookings Institution, 1971); and Aaron Wildavsky, *The Politics of the Budgetary Process,* 2nd ed. (Boston: Little, Brown, 1974).

some of the economists' preferences in budget-making occur; and we, implicitly if not explicitly, (1) rank the relative importance or value to us of the goals served by each potential use of the funds; (2) judge the effectiveness of each use in achieving goals; and (3) assess the efficiency with which administrators apply the funds in each competing use. The return per budget dollar is greater (1) the higher the social priority of the goal, (2) the more effective the given use of the funds in achieving the goal, and (3) the more efficient the application of the funds.[11]

Tax administrators may see their activity as unique in that its product is a flow of additional revenue dollars to the state, dollars that make possible either tax reductions or expanded state services. Budget officials sometimes find the quantitative information that a tax department can supply compelling, but at other times the political appeal of welfare benefits or education or health or highway services may outweigh the tax department's claims. Whatever the political validity of incrementalism or the limitations of quantification, governors and legislators are unwise to overlook the potential increase in revenue from providing additional administrative resources to well-managed tax departments. Or to quote Marius Farioletti,

> We see the fiscally absurd result of the Tax Administrator being denied additional expenditures capable of yielding revenue increases apparently several times the expenditures denied, at the same time that additional tax revenues are sought and budgetary deficits incurred.[12]

Occasionally a governor picks up the challenge and grants a tax agency substantial additional sums for administration. For the fiscal year 1978, New York's Governor Cary did just that.

> Notwithstanding the limits I have placed on State hiring, it is imperative that the State maximize the revenues it receives from all current tax sources. To this end I am recommending 607 new audit and support positions in the Department of Taxation and Finance. We estimate that revenues could increase by as much as $46 million as a result of this effort.[13]

Governor Carey's endorsement of a larger 1978 tax budget to bring in more revenue and help balance the budget was in sharp contrast to the actions of governors in several other states—e.g., Michigan and Wisconsin—who included their revenue department along with all other state agencies when they proclaimed the need for reducing budgets by 5% or more.

[11]One problem with many economists' statements on rational public budgeting is a failure to include the political costs and benefits in their formulas. Once a program and its budget have fought their way through a legislative body, the elected representatives usually have no desire to refight that particular battle, at least not for some years. In repeated defenses of incrementalism, Aaron Wildavsky expands on this idea in *The Politics of the Budgetary Process.*

[12]Marius Farioletti, "Tax Administration Funding and Fiscal Policy," *National Tax Journal* (March, 1973).

[13]New York, Governor, *Annual Budget Message, 1977/1978* (Albany).

Whether because state agency heads are gubernatorial appointees and accept the line that has been laid down, or are naturally conservative, or have not yet learned enough about the gaps in tax enforcement, a surprising number appear entirely satisfied with current programs and budgets. In a 1974 survey, Professor Deil S. Wright showed that nine tax chiefs in states with income taxes reported no need for program expansion, and only five believed an increase of 15% or more was desirable. In accounting for the limits to expansion, eight chiefs stated there was "no need"; four cited "lack of public support"; seven, "lack of fiscal resources"; four, "other agencies more influential"; eight, "lack of legislative support"; and one, "lack of interest group support." These responses of tax chiefs may be realistic in a given state's political climate, but they also suggest an unwillingness to stress publicly or to governors and legislators the gaps in enforcement that affect revenue and equity.[14]

Perhaps the strongest claim for a preferred budget position for tax administrations came some years ago from Charles F. Conlon, then executive director of the Federation of Tax Administrators:

> The decision to allocate resources through the means of government expenditures, a decision essentially that X dollars may more advantageously be spent by the government than by private persons, ordinarily involves the levy of taxes. As I see it, the X dollars available for expenditure for the purposes selected are those which constitute the net yield of the tax. Anterior to and overriding all other criteria relating to the disposition of tax revenue is the principle that provision first be made for the impartial, adequate, and effective administration of that tax. Failure to observe this principle would undermine the fiscal structure of the modern state since the ultimate effect of this omission would be to change the nature of the levy from that of a tax, an involuntary payment, to a contribution that may be made or withheld at will by substantial numbers of taxpayers.
>
> What constitutes impartial, adequate, and effective enforcement? I think that this objective cannot be defined in terms of barely marginal recoveries. It is, rather, a matter of judgment in which consideration must be given to the level of rates, incidence of the tax, number of taxpayers, etc.,—a determination not without some difficulty but one which, on the whole, can be made on the basis of various external and objective indicators.[15]

For the tax department, the ideal income tax budget would set forth (1) the goals of collecting maximum income taxes due under the law consistent with maintaining maximum equity in treatment among all classes of taxpayers; (2) an appraisal of the degree to which the goals are met

[14]These and subsequently quoted survey data have been drawn from a 1974 survey of state administrators conducted by Deil S. Wright, Political Science Research Professor, University of North Carolina. The author wishes to thank Professor Wright and his assistant Mary Wagner for supplying (without individual identification) the data for income tax administrators used here and elsewhere in this chapter.

[15]Quoted in n. 2, pp. 63-64, of Clara Penniman and Walter W. Heller, *State Income Tax Administration* (Chicago: Public Administration Service, 1959).

under present or proposed administrative programs; and (3) an appraisal of the cost of meeting the goals by diverse means. When individual states over the last three decades made the decision to institute withholding, at least some estimates were made as to total wage and salary payments in the state and tax-reported wage and salary payments (point 2 above). The presumed discrepancy convinced administrators and legislators that payroll withholding would provide more revenue at a lower cost (and with equal or greater equity) than had previous administrative procedures (points 1 and 3 above). Few departments or legislatures conducted this analysis with the desired precision, and some legislators were more interested in solving immediate fiscal problems. Nevertheless, discussion centered on the issues of increased collections and equity together with the cost of withholding to the state and the employer.

To set forth fully the goals specified for the ideal income tax budget would require knowledge of the *universe* of individual and corporate income taxpayers, the number of withholding agents, and the total amount of individual, withholding, and corporation income taxes due. No tax department has developed such data since it requires much more sophisticated statistical collection and analysis than has usually been attempted.[16] However carefully state tax departments cross-check IRS Individual or Business Master File tapes with their own master files, this necessarily fails to provide a check on nonresident corporations or on individual taxpayers who may file with the IRS outside the state. And the IRS does not reach every potential taxpayer. Beyond knowing the universe of taxpayers lies the even more complex world of taxes due. But quality budgeting requires at least the establishment of a few goals that are attainable with specified additional resources. Developing and pricing goals is at the heart of the agency budget-making process.

BUDGET ORGANIZATION AND PRACTICES IN THE STATES

Despite differences in state budget procedures and administrative, gubernatorial, and legislative control of budgets, there are many common threads. The majority of states now have annual budgets, all but four of the states elect their governors for four-year terms, and all but eight of the income tax states permit a governor to serve two or more terms. The differences among the states lie largely in the degree of budget analysis and control exercised by the governor and his budget office, the status of the governor's budget in the legislature, and the role of the legislative budget staff. New York has an "executive budget," developed by the governor and

[16] The author found that in posing the question of the state's universe of taxpayers or taxes, most administrators or research specialists did not take the question seriously. California's special management staff members (two) grinned and asked for a few more years to work on their model! The IRS has been working in this direction and has been aided by the wealth of national economic data, which far exceeds that for individual states.

his appointed budget director, which is largely immune to legislative change. In California, both the governor and the legislature have especially active budget staffs. The legislative analyst and assistants review and analyze the budget presented by the governor, and the legislative analyst's analysis is considered with the executive budget. California's provision for legislative budget staffs has been widely acclaimed and copied, although few other state legislators have provided themselves with a proportionate staff.

Notwithstanding the growth in legislative budget organization, in most states the governor's budget remains crucial. In addition to New York, three other income tax states (Maryland, Nebraska, and West Virginia) either provide for no increases or require higher voting majorities to offset the governor's recommendation. Normal practice, the governor's four-year term, and the common provision for an item veto increase the status of the executive budget in a majority of the other states.[17]

DEVELOPMENT OF INCOME TAX BUDGETS

Increased executive and legislative budget professionalization has encouraged or required many state tax agencies in the last decade to improve the quality of their budget requests and internal controls. Yet increased sophistication of budget presentations has not eliminated dependence on (1) the department's experience, (2) its forecast of the work load in returns, or (3) judgments of "what the traffic will stand," "what impossible situations must have attention," or "how far the department is getting behind." Performance budgeting or zero-base budgeting or any other form of cost/benefit analysis cannot change the underlying attitudes of chief administrators, and these attitudes help to set the overall resource goals reflected in their budget requests. Some administrators do not seek more funds, despite enforcement problems, while others with the same or more resources regularly ask for further funding. Political expediency, conservatism, concern for inequities in enforcement, or awareness of gaps in enforcement motivate chief tax executives differently.

Tax department justifications of requests frequently rest on overall cost-

[17] A survey of state administrators by Professor Deil Wright (see note 14 above) indicated that of the thirty state administrators in income tax states who responded, sixteen reported that the governor exercised more detailed review of their budget than the legislature, twenty-three perceived the governor as more sympathetic to agency goals than the legislature, but eleven believed the governor cut their budget more often than the legislature.

A few of the income tax states do not give their governor an item veto: Indiana, Maine, Maryland, New Hampshire, Rhode Island, and Vermont. North Carolina's governor does not have veto power. Unfortunately, studies on the significance of the absence of an item veto for the governor's budget have not been undertaken in recent years. Certainly tax departments generally rejoice when a governor approves their budget requests and celebrate if a governor's budget message selects their budget for a special boost. In 1977, when Governor Carey not only approved a request for additional positions but called attention to the program of the department in his annual budget message, the whole New York tax department rejoiced.

revenue or cost-return ratios. The data are readily available and often impressive. They provide some information as to current achievements and near-future prospects, but they fail to provide any analysis of what administrative effort is productive and what could be improved.[18] At best the cost-revenue ratio may contribute to the general state decision on apportionment of funds among different programs or (even more legitimately) the administrator's choice between two methods of operation. The cost-return ratio provides a work load unit cost and may also furnish an index to choices among competing administrative measures. If properly used, both the cost-revenue and cost-return ratios can be helpful in administrative appraisals. Yet, when used without qualification, both ratios are strongly affected by nonadministrative considerations. No state tax department, for example, no matter how efficient or effective, could compare favorably with the IRS on a cost-return or cost-revenue basis. The much higher rates of the national tax inevitably give the laurel to the IRS.

The general public expects both tax and nontax statutes to be enforced equitably among those affected. In many nontax programs, enforcement cannot be measured in terms of dollars returned; but the program is still considered desirable and is supported in budget after budget. In the case of a tax statute, the program objective is the production of revenue. The fact that this production goal can be measured in dollars should not obscure the parallel objective: enforcement of the tax law in an equitable fashion among all taxpayers. The more citizens can recognize equality of enforcement, the more they will voluntarily comply. Serious attention to general enforcement will optimize but not necessarily maximize cost-revenue ratios. Administrators may have to educate both themselves and governors and legislators to this overriding concern.

TAX BUDGET REQUESTS IN TWO STATES

Preparation of an income tax budget in Wisconsin, one of the leaders in state budget quality, begins with past experience but includes evaluation of current work and methods. The chiefs of all divisions submit to the secretary of revenue estimates of their requirements together with a review of the

[18] A 1943 critique of these measures alone is still valid: "Beside the factor of administrative efficiency involved [overall cost-revenue ratios] are influenced by the following additional factors: (1) Administrative policy, i.e., the degree of thoroughness to which the policing role is pursued; (2) the rates of tax; (3) richness of the tax base (also degree of business prosperity); (4) accounting practices in the distribution of such items as legal expense, capital outlays, local services, research and statistics; (5) lag in administration; and (6) time the tax has been in effect." U.S., Congress, Senate, Committee on Finance, *Federal, State and Local Government Fiscal Relations,* 78th Cong., 1st sess., June 23, 1943, S. Doc. 69, p. 309. The report was prepared for the secretary of the treasury by Harold M. Groves, Luther Gulick, and Mabel Newcomer. If the authors were writing now, they would surely add to item (4) on accounting practices whether or not the cost figure in the cost-revenue ratio includes employee fringe benefits such as retirement and health insurance.

problems and needs of their respective divisions. The revenue secretary has cumulative work load data available on the number and type (individual, corporation, etc.) of returns received. He knows the number of individual and corporation audits made in the office and in the field, the number of additional assessments that result from the audits, and the productivity of employees. Work load forecasts are developed for these same factors. Information on employee productivity and ratios of employees to work loads provide additional data for establishing personnel needs.

Within the framework of work load and cost data, and given some measurements of effectiveness through interstate and federal-state comparisons as well as population figures, gross income, etc., for the state, the secretary of the Wisconsin Department of Revenue arrives at the budget request through a series of divisional conferences. The overall state revenue outlook, the philosophy and disposition of the governor and the legislators, and the availability of qualified personnel may further contribute to the final budget proposed by the department.

Wisconsin income tax budgeting would not meet the canons of a science, but it is valid in the department's world. The secretary has a concept, which he can substantiate to a significant degree, of where the department has been and where it is going. The division director knows the results of matching IRS Individual Master File tapes with the department's master file and he knows the value of the federal-state audit exchange program to the state and to the national government. With such knowledge he has a fair basis for comparison of the state's income tax administration with that of the IRS. The internal budget request includes data similar to (although not as comprehensive as) that published in California.

California budgeting follows somewhat the same general pattern as that of Wisconsin, but is more detailed. The governor's budget meets the concepts of a program budget system more nearly than does the budget of any of the other income tax states. (No state publishes through its budget or in its public reports as much detail on administrative results as California does.) The report of the legislative analyst provides a critical analysis for the benefit of the legislature and the public.[19] The very detailed California analyses reflect the number of work load units, the costs, the amount of tax change, and the amount of revenue per dollar of cost for the major audit and nonaudit activities for the personal income tax and the bank and corporation income taxes. Tables 14, 15, and 16 indicate some of the available data. Unlike most administrative cost figures, the figures for

[19] After the Franchise Tax Board hears and approves the budget of its executive officer, it submits the budget to the governor's Finance Department. As in Wisconsin, budget analysts of the Finance Department analyze the budget and the general situation of the Franchise Tax Board and hold a hearing with the board before the director of finance. In California, a legislative analyst sits in on these hearings as part of the basis for his later recommendations to the state's Joint Legislative Budget Committee.

TABLE 14
California's Income Tax: Summary Cost Analysis for Fiscal Year 1977

Activity	*Total net assessments ($)*	*Cost of operations*	
		Nontax programs ($)	*Tax programs ($)*
Individual and corporation	4,326,173,921	4,542,914	50,831,794
Individual	3,107,893,837		37,881,960
Corporation	1,218,280,084		12,949,834
Senior citizens		2,212,967	
Political reform audit		2,329,947	
Miscellaneous adjustments			−23,088
Net Audits			
Individual	40,377,601		6,189,493
Corporation	80,355,961		7,429,072
Nonaudit Net			
Individual	38,029,750		10,026,447
Corporation	8,098,518		2,850,427

Source: California, Franchise Tax Board, *Operations Report, 1976/77* (Sacramento); figures drawn from exhibit D.

California, with only minor exceptions, represent true cost analysis and cover all possible costs, including the state's contribution to the Retirement Fund and the Franchise Tax Board's share of central agencies' overhead in the state. Since the California Franchise Tax Board has responsibility only for the state's personal income tax and bank and corporation franchise tax (except for the two nontax programs indicated above), it is somewhat easier for the board to isolate the costs of income tax administration than it would be for the general tax agencies of other states.

Income Tax Personnel

Successful administration is attained through leadership and staff personnel who can provide the spark of imagination and the dry log of competence from training and experience. Few more sensitive positions exist in government than those in income tax divisions. The reputation of the state's government may well depend on the effectiveness and fairness of the tax department chief and all others working in one capacity or another to enforce the income tax. Taxpayers find it difficult to relate their tax disbursements to "purchasing civilization"; rather, they require subtle recognition of their standing as taxpayers and assurance that they are receiving fair and equitable treatment under the law and compared with fellow taxpayers. Absolute honesty in money matters and a strong sense of public relations by all those working in a tax agency will aid greatly in securing voluntary compliance in tax matters.

TABLE 15

California: Cost of Personal Income Tax Activities, 1977

Activities	*No. of cases*	*Man-hours*	*Net assessments and prepayments ($)*	*Cost ($)*	*Revenue per dollar of cost ($)*
Self-assessment		1,640,626	3,691,624,369	21,666,020	170.39
Legislation and development		42,492		430,111	
Return forms and instructions		15,204		2,638,788	
Employer withholding			(2,943,748,218)[a]	7,453,346	394.96
Return processing		1,068,841		7,438,328	
Estimate processing		71,608		485,762	
Taxpayer assistance		352,293		2,576,256	
Claims	89,710	90,188		643,429	
Audit		692,568		6,109,493	
Personal income tax audit	1,354,164	360,609	12,001,943	2,959,117	4.06
Federal audit reports	191,083	146,815	19,497,557	1,192,390	16.35
Field audits	29,145	185,144	8,878,101	2,037,986	4.36
Mathematical Verification	8,618,479	250,973	21,840,966	1,905,887	11.46
Filing Enforcement		104,364		1,246,208	
Filing enforcement		66,298	799,457	799,457	11.80
Residency determination		2,167	23,964	23,964	183.60
Investigations		35,899	422,787	422,787	0.33
Collection		678,893	(6,874,352)[b]	6,874,352	(12.34)

Source: California, Franchise Tax Board, *Operations Report, 1976/77* (Sacramento); figures drawn from exhibits B-2, D, D-1, D-2, G, and H. The *Operations Report* provides substantial additional detail. For example, it also shows for each activity listed above the amount of the cost (if any) for the administration, legal, data processing, compliance, operations, departmental costs, and other divisions. Each term that is not self-explanatory has a specific meaning to the California Franchise Tax Board.

TABLE 16

California: Cost of Bank and Corporation Tax Activities, 1977

Activities	*No. of cases*	*Man-hours*	*Net assessments and prepayments ($)*	*Cost ($)*	*Revenue per dollar of cost ($)*
Self-assessment	196,435	305,220	1,554,838,869	2,670,335	582.26
Legislation and development		19,998		265,003	
Return forms and instructions		2,683		199,118	
Return processing		156,212		1,128,548	
Estimate processing		17,670		112,524	
Taxpayer assistance		48,594		446,307	
Claims		60,063		518,835	
Audit					
Federal audit reports	8,969	22,920	14,281,190	205,921	69.35
Nonappor. corp. audits—central	171,772	94,990	4,778,605	819,332	5.83
Nonappor. corp. audits—field	5,984	94,068	3,485,410	1,071,477	3.25
Appor. corp. audits—central	21,481	42,011	601,109	427,873	1.40
In-state, field	5,631	160,412	22,400,691	2,013,854	11.12
Out-of-state, field	6,121	218,868	34,808,956	2,890,615	12.40
Mathematical Verification	256,833	27,868	11,014,301	195,299	56.40
Exempt Corporation		55,832	334,211	543,479	0.61
Filing Enforcement		13,464	2,559,209	126,703	20.20
Collections		202,285	(108,588,418)[a]	1,984,946	(54.71)[a]

Source: California, Franchise Tax Board, *Operations Report, 1976/77* (Sacramento); figures drawn from exhibits B-2, D, D-1, G, and H.

[a]The collection revenue is a memo figure reflecting net assessments that were not paid timely and had to be collected through the collection program.

TAX AGENCY HEADS

State tax administrators accept responsibility in each state for collecting the funds that provide domestic peace, regulate the economy, and otherwise support a multitude of services for which governors and legislators receive applause and win elections.[20] Almost never do governors win re-election on the basis of effective tax administration, whatever the tax administrator may have contributed to the citizens' general satisfaction with government. Tax agency heads seldom move on to political careers; but they and their staffs are often vulnerable to political attacks.[21] They are usually politically dispensable. Who are these people? How were they selected? How much influence do they have on the agency and its enforcement and collection of income taxes? How do they affect income tax policy?

Selection

All but eight of the individuals who head the agencies responsible for state income tax administration are appointed by their respective governors and are subject to state senate confirmation, which would seem to assure appointment of an individual identified with the party in power.[22] Appointment by the governor normally means a term the length of the governor's or shorter. Either the new governor wants a change, or more often the tax administrator finds it advantageous to take another position before the governor's last term is over. Where the same party remains in control of a state over some years, the tax agency head may have a long tenure. And where a tax administrator has held the helm for a number of years, replacement may become inexpedient politically even with a change of party. Certainly Henry Long survived many changes in party control in Massachusetts between 1918 and 1953. Morrisset of Virginia retired in 1970 after serving since 1926. He survived the change in Virginia from a one-party Democratic state through an occasional Republican governor to the shifting control within the state's Democratic Party. Even where the succeeding governor of a different party is not faced with a long-tenured tax chief, he may prefer to leave a respected individual in office. Thus, although Oregon Revenue Director John J. Lobdell was initially appointed

[20]Table 17 identifies the tax agency, its head, method of selection, and recent salary.

[21]A few tax administrators are elected and manage to gain a special kind of popularity, but this is rare. Maryland's Louis L. Goldstein has won election after election, and has even outpolled candidates for governor. North Dakota's current tax commissioner also has proved a successful vote-getter.

[22]The degree of previous political activity of the appointee varies. One would expect substantial activity by appointees in Indiana and Pennsylvania, for example, but states with strong merit systems also tend more and more to have political agency heads. The current California and Wisconsin executives were earlier active political partisans. Earlier political activism may affect *policy recommentations* far more than it affects normal administrative operations in merit-system states.

by Republican Governor Tom McCall in 1971, he has continued in office, under Democratic Governor Robert W. Straub to the present (1978).[23]

Tax chiefs not appointed by governors secure their position in a variety of ways. North Dakota's commissioner is elected. Maryland's director is appointed by the *elected* state comptroller, whose responsibilities include tax administration. In Arkansas, Delaware, and Pennsylvania, where tax administration is handled by an agency with broader responsibilities, the agency head appoints the tax administrator with the approval of the governor. In Michigan, Rhode Island and Utah, where tax administration is also one of several responsibilities of the controlling agency, the tax chief is selected according to civil service procedures. The California Franchise Tax Board executive officer with immediate responsibility for income tax administration is appointed by the board (its membership is *ex officio* and one of the *ex officio* members is appointed by the governor) and confirmed by a two-thirds vote of the state senate.[24]

Control

The majority of state tax administrators would prefer control by the governor (presumably including appointment power, control of the budget, etc.); another majority (but somewhat smaller than that in the preference vote) sees the governor as having more control over the agency than the legislature; and a third majority (larger than that in the preference vote) views the governor as more sympathetic to agency goals than the legislature.[25] Eleven tax administrators perceived the governor as having a "high level of influence" on agency decisions. Only one administrator saw the governor as having no influence, with seventeen reporting "slight" or "moderate" gubernatorial influence on tax agency decisions.

Given the fact that most tax administrators are appointed by the

[23] An administrator appointed by a governor of a different party and continued under a new governor may be respected for his competence and administrative nonpartisanship, and the governor may think it best not to disturb a tax agency that is operating well. Whether the tax administrator finds invisible control strings no doubt depends on the governor and administrator. Although the governor of Oregon appeared to have no qualms about Lobdell's continuing, Democratic leaders in the state legislature did, and it became advisable for other members of the tax agency to make most of the appearances before legislative committees. A North Carolina tax director, initially accepted by the new Republican governor, rapidly found himself replaced for the balance of the governor's term when he attempted to continue business as usual with the Democratic legislative leadership. When Democratic Governor Shapp came into power in Pennsylvania (where patronage remains very much alive), some of his staff were warned of the state's precarious revenue situation and advised to leave the corporation tax bureau personnel alone. The advice was accepted.

[24] Since removal is accomplished in the same way, it should not be surprising that an executive director is likely to determine his own term. The present incumbent is only the second to serve since this appointment and removal procedure was established more than twenty-five years ago. Legislation in 1979 changed this.

[25] From the Wright survey (note 14 above).

governor, most administrators prefer control by the governor and view the governor as sympathetic, and eleven tax administrators see the governor as having a "high influence" on agency decisions, it is surprising to find that most tax chiefs report limited contacts with the governor. Of the thirty administrators in income tax states who responded to the Wright survey, four indicated daily contact, nine weekly, three monthly. Fourteen, however, stated that their contacts were less frequent than monthly. Legislative contacts tended to be more frequent for most administrators, perhaps because of the number of legislators or because individual legislators make frequent inquiries about constituent tax questions. The majority of tax administrators indicated daily or at least weekly contact with other state agencies, with clientele, and with the public at large. Ten state tax administrators reported monthly or more frequent contact with regional federal officials (IRS?); an additional fourteen reported less-than-monthly contact.[26]

Tax administrators do not work in isolation from politicians, administrators with different problems, or the public. Nevertheless, all but one of the responding tax administrators reported that he spent between 50% and 74% of his time on internal management, which also often included policy development. Most reported using much smaller periods of time to promote public support. Responding tax administrators played down other states and professional associations as sources of ideas, and the majority named their own agency as the chief source of new ideas.[27] Nevertheless, whether for exchange of ideas or exchange of information, fifteen state administrators reported monthly or more frequent contact with other state tax administrators.

SPECIAL DEMANDS ON INCOME TAX PERSONNEL

Tax administration in general and income tax administration in particular exert exacting demands on technical, administrative, and public-contact personnel. The duties in these classes demand qualifications that set the income tax service apart from many other government activities.

Types of Personnel

Below the agency chief or chiefs, selected under special statutory provisions, every income tax division employs people with a variety of experience and training—clerical workers to do the many routine tasks; accountants to maintain the necessary internal records; computer pro-

[26]It should be remembered that Wright's survey was sent only to the top tax administrator in each state, so the answers would not necessarily reflect the contacts of auditors, collectors, etc., nor would they in most states reflect the experience of the immediate head of the income tax division.

[27]Since most of the questionnaires were answered by politically appointed tax agency chiefs, who may have had little direct tax administrative experience previously, this reply may not account for the true source of administrative and policy ideas of the agency staff.

grammers and other personnel for the dozens of tasks modern computers perform; auditors or examiners; collectors; perhaps statisticians, economists, management analysts, budget specialists; attorneys; supervisory personnel; public relations personnel; and top administrators. Small tax departments may not have separate positions for all these skills, but the functions represented are nevertheless present.

Auditors (states may use the designation examiner or even accountant) form a key class in any tax department. Although specialization in some departments may make a difference, income tax auditors generally handle money at least occasionally; meet the public on the telephone, through correspondence, or face-to-face in office visits or field investigations; and contribute substantially to the decisions that set the standards practiced by the department. Many times promotions to supervisory and top administrative positions in a career service tap members of the auditor class.

Nature of Special Demands

Attitudes toward the Public. Under the American system of self-assessment in income taxation, the taxpayer is the primary source of tax information. To cultivate that source fully, tax personnel must not only enlist the citizen's good will with tact and fairness but also gain his respect through resourcefulness in ascertaining income and firmness in applying the tax rightfully due. In most government activities, the official offers substantive services to the public, but the tax gatherer has nothing to offer but his claims. Selling such wares requires an unusually gifted salesman.

Auditors who go into a man's accounts and business go to the heart of his financial life. A chip on the auditor's shoulder can create a "come and get me" attitude that will be costly to the state in additional auditing outlays and reduced revenues. Technical competence must be tempered with personality traits that elicit taxpayer cooperation and help to educate him for the future. Administrators generally stress education of the taxpayer as an objective in all audit work.

A sense of fair play is another vital cog in the relationship between tax auditor and taxpayer. An overweaning get-the-tax attitude can destroy taxpayer good will. Chief administrators who give undue weight to tax productivity as the major criterion for promotion of auditors run the risk of creating unfortunate staff attitudes. Still, one administrator at least saw the danger of watering down tax enforcement as a result of current legislative programs that provide an increasing number of social credits or deductions on tax returns and thus often result in a refund to the "taxpayer."

Technical Ability. The discovery of income and its recipients and the proper determination of taxable income are tasks that require a high order of ingenuity and competence. In individual income taxation, adequate coverage can be attained only through the use of many, varied, and often subtle forms of information. Curiosity, imagination, and diligence are needed, especially since few individuals keep good records, and many keep none. Thorough familiarity with the income characteristics of various types of taxpayers will help to forestall evasion, understatement of income, and overstatement of deductions. Experience may be the only reliable teacher.

In verifying business income and in auditing corporations, personnel proficient in legal, accounting, and even engineering and appraisal techniques are needed. Only a combination of ability, training, and experience can successfully disentangle corporate relationships, pull aside the veil obscuring true income, determine a given state's taxable share of a multistate or multinational corporation's income, and wrestle with problems of depreciation, depletion, and obsolescence. The records are available. The crux of the matter is the tax agent's capacity to analyze them.

The full range of techniques available to an income tax administrator today can be put to use only if he has a staff capable of applying them. Few are the states with corporation auditors who have the desired talents. A number of states lack individual income tax auditors with the appropriate qualifications.[28]

Discretion. Substantial discretion is inherent in the auditing function. Applying rules that are necessarily broad and rather flexible, the auditor often functions almost judicially. Even with audit review and appellate provisions, the auditor's initial interpretations and decisions largely determine the amount of tax owed by the individual or corporation. Field auditors in particular exercise broad authority that demands not only competence and balanced judgment but unquestioned honesty and freedom from political taint. Several states permit their field auditors to combine the functions of assessing and collecting taxes. Covert compromises and dishonest settlements—as well as assessing and collecting one amount and reporting and remitting another—are among the possibilities that have to be guarded against. A careful internal audit system can do much to cut down the chances for dishonest manipulation. But such a system is not a substitute for removal of political pressure through merit system appointment of personnel and through establishment of adequate pay scales to lessen pecuniary temptation.

The emphasis in the above paragraph on the individual qualifications and integrity of auditors extends to all personnel in the tax agency. The collector, for example, does not need the accounting skills of an auditor but does need assertiveness to enforce the state's claim properly.

[28]According to a tax supervisor quoted twenty years ago, "We have to adjust our methods to some of the patronage employees we get in order to use them." This statement continues to reflect the situation in perhaps a dozen states. See Penniman and Heller, *State Income Tax Administration*, p. 85, n. 2.

GENERAL MERIT SYSTEM, PATRONAGE, OR A COMBINATION

The competence and leadership qualities of the state's chief tax official will influence the effectiveness of the tax department's program. But department employees selected and protected by a strong merit system may exercise a stronger continuing influence for outstanding tax enforcement. Opposed to the strong merit system in patronage states is the placing of party loyalists in positions of influence, especially in the tax field service, as conduits for voter information and party aid. Appropriate party standing and merit do not have to be opposites, but blatant party activity may undermine public confidence in tax administration.

A majority of the income tax states have statutory or constitutional merit systems designed to remove general personnel selection from party control.[29] The effectiveness of the state merit systems in removing patronage as an employment consideration varies.[30] Without much doubt, California, Michigan, Minnesota, New York, Oregon, and Wisconsin lead the income tax states in avoidance of party patronage and in positive achievements to recruit and keep competent staffs. In other merit states, the examination represents a preliminary hurdle, with some party clearance being the next step before appointment will be considered.

Most patronage states set educational and training requirements for different categories of positions and may require that applicants pass an examination *after* they receive party clearance. A fair generalization is that patronage states, whether or not they require the passing of an examination, set lower minimum experience and educational requirements and administer a less rigorous examination than do the merit states.[31] The absence of higher standards or competence, the higher turnover rate, and the

[29]The states classified as merit-system states are those in which open, competitive examinations are the established means of selection for clerical and technical personnel, including the auditor class of the tax department.

[30]Massachusetts has one of the oldest official merit systems in the nation, but it has not always operated as the state's reformers intended and presumed. Candidates must take the merit examination, but political endorsements commonly follow and strengthen the candidacy. Once in the civil service system, the employee's position is practically impregnable. And, quoting Robert Wood, "It [a self-perpetuating bureaucracy] doesn't protect you from patronage abuses and at the same time it doesn't allow you the techniques of modern management." Neal R. Peirce, *The New England States* (New York: W. W. Norton, 1976), pp. 90-91.

[31]Apart from the clerical class, Ohio's personnel system is quite decentralized. The basic professional class of tax commissioner agent is exclusive to the tax department. Although the classification has existed for some time, the central personnel office frequently does not manage to have lists of applicants available. The personnel office of the department then takes applications, appraises them, and sends desirable applicants to appropriate divisions for interview. If accepted, the agent at some later point would have to pass an exam given by the personnel office. There are several grades of agents, and level and promotion depend on the supervisor's (and his supervisor's) view of the position and the agent's background and proven ability. The State Board of Accountancy does not recognize tax department experience for CPA rating.

general establishment of lower salaries and fringe benefits in the patronage states suggest the probability of less experienced and less qualified auditors and other key personnel.

State boards vary in standards, but one measure of the quality of tax auditors (and auditing) in a state is whether the state's board of accountancy accepts tax department experience for the CPA rating. If the Society of Certified Public Accountants recognizes field or corporation auditing experience in a state's revenue department, the quality of such auditing is presumed to be higher in that state than in states where that experience is not recognized. Recruiting and retention are affected accordingly.

Unionism and collective bargaining are growing in both merit system and patronage states, and they are affecting all personnel systems. Oregon has had a strong merit civil service system for years. In 1971 the governor and legislature "essentially gave employees rights of collective bargaining," according to a tax department administrator. Since then the Oregon Employees Association has secured widespread membership and in 1975 negotiated its first full contract. These developments and others have changed the role of the earlier traditional merit civil service system. In patronage states, unions frequently insist on tenure following probation, regardless of political route to the initial appointment.[32] Unionism may go further and require that seniority apply not only in retention but in promotion to related grade levels. The union push for these changes in Pennsylvania is likely to be copied in Indiana and other political patronage states. How such developments will benefit income tax administration remains unclear.

Presumably the goal of merit systems, and of at least some of the patronage systems, is retention of the quality employee and removal of the misfit. Neither system nor any combination of the two nor the addition of unionism guarantees that this objective will be reached. No one has developed adequate measures to identify all the potential misfits during probation or the means to hold the interest and enthusiasm of all individuals throughout a thirty-year career. Appropriate supervision, in-service training, encouragement of more professional education, and career ladders for promotion and recognition help. Horizontal personnel moves that give individuals a chance to consider different problems provide incentive. Competitive salaries and fringe benefits also help, as does the ability to earn working credit for the CPA.

In the last decade or so the Oregon Tax Department has generally recruited auditors with a bachelor's degree and an accounting major. The audit operation involves few non-college graduates. New recruits go into a

[32] Pennsylvania's legislature, which did not intend to rule out party patronage appointments, approved state employee unionization and collective bargaining on some issues. The long-term results cannot be predicted, but it appears that state employee unions may accomplish at least some of the changes reformers have long sought.

one-month training program, then a month of desk audit activity, followed by another month of training. Trainers use IRS training materials and have had an opportunity to work with the IRS in its own training program. Recruits receive a $45 monthly increase after six months, another after the first year, etc. By the end of three years the individual is assumed to be a journeyman auditor with a monthly salary $500 above the beginning level. The monthly salaries of out-of-state auditors are about $130 higher.

Individual discouragement may still result from arbitrary barriers. Personnel practices and public statutes may limit salary advances for the most dedicated and competent auditor unless he is made an administrator. Yet the auditor whose specialty is examining oil company records, for example, may be more valuable in that position than in any supervisory one. The best professional auditor may be unfit for and uninterested in management. California's Franchise Tax Board has breached the state's traditional salary schedules for auditors by securing authorization for increases in a select number (and to be meaningful the number must be limited) of auditors' salaries above the classification maximum. To qualify, such individuals must meet all IRS educational requirements, have had substantial and varied auditing experience, earned a CPA rating, and utilized these talents in exceptional income tax auditing. Oregon finds that most auditors who stay for three years will make the Revenue Department their career. California's experience has been similar. Without appropriate incentives (including individual dedication), any agency will lose its valued employees and retain only those interested in wages or security.

Recruitment and Selection

Changing labor market conditions and legislated or administrative affirmative action programs, as well as changing job definitions, have modified earlier recruitment and selection procedures within the most professional and least professional state and agency personnel systems. Several of the leading tax departments, including that of New York, have redesigned the position of auditor to make certain the individual has challenging professional work. The more computers can be programmed to make arithmetic and other routine checks of individual returns and sort out for audit consideration only the most complex returns or problems, the more important it is that all auditors receive the appropriate education and training. For the states that take this view, a college degree or reasonable equivalent is the minimum entry requirement. Often these states prefer to take graduates without experience and train them. New York and Wisconsin particularly stress the desirability of training employees on the basis of their college work, the advantage being that they do not have to break the trainees of habits and methods learned in private accounting offices or elsewhere. To recruit college graduates, state tax departments (or occasionally state merit agencies) usually establish liaison with nearby universities and colleges. Wisconsin's Department of Revenue has used some temporary summer positions to attract accounting majors who will be seniors in the fall. The department has also sent senior personnel outside the state to recruit qualified auditors.

Affirmative action programs, reinforcing or reinforced by public opinion, have focused increased attention on the distribution of men and women, on the distribution of races, and on opportunities for the handicapped among auditors. Wisconsin has gone out of state to recruit qualified minority-group auditors. California has probably undertaken the strongest affirmative action program along all fronts. Its executive officer has become personally involved and has pushed to give all peoples an opportunity. New York reports that

> training and employment for disadvantaged persons was undertaken during the year to enable them to assume the duties of Tax Compliance agents in a program partially funded by the Federal government. Staffing the Department's Harlem Branch office was largely accomplished from among local residents and offered significant opportunities in managerial positions.[33]

Greater attention to taxpaying minorities within the state has necessitated the hiring of bilingual or multilingual employees. New York may advertise for a tax compliance agent who is Spanish-speaking. California requires that individuals in its taxpayer assistance telephone program be fluent in one or more languages in addition to English—e.g., Spanish, Chinese, or Japanese.

Employment of women and minorities has not been confined to New York, Wisconsin, and California. The author observed a significant increase in the number of women and minorities in almost every tax department visited, and this change was also observed at national professional tax meetings.

Salary Patterns

Table 17 lists the 1977 salaries of tax agency chiefs and auditors for the states. Inflation alone has significantly affected salary levels in the last decade, and in several states unionization has apparently brought salary increases. Variations among states reflect regional and local economies as well as differing traditions as to whether state employees should or should not be paid according to the practices of private industry. Increasingly the fringe benefits in public employment equal or exceed those in private employment. The critical question for each state and department remains, are the salary, fringe benefits, and conditions of employment (including the career opportunities) sufficient to attract and keep the qualified individuals desired?

[33]New York, Department of Taxation and Finance, *Annual Report, 1974/75* (Albany, 1976), p. 11.

TABLE 17
Salaries for Tax Department Secretary/Director and for Auditors/Examiners, 1978

	Tax agency head[a]		*Auditor/examiner salaries*[b]	
State	*Appointment by*	*Salary ($)*	*Beginning ($)*	*Maximum ($)*
Alabama	G	35,000	13,192	22,975
Alaska	G both H	47,304	18,612	46,716
Arizona	G Senate	39,005	13,212	24,566
Arkansas	Agency head + G	30,194	8,190	16,588
California	G	34,752	11,088	27,180
Colorado	G Senate	38,000	11,136	24,300
Connecticut	G either H	36,531	12,499	15,193
Delaware	G Senate	32,000	9,767	24,240
Florida	G + Cabinet	34,000	11,275	19,085
Georgia	G	32,500	8,976	25,000
Hawaii	G Senate	42,500	10,344	28,608
Idaho	G Senate	20,500	12,168	20,820
Illinois	G Senate	38,000	12,714	33,150
Indiana	G	36,478	10,704	27,288
Iowa	G Senate	32,000	10,452	20,306
Kansas	G Senate	33,000	13,386	25,452
Kentucky	G	32,500	9,384	22,584
Louisiana	G Senate	37,000	11,244	23,232
Maine	Agency head + G	25,200	9,110	15,849
Maryland	Elected	44,856	10,285	13,457
Massachusetts	G	29,352	10,472	12,625
Michigan	Agency head	30,050	13,530	21,402
Minnesota	G Senate	41,000	12,612	24,516
Mississippi	G	25,500	11,160	22,140
Missouri	G Senate	40,000	10,488	15,084
Montana	G Senate	32,400	11,731	17,868
Nebraska	G Senate	26,988	11,253	22,253
New Hampshire	G Council	28,587	—	—
New Jersey	G Senate	42,500	12,529	23,806
New Mexico	G	33,960	9,936	13,440
New York	G Senate	47,800	8,454	16,351
North Carolina	G	38,250	12,108	22,392
North Dakota	Elected	22,500	10,824	21,420
Ohio	G Senate	45,282	9,505	17,056
Oklahoma	G Senate	27,000	7,560	18,000
Oregon	G Senate	37,512	12,240	28,044
Pennsylvania	G Senate	41,250	9,213	14,690
Rhode Island	Civil Service	35,453	13,951	16,282
South Carolina	Commission	33,059	10,487	23,339
Tennessee	G	43,700	—	—
Utah	G Senate	38,880	14,040	23,136
Vermont	G Senate	31,200	11,544	17,290
Virginia	G both H	35,000	8,040	18,700
West Virginia	G Senate	37,500	8,100	23,544
Wisconsin	G Senate	42,000	13,599	31,349

Note: G, Governor; G Senate, governor appoints but Senate approval is needed; G both H, governor appoints but both Houses of the legislature must approve; Agency head + G, the agency head appoints the top tax official with approval of the governor; etc.

[a]Information in the first column abstracted from table on p. 135 (that in second column from p. 131). *The Book of the States, 1978-1979* (Lexington, Ky.: The Council of State governments, 1978).

[b]Data taken from answers to questionnaires mailed to tax departments in August, 1978.

Research and Statistics

New Mexico's description of its tax research division could serve to describe the research programs of many states:

This division provides tax research and statistical support to the Commissioner's Office, the Legislature, other state agencies and the public. It receives and analyzes tax data and prepares monthly reports, for example, on tax receipts and disbursements by the Bureau and on gross receipts tax by industrial category. The Division gathers and interprets information related to, and influencing state revenues. It prepares revenue projections for Bureau taxes, based on existing and proposed statutes. It reviews Bureau regulations and state statutes, and aids in drafting bills suggested by such review or requested by the Commissioner or Deputy Commissioner. The Division prepares the annual report of Bureau operations, is responsible for improving the research library of the Bureau and responds to numerous requests from the public for tax information.[34]

In states with a legal division, the review of regulations, bill drafting, etc., would probably fall within its jurisdiction, not that of the research division.

RESEARCH ORGANIZATION

Every state but California integrates its statistical and research work on income taxes with similar work on other taxes in the tax department. In California, which has a separate agency for income taxes, a separate income tax research operation is carried out by the Franchise Tax Board. In North Carolina, on the other hand, from July, 1942, until October, 1971, a separate Department of Tax Research, with a comparatively large staff, compiled and published all tax statistics and prepared detailed research studies. The size of research staffs and the scope of their undertakings differ substantially among the states. And, as might be expected, the qualifications of personnel in research and statistics also differ. One finds economists with doctorates, academically trained and experienced statisticians, or only glorified clerks. The more professional staffs initiate (as well as prepare at gubernatorial or legislative request) analytical research studies in addition to compiling relevant statistical information from tax reports and returns. Other duties assigned to research staffs include specialized studies to be used as a basis for legislative recommendations by the department; review of all proposals for tax legislation, with some analysis of their revenue, administrative, and perhaps equity effects; preparation of replies to legislators and others on aspects of the state's tax system; and, occasionally, studies directed toward evaluation of administrative effectiveness or gaps in income reporting. In a few states the research director's advice is sought on a wide range of administrative and policy matters.

[34]New Mexico, Bureau of Revenue, *Annual Report, 1975/76* (Santa Fe), p. 18.

Despite care in framing questions, it is possible that in a few instances (e.g., Vermont) salaries are not for strictly comparable range of positions. In most instances, however, the salaries represent 1978 entry level and top level of all departmental auditors or examiners.

STATISTICAL AND RESEARCH REPORTS

Research divisions commonly prepare tax agencies' annual or biennial reports. These reports vary from popularizations (occasionally the comic-strip variety, but more often the slick public relations type) to a careful summary of the work done, an evaluation, and perhaps some recommendations for legislative action or a summary of the previous legislature's action on income tax matters. Still other reports concentrate on the presentation of pages of unanalyzed statistics.

No state matches California in the richness of the data presented in its annual report and in its fiscal year operations report. For policy decision purposes, the annual report provides by aggregate and by adjusted gross income classes such data as (1) income source (salaries and wages, dividends, interest, annuities and pensions, business and professional, partnership, sale of capital assets, rents and royalties, and other), (2) deductions (standard, itemized, medical expense, political promotion, taxes [real estate, gas, sales, in lieu, other], interest on home mortgages, contributions, child care), (3) tax credits for personal exemptions, and (4) taxes withheld and prepaid estimates. Numbers of returns and dollar figures are given and most of the data are subsequently broken down by county.

California's annual report also provides a quick historical review of the income tax in California, including changes in rates and personal exemptions, annual aggregate adjusted gross income, taxable income, and taxes assessed. Since each report provides a summary of major statutory changes, a substantial history of personal income and corporation franchise taxes is readily available.

The aggregate data on income and sources of income could serve as a basis for comparison with other data to provide some estimates of compliance by various sectors of the economy. The only actual comparison made in the report aggregates California income reported on state returns, IRS income reported on the returns of California residents, and personal income reported by the U.S. Commerce Department. The figures are interesting. For one thing, they show that the older gap between California's Franchise Tax Board and the IRS is closing. Differences between Franchise Tax Board and IRS figures or between Franchise Tax Board and Commerce Department figures are not reconciled, however. Nor is any attempt made to establish the number of Californians from whom a tax return is due. The annual report also provides a calendar year summary of the number of cases examined, the number with no change, the number with changes, the amount of money involved, and the return per dollar.

California's operations report (annual on a fiscal year basis) is in effect a productivity report that identifies the major activities involved in administering the personal income and corporation franchise taxes, the man-hours and cost of these activities, and the revenue produced. In other words, handling returns showing self-assessments, auditing, filing enforcement, and collection activities are among the major work load items identified. The report lists the enforcement costs by major and minor activity and the resulting tax revenue. The report provides aggregate accounting and revenue information as well as data on the current and historical productivity of the department's enforcement activities. As in the annual report, no attempt is made to estimate the full dimensions of the compliance problem in income tax administration in California or the gap between activities carried out and those that might be carried out with a larger budget, or to estimate the probable increase in revenue that could result.

The California data provide perhaps the best state base available for analyzing compliance. The reports emphasize for the tax department, the governor, legislators, and the public critical characteristics of the returns filed by taxpayers and the activities undertaken by the department to further enforcement. The Franchise Tax Board planning operation is still at the beginning of developing the data needed to describe the state's aggregate and sector economy and thus to assist in measuring the gap between income presently reported and income actually received by the state's taxpayers.

Administrators generally have not used income tax data to good advantage for administrative purposes. For management purposes and for most needs of the policy-maker or economist, income tax statistics must be related to the actual characteristics of the economy. Neither a legislator nor a citizen gains much from knowing that the department received X returns or collected Y income taxes from this county or municipality compared to others in the state unless he also knows comparative populations, income ranges, etc. Sector tax analysis is equally meaningless without other empirical knowledge of the sector. If, for example, the research division finds that the 23,000 income tax returns filed by the state's farmers reported income of $230 million, a reader might cheerfully say, "Oh, farmers are averaging about $10,000—pretty good!" But if the research division further reports that the state's Department of Agriculture counted 47,000 farms in its census and estimates that the income of farmers last year was $550 million, both the tax department and its readers had better start asking what accounts for the differences. Only with similar data on each economic sector will the public and the department recognize gaps in enforcement and failures to distribute income tax burdens equitably.

Careful analytical designs for collecting and publishing statistics should also permit significant historical comparisons over a period of years and avoid the bane of interested readers who find a fascinating data series dropped after a year or two. Possibly worse are the reports that continue to cite useless statistics year after year because "that's the way they have always been collected and published." More care in determining the desired uses of data will aid in providing quality and continuity. When changes become necessary, the author or authors of the report owe readers an explanation and, if possible, a means to adjustment. As more and more states have at least one university developing a state economic model, tax research division staff can sit on the sidelines or become active partners. As partners, tax research personnel can contribute data and gain information of value for management and policy needs.

Planning

Planning or management analysis exists as a separately organized function within a state tax department only in California, New York, and Wisconsin, though a few other departments carry on the function in the division budget office or in research and analysis. Several other states during the seventies have called in outside management teams under special contracts or have been supplied them as a public service by some of the state's leading businesses (e.g., Minnesota, North Carolina, and Oregon).

The New York Bureau of Planning, working with others within the tax department, has recently assisted in developing and enlarging computer programs and operations to include many more activities of the department, carrying out with outside consultants a taxpayer compliance measurement program that would aid in audit selection, and evaluating programs in whole or in part in varied sections of the department. In New York and in California, where the equivalent bureau also has been very active, such responsibilities can be carried out only with the cooperation and support of many other units or divisions of the department. The success of an internal management planning operation depends on knowledge of individuals and the intimate details of the administrative operation. If the division personnel can also back off and take an objective view and occasionally bring in outsiders, their recommendations are likely to be more appropriate and acceptable than those of the outside "whiz kids," who often lack sensitivity to a tax department's environment.

Conclusion

Unfortunately, despite changes in most revenue departments and the tremendous increase in computer use, a conclusion reached twenty years ago remains essentially correct:

> In surveying the use of staff and management aids in state income tax administration, the authors have been struck by two central facts. In the majority of states, legislators and administrators have yet to be convinced of the contribution that research, statistical, budgeting, and planning activities at the agency level can make to (a) more efficient and equitable allocation of administrative resources

and (b) more informed state tax policy. Inadequate recognition of these functions both in administrative structures and in legislative appropriations has been the rule rather than the exception. . . .

Probably half of the income tax states still do not provide the incentives of salary and promotional opportunities, continuity of tenure, and other conditions needed to staff agencies with suitable personnel for the highly complicated and subtle functions of income tax administration. . . . Much remains to be done to keep pace with—and, in many instances, merely to catch up with—the alternative attractions of private employment in an expanding economy.[35]

Governors and legislatures must bear a major share of the responsibility for the performance of their tax agencies through the leadership, standards, and resources they provide.

[35]Penniman and Heller, *State Income Tax Administration,* pp. 82, 111, 112.

Chapter Five

Processing and Compliance

Income is not a ready-made tax base. Its conversion into a source of tax revenue under the American system of self-assessment depends on the development and use of techniques (1) to bring income and its recipients to light and (2) to verify reported incomes, deductions, and exemptions. The hard core of income tax administration thus consists of income and taxpayer coverage work ("compliance activities") on the one hand and office and field auditing on the other. Before compliance and auditing can occur, "processing" must take place. This chapter will examine processing and several compliance elements. Chapter 6 will review two additional compliance activities: withholding and collection.[1] Chapters 7 and 8 then will consider auditing or verification.

Processing

At the height of the filing season, the somewhat prosaic processing activities of income tax administration take up the time of hundreds of individuals in the largest tax departments. This "paper jungle," stemming from the "paper avalanche" that comes with each day's assortment of mail bags, extends over a two or three month period.[2] Any taxpayer who ever visited a tax agency mail room at such a period would understand if his return could not be located. California officials insist they can locate any

[1]The term "compliance" is used somewhat more broadly here than by some tax specialists. New York, for example, has a compliance bureau that essentially spends its time collecting unpaid tax assessements—whether the taxpayer files but does not pay, or there is an additional assessment for failure to file, or whatever the basis. Here "compliance" includes collection of assessments plus all efforts to secure preassessment collection and relevant information to determine assessments.

[2]These terms come from one of the most graphic descriptions of processing and computer handling of income tax returns this author has read: William R. Surface, *Inside Internal Revenue* (New York: Coward, McCann, 1967), chap. 3, "Into the Paper Jungle." A shorter but good description can be found in *U.S. News and World Report,* April 12, 1976, pp. 81, 83, and 84.

return filed early in the season within fifteen days of receipt. At the peak of the filing season, these officials claim the ability to locate a return within thirty days of receipt. No other state has claimed a better performance.

Processing means emptying all those mail sacks; machine-slitting each of the hundreds, thousands, and eventually millions of envelopes; retrieving from the slit envelopes the returns, letters, checks, money orders, even cash; candling the envelopes to be sure nothing remains; numbering the return and check (not all departments do this) or attaching checks to returns; preparing and verifying deposit statements (possibly sorting checks for deposit statements by banks); ascertaining that deposit statements and return payments balance; making deposits; checking returns for obvious errors (absence of signature, etc.) and returning these to taxpayers with a form letter; editing returns for computer entry; entering via computer the appropriate data for verification, audit, and research, as well as refund claim or deficiency plus batch and file number; clearing refund claims and writing checks.

Only after the above steps have been completed can many of the compliance and audit activities begin. Processing serves three key purposes: (1) to account properly for the moneys received; (2) to get the money into interest-bearing deposits or make refunds with the least possible delay; and (3) to provide the framework for compliance and audit activities.

SPECIAL PROCESSING

In addition to processing individual returns, tax officials must assure timely processing of corporation returns (which may or may not follow a calendar year); quarterly declarations and payments by individuals and corporations; and semimonthly, monthly, or whatever employer withholding tax returns. The volume of such returns is smaller, but each enclosed check is likely to be larger than that in the annual individual returns. To achieve minimal delay in depositing these large funds, states have adopted several techniques. Some states—e.g., New York and Wisconsin—use a "lockbox" system whereby corporation tax payments (including withholding) go to a specified post office box in several cities of the state. An approved depository bank removes the contents of the postal box one or more times each day and minimally processes the contents to assure that the funds therein are deposited daily and the revenue department has a record of each individual item. Records, returns, and papers are immediately forwarded by mail or by messenger to the revenue department.

The director of revenue of the state of Washington has provided a good summary of the "lockbox" procedure for its sales taxes, etc. The procedure for income and withholding taxes paid by businesses would be essentially the same.

> Implementation of the lock-box concept means that returns and remittance of tax are mailed by the taxpayer—in effect—*directly to the bank.* This can be done by

means of a special post office box—in a large metropolitan city—preferably with a Federal Reserve Board clearinghouse. The self-addressed envelope included with blank returns mailed to all taxpayers (registered business firms) carries the post office box address. The bank handles initial processing and deposits the checks immediately. . . . In processing the returns the bank is to: examine each check for negotiability and match the amount remitted with that shown on the tax return, sort by nature of tax return and period covered, batch returns in groups of 100 documents or less, serially number each check for subsequent tie-in with the return (if necessary), microfilm all checks, process check immediately, crediting the state account (at the bank), transmit batched returns to the department of revenue by courier car—at least once daily—with each batch of returns accompanied by a summary slip and adding machine tape, and separately transmit any unprocessable items (returns received without remittance, checks mailed with no return information, etc.). The bank is also to examine opened envelopes for any unremoved contents before destroying, date stamp any returns received five days or more after a delinquent date, and immediately re-deposit (once) any checks, returned marked "not sufficient funds."[3]

Most such bank contracts do not require payment by the state. The bank makes its money through an agreed adjustment in interest rates on all these sizable deposits, and the state still gains through the faster deposit system and earlier-interest-bearing accounts.[4]

Some of the states that do not use the "lockbox" concept have developed internal arrangements for fast deposit. Massachusetts has invented its own machine to assist in the process.[5] California uses special zip codes to secure and process returns with large checks. It supplements these with special post office pick-ups and a bonded messenger service to deliver the processed checks and funds to the banks to assure fast deposit. Colored envelopes are another means to a more rapid sorting of mail that is likely to contain large checks. Whatever works fastest and costs the least should be the chosen instrument. Unfortunately, some states have retained archaic statutes, regulations, or processes and consequently lose substantial interest each year. Ohio, for example, requires that corporation return checks go from the revenue department to the state treasurer for accounting before deposit. Such a delay is costly and serves virtually no purpose.

In addition to special bank arrangements, some states have found it possible to work out advantageous arrangements with local post offices.

[3] Mary Ellen McCaffree, "A New Cash Management Tool: The Lock Box," in *Revenue Administration, Proceedings of the Forty-fourth Annual Meeting of the National Association of Tax Administrators* (Chicago: Federation of Tax Administrators, 1976).

[4] A good discussion of the lockbox is contained in U.S. Advisory Commission on Intergovernmental Relations *Understanding State and Local Cash Management* (Washington, D.C.: Government Printing Office, May, 1977), chap. 3.

[5] For a discription of the Massachusetts system, see Owen L. Clarke, "Use of a Cash Flow Machine," in *Revenue Administration, Proceedings of the Forty-fourth Annual Meeting of the National Association of Tax Administrators* (Chicago: Federation of Tax Administrators, 1976).

Clearly some post office officials are more cooperative than others. Ohio's Personal Income Tax Division has seven different post office boxes and zip codes. This permits the division to code envelopes for varied types of returns, and the post office makes the seven-way sort. The tax office can then more easily make finer sorts. California also has found the post office cooperative in assigning separate postal boxes and zip codes that aid the Franchise Tax Department in its sorting procedures.

COMPUTERS

Before the 1960s, most states implemented filing season tasks by means of a combination of hand operations, bookkeeping machines, adding machines, and typewriters. A few states had some further specialized equipment as well as tabulating and key punch machinery. Only with the advances in computer technology of the last decade or so have more and more of the processing, collection, and audit functions been computerized.[6] Nebraska reports one of the most highly computerized systems in the nation. After machinery has opened the envelopes, clerks extract the contents and send the envelopes through a candling machine to ensure that all enclosures have been removed. Tax documents are sorted by type and batched into groups and an identifying control card, reflecting control and transaction information, is attached. Reconciliation is made of remittances, and an adding machine tape, showing the amount of money involved, is attached. At the next stage of validation, data are taken off, edited, and checked to balance records and deposit slips. Data on documents and remittances are printed to provide lists and journal tapes for future reference. Remittances are then removed and prepared for deposit. ("Money is deposited in less than 24 hours with this system, except for the several days following the April 15th filing deadline." This is the intent of most states, but it is not always achieved.) Each document is examined by an editor for data processing and listed errors are encoded to enable the computer to generate an appropriate letter to the taxpayer. Some identified errors require further review and taxpayer communication during the clearance function. Data entry now proceeds and is merged with information previously entered in the validation process. Errors identified by the computer editing and balancing programs receive attention at this stage. Routine taxpayer inquiries are handled through a computerized correspondence control and calendaring system. Nebraska's Department of Revenue microfilms all returns, and it is the microfilmed return, brought on the screen or printed, that is normally used for further referral.[7]

[6]The IRS changed to a more or less fully computerized system in 1961. Its larger volume of work made the changeover both more feasible and more necessary. As the cost of computers has come down, their feasibility for smaller work loads has increased considerably.

[7]See Nebraska, Department of Revenue, *Nebraska Tax Administration* (Lincoln, June, 1976).

Many state tax computer installations carry out most of the above processing functions and follow up the processing activities with such compliance tasks as (1) taking off data for research and statistical purposes; (2) arithmetically verifying each return; (3) making some inquiries as to previous returns or other indebtedness of the taxpayer; (4) issuing refund checks; (5) selecting returns for questioning or audit; and (6) developing master lists for subsequent cross-checking with the state's previous master list plus the IRS's Individual Master File list; and (7) printing labels for mailing out next year's returns.[8] Computer programs may also (8) identify taxpayers who failed to file last year and then (9) generate inquiry letters. Computers can also (10) handle taxpayer account billing and (11) follow-up. Many states today have on-line computer retrieval capabilities through video terminals in the central office and in the field that (12) permit direct access to any account via social security or employer number, (13) provide the tax official with information as to whether there are any unpaid taxes, and (14) list basic return information. Much of the management and research data utilized are gathered during the computer programming and entry stages of processing returns.[9]

Each of the processing tasks represents a significant part of the compliance setting: identification of the taxpayer; recognition of his filing and payment—or, in the case of his failure to file or pay, follow-up; initial review of his return and correspondence for arithmetic or other routine errors; recording and filing of the return for further reference; and development of next year's return mailing list. Each taxpayer, through the canceled check or agency correspondence, has early assurance that his return was received, his account credited, and general errors noted.

The Nature of the Compliance Problem

Compliance requires the taxpayer to file and to pay his self-assessment plus any further audit assessment. Tax administrators have to overcome not merely dishonesty but negligence, laxity, carelessness, inaccuracy, ignorance, and the like. Even when the taxpayer is honest, conscientious, and intelligent, the assessment process may involve close questions of fact, judgment, and law.

[8]National Association of Tax Administrators, Committee on Administrative Enforcement and Compliance, *The Use of the Computer in Administration: Enforcement and Compliance of State Tax Laws* (Chicago: Federation of Tax Administrators, July, 1975).

[9]Stanley S. Surrey provided an excellent and most complete description of the potential uses of computers in "Automatic Data Processing and Tax Administration: The Potentialities of ADP and Factors Involved in Its Adoption," in *Joint Tax Program: Problems of Tax Administration in Latin America* (1965), pp. 178-200, 200-208, reprinted in Patrick L. Kelley and Oliver Oldman, *Readings on Income Tax Administration* (Mineola, N.Y.: The Foundation Press, 1973). Despite the date when it was written, Surrey's "chapter" should be required reading for tax administrators.

TAXPAYERS' ATTITUDES

During the student disturbances at the University of Wisconsin, Madison, in 1969 the author noticed three particularly long-haired, bearded, and roughly dressed young men engaged in earnest conversation. To her amusement she heard, "But you have to include that in your income tax return under . . ." IRS and state tax officials would have rejoiced. Whatever political ideas they might have had, cheating on their income taxes was not one of them. New York tax officials find that compliance is generally better upstate than downstate. In communities such as the Ithaca-Watertown area, where the early English-German ethic is still dominant, the tax collector is respected as a government man. In contrast, New York City exhibits uniquely difficult tax compliance problems for the state and for the IRS.

Securing or keeping good taxpayer attitudes requires that the tax department prod all taxpayers into attention. The failure of state income taxation prior to this century demonstrated that the unchecked taxpayer is no taxpayer at all. More recently, the states have discovered that the implementation of withholding nets substantial numbers of previously unaware or casual taxpayers. Not that the typical taxpayer is a skilled and scheming evader. On the contrary, tax administrators assert, perhaps even marvel, at the general honesty of taxpayers. But feeble administration converts honesty into dishonesty. Unless the income recipient feels (1) that others in a like position are made to discharge their tax liabilities and (2) that the tax-administering agency is making some effort to protect the state's interests by independently checking his income, he will consider it no great misdeed to underreport his income and adopt a "come and get me" attitude.

In fact, even in a setting of fairly good administration, some taxpayers feel the state is not entitled to their money unless it can discover the income and seek them out to collect the tax. Others, because of laziness or lack of discipline, ignore filing requirements and are willing to pay a penalty for their negligence. (Since withholding tends to overcollect from wage earners, the penalty here may be forgoing a refund due.) In another category are small businessmen whose books do not accurately reflect taxable income and who adopt the attitude that they will pay the tax if the state takes the time and trouble to ascertain the correct income. The dishonesty of these tax delinquents is merely passive, yet it presents a problem of the first magnitude to the income tax administrator, for without the application of techniques that will establish the receipt of income and verify the accuracy of reporting, the tax revenue is as surely lost to the state as it would be were deliberate criminal evasion in question.

Tax administrators must also reckon with the tendency of most taxpayers, especially those represented by accountants or attorneys, to resolve all doubts in their own favor. Dishonesty is not involved, but many doubts are resolved incorrectly, and tax revenues suffer unless the taxpayers' decisions are challenged by the state income tax agency. Ignorance of income tax responsibilities or confusion over income tax law, especially when the law is new, or important changes have been made, or when a taxpayer is new in the state, sets up a barrier to taxpayer compliance. Unintentional errors also arise from confusion over state and federal income tax laws.

Close questions abound in income taxation. By assuming that the taxpayer is always right, the administrator can, of course, create an illusion of full compliance. Some state officials pride themselves on a paucity of income tax disputes and litigation. This paucity may indicate lenience in enforcement of the law or lack of thoroughness in auditing. If taxpayer decisions on close questions are not carefully examined, frequently questioned, and occasionally litigated, the state abdicates its revenue rights and promotes inequities.

MEETING THE PROBLEM

In the face of the incentives and opportunities for noncompliance, misreporting, and erroneous taxpayer interpretations, full use of available compliance devices becomes a vital necessity. The essence of successful compliance work is a comprehensive survey of the many and varied sources of information that will disclose probable taxpayers or serve as an independent check on reported incomes.

The administrator can call on these rich sources of information to aid him (1) in attaining broader coverage of income and its recipients and (2) in auditing the returns, books, and accounts of taxpayers. Some of these sources, by disclosing persons who are probably taxable or actually delinquent, chiefly build up the volume of taxpayer returns. Others yield data on specific types of income and thus build up the volume of reported income.

Some sources will be found unproductive; others will be considered worth utilizing mainly because of the psychological effect of having an inclusive dragnet for the disclosure of income; the majority will pay in tax revenues many times the cost of using them. Beyond such coverage work, which is largely a matter of diligence and ingenuity, lies auditing—a highly technical function that depends on ability and experience in accounting and law and on thorough familiarity with income characteristics and with the means of independently verifying reported incomes.

The following section will examine the taxpayer as the primary information source. The next section will survey information-at-source returns and their use. A final section will deal with a mass of additional sources—many less widely used, but all valuable in guaranteeing proper filing and reporting—to complete the catalog of informational tools at the administrator's command. Withholding programs (see chapter 6) serve both as information sources and as a means of current collection.

The Taxpayer as the Primary Source of Information

The American system of income taxation makes the taxpayer a basic source of information. The tax he pays is based first and foremost on the information he declares on his tax return regarding his income, deductions, and personal status. Even though most taxpayers today have paid a substantial portion of their tax through payroll withholding or quarterly declarations by the time they file their annual returns, it is the information declared on the annual return that initially determines whether they owe any additional taxes or are entitled to a refund on taxes already paid.

A self-assessed tax system based on a concealable subject (at least relative to real property, sales purchased, etc.) like income peculiarly depends on taxpayer education and cooperation for its success. Efforts that make the taxpayer a better source of information pay off in decreased reliance on independent and more expensive information sources. The chief media for making the taxpayer a good source of information are publicity, skillful drafting and careful distribution of returns, broad filing requirements, and official aid in filling out returns.

PUBLICITY

To convert an income recipient into a taxpayer, it is first of all necessary to inform him of his obligations and to jog his memory and conscience. This is achieved through widespread publicity. January withholding statements may encourage many to file, especially if they believe they have a refund coming; but an amazing number of taxpayers manage to forget for days or weeks or months or, if court testimony can be trusted, even years. Whenever a taxpayer believes his return for a particular year has new problems, he may simply delay attempting to fill out the return. Whatever the cause of postponing, the tax agency needs cooperation from the news media to nudge the taxpayer to do his duty.

Few citizens can ignore entirely the news stories on radio or television or in the press during each filing season that call attention to the requirement to file, advertise filing aid by governmental agencies and by private individuals and groups, or discuss particular issues relative to income reporting or deductions that may reduce net taxable income. The IRS puts on a national publicity campaign that provides the news media with official information for their use. Whether strictly news, interpretive discussions, or free publicity as part of a public service contribution, probably no newspaper or radio or television station in the country fails to mention income taxes several times between January 1 and April 15. The state tax agency that provides interviews or well-done information handouts to the representatives of the news media can reinforce both the IRS's efforts and the natural inclinations of reporters in these months.

In addition to encouraging taxpayers to file by emphasizing earlier refunds, better service in the office with earlier filing, or simply obligation, tax officials like to call attention to the penalties for not filing or filing incorrect or fraudulent returns. Whether or not the stories of taxpayer convictions actually increase during the filing season, as some believe, every tax official hopes for front-page publicity when a case is won. Criminal convictions for tax evasion or fraud represent success to the agency. (Tax people, like other people, enjoy the publicity that accompanies their successes but fear public notice of their failures.) The *Milwaukee Journal,* in the largest metropolitan area of Wisconsin, considers convictions of well-known individuals or of persons from the south-central and southeastern parts of the state eminently newsworthy. State officials complain, however, that the newspaper often ignores court convictions of less well known individuals in other parts of the state. The state, of course, prefers publicity for all convictions.

Whether a tax department has a public relations section or not, someone must answer reporter's questions, provide information on request, and be prepared to handle favorable and unfavorable news stories. Adequate interpretation of departmental actions and of departmental statistical information also requires attention by one or more individuals within the agency. The larger states typically have more resources and give more attention to the media than do the smaller ones. The public relations section of New York's tax department handles most interviews and press releases, and during the filing season provides not only releases and spot messages for the news media but also a video tape in which a tax official fills out a tax return while giving detailed explanations. The New York publicity director I spoke with stated that the department receives excellent coverage of its activities. California, in the 1978 filing season, sent seven general news releases and several additional special releases to 160 daily newspapers, 646 weekly newspapers, and 345 radio stations.

Several states carried on substantial publicity campaigns following adoption of property tax circuit-breaker legislation. Often officials found that elderly and low-income taxpayers either were not reached by the usual publicity or for some other reason hesitated to file a return, declare income and property taxes, and claim a refund. Quite possibly Oregon, with a $40,000 publicity budget, achieved the greatest success with the smallest expenditure. The author's interviews and reading confirm the following comment:

> The most comprehensive outreach program is Oregon's, launched in 1973 and continued in 1974 under a special legislative mandate that provided $40,000 for the taxpayer effort. Designed with the assistance of a local public relations firm, the program has had a powerful impact on participation, boosting levels from less than 50% of estimated target population to 87% in less than 24 months. (It was selected in 1974 by the International Association of Assessing Officials as the best tax-

related information program in the country.) The program focussed on homeowners and renters (including mobile homes) and featured posters, mailers, toll-free telephone lines for questions, a short information film for television and speakers' bureau use, bilingual (Spanish and English) television spot announcements and a series of press releases for local and state papers. To eliminate any fears that the program was connected to welfare, its title was changed from "Property Tax Relief" to "Property Tax Refund" program.[10]

TAX RETURN

Make-up of Return Forms

The make-up of return forms[11] depends first on statutory provisions. *Simple forms and complex statutes do not go together.* Within the law, carefully drawn return forms can do much to elicit the maximum amount of information from taxpayers. Skillful drafting of questions, items, schedules, and instructions can simplify and improve compliance and facilitate administrative processing of returns. Putting as many items as possible in question form will press on the taxpayer's memory and conscience. Administrators report that although many taxpayers may find it easy not to tell the *whole* truth when the return does not demand it, few are willing to put a clear falsehood in writing in answer to a specific question. The effectiveness of office auditing depends in no small part on the fullness of information elicited by the tax return.

To elicit information as painlessly and as adequately as possible calls for simplicity in the layout of the return and in the formulation of its items and questions, plus easy continuity in the sequence of items presented to the taxpayer. Skillful drafting can lead the taxpayer by the hand from one item to the next and maximize the chance of his arriving at the correct tax liability. But mechanical simplicity of this kind, however desirable, should not be confused with understandability. The taxpayer may emerge from a simple and accurate process with little comprehension of the law and its purpose. Comprehension is partly a matter of the clarity and phrasing of items on the return and in the instructions.

Not only does formulating a simple but full return present drafting problems, but many taxpayers either genuinely have reading and comprehension problems or prefer to replace their judgment with that of professional taxpayer representatives who advertise the difficulties for taxpayers

[10] U.S., Department of Housing and Urban Development, Office of Policy Development and Research, *Property Tax Relief Programs for the Elderly: A Compendium Report,* prepared by Abt Associates, Inc., Cambridge, Mass., April, 1975, p. 64.

[11] The problem of unusually complex individual income tax reports or of corporation income tax returns is not under discussion here. In both of these cases the taxpayer presumably has access to expert technical advice, and the reporting problem is primarily one of easing the job of the taxpayer's representative in translating taxpayer accounts into a format that will provide the tax agency with the accurate information needed to verify the net taxable income.

in filling out their own returns.[12] There is at least a touch of irony in H & R Block, Inc.'s hiring the Harris Poll to conduct a taxpayer poll in 1977 which tells us that 60% of taxpayers report they find the federal income tax returns difficult to understand.[13] If more taxpayers could be encouraged to go through the tax return carefully, call the tax agency when necessary for questions, and complete the return themselves, the present business of tax preparers would cease to expand almost every year.[14] And taxpayers would fulfill their civic duty with greater understanding.

To ease administration for both the taxpayer and the agency, most states have enacted standard deductions, provided tables for computing taxes, and developed simplified returns that meet the needs of taxpayers with primarily wage and salary incomes. Yet every increase in the number of statutory deductions reduces the appropriateness of these returns for a growing number of taxpayers. As more and more taxpayers have become homeowners, as law-makers have liberalized deductions, and as Sylvia Porter and other newspaper tax pundits have encouraged taxpayers to seek all possible deductions, the proportion of taxpayers using the short forms has steadily decreased.

Whether or not a state legislature encourages the development of its own short form return by statute, many legislatures have attempted simplicity by adopting more or less the IRS Code for defining income and establishing deductions (table 7). Whether this route produces the simplicity sought depends substantially on Congress and the IRS plus the number of modifications to the federal code the taxpayer's own state enacts. Whatever the policy values in the initial decision of the state to go along with the federal code, these may be vitiated and the short return may again become long if the legislature either does not accept all future congressional changes

[12] In the mid-seventies, Oregon hired two individuals to design all returns in terms of the reading and comprehension skills of the less-educated taxpayer. A study of returns and instructions revealed that some of the previous writing was comprehensible only by taxpayers with graduate degrees.

[13] According to a poll taken by Roper Organization, Inc., in May, 1977, for H & R Block, Inc., 60% of the respondents said they had a "not too good" or "very little" understanding of how to fill out the federal tax return. Reported in the *Milwaukee Journal,* July 26, 1977, p. 1.

[14] The author was told by an individual who moonlighted for one of the national tax preparer organizations of an incident where a taxpayer came in with a fully completed return and asked him to make out his federal income tax return. After glancing at the return and asking a couple of questions, the preparer told the taxpayer that if he walked out the door then and mailed the return in his hand, there would be no charge. If the taxpayer wished him to recopy the return, it would cost $15.00. Reluctantly, the taxpayer accepted the implied advice and walked out the door to mail his return. How can taxpayers be reassured of their own capacity to complete returns, and further reassured that neither the IRS nor the state tax agency is going to "jail" any taxpayer for an honest return that may have an error? If the taxpayer seeks assistance because of difficulty with the federal return (the more probable issue), there is little a state can do in terms of simplification that will affect the taxpayer's getting aid for both federal and state returns.

or responds to local special taxpayer lobbying. When Michigan first adopted an individual income tax, it also accepted federal income and deduction definitions. The law permitted a simple, quarter-page return. In the intervening years, the Michigan legislature has responded so often to its own constituents' demands for this change or that that the return has lengthened annually.

Filing Requirements

Given the return forms, what do states do to build up their "tax clientele"? Much depends on the statutory filing requirements and on administrative policy in applying them. Filing requirements (table 10) identify taxpayers with a legal obligation to file. States, unlike the national government, may list filing requirements in terms of net income for both income and personal exemptions. If filing requirements are stated in terms of gross income but personal exemptions are cited in terms of net income, more taxpayers will recognize the responsibility to file. Delaware, Maryland, Minnesota, and New Mexico are among the states that have fixed gross income filing requirements identical to the personal exemption stated in net income. The model state income tax statute requires a return from every taxpayer who is required to file a federal income tax return and from all whose income exceeds adjusted gross income in the amount of present federal personal exemptions.[15] Years ago Minnesota's income tax director emphasized that when Minnesota's filing requirements were lowered to gross income figures identical with the state's personal income exemptions, "the picture changed overnight." Approximately 150,000 more individuals filed returns in the first year the new rule was applied.

Making Returns Available

The fact of human inertia makes it highly desirable to put returns directly into the hands of prospective taxpayers by means of the mail. Several states fail to use this simple means of reminding residents of their obligation to file. Michigan has taken the attitude that not mailing returns to individual taxpayers saves the state some $200,000 annually.[16] One of the difficulties with mailing out returns is the mobility of taxpayers—some 25% in Michigan move each year and returns cannot all be delivered. A number

[15]Changes in the federal income tax could make such a provision inappropriate.

[16]Michigan has attempted to make a virtue of an earlier necessity. Its tax agency's budget was so low a few years ago that it utilized the immediate savings in postage and handling by not mailing individual returns. The *Wall Street Journal* carried an item in a July, 1977, issue that Michigan claimed a savings of $200,000 by its procedure of providing only tax preparers and certain public officials, etc., with returns. No statement followed as to whether the practice had reduced the number of returns received. Some officials in Lansing in 1975 stated that more returns tended to cost the state money in refunds/rebates as a result of overwithholding, property tax credits, etc., so why encourage taxpayers to file? See the discussion of withholding and refunds in chapter 6.

of other states over the years have regularly or occasionally failed to mail out returns to taxpayers. Before the adoption of withholding, the usual result for states that sent out returns after a lapse of several years was a large increase in the number of tax returns filed. But withholding does not eliminate the need to encourage filing. Not everyone is subject to withholding. Even among those who have taxes withheld, the taxpayer may still owe taxes at the end of the year or he may be entitled to a refund. Seldom is the balance of taxes withheld and taxes due zero. Without a return, the tax department cannot know the appropriate tax status of a taxpayer in any given year or collect an additional tax or make a refund. Mailing out returns provides the taxpayer a reminder and the convenience of receiving a form; it provides the department a computer check of returns received and allows the department to place emphasis on locating new taxpayers. (Where agencies prepare labeled envelopes in zip code order, the post office approves a lower bulk mail rate.)

Whether or not returns are mailed individually, departments normally make bulk mailings of forms to public and private offices where taxpayers are most likely to be reminded or to inquire. The usual list of such distributing points includes city halls, county courthouses, banks, and offices of attorneys, accountants, and other tax preparers.

AID TO TAXPAYERS

Individual Assistance

Most states and the IRS have found it profitable, in terms of improved reporting and better taxpayer relations, to furnish extensive services during the filing period.[17] Sometimes the IRS and the state tax department arrange to have their respective representatives in the same or adjoining offices to permit taxpayers to consult both federal and state agencies at the same time.

[17]The IRS has always attempted to aid taxpayers, though the amount and quality of aid have varied. One estimate placed the official cost of taxpayer assistance at 3.5% of the IRS budget in 1973 and 6.4% of the budget in 1975. These figures appear to understate the cost by several percentage points if preparation of returns and their printing and distribution are included. In 1974, 72% of taxpayer assistance contacts were made by telephone, but more than a fourth of the taxpayers seeking aid walked into district offices, satellite offices, or tax mobiles. The IRS also provides varied outreach programs: voluntary income tax assistance for low-income and elderly taxpayers; special education programs for tax practitioners; booklets and other materials for high-school students; special efforts for new businesses; and, of course, speeches before civic groups. IRS officials report that taxpayers often appear to view taxpayer assistance as the most valuable service the agency performs. What the IRS does in taxpayer assistance is often of interest to state officials, and the educational part of the assistance frequently aids in making individuals more aware of the state income tax and their responsibility for it. See U.S., Department of the Treasury, Comptroller General, *Internal Revenue Service Assistance to Taxpayers in Filing Federal Income Tax Returns: Report to the Joint Committee on Internal Revenue Taxation, Congress of the United States, GGD-76-49* (Washington, D.C.: General Accounting Office, April 1, 1976).

The geographic and population distribution of taxpayer assistance usually depends on the state's own characteristics and whether the tax department has field offices. States with few or no fixed field offices may send income tax representatives out on a preadvertised circuit to aid all taxpayers who seek assistance on designated days. Oregon combines the use of its regular field staff and field offices with circuit riders to give every practical assistance to any taxpayer wishing it. California, Massachusetts, New York, and Wisconsin make their geographically distributed field offices serve as focal points of assistance to taxpayers but also provide itinerant service. Pennsylvania, Indiana, Ohio, and North Carolina are among the states that send out an "army" of tax representatives to aid taxpayers during the filing season.

The cost of assistance has continually increased, and both the IRS and many of the states have sought ways to increase effectiveness and hold down costs. The easier and simpler the return, the less the presumed need for assistance, but we have already recognized limits to return simplification. Costs of travel, higher salaries of staff members in the field, and reduction in telephone costs have led some states to replace or supplement field service with telephone assistance for taxpayers during the filing season. California, Minnesota, and a number of other states have adopted a modified version of the IRS's system of providing a toll-free number (some states provide telephone service without a toll-free number or with one in only certain areas) that citizens anywhere in the state may call to ask any income tax question. Usually, one or more sophisticated auditors are available to a group of telephone answerers who are trained to handle the most common requests and questions ("Please send me a return," "Must I file?" "Did my last year's return show __? etc.) and to know when a question should be referred to an auditor. Most states that have utilized the telephone system for a year or more have found that it reduces the manpower needs for taxpayer assistance at the counter—whether in the central office, regional office, or field office—reduces costs, and increases the uniformity of answers provided taxpayers. Taxpayers may still come to the offices of the agency, but many find the telephone service sufficient. A reduction in demands on the time of auditors or other professionals which does not decrease taxpayer services pleases tax officials who have tried the toll-free system.

Special Group Aid

Apart from policies of assistance to individual taxpayers, tax departments view some groups as natural centers for taxpayer education, either because the members are taxpayers with similar problems or because they deal with the general public on tax matters. Changes in statutes and the complexities of the tax in farm matters, for example, make farm organizations or tax advisers to farmers ideal groups for income tax administrators to cultivate.

Minnesota in 1943 set up annual farm tax institutes to present information to farmer tax advisers on tax problems recognized by the tax agency or tax preparers. The institutes, now called "The Farm and Individual Short Course," have been officially sponsored by the University of Minnesota with the cooperation of the state's Department of Revenue and the IRS. Illinois has also been active in providing extensive taxpayer assistance:

> Officers of the Department participated in 52 Farm Income Tax and Urban Tax seminars throughout the state. Nearly 4,500 tax practitioners and other individuals attended these programs. Seminars and classes also were provided to various groups on Department-administered programs like Circuit Breaker, the state's tax relief program.[18]

Many other university agricultural extension centers throughout the country cooperate with state and national tax agencies to provide tax institutes for county extension agents, farmers, and interested taxpayer representatives. With the spread of property tax credits or rebates for the elderly, several states have worked with organizations of the elderly to provide appropriate information for dissemination. California has enlisted representatives of the elderly to contribute time to counsel other elderly taxpayers seeking to file credit/rebate returns.[19] Massachusetts has helped train volunteers from colleges of business to go to nursing homes and assist patients in filing their returns.

Most state administrators accept and often seek opportunities to address organizations where dissemination of tax information may be fruitful. Oregon's tax commissioners hold annual meetings with the state's cattlemen. Wisconsin's income tax director addresses the tax clinic of the state's Society of Certified Public Accountants following each legislative session. Other state directors have held tax schools to which accountants and bookkeepers are invited.

Commercial Tax Preparers

Independent tax preparers or tax preparers working for H & R Block, Inc., or any one of a dozen other national or state tax groups represent a special challenge to tax agencies. Most officials view tax preparers as assistants, not competitors, but as assistants who sometimes must be watched. Reliable tax preparers, whether independent or working for a company, can aid taxpayers with authoritative information often supplied by the tax department. California officials have made a particular effort to

[18] Illinois, Department of Revenue, *Report to Taxpayers, Fiscal 1976* (Springfield, 1976), p. 5.

[19] The IRS has developed "instructional technology" in the form of "a series of thumb indexed decision tables to be used by volunteer (nonpaid) tax assistors in preparing tax returns for low-income, elderly, and non-English-speaking taxpayers. It enables the volunteers to prepare a simple Form 1040A or 1040 and Schedule A without extensive classroom preparation." *Civil Service Journal* 17 (January-March, 1977): 11. A few states also have worked to develop a system of this type.

work with tax preparers—sometimes testing draft returns and instructions with selected individuals and in other ways seeking cooperation with them. When a consistent error turns up in early returns prepared by many or particular tax preparers, a state tax official picks up the telephone and goes over the error to secure correction in subsequent returns filed.

Experience unfortunately has provided most states with evidence that some tax preparers seek only to make a dollar without regard to the quality of information supplied to taxpayers.[20] Personnel hired by the organization are not always screened or trained to provide the needed advice. Or an individual with limited information hangs out a shingle and brings in unsuspecting taxpayers to advise. Almost every state has some evidence of tax preparers conniving with a few taxpayers to secure illegal refunds or to file incorrect returns reflecting no taxes or lower taxes than are actually due. Several states, as well as the IRS, have investigated, prosecuted, and secured criminal convictions of dishonest tax preparers along with dishonest taxpayers.[21]

Oregon in 1973 established the State Board of Tax Service Examiners to license all tax preparers or tax consultants and required that they meet basic education and training standards plus a continuing education requirement for all practicing tax preparers. California adopted registration legislation in 1975.[22] A number of other states have considered such statutes without yet enacting any.

Professional Tax Preparers

The usual differentiation between professional and commercial tax preparers would identify the professional as a lawyer or certified public

[20]See "Where to Go for Tax Help," *Consumer Reports,* March, 1976, pp. 130-37. This article reviews various services, including those offered by the IRS and private practitioners. In the 1978 filing season, a *Milwaukee Journal* reporter went to several preparers with return information and got the same number of different judgments on the amount of taxes due!

[21]U.S., Department of the Treasury, Comptroller General, *No Apparent Need to Regulate Commercial Preparers of Income Tax Returns* (Washington, D.C.: General Accounting Office, December 8, 1975). The accuracy of the title depends on one's view as to the number of cases of fraud and of incompetence that need to be identified before regulation appears necessary. The comptroller general did recommend that "IRS should be able to impose civil penalties on problem preparers. . . . IRS also needs information reports from the preparers to enable it to review any or all of a preparer's returns." The law should further "provide for injunctions against preparers who engage in specific categories of misconduct" (p. 21). Chapter 3 of the above study reports some of the IRS's investigations of questionable returns and the resulting prosecutions. Despite the comptroller general's view, Henry W. Bloch, president of H & R Block, Inc., was quoted in *Taxes,* March 3, 1975, as supporting federal legislation similar to California's licensing requirement: "It would get a lot of people out of the industry who don't belong."

[22]Comptroller General, *No Apparent Need to Regulate Commercial Preparers of Income Tax Returns,* chap. 4. One of the difficulties experienced by California and Oregon is that they have strict secrecy laws and the regulating body in each state lacks normal access to returns. It can, however, insist on registration and can investigate training, continuing education, and, of course, the propriety of advertising names and claims.

accountant—in other words, a member of a recognized profession who as part of that profession will assist client taxpayers with their returns. Presumably the professional begins with a greater knowledge of taxes and hence will give the taxpayer more accurate advice. The professional further holds a professional license that may be revoked if he engages in unprofessional conduct. The state already regulates the professional tax preparer through his profession, and it is not uncommon for certified public accountants to support regulation of their presumably less competent competitors.

Information Returns

The preceding discussion has reviewed a number of devices that can make the taxpayer and his return more productive of information. Most of them are designed to persuade rather than to force the taxpayer to comply. Persuasion should unquestionably predominate in all administration, but independent checking activities and coercion are necessary to apprehend recalcitrant and dishonest taxpayers and to assure the scrupulous citizen that his honesty does not make him the tax goat.

In chapter 2 we briefly considered information returns as a significant tool (table 10 and discussion). Withholding supplants some of the earlier need for information returns but does not eliminate their usefulness. The network of cross-check information theoretically made possible through withholding statements and information returns represents a razor-sharp instrument for laying bare the money transactions that produce the bulk of taxable income. Proof of these income payments, moreover, substantiates an important part of the deductions claimed in the business area and provides clues to the gross incomes of investment income recipients.

The basic systems of information at source differ little from state to state, but there is great diversity in the specific income coverage of the various informational requirements. Examination of information returns for 1976 income payments showed that states most commonly required reports of income payments where these exceeded a specified overall limit or a specific (usually lower) figure for designated income such as interest and dividends. A few states required reports only where the aggregate amount exceeded a specified figure. A few other states showed no aggregate requirements but listed types of payments that were to be reported if they exceeded indicated amounts. Requirements for aggregate income payments to be reported frequently coincided with personal exemptions (tables 6 and 10).[23]

[23] As noted in chapter 2, the Uniform Personal Income Tax Statute gives the tax commissioner authority to require such returns as he deems necessary where the amount of payment is $600 or more or in the case of interest/dividends of $10 or more.

Most states fail to cover valuable at-source information. Only California, Colorado, and Massachusetts require formal reporting of stock ownership where actual and record ownership differ. Only five states require regular at-source reports on capital gains and losses. Wisconsin alone requires all corporations doing business in the state to file a report of all transfers of capital stock made by Wisconsin residents. Oklahoma requires reporting of sales or exchanges of securities of $25,000 or more. Colorado, Minnesota, and Oregon specify that brokers shall report customers' purchases and sales of securities if they exceed stated sums. No state requires at-source reports on interest paid on unregistered bonds.

Measures to Obtain Information Returns

A majority of states automatically send appropriate withholding returns or information returns to all corporations on their tax rolls. A number of states do not specify sanctions to force taxpayer compliance, and even the states with statutory penalties rarely apply them. Noncompliance usually constitutes a misdemeanor punishable by fine or by disallowance of deductions on the payer's business tax return for the items that should have been reported.[24] States report that threats to carry out statutory sanctions usually bring recalcitrant payers to book. But the threats must be made and occasionally carried out to achieve reporting compliance.

Even without information returns filed by payers on many types of special income, auditors (or specially programmed computers) can fill out information returns from tax return deductions claimed for payments by individuals. New York preaudits its fiduciary files and sets up information returns on income distributed to beneficiaries. Fees received by executors and administrators of estates or by attorneys, as well as distributions to beneficiaries, can be recorded by tax officials from fiduciary or estate returns. Ignoring partnership returns as information returns for checking the partners' individual returns is a common error made in many states, but tax officials in states that do match partnership return information with the corresponding individual returns find that the activity pays.

Matching Programs

As discussed in the section of chapter 6 on withholding, the early enthusiasm for computer matching of information returns and tax returns has receded in the face of the ever-increasing volume of returns. The new faith focuses on the possibility of machine-matching employer withholding tapes with individual return withholding statements, but except for random checks in some states, it remains largely a matter of faith up to the present (see chapter 6). Other information returns do not pose the volume

[24]The Uniform Personal Income Tax Statute provides for a modest fine of $2.00 per information return up to a total of $2,000 if the failure to file is due to willful neglect (*Uniform Personal Income Tax Statute*, sec. 75 [b]).

problem of wage and salary withholding statements. Even here, however, full matching is seldom achieved and usually comes only when questions arise from the context of the tax return.

Limitations of Information Returns

Even if state compliance programs fully matched all present information-at-source (including withholding) returns, important segments of income would remain unchecked. First, business, professional, and farm incomes are not easily adaptable to at-source reporting. Second, an important submerged form of income is interest on obligations of state and local governments other than those of the taxing state. In practice, at-source reporting of the home state's interest payments is negligible. If state controllers or treasurers were required to fill out information returns on all such payments, and these returns were exchanged among the states, the gap could be filled. Third, the states, by choice, exclude from their at-source reporting system most small income payments such as interest on unregistered bonds and gains and losses on securities. Fourth, a state cannot exercise jurisdiction over many out-of-state payers of interest, rent, dividends, and frequently wages and salaries. Finally, a state may receive income information too late to bring in the taxpayer who has moved away. How significant state compliance activity (other than withholding and collection) is depends on one's view of the role of the IRS. A state which substantially conforms to the IRS Code and which utilizes the IRS's information exchange of tapes, transcripts, revenue agent reports, etc., may accept the compliance activities of the IRS as adequate for its own enforcement standard. Such states do not attempt to complement or reinforce IRS activities.

Secondary Information Sources

Income tax agencies can tap a wealth of supplementary information sources of which most taxpayers and many administrators are not aware.

GOVERNMENTAL SOURCES

Federal Income Tax Information

Chapter 9 discusses federal-state relations at length, but it can be noted here that every state can secure from the IRS a computer list (the so-called Individual Master File) of all taxpayers in the state which can be matched via social security numbers with the state agency's register of taxpayers to identify individuals filing a federal but not a state return. A number of states find an annual match eminently worthwhile, for the IRS tape includes a substantial number of items for computer match—e.g., adjusted gross income, interest, dividends, capital gains, etc. (see chapter 9). If a state identifies taxpayers filing a state return but not a federal one, it passes this information on to the IRS.

Several state officials have found the IRS's central computer installation a valuable resource for securing the addresses of taxpayers who have moved out of state when none of the common checks produce forwarding addresses. States that require taxpayers to notify the tax agency of any audit changes by the IRS (see table 11) reinforce agreements with the IRS whereby it supplies the state with copies of audit transcripts or the state, e.g., New York, takes appropriate information from the IRS's audit abstracts. In any event, knowledge of federal adjustments aids the states in their compliance efforts.

Information from State and Local Tax Sources

Other state taxes may provide information of great value to the income tax administrator and, of course, vice versa. Inheritance and estate tax returns provide valuable clues on the income of decedents, heirs, attorneys, and administrators. The property and appraised values listed in death tax returns provide (1) an indication of the property income that the decedent should have been reporting in the years prior to death; (2) an index of the income that the fiduciary should report during the period of administration; (3) a net worth figure for the income recipient, especially the propertied farmer who failed to keep records and report income adequately during his lifetime; and (4) bases for determination of capital gains and losses on the future disposition of inherited property. Examination of the distributive shares of the estate yields clues to increases that can be expected in the income of the decedent's heirs.

Property tax records can provide names of out-of-state owners who may receive rental and other income that is subject to the state's tax. And states, such as Wisconsin, that levy a filing fee or tax (the amount varying with the sale price) on the deed for each transfer or sale of property have a built-in check (Wisconsin auditors make up an information return) on such capital gains and on the credibility of earlier income tax returns of the seller as well as a base for the new owner.

Since all but a dozen states now employ both individual income and sales taxes, cross-checks of comparable items on the taxpayer's income and sales tax returns can prove profitable. (Audit investigations of discrepancies sometimes reveal both figures to be wrong.) Occupational and general licensing taxes provide another source of information that is useful in building up tax coverage.

Other State and Local Government Sources

Income tax officials have access to much state information that is required apart from the income tax. The states license and regulate many professions and businesses. The tendency of professional, semiprofessional, and trade groups to seek protective state regulation (reinforced by the state's desire at times to regulate for the general health and welfare of the community) provides tax departments with excellent source lists of numerous taxpayers. Every state has a list of licensed doctors, druggists, and dentists. Given today's omnipresent health insurance companies, cross-checks of insurance reports to the state, etc., with tax returns filed by medical professionals would identify any missing tax returns and provide clues as to medical incomes. Either the state government or the American Bar Association will compile a list of most practicing attorneys. The state usually has lists of registered nurses, chiropractors, osteopaths, optometrists, licensed real estate brokers, watchmakers, plumbers, beauticians, funeral directors, embalmers, insurance brokers, and many others.

Apart from the lists of licensing and registration boards, state health departments or state departments of agriculture may keep lists of every dairy operator in the state, every cheese factory, and every farmer whose cattle have been examined for brucellosis. The highway department will have the names of the contractors holding highway building contracts. Wisconsin requires municipalities to report the names of all contractors to whom contract awards during the year have totaled $25,000 or more and requires state nonresident contractors to file a bond to cover all prospective taxes during the life of the contract. Conservation departments may list resort owners and operators. They also license hunters and fishermen, with differential rates for residents and nonresidents. Wisconsin's Department of Natural Resources and Department of Revenue have found cross-checks of residency declarations mutually beneficial. Occasionally, the state's unemployment compensation and workmen's compensation departments may have information worth checking. While examining unemployment insurance records in Wisconsin recently, a tax auditor identified a number of corporations that had recognized an unemployment insurance obligation but had failed to recognize a similar filing obligation for the state's franchise tax. (California utilizes the same agency for tax withholding.) Municipal or state licensing records provide information on establishments that sell beer and liquor. Whether or not such records are generally public, they are usually available to a sister state department. And even with the matching of withholding, IRS Individual Master File lists, etc., states find that occasional checks of their own official lists turn up nonreporting residents.

Lists of absentee voters provide an incomplete but excellent source of information on individuals outside the state who may have an income tax obligation. This is especially valuable since the federal Individual Master File list will not necessarily identify individuals with addresses outside the state.

NONGOVERNMENTAL SOURCES

Although full use of governmental sources is likely to ferret out most nonfiling taxpayers, there are private reference information sources that can be used for a further check or for verification of earlier suspicions. Most small and large business concerns can be located through trade journals, city directories, or telephone "classified directories." Privately published farm plat maps may give the location and size of every farm and the name of every farm owner or renter. Iowa has used U.S. Farm Bureau lists of farmers, and Maryland has located farm taxpayers through county agent lists. Purchasers of farm products, processors of farm produce, and suppliers of farmers' needs may all have records of value to the income tax agency. Oklahoma at times has secured reports from oil operators on drilling contracts let to nonresident drillers. The oil and pipeline companies also may file information on royalty payments. Brokers' customer ledgers may yield tax-producing information in the states that do not require formal reporting of brokers' transactions. The records of title and trust companies will indicate gains on some transfers of real property. Newspaper stories or anonymous letters or telephone calls provide identification of still other taxpayers or their incomes.

Conclusion

An individual cannot comply with the income tax law unless he knows of its existence, understands his obligation and the return form that is to be filed, and is capable of acting in accord with these demands. The first responsibility of the tax agency, then, is to inform the taxpayer of his obligation through newspaper and other media publicity or personal notice whenever possible; to follow up with a return and instructions that are as clear and complete, yet concise, as trained individuals can devise; to provide the means for answering taxpayers' questions by telephone, personal contact, or correspondence; and in other ways to inform every individual of his tax responsibility and make his obligation to file and to pay as easy as is practical within the law.

To encourage filing and full reporting, tax departments must utilize available resources to verify (1) that citizens who owe a tax do file and (2) that the information supplied on the returns matches that available to the departments from other sources. Pursuing information either to identify the nonfiler or to verify income reported requires time, personnel, and other resources.

Chapter Six

Collections: Current and Delinquent

Until after World War II, U.S. taxpayers paid most of their state income taxes when they filed annual returns in the spring. This spring rite, of harvest rather than sowing, refilled the state's coffers and provided a feast for a few months and a gradually drained treasury by winter. Through the review and audit process, tax departments attempted to identify taxpayers who had failed to file or had understated their taxes, and these assessments, billed to the taxpayers, produced a trickle of further income tax receipts during the year. With the continuous search for certainty in tax collection, equity in administration, and convenience in payment, the possibility of collecting income taxes at the source of income and of simultaneously improving cash flow for the state appealed to many administrators and tax students.

This chapter will first consider collection at the source as a means of current tax payment and then take up the collection of subsequent additional assessments as a result of initial failure to pay, failure to file, mathematical errors on returns, audit adjustments, or the like.

Collection at the Source

Tax administrators in the United States have considered the withholding device primarily in terms of wages and salaries, though some attention has been devoted to interest and dividends. From 1935 through 1951, Wisconsin collected its "privilege dividend tax" on all dividends from corporate earnings in Wisconsin from the issuing corporations without regard to the state of "residence" of the corporate payer or income recipient. Hawaii collected its tax on compensation and dividends at the source until 1956, when it replaced this tax with a general income tax. A few states had statutory provisions for payroll withholding on nonresident wages and salaries or special income before they adopted general withholding statutes.

In 1943, the national government's adoption of tax withholding from wage and salary payments plus quarterly payments of taxes by individuals or corporations on other income stimulated state consideration.[1] In 1947, Oregon adopted general withholding for wages and salaries but did not provide for quarterly declarations or current tax payments on other income. In 1953, Pennsylvania became the first state to require current payment of corporation income taxes. Oregon has not yet gone the full distance in current payments. In 1973, it required corporations to pay one-half of the corporate income taxes due within the given year. Individuals need to declare nonwage and salary income only in the spring after the year in which it is earned. One-half of these taxes due may still be delayed for another six months.

THE SPREAD OF STATE WITHHOLDING

Ten years after Oregon adopted payroll withholding, nine more states had accepted the innovation. By 1967, all income tax states except California, Mississippi, and North Dakota had joined the club.[2] California and Mississippi adopted withholding by the early 1970s. Each new income tax state of the sixties and seventies provided for withholding in its initial statute. Today, North Dakota remains the only state without general wage and salary withholding. Table 18 lists dates of adoption of withholding by the states and whether or not the statutes include quarterly declarations and payments for individuals and corporations. Few states have followed Oregon in its favored treatment of nonwage and salary income. Instead, most states have followed the national government in enacting general pay-as-you-go legislation for individuals without regard to source of income. Also following the national government, the states have not attempted withholding at the source for interest, dividends, etc., but have depended on individual or corporation quarterly declarations and payments for nonpayroll income. As noted in an earlier chapter, almost a dozen states —Alabama, Arizona, Idaho, Iowa, Mississippi, Montana, New Mexico, North Dakota, Ohio, and Utah—favor corporations by not requiring quarterly declarations and current payment of franchise or income taxes. Maryland and Oregon ask only 50% payment in the current year; New Jersey, 60%; and Pennsylvania, 90%.

Before and after adoption of general withholding, several states authorized revenue directors to withhold on special types of income whenever

[1] On a number of occasions tax reform proposals in Congress have included some form of withholding on corporate bond interest and dividends, but no legislation has ever cleared both houses in this century. (The Civil War income tax provided withholding on interest and dividends but not on wages and salaries.) The greatest legislative achievement has been some tightening of information-return reporting in this area.

[2] For a good summary of state withholding as of the early 1960s, see Alan P. Murray, "Wage-Withholding and State Income Taxes," *National Tax Journal* 17 (December, 1964): 403-17.

TABLE 18
Selected Characteristics of State Income Withholding Provisions

State	*Year withholding adopted (individual)*	*Periodicity of deposits (large employers)*	*Quarterly estimates and payments on income (individuals)*	*Quarterly payments required for corporations*[a]
Alabama	1956	Monthly	Yes	No
Alaska	1959 (1949)	Monthly	Yes	Yes
Arizona	1954	Quarterly	No	No
Arkansas	1966	Quarterly	Yes	Yes
California	1971	Monthly	Yes	Yes
Colorado	1954	Monthly	Yes	Yes
Connecticut	No broad-based individual income tax			Yes (if tax over $10,000)[b]
Delaware	1949	Monthly	Yes	Yes
Florida	Corporation income tax only			Yes
Georgia	1960	Monthly	Yes	Yes
Hawaii	1959 (1957)	Monthly	Yes	Yes
Idaho	1955	Monthly	No	No
Illinois	1969	Monthly	Yes	Yes
Indiana	1963	Monthly	Yes	Yes
Iowa	1966	Monthly	Yes	No
Kansas	1966	Quarterly	Yes	Yes
Kentucky	1954	Monthly	Yes	Yes (if tax over $5,000)
Louisiana	1961	Monthly	Yes	Yes
Maine	1969	Monthly	Yes	Yes
Maryland	1955	Monthly	Yes	Yes[b]
Massachusetts	1959	Monthly	No	Yes
Michigan	1967	Monthly	No	No corporation income tax
Minnesota	1961	Monthly	Yes	Yes
Mississippi	1968	Quarterly	Yes	No
Missouri	1961	Monthly	No	Yes
Montana	1955	Quarterly	Semiannual	No
Nebraska	1967	Monthly	Yes	Yes
New Hampshire	No broad-based personal income tax			Yes
New Jersey	1976	Monthly	Yes	Yes[b]
New Mexico	1961	Monthly	No	No
New York	1959	Monthly	Yes	Yes
North Carolina	1959	Monthly	Yes	Yes (if tax over $100,000)
North Dakota	Only for nonresidents	Quarterly	Only for nonresidents	No
Ohio	1971	Monthly	Yes	No
Oklahoma	1961	Monthly	Yes	Yes
Oregon	1948	Monthly	No	Yes[b]
Pennsylvania	1971	Semimonthly	Yes	Yes[b]
Rhode Island	1971	Semimonthly	Yes	Yes
South Carolina	1959	Bimonthly	Yes	Yes
Tennessee	No broad-based individual income tax			Yes
				Yes
Utah	1959	Monthly	No	No

TABLE 18--*Continued*

State	*Year withholding adopted (individual)*	*Periodicity of deposits (large employers)*	*Quarterly estimates and payments on income (individuals)*	*Quarterly payments required for corporations*[a]
Vermont	1951	Monthly	Yes	Yes
Virginia	1963	Semimonthly	Yes	Yes
West Virginia	1961	Monthly	No	Yes
Wisconsin	1962	Quarterly	Yes	Yes

Sources: Column 1 from U.S., Advisory Commission on Intergovernmental Relations, *Significant Features of Fiscal Federalism, 1976-77: Federal-State-Local Finances,* vol. 2, *Revenue and Debt* (Washington, D.C.: March, 1977), table 109. Columns 2 and 3 from information on questionnaires submitted to state tax departments in August, 1978. Column 4 adapted from *Tax Administrators News* 40 (May, 1976); no subsequent changes.

[a]In most of the states with quarterly payments for corporations, all corporations or all corporations with nominal taxable income are required to file and pay. As noted, Connecticut, Kentucky, and particularly North Carolina have higher tax-due levels.

[b]These states in effect require only partial current payment within the year or the first month thereafter. New Hampshire allows last payment in February. Connecticut allows last 30% in following April. Pennsylvania allows last 10% in April. New Jersey allows last 40% in following April, and both Maryland and Oregon allow final 50% the following April.

they deemed it necessary to secure collection. This authority, when used, has resulted in immediate tax withholding for such elusive nonresident income as that from boxing matches, rock star concerts, racing, and lotteries. It applies whether or not the performer is incorporated. California, Illinois, Massachusetts, Montana, New York, Wisconsin, and other states have found such withholding profitable. Advance knowledge of performances and attendance by a tax official to make the collection requires continued attention and an extra policing effort by the tax agency.[3] Licensed or state-operated racing, betting, and lotteries permit more general arrangements to assure tax withholding on nonresident winnings.

Withholding serves as (1) a tax enforcement technique, (2) a means of automatic tax budgeting for the taxpayer, and (3) a fiscal policy measure in the current taxing of current income. The national government's adoption of its pay-as-you-go system in the midst of World War II served all three objectives. The states have likewise claimed improved compliance, taxpayer convenience, and—to a lesser extent—better fiscal policy as beneficial results of the system. The timing of adoption in each state varied with fiscal need, with the extent of personal exemptions, and with state tax rates.[4] In most states—e.g., California—the discussion of withholding stirred political

[3]Current collection of taxes from the nonresident boxer, rock star, or other performer in some circumstances becomes a jeopardy assessment.

[4]The immediate fiscal exigencies of each state influenced its political decision to forgive all or part of the past year's income taxes at the point of making income tax payments current through withholding. Five states provided some degree of forgiveness. See Murray, "Wage-Withholding," p. 404.

ferment that evaporated with actual adoption. Massachusetts, Missouri, and Louisiana "bought off" the opposition of employers by allowing them to retain a portion of the tax for administrative costs.

Although often an innovator, California delayed adopting general withholding until 1971. In the fifties and early sixties, the state's income tax law included rather high exemptions and deductions with low rates. After exemptions and deductions, a net income of up to $10,000 was subject to only a 1% tax. The then executive officer of the Franchise Tax Board saw no need for withholding as an enforcement tool. The state treasury was sufficiently full at all times and thus there was no pressure to adopt withholding. By the late sixties, however, California had reduced its personal exemptions, made many more citizens subject to its income tax, and was rapidly developing a cash flow problem for the treasury. The number of residents with taxable incomes rose rapidly. Governor Reagan, initially a strong opponent of state withholding, recognized the crisis, pushed the legislature to act, and then signed the bill.

ORGANIZATION

In all states except California, responsibility for administering withholding is assigned to the state's tax agency, which is often directly associated with the income tax bureau, if there is one, or is otherwise associated with general receiving, accounting, and collecting. Although Michigan includes the administration of withholding within its tax agency, it places follow-through responsibility in the sales tax section that deals with employers collecting sales taxes. There is a substantial overlap of employers withholding income taxes on payrolls and employers collecting taxes on sales. Yet there are sufficient differences in volume, types of accounting, depositing, and reporting to raise problems of priorities in a combined tax unit.

When California adopted withholding "under the gun," it decided it would be easier and more rational at the commencement of withholding to utilize the agency that was already collecting employer liability and unemployment insurance from the state's employers. Presumably the agency had a complete listing of all employers in the state, and a single audit of an employer to verify his accounting for the several funds would simplify the employer's life and satisfy the state's interests. Over the years, the Franchise Tax Board has found the arrangement administratively costly and less effective than had been expected.[5] Labor interests have outweighed tax interests.

[5]The closest analogy to California's administrative arrangement may be the IRS's collection of social security taxes. Whether a single agency should collect the several state levies on employers for the personnel is a debatable issue. Rationality varies. "Rational organizing principles" carried to the extreme would relate all programs of government and hence lead to a single department. Relating fairly immediate program objectives and priorities may be a better guide to organization.

Wage and salary withholding requires close cooperation with employers in the state. Subject employer lists must be developed more carefully than those used for information return programs, reporting forms must be distributed, and employer accounts must be established to reflect total wages withheld and payments made to the states. Oregon, and every other state that has adopted withholding, has relied extensively on the IRS for its initial register of employers.[6] In addition, most states have supplemented the IRS list with state lists of corporations, lists of unemployment insurance employers, the sales tax lists of all businesses, etc.

California found that employers can successfully begin to withhold on very short notice when they have been duly appraised by the tax department and the media of the probability of withholding's becoming a fact (even though precise knowledge of the actual details and schedules may not be available until later). The Franchise Tax Board developed employer registers during the summer of 1971 and held discussions with key employers (the state's thirty-four largest employers) plus state and national government representatives on procedural matters. (These three groups of employers covered some two-thirds of the wage-earning and salaried employees in the state.) In preceding years, the board had also conferred with other states, and especially with IRS personnel, on the administrative operations involved in handling a withholding system. With the passage of withholding legislation seemingly certain in 1971, the agency secured as much media publicity as possible to avoid surprising any employer with this new responsibility.

California's withholding statute passed the legislature on December 7, 1971, and was to take effect on January 1, 1972. By the night of December 7, mail bags containing all the necessary instructions and forms were in the major post offices of the state. Certification was immediately made to the IRS, and clearance was secured for federal agencies to apply the withholding tax to salaries earned within California.[7] All employers had the benefit of the federal withholding experience to aid them in instituting

[6]IRS lists include all employers obligated to pay social security taxes. This includes households that hire part-time help such as cleaning women, etc. These employers frequently are not required to withhold state or federal income taxes on the small sums involved. Some state tax departments find "cleaning" federal tapes of these employers an arduous job and prefer state lists, although they use both. It is ironic that, without exception, state tax agencies reported fine cooperation from the IRS when the states instituted withholding, yet it was the national government that initially caused Oregon and Vermont the most trouble when it refused its agencies authority to withhold for state income taxes. See Clara Penniman and Walter W. Heller, *State Income Tax Administration* (Chicago: Public Administration Service, 1959), p. 204. Even today states complain that some federal agencies are careless in the reporting and timing of their payments. States in the metropolitan region of Washington, D.C., have particular problems since their residents may be working at federal installations in neighboring states that also have income taxes. Here the national government seems caught up in the resident/nonresident tax and collection problem.

[7]The public seldom gives recognition to those skilled administrators, such as Martin Huff of California, who make new legislation operative despite unrealistic deadlines.

payroll withholding. Despite the short time of three weeks and the normal employee absences at the holiday period, employers managed to institute state withholding with payrolls beginning January 1, 1972.

POLICING WITHHOLDING

As in the case of other income tax provisions, pay-as-you-go and withholding provisions are not self-operating. Withholding shifts the tax agency's burden from collecting small sums from numerous individual wage earners to collecting much larger sums from their employers. For the tax agency, the number of taxpayers to be collected from goes down while the individual amounts to be collected from the fewer withholding agents go up. The loss to the state through the failure of any one withholding employer to pay normally far exceeds the revenues that would be lost through the failure of any single taxpayer to pay. The administrative arrangements for withholding replace the need for securing and matching employer information returns and wage earners' tax returns with matching withholding statements and tax returns. Withholding cannot ensure the accuracy of individual exemption and deduction claims or the fullness of reporting of nonwage income. Erroneous taxpayer refund claims must be identified. Additional assessments must be collected. Nevertheless, all indicators suggest that taxpayer delinquencies have gone down under the withholding system, even in states with the best record of income tax administration. No legislature has proposed the abolition of withholding once it has adopted the plan.

Accounting and Reporting

Only Louisiana, Massachusetts, and Missouri provide for any cost reimbursement for the additional effort by employers to withhold, deposit, and report taxes withheld. For the large employer with computerized payrolls, the additional costs presumably are not large and, of course, are deductible as a business expense on both federal and state income tax returns. Small businesses without computers and without accounting employees may find state income tax withholding to be another of the governmental controls and regulations that make operating a small business increasingly difficult. The number of such businesses usually exceeds the number of large businesses and thus, from a narrow, state agency "efficiency" point of view, constitutes a nuisance out of proportion to the number of individual taxpayer accounts and funds withheld. State tax departments often recognize the potential hardship for small businesses and make every effort to provide them with detailed information, periodically sending an official to assist or to answer questions. In this and other ways the departments attempt to aid the small businesses as well as the large. Aiding and encouraging cooperation from all withhholding employers in the state improves the standing of the tax agency and presumably produces closer adherence to the law and appropriate rules and regulations.

State law or the relevant rules and regulations determine the schedule for taxpayer withholding and the periodicity of employer deposits and reports of taxes withheld. Table 18 indicates the types of schedules required and the depositing and reporting times. States normally require more frequent reporting by employers withholding the largest amounts of taxes and make fewer reporting demands on the small employer.

Large employers withhold thousands of dollars in taxes each pay period, and it is in the state's interest to have these funds paid in currently. All but nine income tax states require larger corporations to make at least monthly deposits of all taxes withheld. Even the days and hours of deposit can affect who earns what interest. Several states have established specific banks as depositories for state funds and instruct employers to make their payments directly to these banks. This procedure may easily add from one to three days additional interest on the deposit (a million dollars earns $136 each day at a mere 5% interest rate). States that do not use a bank depository arrangement may still provide for immediate clearance of all checks together with special messengers to make the bank deposits (see discussion in chapter 5).

Matching Withholding Statements

The sheer volume of withholding statements has to date defeated efforts of tax agencies in both large and small states to match fully employer withholding statements and those attached to individual returns. New York reports that in the days when the state and city submitted separate slips for each taxpayer on their payrolls, trucks or vans arrived with bag after bag of individual statements. Neither manpower nor computer time, nor both, have been adequate to meet the task. Computerized payrolls are changing the dimensions of the problem and may solve it if the major employers, the IRS, and the states can agree on a reporting tape format that can be matched with the data from the employee's return as well as reconcile the periodic deposits and reports of the employer to the tax agency. New York's Department of Taxation and Finance and most tax departments with substantial computer operations are already accepting computer tapes in lieu of separate paper withholding statements from the state, its large cities, federal agencies, and large private corporations.[8]

Matching employer withholding statements with taxpayer copies attached to returns serves several verification purposes. It helps to ensure individual taxpayer honesty in reporting and to ensure that all employers who withhold

[8]New York recently described its withholding efforts as follows: "The Withholding Tax Unit maintains and updates a master file of employers, and processes and balances year-end reconciliation reports and 14 million wage and tax statements against withholding tax accounts. Information on Wage and Tax Statements attached to income tax returns is verified on a sample basis against copies of Wage and Tax Statements forwarded by employers." New York, Department of Taxation and Finance, *Annual Report, 1975/76* (Albany, 1977), p. 6.

report fully to the tax department. It identifies individuals who fail to file returns and who may either owe taxes or be entitled to refunds on taxes withheld. (A matching of IRS Individual Master File tapes with a tape of state taxpayers will provide additional aid.) Matching of employer quarterly and annual figures with totals of withholding tapes submitted by the employer and totals extracted from employee statements will help to identify employers who fail to deposit taxes withheld.

Despite the volume problems of matching individual withholding statements of taxpayers with those submitted by employers, every state needs to make an effort at least to check occasionally. Some states regularly sample, as New York does, and other states at least attempt to match if any question arises concerning the W-2 attached to the return. Failure of states to check employers' annual reconciliation statements against intervening reports and deposits is particularly difficult to justify. Yet some states, at least in some periods, fail this test.

Delinquency

Although the bulk of employers pay the total taxes withheld and make the required reports within the time periods specified, some employers are tardy or attempt to defraud the state by retaining tax funds. Few states maintain such up-to-date files that on any given day an official could specify the number of employer accounts in arrears either in reporting or in making payments. State law or rules and regulations specify dates, but normal administrative judgment decrees that any withholding agent be given a few days leeway—the mail may have been late or an excusable crisis may explain the delay. The problem is to determine a reasonable time point for follow-up and then to follow through until the account is settled or canceled (see discussion later in this chapter). Employers may be careless, may temporarily "borrow" from the tax fund, go into bankruptcy, go out of business, move out of state, etc. The tax department has a responsibility to keep the number of debtor employers in any of these categories as low as possible.[9] Jeopardy assessments may be needed where an employer's financial situation is particularly cloudy.

The number of employers who "borrow" from their tax funds by fully reporting taxes withheld but failing to include the appropriate check inevitably rises when the economy is slow. As one employer-friend explained to the author, "it was great to be able to borrow from both the federal and state payroll withholding last winter, the interest was lower and I didn't have to go through the hassle of a bank loan." In 1974 and 1975, many tax departments experienced delays in receiving payroll withholding

[9]U.S., Department of the Treasury, Comptroller General, *IRS Can Improve Its Programs to Collect Taxes Withheld by Employers: Report to the Joint Committee on Taxation, Congress of the United States, GGD-78-14* (Washington, D.C.: General Accounting Office, 1978). Although not fully relevant to the situations of the states, this report may be helpful.

deposits, but in most cases, the states eventually received the appropriate funds with interest.[10] The problem will always be aggravated in an economic slow-down unless the interest rates are unusually high and collection with interest is assured. Minnesota in 1977 adopted 8% rates for delinquent individual and corporation income taxes but 10% rates for delinquent withholding and sales taxes—apparently on the reasonable premise that delinquent "trusteed" funds should carry a higher interest rate.

States with major border cities, areas bordering other states with major border cities, or small states may have particular problems in enforcing withholding. Maryland, for example, finds it difficult to maintain current knowledge of and reporting by every out-of-state employer, e.g., building or road contractors operating in Maryland. Even where the contractor does register, nonresident employees may fail to file returns and pay any tax owed or to claim probable refunds at the end of the year. A further problem for Maryland, and one shared by the District of Columbia and Virginia especially, concerns the unwillingness of some federal agencies to withhold taxes for all employees working in the jurisdiction in which the agency is located or for residents of a jurisdiction levying income taxes.

Oregon, Wisconsin, and some other states have developed at least a partial solution to the out-of-state contractor problem. Whenever the state awards a contract for building, for highway construction, etc., the nonresident contractor is required to file a bond to ensure that any taxes due the state will be paid. Under these circumstances, the state will not release the bond until it is satisfied the contractor no longer owes income taxes, withholding taxes, sales taxes, etc. No state should pay a contractor for work done and then discover that the contractor has left the state's jurisdiction without clearing up tax indebtedness. Unfortunately, when the state is left out in this fashion, only a few individuals know about it. There is seldom a public red face, and corporations are rarely black-listed for future contracts in the nation (or even in the same state). Wider knowledge of the losses that result from such delinquency or fraud might tighten tax supervision and lessen public losses.

Minnesota charges a higher interest rate for delays in turning over trusteed tax funds than for other types of tax delinquency. In addition, the

[10]The rapid changes in interest rates in the seventies caught the national government and most of the states unprepared. The standard 6% rate for delayed payments had become a bargain for the taxpayer who faced 8%, 9%, or higher interest rates at the bank. The IRS and several states have shifted to a variable rate that is intended to reflect the going rate at any given time. Taxpayers may still find it advantageous at times to "borrow" by delaying withholding payments, but they will not get the interest bargain they once did.

Tax officials sometimes complain of "delinquency" or delayed payments/reports by federal, state, and local government agencies. Delays may be a nuisance to the tax department, but they do fall into a different category from delinquency by private business. Eventual reporting and payment by the government agency are a foregone conclusion. In the meantime, some government is presumably earning interest.

legislature has given agencies authority to subtract from any payment due from the state to any individual or company such amount as is needed to satisfy any uncontested tax delinquency.[11] This applies to individuals' personal taxes and to businesses' direct business taxes and trusteed taxes. In order for this system to be fully effective, all state checks to individuals or corporations must go through a computer that has been programmed to reflect all uncontested tax delinquencies.

Refund Claims

Employers, using the withholding tax tables provided by most states, overwithhold taxes for many employees. Not only do the tables encourage overwithholding, but some taxpayers apparently like to "save" by understating their personal exemptions. Verifying, writing, and mailing thousands (and in the larger states, millions) of refund checks is a major spring activity in most revenue departments across the country. And at this stage, taxpayers want immediate action. All state tax officials recognize the public relations advantages of making rapid refunds. Calls from indignant taxpayers or critical questions from legislators concerning the whereabouts of a tax refund check add to the strains on officials. Agencies usually attempt to clear returns as they come in whether checks are attached which require deposit or refunds are due which must be processed. Yet delays occur, and a number of state legislatures have provided that refunds not handled within a specified number of days from the end of the filing season earn interest.

Processing that is too rapid has its own dangers and also brings legislative criticism. Before the refund check is issued, a computer program should verify the arithmetic, check social security number for possible duplicate claims, make a general plausibility check, and set aside for further review or even substantial audit any return that does not meet these standards or involves an unusually large refund.[12] Any refund that appears legitimate after these reviews should be further checked against possible unpaid taxes due from the claimant. More and more states find it increasingly practical to run refund claims through such computer programs and still make refunds within a reasonable period. Even the necessity to pay out occasional interest may be an appropriate trade-off for the loss of revenue that would result from an inadequate review. Publicity on the payment of improper refunds or of refunds to recipients owing other taxes creates the possibility

[11]Minnesota, Department of Revenue, *Laws of 1975,* chap. 377, quoted in the state's *Biennial Report, 1975/76* (Saint Paul, 1976), p. 27. Medical assistance or welfare payments are exempt from the provision.

[12]The cut-off amount for attention by a supervisor or top administrator will vary with a number of factors and probabilities. California's executive officer must approve all refunds over $10,000. The immediate reviewer or a succession of supervisors have the authority to approve lesser refunds. Other states may have lower limits for top clearance.

of a scandal (even if the tax department's role was simply ineffectiveness) that no official wants.

Some state statutes provide that refunds may be applied not only against income tax indebtedness but against other unpaid taxes or against any liabilities of the taxpayer to the state. Minnesota's provision for this was mentioned earlier. California processes all refund checks through a computer that is programmed to throw out any refund if either the tax department or some other state department has filed a claim that a citizen owes it funds. Checks are not written for such refunds and each tax claimant is advised that he must settle with the particular state agency before the refund can be made.[13] There need be no violation of secrecy in this arrangement since the state agency seeking to collect does not know whether its claim will find any refund due the individual or corporation. It is simply a clearance procedure for collecting debts owed the state.

Locating Refund Claimants

Locating the legitimate tax refund claimant or potential claimant presents problems on occasion. Early in its experience, Oregon received from a state prisoner multiple refund claims based on taxes withheld under several aliases. Eventual verification that indeed the prisoner was the individual from whom taxes had been withheld under several payroll names resulted in the Tax Commission's sending a check to the state prison address. Too often tax refund claimants give an incomplete or inaccurate address or move between the day of filing and the day the refund check arrives. Where the problem is moving across state lines without leaving a forwarding address, a locating inquiry to the IRS may solve the address problem.[14] Since journalists find human interest stories in the existence of unclaimed checks, newspaper and wire services may print without charge lists of check owners whose current addresses remain a mystery to the tax department. The publicity may aid the state in delivering refund checks.

A different problem presents itself when a taxpayer fails to file a return to claim a refund due. In the first year of the Oregon withholding law, the Tax Commission estimated receipt of $600,000 in taxes withheld from individuals who did not file returns. Although a part of this $600,000 may have been due the state, the commission believed the bulk of the amount

[13]Despite the seeming desirability of such a collection system, several tax administrators expressed reservations about a system that permits other agencies to collect through tax refunds. Some questioned the equity of the arrangement. Others feared taxpayers would reduce the amounts they now authorize for withholding. Since some taxpayers regularly understate exemptions so that their refund check will be larger, the author believes it doubtful that many taxpayers would take the actions predicted by critics. California and Michigan, among the states that have particularly comprehensive collection systems, have not seen these problems over the past decade.

[14]See U.S., Department of the Treasury, Internal Revenue Service, "Instructions for Requiring Last Filing Data and/or Address Information," May, 1975.

was due in refunds to individuals who were either ignorant of or careless about their responsibility to file a return. Statutory elimination of seasonal and temporary farm workers from the withholding act, a change in the reporting of income of minors, and greater taxpayer awareness of withholding provisions reduced the state's windfall gains to a "negligible amount." In the first years of the Pennsylvania income tax, state officials thought they might face a situation similar to Oregon's; and Michigan and North Carolina officials, among others, indicated some net gain in revenue from the tax balances of nonfiling taxpayers. But these states were unable to put a precise figure on the amount of their windfalls. Officials in other states with whom the author talked doubted the existence of much unclaimed refund moneys from withholding. The fact is, few if any officials know.[15] More overall matching of withholding slips and more extensive investigation would give a state greater knowledge of the dimensions of the problem of refunds and unpaid taxes.

Collecting Assessments

Payments that accompany employer withholding reports, taxpayer returns (whether quarterly or yearly declarations), or that are the taxpayer's response to departmental billings for additional assessments are not "collections" in the usual use of this term in most tax departments. In fact, in the usual terminology, departmental "assessments" become collectable assessments or collections only after the taxpayer ignores his appellate deadlines or loses his contesting of the assessment on appeal. Tax agencies generally define "collection activities" as those activities developed for the purpose of securing taxes due from businesses or individuals who have failed to respond to normal departmental billings for taxes due. Only then is a tax delinquent and only then does the "collection" activity come into play.

Every successful effort to enforce current payment reduces the delinquent account load. Although the states differ in their deposit demands on income taxes withheld, none requires deposit of taxes more often than semimonthly, and the majority do not require even the largest employers to deposit withholding taxes more frequently than once a month (see table 18). The Uniform Personal Income Tax Statute provides for monthly deposits of withholding taxes by larger employers.[16] The IRS, with more

[15] Until the state secures a tax return from every individual from whom any employer has withheld taxes, it cannot know whether there are substantial taxes or refunds due. And this process requires a more comprehensive match than tax departments currently undertake.

[16] *Uniform Personal Income Tax Statute,* sec. 22, p. 228. The statute also authorizes the commissioner, when he deems it necessary to protect the state's interest, to require more frequent reports and deposits.

money at stake, requires the largest employers to deposit withholding taxes in a Federal Reserve bank or in designated commercial banks within three banking days after employees have received their pay.[17] Quite apart from any delinquency problem, the U.S. Treasury, like the states, is constantly seeking ways in which to increase daily balances and to reduce the amounts involved in necessary borrowing. Hence, the faster the Treasury receives withholding taxes, the better off it is. Frequent deposits of withholding taxes and faster and more comprehensive checks of the status of all employer reports and payments not only increase the amount of cash available to the government but also identify delinquents faster. Bonding, faster deposits, and earlier reports are other potential aids.

ORGANIZATION

A single collection division in the tax department will ease any possible communication barriers concerning a given taxpayer's delinquency status for all state taxes. More or less identical statutory language for all tax delinquencies also helps. Tax departments have increasingly established a single collection division, at least in the field, to replace the older system of attaching separate collection units to each tax program (chapter 3). Field collectors work more effectively if one collector can act to locate the debtor-taxpayer and attempt to collect or arrange a settlement on open accounts for withholding, income, sales, or other taxes. On-line computer accounts available to collectors are a further aid. As New York shifted toward a more integrated tax organization in the mid-seventies, it first merged collection functions in the field and later integrated collection in the Albany office.

THE PROBLEM

Size

Most tax departments do not publicly report the exact status of their income tax accounts receivable or the number and amount of delinquent tax assessments. And among those which do not report, at least some appear not to know the number of employer withholding delinquencies or the amount or number of individual or business income tax delinquencies.

A few states provide statistics on income tax accounts receivable in terms of numbers and (sometimes) amounts, the number of accounts cleared in a given year, and whether the backlog is growing or declining.

[17] As a recent report from the General Accounting Office stated it: "While the requirements for using the Federal Tax Deposit System are fairly complex, employers are generally required to deposit withheld taxes when the accumulated amount during the month reaches $2,000, or at least monthly if the withheld taxes are over $200. If quarterly liability is less than $200, then taxes may be paid with the quarterly return." Comptroller General, *IRS Can Improve Its Programs to Collect Taxes Withheld by Employers,* p. 1. The report is valuable for insights into IRS problems that are also relevant for the states.

The data seldom separate withholding taxes from income taxes generally. "Closed accounts" may mean several things: closed as a result of clearing legitimate answers to legitimate questions; closed as a result of the statute of limitations running out (six years is fairly common); or closed as a result of being declared "uncollectable," which may mean uncollectable after a substantial search and investigation of employment or property claim possibilities or uncollectable after a casual letter or two failed to elicit a response from the taxpayer.[18]

"Clientele"

There appears to be little statistical analysis with which to identify the most probable tax delinquents. The author would echo John F. Due: "No state currently has data of delinquencies by type of business, though administrators are well aware that the problem concentrates in certain fields."[19] It is reasonable to assume that the same business taxpayers who fail to pay sales taxes on time will also delay payment of employer withholding taxes or taxes on income from the businesses. Tax officials have confirmed problems with such repeat delinquents. The IRS indicates that *almost three-quarters of its tax delinquents are businesses,* with large businesses being the least delinquent. Ignorance, carelessness, lack of accounting, shortage of funds, need for capital, or evasion account for these delinquencies. Since these businesses may owe withholding payroll taxes and sales taxes collected from customers plus other taxes, they require particular attention from state tax departments. Every new business must receive some attention—if only a letter outlining tax responsibilities—if the department is not automatically to have an additional tax delinquent on its hands. An official call and explanatory bulletins also are helpful to new businesses. The IRS and several of the states consider taxes withheld on payrolls a trusteed account and may enforce a separate bank account for the taxes. It was noted earlier that Minnesota charges a higher interest rate on such delinquent accounts than on others.

Businesses in financial straits are an automatic concern to the tax department. If paying taxes means bankruptcy, nonpayment appears to be a reasonable alternative to the business. Even the tax collector may recognize

[18] In the early seventies, according to one report, the IRS failed to collect less than $100 million per year in delinquent accounts—some 2.5% of all delinquent accounts and some 0.05% of all assessments, a minuscule amount. If the percentage of uncollectable assessments normally runs 0.05%, the IRS should be the envy of the states and private bill collectors. Such statistics are particularly slippery and depend very much on classifications and assumptions.

Whatever the state's statute of limitations, it does not apply to judgments or liens filed against the taxpayer's property. If such action is taken within the six-year (or whatever) period, it may produce collection years later. This is one reason why even the most careful accounting may fail to provide a complete collection picture.

[19] John F. Due, *State and Local Sales Taxation* (Chicago: Public Administration Service, 1971), p. 199.

this and attempt to provide time payments to permit the business to regain its financial footing. Continued operations may only deepen the debtor's hole, but collectors and the tax agency may hesitate to be the imminent cause of bankruptcy.

Other nonpayers (individuals or businesses) may fail to understand the department's action to date or question the legitimacy of the action and simply await the tax collector's arrival for information. Regardless of the desirability of such action from the point of view of either the taxpayer or the tax department, "confrontation" will usually bring about settlement of these accounts.

Some nonpayers are tax evaders who first file an incomplete, late, or inaccurate return, or do not file at all, and when that ploy does not work, try to wait out any collection action. The department that fails to follow through on its billings and subpoenas aids this nonpayer, who may subsequently move out of state with his assets. All tax debtors (whether deliberate tax evaders or not) who move out of state leave the state with a difficult practical problem of collection. Newcomers to the state may prove delinquent until the department identifies them.

A final group of tax delinquents (sometimes tax evaders) consists of businesses and individuals involved in illegal or questionable operations —gambling, prostitution, drugs, etc.—who fail to file or fail to disclose all income fully in order to avoid other possible criminal action, even though the secrecy of the tax return is assured. When confronted with a tax assessment and a tax collector, however, they may pay any amount they consider reasonable in order to avoid further investigation. To the tax collector, this group is not necessarily hard core if the individuals can be located and currently have funds.

ENFORCING PAYMENT

Timeliness

To avoid delinquency in the first place or to collect from the delinquent taxpayer, every agency's motto should be "Collect Taxes Now." Always, the older account is the more difficult account. When an additional income tax assessment is generated in the course of processing, reviewing, or auditing a return, the taxpayer is sent a computer notice and a bill, which the majority of taxpayers pay. Those who do not pay (and do not protest or appeal) after reminders become part of the work load of the collection division. A properly programmed computer can identify the delinquents within a short period and not only provide the collection division with lists of delinquents but go on to issue subpoenas. Pennsylvania's Department of Revenue reported an increase of 82% in the collection of delinquent corporate taxes for 1975/76 after it developed a computerized notification system and activated more diligent collection efforts involving telephone calls to taxpayers and increased use of liens.[20] The computer can calendar each subpoena and, if the subpoena is ignored, can follow in due course with a notice to a field agent to go out and collect. Failure to collect through personal taxpayer contact can be followed by wage or bank account garnishment or by lien and seizure of property. Close and timely monitoring of each account in this calendar sequence of actions adds to the probability that the field agent will collect.

A full panoply of legal powers would include (1) assessment, (2) jeopardy assessments, (3) subpoena, (4) tax warrant and seizure of property, (5) judgment and lien, (6) wage or salary garnishment, (7) "stop" on any moneys due from the state or other privileges of the state (e.g., withholding a liquor license), and (8) attachment of bank account. The Uniform Personal Income Tax Statute, the IRS Code, and some state statutes make certain officers of a business personally responsible for nonpayment of income taxes *withheld*. Thus, for example, if one partner or officer absconds, the agency may take action against another to recover the taxes withheld. Another provision in some state statutes requires that the purchaser of a business secure a tax clearance. If the purchaser neglects to do so, he becomes responsible, under the state's successor liability provision, for any withholding taxes not paid the state by the former owner.

Successful collection by any or all of the means available usually involves payment not only of the taxes due but also of a variety of civil penalties and interest; and in the criminal case, conviction for fraud may bring a prison sentence. Only where neither the taxpayer nor any of his assets nor any other responsible individual nor his assets can be located does the tax agency reach an impasse in collection. Tax officials must utilize all the tools at their command and have adequate staffing to achieve optimum collection.

Case Studies

Michigan. The state had an effective sales tax collection function before the tax agency assumed responsibility for the new income tax in 1967. Collection of delinquent withholding and income taxes has presented an additional challenge. The recession of the seventies hit the automobile industry, and therefore Michigan, unusually hard. Delinquent withholding taxes (and sales taxes) became the great problem for the collections division as every small business dependent on automobile prosperity suffered.

Michigan gives taxpayers every opportunity to pay before taking more serious action. Whenever a return is filed without payment or with incomplete payment or there has been an office addition to the amount of the tax without action by the taxpayer, the computer is programmed to prepare a twenty-day notice of intent to assess and subsequently to send a final

[20] *Tax Administrators News* 40 (November, 1976): 127.

assessment notice if the taxpayer fails to reply within twenty days. If no payment comes in within thirty days, personnel in the central office review the taxpayer's file for collectability—is there evidence that the taxpayer owns property or other probable assets? Another polite letter may be sent at this point or the account may be sent to the field for collection. Quite possibly the first action of a field collector will be to telephone; some 50%-60% of accounts sent to the field are collected as the result of telephone calls. These are the easy cases. Collectors tend to be more successful over the phone in rural areas than in large urban areas. One collector on the Upper Peninsula averaged $25,000 per month in the mid-1970s.[21]

Accounts that do not produce payments after telephone or personal calls may require full use of the department's authority. When a collector fails by persuasion or threats of departmental legal action to collect or to arrange for collection over time, and if there is property or the prospect of property of any type that could be used to pay off the tax debt in whole or in part, he recommends filing judgment and lien. This drastic action can be taken only with central office clearance and the actual signing of the warrant by a central office official. A district office warrant officer then serves the taxpayer with the appropriate warrant to collect the tax from any available assets. Michigan files some 10,000 tax liens a year—"a good proportion for nonpayment of payroll taxes withheld" by small employers.[22]

Where the district office warrant officer has "seized" the property, the state must safeguard it until a sale takes place. With the present rifeness of vandalism in large cities, this can be difficult. Both Michigan and New York report hesitance at times to "seize" property since an appropriate sign on such property almost constitutes an invitation to vandalism.

New York. In the mid-seventies, New York established a consolidated collection operation in its central tax office and in the districts. Along with the organizational change, accounts receivable and the necessary calendar of collection steps were computerized for faster action and better control. "Processing" or "auditing" generates an income tax bill for employer withholding taxes, individual income taxes, unincorporated business tax, or corporation income tax and this bill is sent to the compliance division for action. Taxpayers are then billed from the central office, and more than 80% pay at this time. After forty-five days, unpaid accounts are sent with a collection packet, including a warrant, to the appropriate district office and a demand letter, subpoena, is sent to the delinquent taxpayer. After another forty-five days, a district officer will visit the taxpayer and attempt to enforce the warrant against any available assets of the taxpayer. With

[21]The state official who described the collection process to the author suggested that taxpayers in rural areas are more impressed than their urban counterparts by the possibility that "a man in blue" will appear to collect if payment is not made after the telephone call.

[22]A Michigan official told the author that though liens are public records, news media representatives seldom make any inquiries or comment publicly on such taxpayer problems. More media attention might aid in collection.

full computerization of all tax accounts and with all liabilities on a single disc, the central office will assign field cases weekly by zip code.

Tax collection in New York is a major undertaking. In a recent year some 90,000 warrants were issued, about 5,000 levies were made on bank accounts, and over 15,000 garnishments were issued. About half of the collection accounts are for sales taxes. Several years ago each individual in the program averaged more than $1,200 per day in collections.

Oregon. Oregon has attempted to improve its collection of withholding taxes through an account services program which endeavors to distinguish between the routine tax collection problem and the true delinquent. In practice this has involved extensive use of in-state WATS lines to call employers as soon as a problem shows up. Within a year and a half, telephone calls or personal visits to delinquents have reduced first notices by 37%, second notices by 83%, and liens by 78%.[23] Where the telephone or personal visit fails to bring results, the department proceeds to more radical steps to collect the taxes owed.

Rhode Island. The small state of Rhode Island claims an unusually successful program of enforcing collection of withholding taxes:

We pay special attention to category number one (semi-monthly filers who withhold $400 or more each month) since eighty percent of our withholding revenue is from this group. In this category, when the print-out (of non-payment) is received on the sixth business day following the due date, the taxpayer is contacted by the contact unit of the collection section. If payment is not received within forty-eight hours, a revenue officer will call on the taxpayer to effect such collection. If he is unable to make collection at that time, he will make a forty-eight hour demand to hand deliver such payment to the collection section. If the taxpayer fails to pay, liens are placed against the taxpayer's assets and those of responsible officers, if any. Finally, it is referred to the legal section for immediate action.

Except in the case of bankruptcy, receivership, or cessation of business, it has not been necessary to implement collection by legal means with one exception. With reference to that one exception, the case was referred to the attorney general's office, and the taxpayer was arrested and charged with misuse of corporation trust funds. The liability was promptly settled on immediate payment by a responsible corporate officer.

During the three years that this tax has been in effect, we have collected some $222 million. Our bad debt losses or write-offs amounted to $142,000; of this amount $113,000 is attributable to receiverships and bankruptcies. The bad debt ratio of dollars write-off to dollars collected is .06 percent.[24]

Wisconsin. In addition to many of the usual efforts and tools for collecting delinquent taxes, Wisconsin law since 1963 has provided that any employer

[23] Oregon, Department of Revenue, *Biennial Report, 1974-76* (Salem, 1976), p. 4.

[24] John H. Norberg, "Minimizing Delinquencies of Withheld Taxes," in *Revenue Administration, Proceedings of the Forty-third Annual Meeting of the National Association of Tax Administrators* (Chicago: Federation of Tax Administrators, 1975).

with taxable situs in Wisconsin may be required to withhold delinquent income and withholding taxes from an employee (in addition to regular wage tax withholding). The law applies to tax delinquent employees whether they are currently living in Wisconsin or not. An employee is notified before an employer is advised of the official requirement to withhold for the tax delinquency, and many employees then pay up to avoid having notification of their tax debt sent to the employer.

Since the passage of this special delinquency tax collection statute, Wisconsin estimates that some 2,500 employees have had taxes so withheld each year and that the amount collected has exceeded $500,000. The state profits from the low administrative cost of the action, and the taxpayer is provided with an orderly installment payment plan. This has also proved an effective means of collecting from taxpayers who have moved out of state.[25]

UNCOLLECTABLE ASSESSMENTS

Successful collections depend on staff effort, ingenuity, available legal tools, and the state's statute of limitations. Not all taxes are collected even when conditions are optimal. The laws of each state, as well as the types and habits of taxpayers, make for differences in the exact procedure for working through the collection process, but all states have one problem in common: under what circumstances should a state write off a tax as uncollectable and cease further effort? Where a tax department makes either an insignificant or a modest effort but then automatically clears every account after a period (whether on the basis of statutory limits or administrative policy), it can keep the backlog of accounts receivable down. It may also be encouraging the dilatory tax debtor simply to wait out the time. Again the conscientious taxpayer suffers.

The older the tax debt, the greater the necessary effort and the lower the probability of collection. Thus, at some point, even where a diligent effort has been made to locate the taxpayer or any attachable property, writing off the unpaid tax becomes the only appropriate action. Most state statutes and agency practices allow for cancellation of taxes where collection would mean dire hardship. Judgment here requires a genuine distinction between dire hardship and mere inconvenience.

Finally, as in all tax department activities, the question arises as to the need to add staff to increase collections by means of earlier and more effective action by the department. In 1975, when the Office of the Auditor General of California found 245,000 individual delinquent tax accounts representing approximately $100.2 million owed to the state, the auditor

[25] A court in Washington State, however, ruled against Wisconsin in 1977 when it attempted to collect from a resident (who had moved from Wisconsin) through his employer.

general recommended additional collection staff as an economy to the state.[26] Other state auditors and budget officials might take note that sometimes economy requires greater state spending.

Conclusion

By the 1970s every income tax state but one had adopted wage and salary withholding, and the majority of states had adopted quarterly declarations and current payments for individuals with other income and for corporations. Withholding has proved a boon to improving collections generally and to easing the budget strain for taxpayers, but it has produced its own problems. Policing withholding adds to the general collections enforcement load of all tax departments. The key to reducing tax delinquency remains timeliness of department action; and timeliness in turn depends on appropriate computer programs, adequate staffing, and departmental allocation of effort. Finally, appropriate statutory provisions aid the tax department in forcing tax payments from delinquents who choose to ignore reminders of tax indebtedness. Some uncollectable tax debts will remain, but equity requires that these involve mostly taxpayers whose dire need earns them forgiveness.

[26] California, Office of the General Auditor, "Operations of the Franchise Tax Board," *Report to the Joint Legislative Audit Committee* (Sacramento, 1975).

Chapter Seven

Office and Field Auditing: Individual Income Tax Returns

Tax administrators operate within the same general framework as administrators in specific regulatory fields of government. In each case the job could not be done without public acceptance of the statutory policy and its actual implementation. To establish understanding and maintain acceptance, the income tax administrator must divide his enforcement forces among efforts to publicize reporting requirements: teach the taxpayer his specific responsibilities; process the returns; establish the fact of filing and generally inspect at least a representative number of returns to verify compliance; and, finally, apply sanctions directly or through the courts to the continuous or deliberate malefactor.

The tax administrator carries a greater burden than his fellow administrators. He does not directly provide any specific government service. Traditionally he must contend with much public apathy as well as the antagonism of particular taxpayers toward his accomplishments. In contrast, even the early factory inspector had at least a small militant public on his side and increasingly won the support of the employees who benefited from his action and, eventually, of the employers who also recognized a service performed. The tax official's service can be generalized only in terms of the value of the revenue he collects for the operation of all government and in the fairness with which he collects such revenue within the state's tax framework.

Teaching the taxpayer his general reporting responsibilities and verifying his compliance in filing will not by themselves guarantee taxpayer equity and full tax collection. These activities do not assure that deductions and exemptions are properly claimed; that business, professional, and farm incomes are accurately reported; that business income has been allocated correctly among states; that the tax return reflects the basic situation of the taxpayer rather than some illegal fiction; or that taxpayer books and accounts are properly kept. Adequate income tax administration demands more than mechanical coverage work. It demands analytical review of tax returns and of at least some taxpayers' records as well. The taxpayer must be assured that his return is not filed away without examination. He will otherwise find it increasingly easy to forget income items, exaggerate deduction items, and feel that his conscientious reporting is rewarded by personal loss of equity compared with other, less responsible taxpayers.

The comment of a Mississippi income tax director more than twenty years ago that "it's staff and time, not information, that we are lacking," remains true of the availability of income tax information in the American economy today. The computer has added a valuable means of extending the check of each return against information available to the tax department. Yet with present resources of staff, time, and machinery, officials still cannot check a representative number of claims for medical or dental expense deduction against the doctor's or dentist's income; payments by grain elevators, cotton gins, tobacco warehouses, creameries, and cattle buyers against farm returns; or commission, dividend, interest, rent, and royalty payments made against payee returns. And almost every legislative session adds further deductions or exemptions that require verification if income payments reported by taxpayers and expenditures claimed by taxpayers are to be cross-checked. Individuals and groups lobbying for specific changes regularly drown the cries of both federal and state administrators that equity will be served better by simpler statutes that can be understood more easily by taxpayers and more fully verified by administrators.

Auditing goes beyond compliance activities to establish the accuracy of the taxpayer's reporting of income, deductions, and exemptions within the statutory provisions of the state's income tax act. The scope of audit activities extends from an office review of returns (the "office" or "desk" audit done manually or in part by computer) for internal consistency, consistency over years, and reasonableness of deductions claimed, to the full field auditing of an individual's or corporation's accounts or the special investigation and construction of accounts where the taxpayer has failed deliberately or otherwise to maintain records. Verification of arithmetic calculations and some matching of salary and wage information and other data with tax returns are usually accomplished today (often by computer) before tax returns go to audit. Increasingly, in fact, auditors get only those returns the computer program sets aside after such verification and matching efforts are completed.

This chapter will consider audit organization and the several functions of individual income tax auditing both in the office and in the field. Chapter 8 will examine corporation audit organization, the auditing of corporation returns, and special investigative work on income tax cases, whether individual or corporate, involving evasion and fraud.

Audit Organization

Twenty years ago, three states did not audit individual income tax returns on a completely centralized basis. All state tax agencies organized the office audit function for income tax returns without attempting to integrate it with the audit activity for other taxes. Most of the states with both individual and corporate income taxes had separate audit bureaus for these two taxes.

Today, all states except Virginia have centralized all office auditing of their individual income tax returns and have increasingly integrated auditing not only of corporation and individual income tax returns but also of sales tax returns. As noted in chapter 3, the earlier tax-by-tax organization is giving way in a growing number of states to a functional organization whereby such major divisions as processing, auditing, statistics and research, legal, etc., comprise an all-inclusive tax department. California is the only state employing both a sales tax and an income tax which retains separate agencies, and hence the state's Franchise Tax Board is organized much as most other state income tax divisions were organized in the 1950s. Both Massachusetts and New York in the mid-1970s shifted from a largely tax-by-tax division organization to a functional or process division organization. (Again, see chapter 3 for further discussion of organization.)

Despite the seeming dominance of the process or functional organization pattern in most tax departments, audit specialization—planned or unplanned—is common. The individual income tax is sufficiently different that auditors trained to handle these returns are not necessarily able to handle either corporation income or sales tax returns. And corporation income taxes differ sufficiently from sales taxes to again make audit specialization desirable. Oregon, for example, has a single audit division but separate sections for the several taxes (see chart 15).

Minnesota's Department of Revenue attempts to integrate field audit operations, but its income tax division is its office audit division for income taxes. The division carries responsibility for office and correspondence auditing for individual, withholding, and corporate income tax returns. The division also acts somewhat as a focus of general income tax administration since it handles taxpayer assistance and operates in liaison fashion (including assignment of assisting examiners) with the administrative services division for immediate return review and related correspondence in the cashier section, the editing and machine audit section, and the refund section. The income tax division also necessarily cooperates directly with the field operations and compliance divisions in direct enforcement activities. The latter divisions also have responsibility for other taxes administered by the department. (See charts 14 and 18.)

CHART 18
Minnesota Department of Revenue—Audit Division

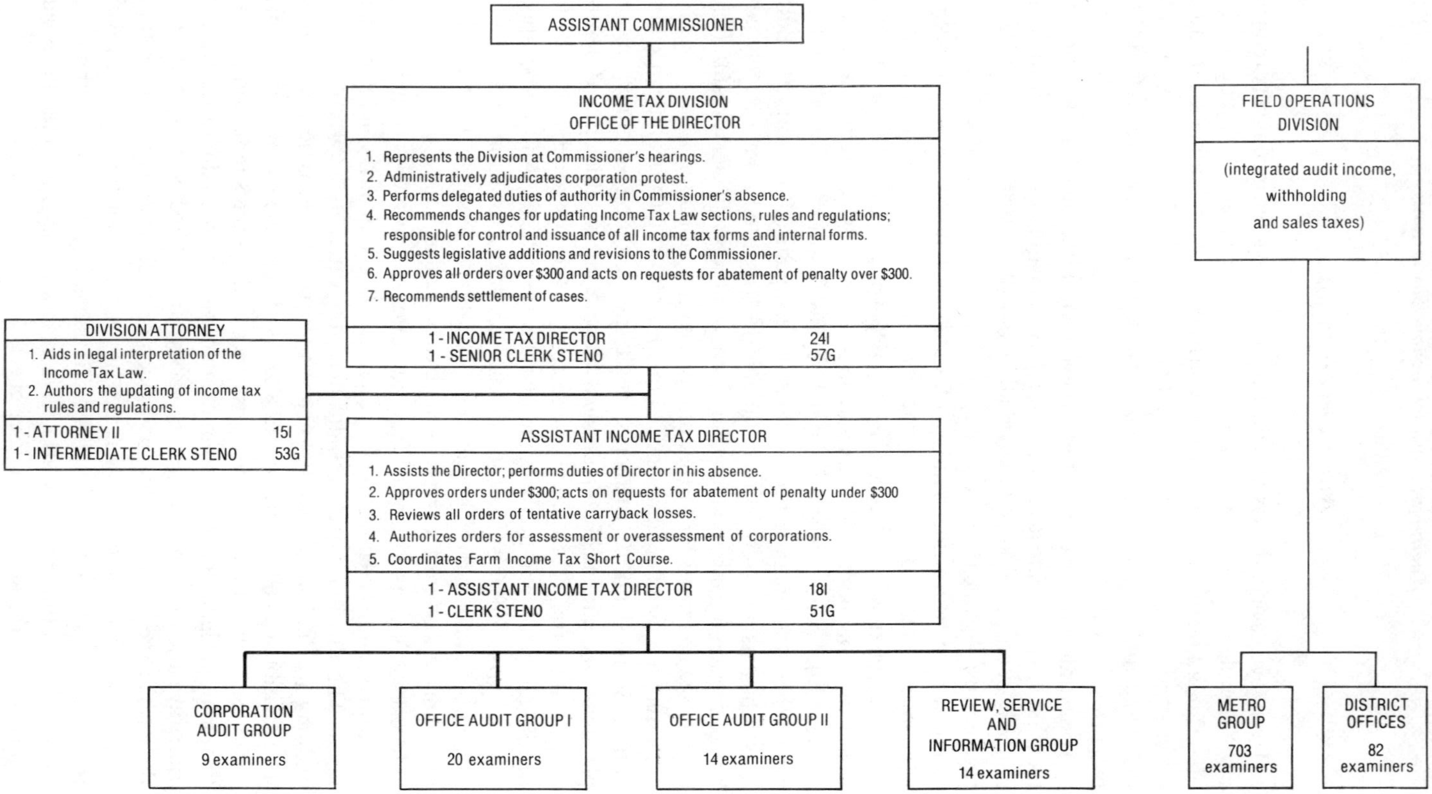

ASSISTANT COMMISSIONER

INCOME TAX DIVISION
OFFICE OF THE DIRECTOR

1. Represents the Division at Commissioner's hearings.
2. Administratively adjudicates corporation protest.
3. Performs delegated duties of authority in Commissioner's absence.
4. Recommends changes for updating Income Tax Law sections, rules and regulations; responsible for control and issuance of all income tax forms and internal forms.
5. Suggests legislative additions and revisions to the Commissioner.
6. Approves all orders over $300 and acts on requests for abatement of penalty over $300.
7. Recommends settlement of cases.

1 - INCOME TAX DIRECTOR 24I
1 - SENIOR CLERK STENO 57G

DIVISION ATTORNEY

1. Aids in legal interpretation of the Income Tax Law.
2. Authors the updating of income tax rules and regulations.

1 - ATTORNEY II 15I
1 - INTERMEDIATE CLERK STENO 53G

ASSISTANT INCOME TAX DIRECTOR

1. Assists the Director; performs duties of Director in his absence.
2. Approves orders under $300; acts on requests for abatement of penalty under $300
3. Reviews all orders of tentative carryback losses.
4. Authorizes orders for assessment or overassessment of corporations.
5. Coordinates Farm Income Tax Short Course.

1 - ASSISTANT INCOME TAX DIRECTOR 18I
1 - CLERK STENO 51G

CORPORATION AUDIT GROUP
9 examiners

OFFICE AUDIT GROUP I
20 examiners

OFFICE AUDIT GROUP II
14 examiners

REVIEW, SERVICE AND INFORMATION GROUP
14 examiners

FIELD OPERATIONS DIVISION
(integrated audit income, withholding and sales taxes)

METRO GROUP
703 examiners

DISTRICT OFFICES
82 examiners

New York has achieved both a functional organization and specialization within that structure. Its Department of Taxation and Finance has established a single audit division for all taxes (chart 19) that identifies distinct functions within the division with separate bureaus: its audit services bureau provides administrative, filing, and stenographic support; a central office audit bureau is responsible for desk audits and other reviews conducted in the central office; the district office audit bureau is responsible for all field office activities; and there is an audit evaluation bureau. Additionally, a technical directive section, responsible for the development and dissemination of documented audit policy, reports directly to the office of the director of the division. This common audit division for all taxes has not meant joint audits of all tax returns either in the office or in the field. The district office audit bureau, for example, has an audit section for each of the previously organized taxing bureaus.[1] The audit evaluation bureau is responsible for continually evaluating audit operations through an audit effectiveness section, an audit quality control section, an assessment review section, and an audit selection section.

Audit Function

SELECTION FOR AUDIT

"The most efficient use of auditing time would single out and deliver only the incorrect returns . . . into the hands of the auditors. Yet no preaudit magnet can infallibly pull out only those returns which require audit attention."[2] Today's computer engineers and programmers can bring this wish closer to reality. Properly programmed computers have become the "magnets" that can identify many of the returns that require audit attention and set others aside. The fully used computer first verifies the arithmetic accuracy of the return (increasing or reducing the assessment if necessary and advising the taxpayer of the change), checks the returns for internal consistency, and manages at least sample matchings with withholding statements and interest, dividend, royalty, and rent information returns. The computer can further match the returns against other selected information: data on property sales and gains; previous returns of the taxpayer; the IRS's Individual Master File list of the state's taxpayers and their major characteristics; etc. None of this is done automatically, any more than manual preauditing and auditing were done automatically and

[1]This description of the reorganized audit function in New York's Department of Taxation and Finance was drawn from the address of Thomas F. Hogan, Assistant Administrative Director, to a general session of the National Association of Tax Administrators in Boston on June 20, 1978.

[2]Clara Penniman and Walter W. Heller, *State Income Tax Administration* (Chicago: Public Administration Service, 1959), p. 148.

CHART 19
New York Department of Taxation and Finance—Audit Division

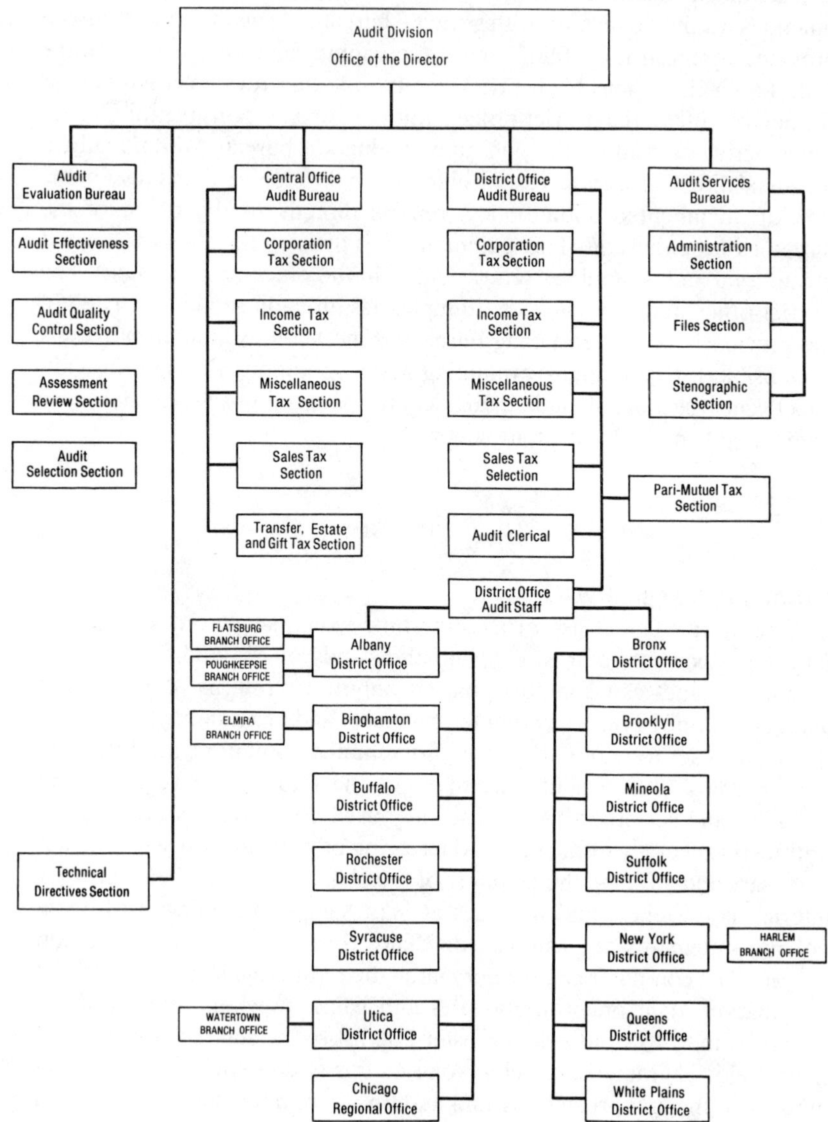

without cost. The state tax department requires resources to utilize its numerous information sources, to put the data into the computers, and to program the computers to attempt to match these data with the taxpayer's report on his return. But the fact remains that if a tax department has the necessary resources, preauditing can include much that auditors previously had to accomplish manually.

Selection Programs

Computers can be programmed to go beyond the unmatched returns in the several verification and checking operations above and to select all returns with particular characteristics, e.g., all returns with income above a specified level, all returns with certain types or heights of deductions, all business returns with selected ratios of income to sales, etc. With or without computers, some states have used such criteria for decades to reduce the total number of returns to a more manageable number for auditing. Computers have simplified the selection process and made feasible more sophisticated audit selection programs.

The IRS has programmed its computers (sometimes referred to as the DIF or Discriminate Function System) for two decades or more to select returns according to sophisticated statistical criteria developed from studies referred to as the Taxpayer Compliance Management Program (TCMP). Based on a careful statistical sampling procedure, returns are selected for full office and field audits. The findings from these audits indicate the types of returns, taxpayers, income, etc., that are most likely to produce the largest number and amount of tax changes. These characteristics are then made into a computer program (DIF) for the selection of returns for auditing for the next several years. No such audit program is productive indefinitely—characteristics of the taxpaying population change or the public begins to recognize the characteristics of those whose returns are audited and those whose returns are not.[3]

In 1974 and 1975, under a special legislative mandate and a special appropriation, New York employed a private consulting firm and undertook a major analysis along TCMP lines to gain knowledge of the types of taxpayers and types of errors in state returns that most frequently require examination and full audit. On the basis of the findings of this study, New York established its audit selection program in 1977 for 1976 returns.

California has developed its own computer selection program, ASTRA. As in all good programs, this one has been used, tested, modified, and again used. California officials express satisfaction with the results.

[3]U.S., Department of the Treasury, Comptroller General, *Repetitive IRS Audits of Taxpayers Are Justified: Report to the Joint Committee on Taxation, Congress of the United States, GGD-77-74* (Washington, D. C.: General Accounting Office, November 18, 1977). This report describes IRS policies and procedures for selecting returns for audit.

The growing number of returns filed each year requires continuing development of computer programs by the states to identify returns with more or less routine errors that can be handled readily by programmed correspondence. Audit selection must become ever more sophisticated to select for review by professional examiners only those returns that are most likely to need audit, whether for reasons of significant underpayment or overpayment.

Aid from the IRS for Audit Selection

The IRS has not established state by state either the Taxpayer Compliance Management Program or its companion computer audit selection program. To do so would add considerably to operational costs and would not particularly aid the national tax administration effort. In the best of all possible worlds, each state tax agency would periodically develop and undertake its own Taxpayer Compliance Management Program, as New York did in 1974 and 1975, and develop its own audit selection program based on TCMP findings. The inevitable overlap with IRS audit selection could be reduced, if not eliminated, by mutual consent and could result in a broader coverage of the returns most in need of audit than either the state agency or the IRS could achieve alone. This nirvana has not yet arrived.

Yet the states have profited from the IRS audit selection process, which tends to select out more returns than IRS field staffs can audit within the three-year statute of limitations. District directors in several states, including California, Minnesota, North Carolina, and New York, have provided the state tax agencies with names of taxpayers selected for audit in the state that the IRS will not be able to cover. The states then make their own audits of these tax returns and under the mutual exchange program advise the IRS of changes required. The arrangement serves the interests of both federal and state tax agencies.

Volume

The ratio of audit staff to volume of income tax returns and the length of the state's statute of limitations condition the state's audit program and the effectiveness with which desk auditors use available resources and select returns for desk, correspondence, and field audit. A number of states have never employed large enough audit staffs to attempt anything more than the most routine review of returns, and their tax departments have depended on the activities of the IRS for audit coverage. The spread of federally adjusted gross income (or federal net income or tax) as the state's beginning base, together with the availability of IRS tapes, abstracts, and revenue agent reports, has perhaps further encouraged some states to minimize their individual audit efforts.

At one time or another several states have fallen hopelessly behind in audit review. This has also happened to some of the new income tax states, e.g., Illinois and Ohio, in one or more of the early years of administration. The solution has usually been to "forget" auditing for such years. Any department can, of course, keep current despite an insufficient audit staff by the simple expedient of selecting few returns for audit and by questioning even fewer. Instructions to auditors not to bother with assessments on business schedules involving additional income of less than $500 or $1,000; to ignore errors of less than $10; or not to question contribution items unless they exceed $1,000 or 10% of gross income, etc., will control the audit load but may encourage equally casual reporting by taxpayers in the future. Nevertheless, the audit selection program has to be realistic in terms of the resulting work load for the available staff.

OFFICE AUDITS

The glories of the computer for checking and for audit selection do not replace human review. Whether it follows or incorporates preaudit activities, the office audit (also called the desk audit) is designed to correct errors in interpreting or applying the law, to uncover deliberate misreporting of income, and to unmask various subterfuges designed to conceal income. Office audits either supplement the selection of returns for field audits or serve as the field audit selection process.

Desk Audit Resources

Files. Although once common practice, few states today maintain historical files that place together the returns of a taxpayer for the past several years. In most states today, the processing operation involves numbering returns, establishing a master alphabetized list for the year, and filing returns annually by number. Wisconsin, which still maintains historical files, provides that office auditors shall go through all files in the course of three or four years (Wisconsin's statute of limitations is four years) and automatically review the consistency of taxpayer reporting over the years. An auditor in a state that uses numerical filing has a single return of the taxpayer on his desk and must judge the need to call for earlier files to test consistency or to answer questions raised by the current return.

Historical filing uses more resources than annual filing and is becoming more difficult to justify wherever departments (1) make sophisticated tests of compliance along the lines of the taxpayer compliance program of the IRS, (2) utilize computers extensively to match return information with returns filed with the IRS and with other available data, and (3) carefully program computers for audit selection.

Internal Technical References. Copies of the state's income tax laws, the department's rules and regulations under the law, perhaps additional legal interpretations of the law or rules and regulations, and department audit manuals or occasional audit memoranda are the auditor's technical guides.[4] Given the states' increasing dependence on the IRS Code as the basis for many of their income tax laws, the code has become a necessary reference for the auditor.

Although some states are excessively casual in developing rules and regulations or keeping them current, others consider such an effort a major responsibility of the agency. Minnesota publishes revised rules and regulations following each legislative session. California continually publishes revisions of its formal rules and regulations. Oregon regularly prepares for its auditors and for the professional tax public legal abstracts, which are interpretations of various tax questions by the Tax Commission's legal staff. Most states provide something in the way of instructions to auditors whether mimeographed audit instructions, occasional policy notices, or oral instructions on general auditing policies. New York makes this an assigned responsibility for the technical directive section of the audit bureau. The more comprehensive the technical guides, the more useful they will be in training new auditors and in achieving consistency in the application of audit policies.

Federal Audit Information Exchange. Without going into the history of federal-state relations in income tax administration now (see chapter 9), it is important to recognize that federal audit abstracts and revenue agent reports constitute a major source of audit strength for state tax agencies. Even the most active and best-supported state agencies find that federal audit reports are a significant supplement to their own efforts, and a majority of the states may well secure more additional audit assessments from IRS transcripts than from any separate audit effort of their own. Many states require taxpayers to attach a copy of their federal return and to advise the tax agency of any changes made by the IRS in adjusted gross income and net tax (see table 11). Usually, if the taxpayer neglects to inform the state of such changes, the statute of limitations for state auditing does not run. Since the state is also receiving audit abstracts or revenue agent reports from the IRS, the agency has the advantage of knowing about the changes even if the taxpayer fails to advise the department. Upon review of these changes, auditors or other reviewers can either immediately bill the taxpayer for additional state taxes due (or make a refund) or telephone, correspond with, or visit the taxpayer in the field to obtain the information needed to determine the effect of the federal audit finding on the taxpayer's indebtedness to the state. Table 35 provides data

[4]Given the low cost of small calculators, this mechanical aid also can be helpful. The author was surprised to learn how frequently auditors in departments across the country in the mid-1970s either had to check calculations manually or get up to use a calculator that was somewhat centrally located. Several auditors with small calculators stated that they had personally bought them.

on the number of audit transcripts provided the states for selected years by the IRS. Table 35 adds data on the value of these transcripts to selected states.

Other Resources. Most information returns, if utilized today, become a part of the preaudit computer check, but occasionally the nonwage and salary information returns for dividends, interest, rent, royalties, and similar income are filed with the return for office review by the auditor. Office audits also may include cross-checks with partnership returns and with inheritance and estate tax returns. Where states require property sales to be taxed and reported, these constitute an information source of value that is normally incorporated in the tax agency's files.

In either historical or annual filing, any taxpayer correspondence accompanies the return for audit examination. Occasionally newspaper clippings or informer letters also are given to the auditor to review. Although most informer letters add nothing to tax returns or the agency's knowledge, there is always one that may open up a whole case for field audit or fraud investigation.

If state law permits deduction for the federal income tax, such deductions often deserve attention. The desk auditor may find that these have already been checked through a computer match with the federal tape or with the copy of the withholding statement. Otherwise verification requires correspondence or field effort. Even with no intent to defraud, taxpayers on a cash basis may confuse the timing of payments of federal taxes and may doubly deduct last-quarter payments. Or the taxpayer may forget about a refund on federal overwithholding. If state law permits deduction of the state income tax against itself, similar timing problems may arise that require checking. Another significant internal check concerns differences in deductions permitted by state and federal law. Wisconsin auditors, for example, check to be sure the taxpayer has not deducted half of his capital gains, as permitted under federal, but not state, law.

The Audit Process

Ideally returns can be processed, cleared through computer verification programs, selected for audit, and still reach desk auditors not later than one year following the taxpayer's reporting year. More commonly today, the better departments probably begin review at least a year and a half following the reporting year, since many preaudit computer matching programs are not completed earlier. As in every aspect of income tax enforcement, the earlier the audit is begun, the better the chance of finding a satisfactory solution to any problems uncovered. Taxpayers are likely to have better recall and better records. If an investigation is necessary, this too will proceed more easily with the more recent memories of those with whom the taxpayer did business. Finally, the earlier the audit, the more likely it is the taxpayer will be at the address shown on the return.

With varied resources at his command, the auditor examines returns in detail for all the items suggested under preaudit, matches information and tax returns not previously matched, utilizes unused but available federal information, including, of course, abstracts and revenue agent reports, and brings to bear such additional information sources as inheritance and estate tax information, sales tax reports on business income, informer letters, and newspaper stories. In addition the desk auditor applies his training, experience, common sense, and ingenuity in testing items on the returns for reasonableness, internal consistency, and accounting validity. Whether working from a historical file that contains several years' returns or from assembled files called for, the auditor can verify the consistency of opening and closing balances, of previous and current depreciation adjustments, and of capital gain or loss carry-overs. The auditor can identify unusual increases in wealth as dividend income changes. He can note the failure to show interest or dividend income regularly reported in the past, unusual changes in business gross receipts or in the gross-to-net ratio. He can follow the deduction and exemption patterns of the taxpayer. Finally, the auditor achieves a general sense of the continuity of the taxpayer's financial affairs and whether the picture appears consistent.

Audit Action

Telephone/Correspondence. Information on returns does not always permit a decision to make a deficiency assessment, to make a refund, or to close the audit. A telephone call or a letter to the taxpayer may provide the data that will permit such a decision. Auditors can supplement their office review significantly by telephoning or writing taxpayers for answers to questions that develop in the course of the desk audit. Tax departments in the last decade generally have increased their use of the telephone as a means to faster, and often better, communication with individual taxpayers. Use of special DAIN or WATS lines for taxpayer assistance during the filing season can contribute to office audits where questions require fairly simple types of information from the taxpayer. In these instances the telephone can save the agency time and money if the taxpayer can be located and the information secured in a matter of minutes. (Some departments provide for evening calling to increase the chances of reaching the taxpayer.)

Questions that require the taxpayer to check his records may necessitate the auditor's writing the taxpayer for the information needed to complete the desk audit. Occasionally the letter may invite the taxpayer to bring his records to the central office or to a field office to answer more fully the questions that have arisen. And, of course, sometimes the taxpayer prefers to act in this fashion even though not requested to do so. In some states the desk auditor simply writes the taxpayer, but in others he prepares questions and makes recommendations for correspondence or field audit. Dictating examiners then review the audit program and, as appropriate, initiate correspondence with the taxpayer. These examiners handle all answers from the taxpayer and all subsequent correspondence with him. Audit questions can sometimes follow a predeveloped form letter or standard paragraphs. Prepared paragraphs save staff effort and over time undergo the test of taxpayer comprehension.

The effectiveness of correspondence audits depends on the type of information requested from the taxpayer, the clarity and tenor of the request, and the faithfulness with which a follow-up is made of all unanswered correspondence. Overly technical language may confuse and even frighten taxpayers, who may then answer vaguely or hesitate to answer at all. Letters suggesting that the tax department has any doubts about the citizen's integrity can be very damaging. Most states attempt to couch letters in terms designed to gain taxpayer cooperation and good will.

Cultivating taxpayer good will requires a serious follow-up program. Demands made of the taxpayer for information or payment, however courteous and reasonable, are valuable only when followed through. To assert in writing that definite, even dire, action will be taken in ten, thirty, or sixty days unless the taxpayer complies with demands reasonably made, and then to let the matter slide, invites disrespect for the law and its administration. Some states have no follow-up system other than "going through the file when somebody has time." Even though work load pressure may seem a good excuse in the tax department, delay to the taxpayer means disinterest and encourages carelessness or delinquency. Computer programs or even systematically used tickler files can provide an automatic follow-up to telephone calls or correspondence and threatened penalties.

Field Referral. Depending on the selection program of the tax department, the desk audit may or may not be an important source of return selection for field audit. Generally speaking, the more sophisticated audit programs select independently for desk audit and field audit. Only occasionally in such circumstances does the desk audit turn up problems that require sending returns to the field. Other tax departments rely almost exclusively on desk auditors to set aside returns with serious questions that the reviewing auditor believes should receive field attention. And the number that actually receive field attention depends as much on the size of the field staff as on the problems found in the returns. Where tax departments do not field audit personal income tax returns, the telephone and correspondence must provide all answers.

Audit Review

Tax departments commonly provide that the section, unit, or bureau supervisor review all office (and field) audit assessment proposals before they are sent to the taxpayer. Minnesota's Department of Revenue designates two office audit groups. Group II reviews assessment proposals in the office and handles taxpayer protests of field audit decisions. (Each field auditor's assessment recommendations are reviewed within the administrative unit of the field operations division before they are sent to the taxpayer.) Further, the division director must sign any assessment proposal (or abatement of penalties) where the amount exceeds $300.

California, Minnesota, New York, Oregon, Wisconsin, and several other states further provide for a review staff which goes over all or selected audited returns. Such continuing examination of the work of auditors promotes uniformity of decisions and hence of taxpayer treatment. It can serve to raise questions for discussion and develop consensual interpretations. And it can aid in the training of new auditors and refresh the memories of older ones. Finally, such internal review helps to guard against improper action on the part of any auditor.

FIELD AUDITS

A broad-gauged office audit program—one combining full use of available information resources, skillful desk auditing of returns for accuracy and internal consistency, and well-managed telephone and correspondence programs—can reduce the sphere of field auditing to manageable proportions. Agencies must maintain a minimum field audit program to avoid chronic misreporting in those corners which the office audit broom cannot reach. Such items as capital gains and losses, fiduciary incomes, rents, and large and questionable deductions, and most items involving distinctions between income and capital, abound in problems calling for field investigation. But the most general and pressing need for individual field audits lies in the area of business and professional income.

Field auditing raises the same basic questions of audit planning and philosophy that occur in other areas of income tax administration. In what ways can the effort and moneys available be expended to produce the greatest revenue and the greatest equity? What selection process will produce the cases in greatest need of investigation as judged by the criteria of (a) securing maximum revenue returns and (b) educating and aiding the taxpayer and his friends in proper compliance with the income tax? Field auditors typically represent the most experienced and the highest salaried auditors in the agency. Some of their time is inevitably eaten up in travel to the taxpayer's place of business or residence. These cost factors limit the types of return problems that permit field attention. Further, the general lack of budget support for an adequate field audit staff also helps to define the returns "worthy of field attention." Unless field personal income tax auditors are designated separately from field corporation income tax auditors, most or even all field audit time will be absorbed by the latter, more immediately profitable efforts. In the modern, integrated tax agency the central office field supervisor, the district directors, or the field auditors recognize the greater productivity of corporation audits to the detriment of attention to individual audits. And honest individual income taxpayers lose in equity.

Selection for Field Audit

States differ on whether returns for field audit come from (1) a special field audit ("scientific") selection process; (2) desk auditors; or (3) leads generated in the field. Where a field audit selection process exists, the computer may identify these returns directly and route them immediately to the field supervisor without an intervening desk audit. In other cases the desk auditors may select returns on the basis of objective criteria or individual judgment for referral to the field supervisor for field audit attention. A few states leave most of the selection process to the field auditors, who follow up on local leads or particular categories of taxpayers.

Earlier in this chapter some of the elements in audit selection and the efforts of the IRS to develop a more sophisticated selection pattern were reviewed. Most of the IRS's efforts have concerned field audit selection. To the extent, then, that IRS district offices share their audit selection lists with the states, they provide information for field audit selection. Any state field follow-up on federal revenue agent reports would again be a part of such field audit selection. Only New York, with its recent taxpayer compliance management study, has developed a similarly sophisticated base.

Lacking the equivalent of the IRS's Taxpayer Compliance Management Program, some states still attempt "scientific" methods of selecting returns for referral to the field. By carefully studying previous field audit experiences to determine which characteristics of the audited returns were associated with productive field audits, states can establish quantitative criteria to aid in future audit selection. These criteria typically take the form of (a) specified amounts of total reported income and of particular income and deductible items and (b) ratios of one item to another (e.g., net-to-gross business income). Returns with items or ratios exceeding the specified figures are automatically marked for field verification. A few years of experience inform many tax administrators or auditors that particular types of businesses or professions provide more than their share of enforcement problems for the agency. This judgment of experience further indicates that there is a strong overlap between the types of taxpayers that give trouble for both the individual income tax and the sales tax. A study of one provides data for the other. Even a "seat of the pants" judgment of one is a judgment of the other in terms of selecting returns for field audit. The possibilities for enforcement and recovery of both taxes automatically make some businesses good audit prospects.

Desk audit selection remains the most common means of developing the field audit work load. Rarely has a state limited field auditing to a selection program that excludes office audit questions. The states differ greatly in whether selection depends primarily on the individual judgment of the auditor or on objective criteria established by the tax department. When selection is not based on well-developed objective criteria, whatever questioned returns are left over after others have been readily checked through office reference resources or through a telephone call or a letter or two to the taxpayer tend to be candidates for field audit. Thereafter, either the field supervisor in the central office or the field offices themselves select according to their personal preferences or judgment of productivity within the time available.

Only occasionally do states depend on field operations for selection of returns for audit there. The central office provides an inevitably broader perspective for effective use of field time. Yet the field auditor's intimate knowledge of an area of the state sometimes needs recognition. Oregon's auditors are free to judge between the importance of cases assigned by the central office and their own current investigations. Other states give the field auditors some flexibility without such complete freedom of choice.

Field Audit Procedures

States typically grant their income tax administrators extensive powers to commandeer and examine taxpayers' books, papers, accounts, records, bank statements, safe-deposit boxes, and the like. Early income tax laws lacked such teeth, but most tax agencies can no longer complain of any lack of authority to get at the records that are vital to a comprehensive audit. Armed with broad powers, the auditor either summons the taxpayer to appear at some central point with his books and records, or, especially in the case of business and professional returns, goes into the taxpayer's establishment for the audit. His investigation may be (1) a simple interview to clarify a few questions and to ascertain the taxpayer's understanding of his obligations; (2) a full examination of the taxpayer's accounts; or (3) where the taxpayer has kept no records or inadequate records of his fiscal affairs, an all-out attempt to build up his income record through "net worth," cost-of-living, or similar techniques. Other investigations may concentrate on locating types of underreported income or classes of nonreporting taxpayers.[5]

In instances where taxpayers present wholly inadequate books and records, states occasionally turn to the net worth assessment as a last resort. This device employs a balance sheet approach. The auditor attempts to build up a net worth figure for the individual at two different points in time. The increase in net worth between the two points is then adjusted for

[5] For a somewhat tongue-in-cheek description of a revenue agent's experiences in field auditing, see Diogenes, *The April Game* (Chicago: The Playboy Press, 1973).

probable living expenses. Net worth figures may be developed from (1) a previous audit, if one has been made; (2) information on the taxpayer's wealth; (3) previous income tax returns, especially the interest and dividend income items shown therein; (4) appraisals of estates for death tax purposes; and (5) bank statements, contents of safe-deposit boxes, and the like.

The net worth technique is especially applicable to illicit businesses such as drugs, bootlegging, prostitution, and gambling, and to legitimate businesses like construction contracting where books and accounts may be skimpy or nonexistent. It may be used more often in investigations of fraud than in general auditing. One flaw in the net worth method is that it automatically allows deduction of all the taxpayer's losses, since they decrease rather than increase his assets; gamblers, for example, are thereby allowed, in effect, to deduct their nondeductible gambling losses. But, given auditing competence and ingenuity, the net worth method can produce impressive results.

In the case of particularly recalcitrant taxpayers who have not filed returns, failed to produce books, and in every respect have been uncooperative, some state statutes permit the levying of "doomage" assessments. In such an instance, the auditor makes an estimate of taxable income based on any information available anywhere and makes the tax assessment. This administrative assessment, usually made intentionally high, is levied on the taxpayer, who then has the choice of paying it or upsetting the assessment by producing the facts to substantiate a lower one. An allied weapon is the jeopardy assessment, which may be used to enforce the "doomage" or to protect the state's interests on other occasions when speedy action is required, e.g., before the taxpayer moves out of state, declares bankruptcy, or in some other fashion appears to endanger payment of taxes due. Again, these techniques are used most often by the state's intelligence unit.

TIMING

In the case of the ordinary taxpayer, the tax department may not question a return after two, three, or four years—whatever length of time the state's statute of limitations provides (table 11). This, of course, means that office and field auditing and any resulting assessments must be completed within this period. State administrators can and often do ask taxpayers, whether individuals or corporations, to grant waivers extending the time available for review. The request is normally granted, since if it is refused, the department has the power either to make an immediate audit and assessment or to make a jeopardy assessment. Moreover, state statutes usually allow for extension of the review time if the taxpayer has grossly understated income, and may leave the review period wholly open if the taxpayer has not filed or has committed fraud in reporting.

Productivity of Audit Programs

No reasonable audit program fails to recover several times the salaries of the staff, together with a liberal allowance for other administrative expenses. Neither the IRS nor any state comes close to equalizing marginal costs and marginal revenues in its audit efforts. There continues to be more "audit gold" in the hills than it would cost to mine and produce. The volume of gold remaining depends on tax rates and on the tradition of compliance and enforcement in each state. Where most citizens fully report their income and pay their taxes willingly, or have learned to do so as a result of tax agency enforcement action, the amount of "audit gold" will be less than where acceptance and enforcement activity have been low. "Audit gold" may also increase where frequent changes in the tax law confuse taxpayers as to their reporting responsibilities or as tax rates increase rapidly. Just as the amount of gold available for mining varies with different characteristics of the tax law, taxpayers, and the activities of the tax agency, so does the cost of "audit mining." In auditing, as in most mining, the less gold there is out there, the more expensive it is to mine; or the less unreported income and the lower the tax rates, the more expensive the auditing to recover the remainder. Since we have today only hazy estimates as to the total amount of taxable income in any state, estimates of the amount of unmined audit gold also must remain hazy.

The IRS—with its more comprehensive view of all tax returns, its more scientific selection of returns for audit, and its tighter definition of what constitutes auditing—has for the last decade or so projected a goal of auditing about 5% of all income tax returns. In the mid-seventies, however, actual IRS audits covered only about half that number (2.2% for fiscal year 1977). Audit recoveries (recommended additional tax and penalties) by auditors and revenue agents totaled $1.6 billion in fiscal year 1977,[6] or under 1% of individual income tax collections. Since most returns audited probably were for earlier calendar years and refunds were not deducted, the ratio of audits and recoveries to net collections is in reality somewhat higher than these figures indicate. In comparisons among the states, or between any state and the IRS, one stumbles over the noncomparability of audit activities and available statistics. To the degree that state auditors perform audit functions of the same type as IRS auditors and revenue agents, the foregoing IRS ratios have some relevance to state ratios, but anyone should hesitate to make such conversions from the available statistics. Even if that stumbling block were removed, the higher tax rates of the national income tax compared with state tax rates often make comparisons irrelevant.

[6]U.S., Department of the Treasury, Commissioner of Internal Revenue, *Annual Report, 1977* (Washington, D.C.: Government Printing Office, 1977), pp. 23 and 25.

PRODUCTIVITY OF SELECTED STATES

California

No other state has consistently made a public report of its processing, collection, preaudit, and audit activities and their results that is as detailed and resourceful as California's. Only a close review of the annual (since 1952) *Operations Report* publilshed by California's Franchise Tax Board can provide an adequate sense of the wealth of *administrative* information provided in its twenty-five or so pages. Tables 19 and 20 excerpt some of the data on individual income tax auditing. California follows the IRS in reporting on "tax changes" as well as assessments. Such reporting gives equal credit to audit efforts that make refunds to taxpayers and those that produce additional revenue for the treasury. California also gives credit to the IRS for almost a third of its audit recoveries by separately identifying changes resulting from federal audit reports.[7]

California reports some activities under the heading "audit" that the IRS catalogs as part of its service centers' preaudit operations, e.g., mathematical verification. California does not consider filing enforcement, residence verification, or investigations to be audit activities. Neither does the state's auditing program at any point include withholding audits, since withholding administration is not a responsibility of the Franchise Tax Board. All audit activities summarized in tables 19 and 20 indicate productivity on a net assessment basis, after cancellations and abatements, but not after collection. Table 19 lists the number of cases examined and table 20 shows the *net* assessments or productivity of California auditing for six years.

In the fiscal years 1972 through 1977, California collected individual income taxes in the amounts of $1.8 billion, $1.9 billion, $2.8 billion, $2.5 billion, $4.2 billion, and $3.6 billion. For fiscal year 1977, then, total net audit assessments of $61.2 million represented 1.7% of total collections that year.

Massachusetts

The Massachusetts Department of Revenue provided the author with field audit and federal change productivity figures as follows:

Personal Income	1973 ($)	1974 ($)	1975 ($)	1976 ($)	1977 ($)	1978 ($)
Field Audit	273	—	3,181	2,064	1,695	1,553
Federal Change	981	1,450	3,452	3,979	4,831	2,487
Total	1,254	1,450	6,633	6,043	6,526	4,040

[7]States that do not follow this practice, but utilize federal reports, overstate audit recoveries from their own efforts.

TABLE 19
California: Personal Income Tax Cases Examined for the Years 1972-77

Fiscal year	No. of cases examined: Desk audits	Federal audit reports	Field audit	Mathematical verification
1971/72	6,695,264	62,532	13,032	254,845
1972/73	8,194,593[a]	56,244	11,137	1,770,421
1973/74	1,684,037	67,532	11,056	6,908,804
1974/75	1,721,161	201,061	28,883	7,284,180
1975/76	1,062,362	180,546	24,755	7,130,276
1976/77	1,354,164	191,083	29,145	8,618,479

Source: California, Franchise Tax Board, *Operations Report* (Sacramento, fiscal years indicated), exhibit B-2, col. 3.

[a]The substantial shift in statistics after fiscal year 1973 is partly accounted for by the fact that California payroll withholding had become effective in 1972 and the "small return" audit apart from computer checks almost disappeared after examination of 1971 income returns in 1973. Beginning with fiscal year 1974, California turned to a computer check and mathematical verification of all returns and selection of returns for audit.

TABLE 20
California: Personal Income Tax Net Audit Assessments for the Years 1971-77 (in millions of dollars)

Fiscal year	Office audit assessments	Federal audit reports	Field audit assessments	Mathematical verification
1971/72	6.0	19.5	7.3	11.9
1972/73	11.7	13.4	2.6	14.9
1973/74	4.7	15.9	4.4	(11.2)[a]
1974/75	5.6	16.5	6.5	3.5
1975/76	8.7	19.0	9.5	11.8
1976/77	12.0	19.5	8.9	21.8

Source: California, Franchise Tax Board, *Operations Report* (Sacramento, fiscal years indicated), exhibit B-1, col. 5.

[a]According to the report, the large negative for this year was "principally due to the allowance of unclaimed special tax credits as abatements of the self-assessed tax."

Minnesota

Minnesota reported individual income tax collections of $849.5 million in fiscal year 1976. Its office auditors made 19,000 assessments for a net increase in revenue of $4,795,684. Additionally, primarily office auditors reviewed 9,217 revenue agent reports and made assessments totaling $2,519,219. In the field the state's auditors made 3,664 assessments representing $2,205,010 in revenue. Table 21 shows the data for fiscal years 1972-76. In that last year audit productivity represented 1.1% of total collections.

Montana

Montana reported for 1975, a fairly typical year, individual income tax audit assessments of $2.5 million, or 3.2% of the $73.7 million collected. In that year the state employed fifty-three staff members (five of whom were auditors) to handle income and inheritance taxes.

New York

With individual income tax collections of $4.5 billion in 1977, 202 office auditors and 160 field auditors made assessments of $90.1 million (including those from IRS revenue agent reports), or 2% of total individual income tax collections. It will be recalled that New York's budget and other resources directed toward income tax auditing increased substantially after the mid-seventies. Table 22 reflects some of this activity.

North Carolina

North Carolina reported individual income tax collections of $657.6 million in fiscal year 1977. Its sixty-two office auditors made 316,496 changes during their review of returns and these changes yielded $7,666,450 in net assessments. Additionally, the office auditors' review of 12,186 changes shown on IRS revenue agent reports produced net dollar changes of $2,101,984. In the field the state auditors' examination of 2,291 accounts brought net changes of $1,577,700, while 377 field examinations from IRS revenue agent reports added $676,464. The combined audit adjustments represented 1.5% of collections in 1977. Table 23 provides statistical data for the years 1972-77.

Oregon

Oregon collected $686.2 million in individual income taxes for fiscal year 1978. Its 143 income tax auditors (individual, corporation, and field) assessed almost $5 million in additional taxes (not necessarily collected in 1978). In other words, audit assessments represented 0.7% of the 1978 collections. Table 24 provides some audit data for Oregon for the fiscal years 1972-78.

Wisconsin

Beginning with fiscal year 1972 and continuing through fiscal year 1978, Wisconsin's individual income tax collections have been: $594.7 million; $727.9 million; $803 million; $873.7 million; $959.9 million; $1.1 billion; and $1.3 billion. The number of office auditors totaled eighty-seven in 1978; field auditors, forty-five. Federal information accounted for somewhat more than 20% of collections each year. The ratio of assessments to tax collections was 1.9% in 1972, 1.3% in 1974, 1.6% in 1977, and 1.9% in 1978. Since assessments are actually additions to earlier years, the true assessment-collection ratio is somewhat higher in a period of years when collections have risen each year. On the other hand, assessments are higher than net

TABLE 21
Individual Income Tax Audit Data—Minnesota

		Office activities				*Field activities*			
				Changes, RARs				*Changes, RARs*	
Fiscal year	*Total personal income taxes collections (million $)*	*No. of changes*	*Net amount of changes ($)*	*No. of changes*	*Net amount of changes ($)*	*No. of changes*	*Net amount of changes ($)*	*No. of changes*	*Net amount of changes*
1972	483.2	8,040	2,085,035	12,455	2,293,007	—[a]	—[a]	Included	
1973	586.2	8,530	4,136,842	8,214	1,721,118	—[a]	—[a]	in	
1974	701.4	7,550	3,318,311	9,872	1,900,071	4,417	169,808	office	
1975	807.1	13,487	4,550,073	9,826	2,698,173	8,841	2,488,494	activities	
1976	849.5	19,000	4,795,684	9,217	2,519,219	3,664	2,205,010	figure	

Sources: Column 1 from table 7, U.S., Department of Commerce, Bureau of the Census, *State Government Finances in 1972* (Washington, D.C.: Government Printing Office, 1973), and volumes for succeeding years. Data for other columns supplied by the Minnesota Department of Revenue, October 13, 1978.
Note: RAR = revenue agent report.
[a]Separate field auditing group not formed until 1974.

TABLE 22
Individual Income Tax Audit Data—New York

Fiscal year	Total personal income taxes collected (million $)	Office activities[a]		Field activities[a]		RARs	
		No. of cases	Amount of assessments (million $)	No. of cases	Amount of assessments (million $)	No. of cases	Amount of assessments (million $)
1972	2,514.6	NA	NA	2,982	2.7	NA	NA
1973	3,211.9	NA	NA	2,969	3.1	NA	NA
1974	4,306.4	NA	NA	14,996	8.4	NA	NA
1975	3,588.6	546,081	49.3	14,959	10.8	NA	NA
1976	3,948.8	377,174	49.6	25,303	12.7	109,983	14.5
1977	4,527.0	388,515	58.5	20,381	12.3	153,380	19.3
1978	4,506.0	440,102	59.5	17,077	17.1	150,344	21.5

Sources: Column 1 from table 7, U.S., Department of Commerce, Bureau of the Census, *State Government Finances in 1972* (Washington, D.C.: Government Printing Office, 1973), and volumes for succeeding years. Data for the other columns provided by Gayle M. Hatch, Director of the Office of Tax Systems, New York Department of Taxation and Finance.

Note: RAR = revenue agent report.

[a]New York's budgeted auditors for individual income tax field audits totaled 47, 42, 94, 105, 147, 160, and 175, respectively, for the years 1972 through 1978. Desk auditors totaled 234 in 1975, 196 in 1976, 202 in 1977, and 223 in 1978.

TABLE 23

Individual Income Tax Audit Data—North Carolina

Fiscal year	Total personal income taxes collected (million $)	Office activities[a]				Field activities[a]			
				Changes, RARs				Changes, RARs	
		No. of changes	Net amount of changes ($)	No. of changes	Net amount of changes ($)	No. of changes	Net amount of changes ($)	No. of changes	Net amount of changes ($)
1972	361.8	150,017	2,760,081	10,898	1,007,046	2,102	717,073	862	347,419
1973	431.2	141,042	2,989,664	12,178	1,246,790	2,159	754,457	766	572,910
1974	504.3	157,193	3,561,413	26,680	2,653,191	2,280	1,089,670	560	317,848
1975	549.9	174,216	4,107,578	13,772	2,033,847	2,561	1,082,607	527	295,803
1976	604.8	265,524	5,816,901	19,670	2,761,752	2,480	1,256,900	563	634,676
1977	782.0	316,496	7,666,450	12,186	2,101,984	2,291	1,577,700	377	676,464

Sources: Column 1 from table 7, U.S., Department of Commerce, Bureau of the Census, *State Government Finances in 1972* (Washington, D.C.: Government Printing Office, 1973), and volumes for succeeding years. Data for other columns provided by H. C. Stansbury, Director of the Tax Research Division, North Carolina Department of Revenue, in a letter to the author dated September 8, 1978.

Notes: For full recognition of the net amount of audit changes, columns 3, 5, 7, and 9 must be added.

RAR = revenue agent report and indicates the value of that part of the exchange agreement with North Carolina for the indicated years.

[a]North Carolina employed 54 office auditors in 1972; 56 in 1973; 58 in 1974, 1975, and 1976; and 62 in 1977. Field auditing was assigned to a combined field office operation and no audit man-hours were computed.

TABLE 24
Individual Income Tax Audit Data—Oregon

Fiscal year	Total personal income taxes collected (million $)	Office activities: No. of cases	Office activities: Amount of assessments ($)	Field activities[a]: No. of cases	Field activities[a]: Amount of assessments ($)	RARs: No. of cases	RARs: Amount of assessments ($)
1972	251.2	NA	NA	NA	NA	NA	708,225
1973	300.6	NA	NA	NA	NA	NA	806,228
1974	438.1	NA	NA	NA	NA	NA	575,376
1975	427.0	16,291	1,798,338	6,445	1,673,076	8,659	1,504,838
1976	538.8	28,515	2,012,818	6,721	1,313,541	5,425	873,892
1977	561.9	35,306	2,742,577	6,427	1,285,573	7,739	1,282,884
1978	686.2	27,526	2,145,733	6,891	1,670,087	6,671	1,086,810

Sources: Column 1 from table 7, U.S., Department of Commerce, Bureau of the Census, *State Government Finances in 1972* (Washington, D.C.: Government Printing Office, 1973), and volumes for succeeding years. Data for the other columns provided by John J. Lobdell, Director of the Oregon Department of Revenue, in a letter to the author dated September 12, 1978.

Note: For full recognition of audit assessments, of course, columns 3, 5, and 7 must be added for each year.

[a]Oregon's budgeted auditors numbered 130 in 1972, 134 in 1973, 145 in 1974, 144 in 1975, 140 in 1976, 141 in 1977, and 143 in 1978. These auditors handled office and field auditing for both individual and corporation returns.

TABLE 25
Individual Income Tax Audit Data—Wisconsin

Year ending	Field audit				Office audit					
	Total		*RARs only*		*Total*		*RARs only*		*IMF only*	
	No.	*$*	*No.*	*$*	*No.*	*$*	*No.*	*$*	*No.*	*$*
6/30/72	904	2,005,389	185	297,128	47,127	9,252,687	4,437	1,015,239	3,289	1,150,456
6/30/73	780	2,240,155	159	305,490	46,864	9,471,505	4,323	1,005,135	2,722	1,237,923
6/30/74	731	1,973,323	55	204,367	42,306	8,820,086	4,986	1,022,041	520	327,641
6/30/75	818	1,957,883	68	211,719	50,581	10,237,524	6,555	1,158,829	2,183	798,617
6/30/76	898	2,189,904	202	403,555	51,515	11,609,432	11,392	2,520,760	1,803	1,116,298
6/30/77	858	2,414,546	273	700,935	49,459	15,542,999	7,583	2,029,827	153	123,880
6/30/78	632	2,095,457	226	771,891	66,277	18,504,142	8,411	2,236,501	1,793	1,804,849

Source: Data provided the author by the Wisconsin Department of Revenue, October 19, 1978.
Note: RAR = revenue agent report; IMF = individual master file.

assessment collections, since in Wisconsin's experience decisions on appeals reduce them by about 20%. Table 25 provides data on Wisconsin's office and field audit assessments for 1972-78.

The foregoing tables for several income tax states illustrate the types of audit productivity data that are currently available in these states. Since the data are not gathered with the intent of reflecting either fully comparable definitions or even similar types of information, it is not feasible to make comparisons or to dwell too heavily on the tables. They do indicate something of what can presently be known. All suggest that active state tax departments can more than justify the resources represented by their auditors. They also indicate the value of IRS information, which accounted for 31% of California's additional assessments in 1977; 62% of Massachusetts's field assessments in 1978; 26% of Minnesota's assessments in 1976; 22% of New York's assessments in 1978; 28% of North Carolina's assessments in 1977; 22% of Oregon's 1978 assessments; and 23% of Wisconsin's 1978 assessments.

Chapter 8

Office and Field Auditing: Corporation Income Tax Returns and Fraud Investigations

Although corporation returns represent less than 5% of the volume of individual income tax returns in most states, they present far more difficult problems to drafters of legislation and to administrators. State legislators early in this century considered the income of domestic corporations taxable and applied the same principle to out-of-state corporations doing business in the state. Legislative statutes and both state and national judicial interpretations of these statutes and of implementation measures have formed a substantial body of law on what business activities within the state can be taxed by the state. *Doing business* has come to have a highly technical meaning that turns on specific characteristics of the corporation's activities.

As corporations have increasingly become multistate and multinational, state tax statutes have changed to define the corporation's taxable base. In the first place, states adopt an apportionment formula that defines those factors which will be considered in determining the portion of the corporation's business that is "carried on in the state." The most common formula, and that incorporated in the Uniform Division of Income for Tax Purposes Act, is a three-factor formula which considers the ratio of sales in the state to total sales, the ratio of payrolls in the state to total payrolls, and the ratio of property owned in the state to total business property.[1] The arithmetic average of these factors is then applied to the net taxable income of the corporation to determine the base for the state's taxation. If this apportionment formula were applied to *all* income and business of all corporations, and if *all* states levied a corporation income tax and adopted the same formula, presumably national corporations would be taxable by all fifty states on 100% of their net income, no more and no less.

However, only twenty-five of the forty-four states with a corporation income tax have adopted the Uniform Distribution of Income for Tax Purposes Act (table 26). Even within these states, perfect uniformity slips away through differing judicial and administrative interpretations or sub-

[1]The Advisory Commission on Intergovernmental Relations has not published a model corporation income tax as it has done for the personal income, sales, and property taxes. It has generally supported the Uniform Division of Income for Tax Purposes Act, which forms the basis for auditing by the Multistate Tax Commission.

sequent legislative amendments. Several other states generally follow the Uniform Distribution of Income Act but have not formally adopted it, and the states that choose to place different emphases on the formula factors add further to the confusion. Wisconsin first adopted a corporation income tax in 1911 and some fifty years later added a franchise tax to include some income exempted under the corporation income tax alone. During most of those years its apportionment formula for multistate corporations approximated the Uniform Distribution of Income Act, but in 1973 it revised its statutory formula to give double weight to sales within the state. (Florida, Massachusetts, and New York have similar provisions.) This changed formula aids Wisconsin, where corporations tend to have more sales than payrolls and property within the state, but it poses problems across the nation.

Corporations from time to time have sought congressional action to achieve uniformity in state apportionment formulas or in the allocation of income. Most state tax administrators, presumably speaking for themselves and the states' legislators and governors, have opposed congressional action as an invasion of a field that under the Constitution has so far been left to the states.[2] Many administrators also fear that congressional action would favor corporations and fail to recognize the legitimate taxing interests of the states. An even more complex issue—multinational corporations and executive tax agreements or tax treaties—has faced the states and involved them in congressional lobbying. For several years President Ford and then President Carter sought Senate approval of a tax treaty with the United Kingdom. The business community, multinational corporations, and newspapers such as the *Wall Street Journal* supported the treaty. The Senate responded to state pressures and amended the treaty (1978) to permit any state to require a corporation to account for *all* foreign and domestic net income on a unitary basis as the starting point for application of the state's apportionment formula for income tax purposes (see chapter 9).[3]

[2]References on the problem ot state taxation of multistate corporations are numerous. See the proceedings of the annual meetings of the National Tax Association and the National Association of Tax Administrators, the latter entitled *Revenue Administration.* See also Donald P. Simet and Arthur D. Lynn, Jr., "Interstate Commerce Must Pay Its Way: The Demise of Spector," *National Tax Journal* 31 (March, 1978): 53-58, which provides a summary of U.S. Supreme Court decisions on the matter as of that date; and Jerome R. Hellerstein, "State Tax Discrimination Against Out-of-Staters," ibid. 30 (June, 1977).

[3]State statutes establish apportionment formulas, but the statutory provisions also establish whether a corporation is free to allocate certain types of income or all income from particular subsidiaries to sources outside the state. States such as California and Oregon insist that the corporation is the *whole* corporation and that the fact that a conglomerate may carry on one type of business in California or Oregon and other types of business outside the state or have investment income outside the state at its "commercial headquarters" is immaterial. States fear that corporations might otherwise shift income and expenditures around to minimize taxes due in states with corporation income taxes, and particularly in states which have higher rates and also audit carefully.

TABLE 26
Selected Administrative Characteristics of Corporation Income Tax

State/ other jurisdiction	Tax rate[a] as of 1/1/79 (%)	Federal income used as tax base	Uses UDITPA formula	Member Multistate Tax Commission
Alabama		No	Yes	Yes[b]
Business corps.	5.0			
Banks and financial corps.	6.0			
Alaska		Yes	Yes	Yes
Business corps.	5.4[c]			
Banks and financial corps.	7.0[d]			
Arizona		No	No	Yes[b]
$0-$1,000	2.5			
Over $6,000	10.5(7)			
Arkansas		No	Yes	Yes
$0-$3,000	1.0			
Over $25,000	6.0(5)			
California		No	Yes	Yes
Business corps.	9.0[e]			
Banks and financial corps.	9.0-13.0[f]			
Colorado	5.0	Yes	Yes	Yes
Connecticut	10.0[g]	Yes	No	No
Delaware	8.7	Yes	No	No
Florida	5.0[h]	Yes	No	No
Georgia	6.0	Yes	No	Yes[b]
Hawaii		Yes	Yes	Yes
Business corps.				
$0-$25,000	5.85[i]			
Over $25,000	6.435(2)			
Banks and financial corps.	11.7			
Idaho	6.5[j]	Yes	Yes	Yes
Illinois	4.0	Yes	Yes	No
Indiana	6.0[k]	Yes	Yes	No
Iowa		Yes	No	No
Business corps.				
$0-$25,000	6.0[l]			
Over $100,000	10.0(3)[l]			
Banks				
$0-$25,000	5.0[l]			
Over $100,000	8.0(4)[l]			
Kansas		Yes	Yes	Yes
Business corps.	4.5[m]			
Banks	5.0[m]			
Trust cos. and savings & loan assocs.	4.5[m]			
Kentucky		Yes	Yes	No
$0-$25,000	4.0			
Over $25,000	5.8(2)			
Louisiana		No	No	Yes[b]
$0-$25,000	4.0			
Over $200,000	8.0(5)			

TABLE 26—*Continued*

State/other jurisdiction	Tax rate[a] as of 1/1/79 (%)	Federal income used as tax base	Uses UDITPA formula	Member Multistate Tax Commission
Maine		Yes	Yes	No
$0-$25,000	4.95			
Over $25,000	6.93			
Maryland	7.0	Yes	No	Yes[b]
Massachusetts		Yes	No	Yes[b]
Business corps.	9.4962[n]			
Banks and trust cos.	12.54			
Utility corps.	6.5			
Minnesota		No	No	No
Business corps.	12.0[o]			
Banks	12.0			
Mississippi		No	No	No
$0-$5,000	3.0			
Over $5,000	4.0(2)			
Missouri		Yes	Yes	Yes
Business corps.	5.0			
Banks and trust cos.	7.0			
Montana	6.75[p]	Yes	Yes	Yes
Nebraska		Yes	Yes	Yes
$0-$25,000	4.0[q]			
Over $25,000	4.4(2)[q]			
New Hampshire	8.0[r]	Yes	No	No
New Jersey	7.5[s]	Yes	No	Yes[b]
New Mexico		Yes	Yes	Yes
Business corps.	5.0			
Banks and financial insts.	6.0[t]			
New York		Yes	No	No
Business corps.	10.0[u]			
Bank and financial corps.	12.0[v]			
North Carolina		Yes	Yes	No
Business corps.	6.0			
Building & loan assocs.	7.5			
North Dakota		Yes	Yes	Yes
Business corps.				
$0-$3,000	3.0[3w]			
Over $15,000	6.0(4)[w]			
Banks and financial corps.	5.0[x]			
Ohio		Yes	No	Yes[b]
$0-$25,000	4.0[y]			
Over $25,000	8.0(2)[y]			
Oklahoma	4.0	Yes	Yes	No
Oregon	7.5[z]	No	Yes	Yes
Pennsylvania	10.5	Yes	Yes	Yes[b]
Rhode Island	8.0[aa]	Yes	No	No
South Carolina		No	Yes	No
Business corps.	6.0			
Banks	4.5			
Financial assocs.	8.0			

TABLE 26—*Continued*

State/other jurisdiction	*Tax rate*[a] *as of 1/1/79 (%)*	*Federal income used as tax base*	*Uses UDITPA formula*	*Member Multistate Tax Commission*
Tennessee	6.0	No	No	Yes[b]
Utah	4.0[bb]	No	Yes	Yes
Vermont		Yes	No	No
$0-$10,000	5.0[cc]			
Over $250,000	7.5(4)[cc]			
Virginia	6.0	Yes	Yes	No
West Virginia	6.0	Yes	Yes	Yes[b]
Wisconsin		No	No	No
$0-$1,000	2.3			
Over $6,000	7.9(7)			

Sources: Column 1 from corporate income tax rates, *The Book of the States, 1978-1979* (Lexington, Ky.: The Council of State Governments, 1978), p. 312; and letter from the Executive Secretary, Federation of Tax Administrators, containing 1979 information. Columns 2, 3, and 4 adapted from table 114, p. 223, of U.S., Advisory Commission on Intergovernmental Relations, *Federal-State-Local Finances: Significant Features of Fiscal Federalism, 1976-77*, vol. 2, *Revenue and Debt* (Washington, D.C.: Government Printing Office, March, 1977).

[a]Figures in parentheses indicate number of steps from lowest to highest tax rate.

[b]Associate member only.

[c]Plus a surcharge of 4% of taxable income; the state surcharge exemption follows the federal surcharge exemption.

[d]Banks and other financial institutions are subject to a license tax.

[e]Minimum tax is $200.

[f]Rate adjusted annually: maximum, 13%; minimum, 9%; minimum tax, $200.

[g]Or 0.31 mills per dollar (maximum $100,000) of capital stock and surplus, or $50, whichever is greater.

[h]An exemption of $5,000 is allowed.

[i]Taxes capital gains at 3.08%.

[j]An additional tax of $10 is imposed on each return.

[k]Consists of 3% basic rate plus a 3% supplemental tax.

[l]Fifty percent of federal income tax deductible.

[m]Plus a surtax of 2.25% of taxable income in excess of $25,000.

[n]Rate includes a 14% surtax, as does the following: a tax of $2.60 per $1,000 on taxable tangible property (or net worth allocable to state for intangible property corporation). Minimum tax of $228 including surtax. Corporations engaged exclusively in interstate or foreign commerce are taxed at 5% of net income and are not subject to surtax.

[o]Minimum tax is $100.

[p]Minimum tax is $50; for small business corporations, $10.

[q]Twenty-five percent and 27.5% of individual income tax rate, determined annually by Board of Equalization and Assessment, imposed on net taxable income.

[r]Business profits tax imposed on both corporations and unincorporated businesses.

[s]This is the corporation business franchise tax rate, plus a net worth tax at millage rates ranging from 2 mills to 0.2 mill; minimum tax is $250. Corporations not subject to the franchise tax are subject to a 7.25% income tax.

[t]Minimum tax is $100.

[u](1) 10% tax on allocated net income; or (2) 1.78 mills per dollar on business or investment capital allocated to New York; or (3) 10% of 30% of allocated net income plus certain salaries; or (4) minimum flat rate of $250, whichever is greater.

[v]Minimum tax is $250 or 1.6 mills per dollar of capital stock; for savings institutions, the minimum tax is $250 or 2% of interest credited to depositors in preceding year. A 30% surcharge, less $50,000, is imposed on 1978 tax years.

[w]In addition to the tax shown, North Dakota imposes a privilege tax of 1% on income in excess of $2,000 on corporations not subject to (or in lieu of) personal property taxes.

[x]Plus an additional 2% tax; minimum tax is $50.

[y]Or 5 mills times the value of the taxpayer's issued and outstanding shares of stock as determined according to the total value of capital surplus, undivided profits, and reserves; minimum tax is $50.

Corporation-Return Filing

Given the legislative, judicial, and economic environment suggested by the preceding discussion, administrators face out-of-the-ordinary problems in rigorously implementing corporation income tax laws. The problems begin with determining who must file returns and securing these returns. Most of the established corporations with substantial investments in a state have no desire to indict themselves through failure to file. Large corporations normally have legal departments and tax counselors who are reasonably well acquainted with the state's filing requirements.

Delinquencies will occur most frequently among marginal or bankrupt corporations and corporations which find in the law a basis for exemption. Where corporation counsel advises that the particular interstate corporation has no obligation to file a return, only active identification of all corporations *doing business* within the state by the state's tax officials will bring forth returns (or court cases). The more active the administration of state corporation income taxes, the fewer the temptations for corporation counsel to interpret state regulations on filing requirements and other matters too loosely or generously. Yet even the best-administered state corporation income tax statute permits many honest differences. Either as part of the audit process or in a separate operation state tax officials check for filing conformance by corporations.

FILING OBLIGATIONS

State laws differ as to whether all corporations must file without regard to profit, whether tax-exempt educational or philanthropic corporations must file, and what constitutes "doing business in the state." Whether the state has a corporation net income tax or franchise tax measured by net income determines the filing requirements for most business corporations. States such as California, Oregon, and Wisconsin (table 1), which levy both corporation income and franchise taxes, have the broadest sweep and require proportionately the largest number of corporations to file. Several states require corporations not only to file without regard to whether they had a net profit in particular years but to pay a minimum tax with the return. Requiring all corporations to file has the same merit as requiring individuals to file on the basis of gross income that is as low as the net taxable income. The corporation or individual cannot then make a unilateral determination of no profit. Additionally, this requirement provides the tax department with a continuous record of corporation affairs.

---

[z]Minimum tax is $10.

[aa]Or, for business corporations, the tax is 40¢ per $100 of corporate excess, if greater than the tax computed on net income. For banks, if a greater tax results, the alternative tax is $2.50 per $10,000 of capital stock; minimum tax is $100.

[bb]Minimum tax is $25.

[cc]Minimum tax is $50.

Requiring tax-exempt corporations to file also permits the state to police the tax-exemption claim. Since 1951, California has required tax-exempt corporations to file a simplified "information" return on corporation activities. In its early years this filing requirement turned up a number of corporations that had assumed a tax-exempt status under the corporation's interpretation of the California statutes, an interpretation which was at odds with the tax department. In a few cases, California collected taxes it had been due since 1928, the year of enactment of its corporate franchise tax law.

A new class of corporations has been authorized under California law; and in that state, and in any other state that makes such provisions, the volume of obligated corporate income tax filers will increase. Professional corporations, almost unknown until the 1960s, have expanded rapidly in the last decade. Since 1968, California has allowed physicians, lawyers, and dentists to form corporations; through subsequent amendments, the incorporation privilege has been extended to psychologists, physical therapists, accountants, optometrists, and other licensed professional groups. Some 10,000 professional corporations, more than 80% of which are medical or dental, now file returns in California.

FILING COMPLIANCE

Tax departments have no single source for annual verification of corporation filing compliance that is as complete as wage withholding statements for individuals or the IRS's Individual Master File list. The IRS is currently arranging to provide a tape of its Business Master File to states that request it. (If a state uses the IRS's Federal Employer Identification Number, it will assist computer matching.) Although this master file list will be helpful, it is unlikely to be as complete as the individual list, since corporation addresses do not follow all state business locations. The majority of states require quarterly estimates and payment of corporation income taxes quarterly, but again there is no cross-check as there is with wage withholding statements for individuals.

States normally require corporations doing business in the state to register with a state official, frequently the secretary of state, but some corporations fail to register. And some corporations that are liable for taxes are not required to register. Others that do register may not notify the agency when the corporations cease to do business in the state or cease altogether to do business. Nevertheless, this remains the central registry for tax department review. Beyond the state's central registry of corporations and the IRS's Business Master File tape, tax departments have found workmen's compensation or unemployment compensation records valuable in identifying nonfiling corporations. State or local personal property tax records also may aid in detection.

Wisconsin utilized the state's unemployment compensation employer list in 1976 to check whether any corporations headquartered in another state but subject to Wisconsin unemployment compensation laws had an unfulfilled franchise or sales-and-use tax return filing obligation. As a result of sending a questionnaire to all companies listed for unemployment compensation but not on the Corporation Tax Master List, the state collected within about twelve months an additional $29,000 in franchise taxes (and $24,400 in sales-and-use taxes) at a project cost of $4,000. Not only did the department expect some additional tax assessments but the assessed corporations represented future taxpayers, which made the project doubly valuable.

Usually tax officials must use their own resources to secure the list of corporations that are registered to do business in the state. Georgia's *Statutes,* however, require that the secretary of state provide the income tax division with a list of corporations that are qualified to do business in the state. New York's tax department receives daily a copy of the list of domestic and foreign corporations registering in the state. When Oregon's Department of Revenue receives its monthly listing of newly chartered or registered corporations from the state's Department of Commerce, it not only updates its master corporation list but sends out a "get acquainted letter," a general statement of the corporation's state tax obligations, and a request to be advised of the corporation's accounting period.

Apart from government sources, officials find that financial pages in the leading newspapers in the state provide useful leads to corporations earning income in the state. California's Franchise Tax Board has checked regional and national trade meetings in the state for directories that may list agencies operating in California. Catalogs of construction companies or corporations handling construction machinery also have proved to be a helpful source. Sweet's Catalogue Service, especially those volumes dealing with engineering and industrial building, has proved especially valuable. Not to be overlooked are any construction, building, or other corporations temporarily doing business with the state.

In 1973, an Oregon auditor suggested a miscellany of sources for identifying corporations that should be filing state income tax returns: telephone book yellow page listings, advertisements, financial pages, and general news sections of local and large metropolitan newspapers that report the opening of a sales office, enlarging a plant, the purchase of a local firm by a foreign corporation, and even personnel promotions or transfers.[4] These stories or references could help locate corporations that

[4]Paper entitled "Discovery," by Gordon C. Wells of the Oregon Department of Revenue, presented at the Multistate Tax Commission Seminar on Tax Jurisdiction, Portland, Oregon, April 24-25, 1973. Mr. Wells described a number of fascinating incidents that had resulted in new filers and more corporation income taxes. For example: "One day in the basement of our State Office Building cafeteria, I picked up a soda straw and on the paper cover it listed the company name and the names of several cities, including Portland. I wrote them and learned they had an inventory in Portland and they had never filed returns. They filed returns and paid the tax that was due." However sophisticated a state's compliance and audit measures, human alertness also plays a role.

have not filed or help in actual auditing. This same Oregon auditor recommended *Moody's Industrials* as the number one reference for a listing of companies operating in a state and for the wealth of audit information it contains. In addition, for Western corporations, whether securities, industrial, or general corporations, he recommended *Walker's Manual* (published in San Francisco). Trade magazines are another helpful source.

Corporation Auditing

ORGANIZATION

Tax departments generally organize corporation income tax office audit functions apart from office audit activities for individual returns or for other corporation taxes. Where a state such as New York has organized along functional lines, the audit division still shows tax specialization in its bureau (chart 19). Although field audit operations may include corporation income and sales taxes or even individual income taxes, specialization in corporation income tax work remains common. Both timing and the nature of the audit make full integration of corporation sales and income tax auditing difficult. New York and California tax officials told the author that either they receive no complaints from corporations about duplicate audits or the complaints are not serious. Tax officials in several states stressed the complexity of corporate income tax auditing and the differences in timing, etc., that often make joint audits for multiple taxes impractical.

DESK AUDITS

Selection

Most states restrict preaudit checks of corporation returns to general verification of compliance in filing, an arithmetic check of calculations on the return, and verification that the quarterly payments (if required) balance with the total tax due. States that have adopted current payment of corporation income taxes through quarterly declarations have presumably reduced tax delinquency, reduced their cash flow problems, and provided equity with individuals under payroll withholding or quarterly declarations.

Writing in 1975, New York's director of corporation tax commented:

> In the recent past, during a normal three-year audit cycle, all corporations are audited, either by a screening process (57%), by "Folder" or desk audits (42%), or by field audit (1%). However, recent changes to improve computer processing and analysis of returns, plus increased audit staff, will allow us to substitute computer for manual screening, produce greater in-depth desk audits, and an increase in field audits.[5]

[5] Letter to the author from William A. Craven, then Director of Corporation Tax, New York Department of Taxation and Finance, September 15, 1975.

Minnesota's corporation tax examiners follow a preaudit program each year that reviews all corporation returns to check particular points and to classify the returns primarily according to size and interstate and intrastate business. They compare opening inventory with closing inventory on the previous year's return; check each corporation's income for the previous years; consider gross income and net profit from the point of view of type of business operation; check the relationship of a given corporation to its affiliates, especially for possible diversions of income; reconcile surpluses and verify that proper items have been included in taxable income; review deductions; compare federal income tax payments claimed with the size of the previous year's income; review balance sheet items and capital gains; and check contributions and dividends-received credits for agreement with state law.

Minnesota's examiners automatically select for further review all returns from corporations receiving out-of-state income and other returns in which the preaudit check has turned up discrepancies. Evidence of federal audit adjustment, either through a return or a federal audit report in the file or a history of difficulty with the taxpayer, will flag a return for further attention. Finally, examiners select some returns from particular classes as determined by office policy and a few other returns on the basis of intuition. Minnesota's audit system concentrates on selecting domestic corporations one year and foreign corporations the next year for a two-year work cycle.

As in the case of individual returns, the number of field auditors is the decisive factor in determining selection of returns for field review. In recent years, states belonging to the Multistate Tax Compact have been able to extend their out-of-state field auditing somewhat. Field audit assignments stem from (1) the complexity of questions raised; (2) questions of corporate understanding or application of state allocation formulas; (3) doubts about whether the return reflects the true accounts of the corporation; and (4) policy decisions to undertake field investigations of all returns falling into particular income, geographic, or business classes.

Resources

Despite the complexity of corporation returns and the frequent desirability of examining actual accounts, office review time can be well spent. State laws, state rules and regulations, special office policy statements, and legal abstracts are valuable aids. A good reference shelf would include such items as *Standard & Poor's Corporation Records;* Prentice-Hall's *Capital Adjustments Service; Moody's Industrials;* the Commerce Clearing House's *Capital Changes Reports;* Robert D. Fisher's *Manual of Valuable and Worthless Securities;* Dun and Bradstreet's *The Reference Book,* a guide to average gross-to-net ratios; professional trade journals; etc.[6]

[6] Some of these same references are useful in verifying corporation filing compliance and some have value in auditing personal income tax returns.

Fortune magazine and its appraisal of corporations also can be of assistance.

States file their corporation returns chronologically, and frequently a single folder will hold five or more years' returns. Some states have not destroyed any corporation returns since inauguration of their corporation income tax. This historical continuity of returns permits easy checking of closing and opening balances, treatment of reserves, handling of depreciation, and other related accounts from one year's return to the next. The tax department also receives federal audit reports from the IRS and quite possibly from the corporations themselves.

Process

Typically, desk audits of corporation returns follow the same general pattern as Minnesota's preaudit. Desk auditors use all available office resources at the time of their examination to determine whether correspondence or a field audit is warranted. Detailed attention is given to the internal consistency of the return, as well as to the consistency of returns over time. Every auditor watches for evidence that items such as capital gains or depreciation have been handled properly in accordance with state law. Available federal returns and federal audit reports are checked. (New York's recent experience indicates that about half the corporations reporting to New York show IRS revenue agent reports.) The IRS's audit report for a corporation doing business within only one state often serves as a substitute for detailed state attention to the company. In the case of the interstate or multinational corporation, the federal audit report may affect the tax base reported or may alert state auditors to other possible changes.

IRS audits of corporations are of greatest assistance to states that have adopted the same general definition of net income as the national government (table 26). California has adopted part of the federal corporation return form in an attempt to improve the quality of reporting and to decrease the burden on the corporation. The state regularly incorporates the federal return in the first thirty-two items of its return. Some other states have done the same.

No matter how closely state laws conform to federal statutes, however, the usefulness of federal audit reports on interstate corporations still ceases just short of interstate apportionment of income. In applying a state's apportionment formula, corporation auditors utilize all information presented with the return but then must resort to correspondence or field auditing for any unanswered questions. And these questions will abound if the desk auditor is knowledgeable and carries out a critical review. The absence of a uniform apportionment formula for all the states plus differences in state laws relative to corporation allocation of income provide innumerable opportunities for honest mistakes, resolution of doubtful questions in the taxpayer's favor, and outright manipulation of income. Desk auditing often reveals misinterpretations and/or discrepancies.

CORRESPONDENCE AUDITS

For the most part, corporation correspondence audits consist of requests for clarification of certain items (where the corporation's report suggests inconsistencies or omissions), requests for a copy of federal audit report, and questions on the corporation's particular method of apportionment or income allocation. Since many states undertake little, if any, corporation field auditing, they must rely on correspondence to bring in answers to questions raised during office review. (The complexity of corporation accounts makes the telephone less valuable here than for personal income tax returns.) As in the area of personal income returns, success will depend upon the nature of the questions raised, the clarity of the letters, the regularity of follow-up, and the application of penalties for refusal to comply. The corporation's correspondent normally will have a reasonable knowledge of accounting as well as detailed books from which to gather answers to tax department questions. Without a state field audit, or at least a federal audit report, the tax department must very largely accept both the corporation's word for reported items and its knowledge of the application of the tax law.

FIELD AUDITS

"'It is unfortunate, but true, that some of our corporate citizens have not been entirely honest.' As that comment by an Internal Revenue Service official partly suggests, our nation's corporations have bribed, kicked back, illegally contributed and engaged in sundry other illicit acts to gain business."[7] These words from the April 25, 1977, *Wall Street Journal* should convince any doubter among state tax administrators that corporation returns require attention.[8] Chicanery, ignorance, and self-interested interpretations of state statutes, as well as honest differences of opinion over statutory intent, can be uncovered only if a substantial number of corporations are field audited on some regular cycle. Unfortunately, a judgment made twenty years ago, that "inadequate field auditing of corporation returns prevails," cannot be modified. The volume of returns, the volume of business, and even the tax rates in some states have increased, but there is no evidence of a substantial increase in general efforts to develop an energetic in-state or out-of-state professional field audit force.

Field audits should play a much more significant role in determining the adequacy of the overall audit for corporation income taxes than they do in the review of individual income taxes. No checks comparable to matching

[7]Sanford L. Jacobs, "'Eleven Questions' Get Results, Stir Company Ire," *Wall Street Journal*, April 25, 1977.

[8]Legend has it that there once was a New York corporation income tax director with such faith in the integrity of American corporation officials that he thought any real investigation insulting. Basically he and his auditors checked for filing and then reverently placed the returns in their appropriate dockets. However extreme this may sound, some state tax departments still appear to act on such a premise by doing little or no corporate auditing.

individual withholding returns or other numerous possible information sources can be made in the review of corporation returns. Only regular audits at the home offices of corporations can provide the needed verification of most corporation income tax returns. This means field auditing, often out-of-state field auditing. Corporation field auditing also requires the most highly trained and experienced auditors the tax department can afford to hire and is able to recruit. Corporation accounts are complex, and most corporations of any size employ well-trained accountants, comptrollers, and tax counselors who necessarily know the corporation's business better than the state tax auditors who come in for a few days or at most for a couple of weeks or so annually. States with qualified auditors who are allowed adequate time for examination of corporation accounts and records find field auditing eminently worthwhile. States whose auditors have had experience with specific types of corporations, e.g., oil, are particularly fortunate. Even the less-qualified state auditor who spends only a short time in a corporation headquarters office is likely to pick up additional taxes far in excess of his salary and expenses. The auditor's presence reminds the corporation of its state tax responsibility, and the auditor may provide information or interpretations the accountants need in order to develop and file correct tax returns with the state. Any given field audit should cover all open tax years. Details of state laws play a role in the complexity of required audit reviews and may determine the feasibility of joint audits of corporations for withholding, sales, and income taxes.

A significant state action in the field of corporation auditing was initiated in 1966 and resulted in the formation of an interstate compact that in turn produced the Multistate Tax Commission for joint audit of major multistate corporation accounts to determine the accuracy of income and sales tax returns filed with member states.[9] Tax administrators in states that have joined in the compact express satisfaction despite continuing problems (see chapter 9). Oregon estimates that it has collected "about $500,000 from several corporations as a result of MTC audits."[10]

In 1978, fifteen of the forty-four states with corporation income taxes remained outside the compact. It is possible that the favorable decision by the U.S. Supreme Court (1978) in the United States Steel Corporation case challenging the auditing powers of the Multistate Tax Commission will bring more states into the compact. At the moment the commission is more a symbol of hope for the adoption of audit activities by the fifteen

[9]For about four years in the 1940s, several of the states, with the special blessing of the National Association of Tax Administrators, attempted cooperative out-of-state sales tax auditing. Unfortunately, only one or two of the cooperating states were willing to assign auditors full time to develop a consistent program and the cooperative agreement lapsed. See Vernon M. Ekstrom, "Interstate Cooperation in Income Tax Administration, in *Proceedings of the National Tax Association, 1946* (Sacramento, Calf.: National Tax Association, 1947), pp. 111-17. See also chapter 9 for several bibliographical references on the Multistate Tax Commission.

[10]Oregon, Department of Revenue, *Biennial Report, 1974-76* (Salem, 1976), p. 6.

nonmember states than an effective audit force. It has suffered from the deficiencies of member states that lack experienced corporation auditors and it has required greater contributions of resources from a few member states such as California, Michigan, and Oregon. These states have continued their own sophisticated corporation auditing programs while loaning one or more auditors to the commission's audit force and in other ways giving aid and support. The Multistate Tax Commission has secured national press attention from time to time in the *New York Times,* the *Washington Post,* the *Wall Street Journal,* and regional newspapers such as the *Milwaukee Journal,* etc. (see chapter 9).[11]

The nonmember states include such leaders as Massachusetts, Minnesota, New York, and Wisconsin, which have long levied corporation income taxes and maintained fairly effective field operations. They apparently have feared that the quality of auditing the commission could develop would not meet their own standards, have feared losing some independence, and at times have feared the possibility of federal takeover either in placing constraints on the states in their taxation of corporations or in federal auditing of state taxes.

The Field Audit Process

Unlike auditors of individual tax returns, corporation tax field examiners generally can expect to find full accounting records. Verification is in large part a matter of legal and accounting analysis. Where the IRS auditor or auditors have examined the company's accounts, most state administrators believe it is unnecessary for the state to review the net income thus established except in cases where there are specific differences in the federal and state laws. States may deliberately plan auditing programs for interstate corporations so that state examiners will check corporation accounts after the IRS has made its audit. Attention is then concentrated on the corporation's accounting under the state's apportionment formula. Review and auditing for this purpose alone require time and audit experience. As stated in a recent New Jersey annual report:

> The auditing process is becoming increasingly more difficult and complex due to greater utilization of computer reporting by businesses and increased number of conglomerate type corporations. In addition, changes in methods used by corporations and other businesses in day-to-day financing of their operations, such as lease-back arrangements increases the complexity of audits, and of necessity results in an increase of the time spent on each audit.[12]

[11] For example, the "Business News" section of the *Milwaukee Journal* for September 18, 1977, carried a four-column article with the large-type headline, "Corporations Target of States." It was an AP story with a local angle.

[12] New Jersey's auditors now audit for all state taxes when in corporation offices, and the state's annual report indicated additional assessments per auditor of $168,856 in 1975 and $212,752 in 1976! See New Jersey, Department of Revenue, *Annual Report, 1976 Fiscal Year* (Trenton), p. 42.

The general reliability of accounts—apart from technical interpretations of each state's laws—may depend on the degree of independence of the company's accounting staff. Careful audits are often needed of closely held corporations, often relatively small, where there are temptations (1) to bypass the corporate tax by padding owner-operator's salaries and (2) to charge the corporation with essentially personal deduction items. Again, if the IRS has audited such a company, the state's responsibility may be diminished.

Out-of-State Auditing

Although individual income tax auditing seldom requires examination of out-of-state records, the states find that the headquarters and main accounts of many of their major interstate corporations are located outside the state. Out-of-state auditing is only one facet of corporation field auditing, but it is characterized by two differences in emphasis from in-state field auditing. First, the immediate cost in manpower and travel expenses exceeds that for in-state field auditing. Second, the need to field audit corporations with out-of-state headquarters is often more acute than that for domestic corporations. Several state administrators expressed to the author the belief that a corporation's tax man, unless he is called to account, has a tendency to overlook differences in state laws and at a point of doubt is likely to follow the federal law or the law of the state in which the corporation is headquartered. To the extent that states utilize the federal base as a starting point, the federal law is applicable (table 26). But proper apportionment (and income allocation) of the formula factors depends on detailed knowledge of the state's statutes and their interpretation in the courts and by the tax agency.

Apart from the auditing carried out by the Multistate Tax Commission, few states regularly engage in out-of-state auditing. California, Georgia, Massachusetts, Minnesota, New York, Oregon, and Wisconsin are among the states that have done so within the last decade. Some out-of-state field examinations would more accurately be called "checks" than "audits." California, Massachusetts, New York, Oregon, and Wisconsin have found it desirable to station auditors full time in distant cities. Other states send auditors to New York, Chicago, or other major corporation headquarter cities for varying periods of time.

States differ on the question of the desirability of maintaining an out-of-state office. The out-of-state office provides a base of operation, may reduce costs, and gives the one or more auditors stationed there better working space than a hotel room provides. In the case of California, for example, the cost of traveling may exceed that of maintaining a more permanent office in New York City. Yet field auditors who visit corporation headquarters for a period of weeks and then return to headquarters may keep in better touch with the decisions and policies of the home office. Which choice is preferable varies with the geographic location of the corporations and the states. New York has sent teams of auditors to corporation headquarters located outside the state. California has found it desirable to locate small offices in New York City and Chicago. The changing location of corporation headquarters may affect future New York State decisions, and California may at some future date find it desirable to set up an office in Houston, Texas, for example. California has shared its New York and Chicago (as well as its Los Angeles) offices with Oregon auditors stationed outside that state. Wisconsin has generally maintained out-of-state offices in New York, Chicago, and Minneapolis. Massachusetts has a New York office. All these states also send one or more auditors to other cities where corporation headquarters are located. The Multistate Tax Commission has offices in Chicago and New York City, plus its headquarters in Boulder, Colorado.

Productivity of Audit Programs

Strictly in terms of direct revenue, corporation audit activities produce more revenue per dollar of administrative costs than do individual audit activities. This is true despite the fact that corporation auditing frequently requires higher salaries for more specialized skills, more time, and greater travel costs. Tables 27 and 28 provide some evidence of the profitability of corporation office and field auditing by selected states. The data are not strictly comparable because hardly any two states divide up functions in the same way or report in the same fashion. Even if the data were comparable on such grounds, they would not be fully comparable because of differences in tax base, formula, rates, and in the characteristics of the states' economies. Even a state's tradition of strict or casual enforcement or auditing of its corporation income tax will presumably affect audit productivity. Thus the records of these selected states must be weighed against such differences, and few comparisons are valid.

As in the case of the personal income tax, California presents substantial data in its annual *Operations Report.* Table 27 provides information on the number of corporation returns examined. Table 28 reflects the productivity of these audit examinations in net assessments. In the six fiscal years noted, California collected bank and corporation income taxes in the amounts of \$661 million, \$866 million, \$1.1 billion, \$1.3 billion, \$1.3 billion, and \$1.6 billion. For fiscal year 1977, then, total net audit assessments represented 5.6% of total collections that year.

The Massachusetts Department of Revenue provided field audit and federal change productivity figures as follows:

Corporation Income Tax	1973 ($)	1974 ($)	1975 ($)	1976 ($)	1977 ($)	1978 ($)
Field Audit	—	—	1,070	3,728	2,539	6,426
N.Y. Office	NA	NA	1,423	4,241	8,600	9,371
Federal Change	NA	5,760	5,756	6,235	5,448	4,215
Total	—	5,760	8,249	14,204	16,587	20,012

Minnesota collected $196.4 million in corporation income taxes in 1976 and gained a total of $17.4 million in audit assessments for a ratio of 8%, unusually high as a glance at table 29 will show. The table reflects Minnesota's corporation audit assessments for 1972-76.

Montana reported for 1974, a typical year, collections of $15.6 million in corporation license (income) taxes and additional audit revenues of $2.6 million, or 16.7% of total collections. The corporation license bureau employed an average of 10.5 people that year, 6 of whom were auditors, and the department urged an "orderly increase in manpower for field audit."

New York reported total corporation income and franchise taxes for fiscal year 1977 of $1.3 billion and additional audit assessments of $39.3 million, or 3% of total collections in that year. Table 30 provides further data on the productivity of New York's corporation income and franchise tax audit activities. The reader will note that IRS revenue agent reports produced roughly 20% of the total audit assessments in most years.

North Carolina, with total corporation income tax collections of $204.3 million and audit assessments of $5.9 million in 1977, showed a ratio of 2.9%. Table 31 provides data on the productivity of the state's audit efforts for the years 1972-77. It will be noted that additional assessments from IRS revenue agent reports have usually equaled or exceeded the state's corporation audit assessments and thus make the exchange very valuable to North Carolina.

Oregon reported corporation income and franchise tax collections of $125.5 million in 1978, and its corporation audit assessments totaled $3.9

TABLE 27
California: Bank and Corporation Tax Examinations for Fiscal Years 1972-77

	No. of cases examined				
			Field		
Fiscal Year	*Desk audits*	*Federal audit reports*	*In-state*	*Out-of-state*	*Mathematical verification*
1971/72	144,844	5,675	17,519	5,653	40,435
1972/73	139,286	5,665	15,675	6,114	53,061
1973/74	137,523	7,522	18,348	7,636	244,406
1974/75	154,238	10,280	16,435	6,886	238,001
1975/76	136,171	13,297	11,695	5,273	253,365
1976/77	193,613	8,969	11,615	6,121	256,833

Source: California Franchise Tax Board, *Operations Report* (Sacramento, fiscal years indicated), exhibit B-2, col. 4.

TABLE 28
California: Bank and Corporation Tax Net Audit Assessments for Fiscal Years 1972-77

Fiscal Year	Office audit assessments ($)	Federal audit reports ($)	Field audit assessments In-state ($)	Field audit assessments Out-of-state ($)	Mathematical verification ($)
1971/72	2,511,671	9,082,347	12,031,092	21,512,548	2,061,269
1972/73	4,555,144	15,800,098	10,857,715	19,753,848	1,602,558
1973/74	7,092,773	16,636,820	23,090,676	31,516,825	3,882,915
1974/75	5,343,925	8,804,884	18,759,339	41,863,784	3,571,610
1975/76	5,894,752	14,366,621	24,171,038	25,852,594	6,060,358
1976/77	5,279,714	14,281,190	25,886,101	34,808,956	11,014,301

Source: California, Franchise Tax Board, *Operations Report* (Sacramento, fiscal years indicated), exhibit B-1, col. 5.

TABLE 29
Corporation Income Tax Audit Productivity—Minnesota

Fiscal Year	Corporation income taxes collected (million $)	Type of audit	No. of assessments	Value of assessments ($)
1972	112.4	Office	3,851	2,618,730
		Field	420	3,228,743
		RAR	567	1,223,567
1973	170.7	Office	3,657	2,787,719
		Field	658	2,822,575
		RAR	466	1,229,747
1974	190.3	Office	3,449	3,528,170
		Field	403	3,695,592
		RAR	314	862,892
1975	195.9	Office	4,087	4,263,447
		Field	463	3,216,547
		RAR	482	1,032,059
1976	196.4	Office	3,489	3,807,373
		Field	452	11,927,433
		RAR	706	1,665,249

Sources: Column 1 from table 7, U.S., Department of Commerce, Bureau of the Census, *State Government Finances in 1972* (Washington, D.C.: Government Printing Office, 1973), and volumes for succeeding years. Other data supplied to the author by the Minnesota Department of Revenue in a letter dated October 13, 1978.
Note: RAR = revenue agent report.

million, or 3.1% of collections in that year. Table 32 indicates the state's corporation audit productivity in the fiscal years 1975-78.

Wisconsin collected $251 million in corporation income taxes in 1977 and reported additional audit assessments of $9.7 million, or 3.8% of total collections. The ratio in 1978 was 4.5%. The state paid the equivalent of 10.8 office auditors and 30.5 field auditors in 1978. Table 33 provides further data.

Repeating earlier warnings, the tables for seven of the states with corporation income taxes are not comparable. They do illustrate, however,

TABLE 30
Corporation Income Tax Audit Productivity—New York

Fiscal year ending March 31	Corporation income taxes collected (million $)	Type of audit	No. of assessments	Value of assessments (million $)
1972	781.0	Office	50,188	21.2
		Field	589	5.8
		RAR	7,128	5.2
1973	874.6	Office	34,330	14.6
		Field	512	15.1
		RAR	5,704	6.1
1974	874.4	Office	21,601	14.2
		Field	438	11.9
		RAR	4,972	4.5
1975	967.4	Office	27,611	14.7
		Field	502	8.4
		RAR	5,154	6.3
1976	1,132.7	Office	16,865	18.9
		Field	595	18.6
		RAR	5,210	2.9
1977	1,295.0	Office	140,308	17.0
		Field	739	22.3
		RAR	NA	NA
1978	1,344.6	Office	96,539	26.4
		Field	58	30.9
		RAR	NA	NA

Sources: Column 1 from table 7, U.S., Department of Commerce, Bureau of the Census, *State Government Finances in 1972* (Washington, D.C.: Government Printing Office, 1973), and volumes for succeeding years. Other data supplied to the author by Willian A. Craven in letter of March 30, 1977, and by Gayle Hatch in letter of October 23, 1978.
Note: RAR = revenue agent report.

the types of audit productivity data currently gathered. Definitions and types of information differ, and it would be inaccurate to make any general comparisons. Again, the data suggest that auditing efforts produce a substantial return on budgeted resources and that federal audit information contributes importantly to assessments: California gained 15.7% of its collections in 1977 thereby; Massachusetts gained 24% of its 1978 field collections in this way; Minnesota, 9% in 1976, although in most previous years it had averaged about 18%; New York gained 7% in 1976 (closer to 20% in previous years); North Carolina attributed 49% and Oregon 7.8% of 1978 tax collections to the federal audit exchange; and Wisconsin in 1978 gained 6.5% (though in 1977 the gain from federal audit information was 15.5% of assessments).

Special Investigations

Income tax compliance and auditing cover a number of different problem areas, each requiring specialized knowledge and techniques. Personal

TABLE 31
Corporation Income Tax Audit Productivity—North Carolina

Fiscal year	*Corporation income taxes collected (million $)*	*No. of auditors*	*Type of audit*	*No. of assessments*	*Annual value of assessments ($)*
1972	123.5	12	RAR	1,106	1,867,110
			Office and Field	888	1,195,660
1973	139.2	13	RAR	1,341	1,962,529
			State	1,065	1,563,041
1974	153.3	11	RAR	1,393	2,649,417
			State	1,126	2,111,412
1975	166.4	11	RAR	1,339	2,628,106
			State	1,425	2,337,548
1976	156.7	11	RAR	1,327	2,911,726
			State	1,443	3,006,687
1977	204.3	11	RAR	1,402	2,959,926
			State	1,556	2,963,754

Sources: Column 1 from table 7, U.S., Department of Commerce, Bureau of the Census, *State Government Finances in 1972* (Washington, D.C.: Government Printing Office, 1973), and volumes for succeeding years; 1977 figure from table 3, U.S., Department of Commerce, Bureau of the Census, *State Tax Collections in 1977* (Washington, D.C.: Government Printing Office, 1978). Other data provided by H. C. Stansbury, Director of the Tax Research Division, North Carolina Department of Revenue, in letter to the author dated September 8, 1978.
Note: RAR = revenue agent report.

income tax return review and auditing differ from corporation return review and auditing. The characteristics of personal income tax returns for salaried individuals differ from those of returns for the independent business or professional individual. Corporation returns for the small, closely held corporation differ significantly from the multistate, multinational corporation conglomerate. The oil corporation differs in its accounting and returns from the manufacturing corporation. And farm corporation returns differ from the returns for other corporations and from the individual farmer's return. Tax auditor specialization depends on the number of auditors and the number of returns received and audited in any of these areas. Taxpayers who deliberately fail to file or file fraudulent returns create another area of audit specialization. Fraud may, of course, occur in returns from any taxpayer classification. Wage-earning and salaried individuals and individuals or corporations in any occupation or business may file intentionally incomplete or misleading returns, but the incidence of fraud appears to run higher among taxpayers involved in illegal pursuits or in businesses on the fringes of the law.[13]

[13]The difficulties of establishing total personal or corporate income in any given state (or the number of such taxpayers) are multiplied in the case of fraud if we presume that "underground" income is the greatest source of fraudulent returns, for "underground" income does not appear in standard econometric models that attempt to establish personal income.

TABLE 32
Corporation Income Tax Audit Productivity—Oregon

Fiscal year	Corporation income taxes collected (million $)	Type of audit	No. of assessments	Value of assessments ($)
1972	40.6	Office		
		Field	NA	NA
		RAR		
1973	51.1	Office		
		Field	NA	NA
		RAR		
1974	85.7	Office		
		Field	NA	NA
		RAR		
1975	90.7	Office	2,434	1,302,099
		Field	1,037	3,557,683
		RAR	573	383,202
1976	66.7	Office	2,614	1,266,635
		Field	1,327	2,983,269
		RAR	664	448,404
1977	91.1	Office	1,733	895,648
		Field	1,362	2,202,949
		RAR	439	247,641
1978	125.5	Office	1,714	957,985
		Field	1,094	2,499,617
		RAR	630	542,253

Sources: Column 1 from table 7, U.S., Department of Commerce, Bureau of the Census, *State Government Finances in 1972* (Washington, D.C.: Government Printing Office, 1973), and volumes for succeeding years; 1977 figure from table 3, U.S., Department of Commerce, Bureau of the Census, *State Tax Collections in 1977* (Washington, D.C.: Government Printing Office, 1978). Other data supplied by John J. Lobdell, Director of the Oregon Department of Revenue, in letter to the author dated September 12, 1978.
Notes: It should be recalled that the number of auditors shown on the individual income tax table also have responsibility for corporation income tax auditing: 130 in 1972; 134 in 1973; 145 in 1974; 144 in 1975; 140 in 1976; 141 in 1977; and 143 in 1978.
RAR = revenue agent report.

Citizens, and the courts, often view tax fraud (especially tax fraud by otherwise upstanding individuals or businesses) as a different category of crime from burglary or crimes of force and as a different category from embezzlement. Sometimes it appears to be a game of trying to beat the government in a test of wits—with the reward going to the victor—rather than a moral issue of breaking the law. Yet the other side of the coin of politically unpopular stricter tax enforcement may be the politically unpopular tax increase needed to supplant the lost revenue from undetected carelessness, negligence, or fraud in taxpayer reporting. When the governor and legislature of New York in 1977 provided significant additional administrative funds to the Department of Taxation and Finance, several administrators (and the public?) interpreted the appropriation as a directive for stricter enforcement to avoid the necessity of raising taxes.[14]

[14]One ongoing argument among tax administrators, legislators, and citizens concerns whether a proportionately greater enforcement effort should be concentrated on "criminals" or whether all taxpayers who engage in tax fraud are equal. Is the tax fraud, tax fraud

TABLE 33
Corporation Income Tax Audit Productivity—Wisconsin

Fiscal year	Corporation income taxes collected (million $)	Type of audit	No. of assessments	Value of assessments ($)
1972	116.8	Office	2,081	1,133,508
		Office RAR	559	484,727
		Field	193	4,832,802
		Field RAR	8	297,128
1973	136.1	Office	2,221	1,172,102
		Office RAR	314	294,605
		Field	201	5,121,234
		Field RAR	14	85,509
1974	160.3	Office	2,173	1,976,156
		Office RAR	300	290,988
		Field	210	6,695,084
		Field RAR	9	117,934
1975	153.4	Office	1,427	1,720,443
		Office RAR	282	330,627
		Field	231	8,999,126
		Field RAR	5	22,688
1976	190.4	Office	1,100	1,797,784
		Office RAR	303	352,050
		Field	269	8,540,844
		Field RAR	15	113,474
1977	251.7	Office	1,235	1,347,774
		Office RAR	738	847,210
		Field	256	6,818,936
		Field RAR	35	676,076
1978	284.9	Office	1,341	1,510,321
		Office RAR	1,074	646,639
		Field	239	10,585,210
		Field RAR	48	200,957

Sources: Column 1 from table 7, U.S., Department of Commerce, Bureau of the Census, *State Government Finances in 1972* (Washington, D.C.: Government Printing Office, 1973), and volumes for succeeding years; 1977 figure from table 3, U.S., Department of Commerce, Bureau of the Census, *State Tax Collections in 1977* (Washington, D.C.: Government Printing Office, 1978). Other data was provided the author by the Wisconsin Department of Revenue, October 19, 1978.
Note: RAR = revenue agent report.

IRS officials share the layman's view that illegal pursuits have increased in the last decade, as has income tax fraud. The quotation from the *Wall Street Journal* cited on p. 211 suggests an increase in "fraud," or at least its close cousin, by corporations. The growth in population, growth in wealth, "Watergate," individual decisions as to which government activities a person's taxes may be used for, and a seemingly greater casualness toward

without regard to who commits it? Always the Al Capone tax case is cited or the recent increase in tax convictions of narcotic dealers is noted. There is reality to the issue, as to all questions of comparisons between "white-collar" crime and other crime, yet it can also be a red herring. If deterrence is the major objective of fraud investigations, then selected cases will bring in malefactors from all professions and businesses as well as those engaged in illegal activities. Yet proportionately, we presume the latter will show a heavier incidence of tax fraud.

moral values of the past suggest some of the explanations for increased income tax fraud. And few states have responded. No states have ever approached the IRS's intelligence effort, and that is inadequate in the minds of knowledgeable IRS officials.

Organization

The IRS recognized from the start that taxpayer fraud requires different audit techniques than do the standard tax returns of individuals or corporations. In any given year, close to a dozen state income tax departments have a separately organized intelligence, special investigations, or fraud unit. Half a dozen states have carried on a special investigations operation more or less continuously for several decades. State administrators differ on the need for a special bureau and on the question of whether the regular audit bureau can adequately identify and handle fraud cases. The economic, political, and social characteristics of each state, together with statutory definitions of fraud, including whether the statute makes deliberate nonfiling or deliberate misreporting of income or expenditures a felony or a misdemeanor, condition the decision for organizational arrangements (table 11). Not all states make the division between civil fraud and criminal fraud for taxpayers and their returns that the IRS does.[15] IRS intelligence handles only the latter, whereas the audit division handles civil fraud.

A 1950 statement by a New York official still states the case well for a special investigations unit:

> Because of the complex nature of the cases and the large amount of money at stake, we have found it desirable to handle fraud through a separate Bureau of Special Investigations within the Department of Taxation and Finance. In this bureau, men trained in criminal as well as in civil aspects of the law concentrate their efforts on the most serious type of tax violator, usually an individual engaged in an illegal enterprise. We have found that it is good administrative economy to segregate this type of evader from the great mass of lesser violators.[16]

National activities inspired the formation of the New York and California special investigations units. Thomas E. Dewey, Special Prosecutor for New York State in the mid-1930s, believed that the state, like the federal government, might find income tax prosecution an aid to prosecution of

[15] The term "fraud" has a very precise meaning under federal law, but the meaning differs among the states. In layman's language, criminal fraud is distinguished from civil fraud depending on the evidence of the degree of intent, conspiracy to commit fraud, and sometimes on the amount and period of time. Civil fraud is also distinguished from "negligence" and other terms identifying taxpayer behavior, e.g., failure to file, incomplete reporting, or errors in reporting. Some states have not provided criminal fraud penalties under their income tax statutes, but may prosecute taxpayers under general fraud provisions of the statutes.

[16] From an address by Spencer E. Bates, President of the New York Tax Commission, to a 1950 meeting of tax administrators, reprinted in *Annual Report of the State Tax Commission, 1950/51* (Albany: Williams Press, 1951), p. 142.

criminals. He sought the assistance of Governor Lehman and Tax Commissioner Graves. The informal cooperation continued among the special prosecutor, the governor, and the tax commissioner for almost a year before the public learned of their efforts. Thereupon the state's tax department developed its own formal organization for continuance of such investigations.

In 1950, California decided that the disclosure by the Kefauver Committee of rackets and criminal activities in the state warranted additional efforts from the income tax administration. The Franchise Tax Board recommended in its 1950 *Annual Report* that a special fraud unit be set up, and the legislature accepted the suggestion and provided the necessary appropriations in 1951.

Michigan established its special bureau in about 1970, initially to investigate sales tax fraud, and later to cover income tax fraud as well. Colorado, Massachusetts, Minnesota, Oregon, and Wisconsin are other states that have had special investigations units. With or without a special unit, state tax departments may engage in special investigations and criminal fraud prosecutions. State tax departments, either because they lack the manpower or because of the limited penalties provided under their statutes, may advise IRS officials of suspected cases. Rarely, but still occasionally, the IRS provides information on criminal investigations to a state.

New York, with the oldest formal investigative unit, has the largest bureau of special investigations among state tax departments.[17] The bureau's largest operation is in New York City and its director reports to the executive deputy commissioner. (The audit division reports to the administrative director, or a line below the executive deputy commissioner.) Professional investigators require accounting training and experience, knowledge of the appropriate tax law and criminal code, and the skills of a policeman and detective. They may be recruited from outside the tax department (Alaska, New York, California, and other states welcome former FBI or IRS intelligence officials) or from the collections or audit division of the department.

WORK ASSIGNMENTS AND METHODS

Although each state's special investigations unit receives referrals from the general audit division, where officials identify suspicious returns, other sources must be developed. A New York bureau director once listed case sources as investigations conducted by other agencies, e.g., by attorneys-general, district attorneys, special commissions; anonymous tips and other communications from private individuals; publicity accorded to police cases

[17]The IRS has approximately 2,000 agents in its intelligence division, whereas most of the states have a half-dozen or fewer. Such figures alone dramatize the difference in attention. Eventually, of course, most states can collect some of the taxes due, if not always prosecute the offender, on the basis of IRS-supplied data.

and lawsuits; the IRS; and prosecutions by federal agencies. Further, companies in any industry are so interlaced with the same suppliers and customers that investigation of one opens an entire field, and similar interrelationships between different industries are frequently found. Taxpayers caught in violations often furnish information about other violators. The California director stressed the desire of district attorneys to investigate individuals thought to be involved in economic crime. Frequently the district attorney sees an income tax investigation as the best opportunity to gain information and prosecution and so advises officials of the Franchise Tax Board.

Whereas the auditor has a tax return to examine, the investigator may have to begin with only a question. Depending on the type of case, the agent may ask the taxpayer to turn over all his accounts and records or may generate inquiries with others who may know something about the taxpayer's work or living habits. If state or federal income tax returns exist, these will be examined. During the review of a business, every check, invoice, and entry, and sometimes computations, are checked; unusual transactions are verified; endorsements are carefully scrutinized and bank accounts verified. The investigator communicates with vendors and vendees to check the accuracy and completeness of records. Accountants' work papers may be examined. And at some point the taxpayer is interviewed and may be questioned under oath on any new income items disclosed, an unexplained incomplete entry, the absence of records, or apparent living expenses beyond the income reported. Many times the lack of accounts or the lack of full accounts necessitates extensive use of the net worth device to approximate income received in given periods.

ACCOMPLISHMENTS AND EVALUATION

Few states have maintained investigative units for a long period of years; therefore both historical and comparative statistics are limited. Since state tax investigative units, except in California, are responsible for more than individual and corporation income taxes, most of the statistics on staff and on investigation results are further limited. And there is no way to establish what would have been accomplished by a regular audit if no specialized unit had existed.

The California Franchise Tax Board (FTB) employs nine special agents in the major population centers of the state. "The primary objective is to maximize voluntary compliance with the state income tax laws by enforcement of the criminal statutes."[18] During 1976, six prosecutions were successfully concluded and seventeen cases were pending in the judicial system at year's end. Special agents had investigated eighty-six other cases during the year, including twenty cases involving internal department matters. The

[18]California, Franchise Tax Board, *Annual Report, 1976* (Sacramento), p. 15.

following figures provide a summary of the department's special investigations activities from January 1, 1968, through December 31, 1977:[19]

Preliminary investigations completed (Prior to withholding on 1/1/72, investigators examined many source documents to develop cases for investigation potential. These have been discontinued.)	7,885
Assigned cases completed	786
Prosecutions completed (129 cases for tax evasion, 4 multiple filing fraud, 2 prosecutions of employees for theft, 3 penal code violations affecting the department)	138
Cases that went to trial	8
Violation-of-probation hearing completed	3
Administrative hearings completed (Investigation of complaints during 1968 and 1969 of FTB impersonation calls determined that 4 private investigative agencies were involved. Following hearings before the Bureau of Private Investigators and Adjustors, the licenses of 3 were revoked.)	3
Revenue (tax and penalties assessed, restitutions and fines)	$5,836,724

Investigations of fraud are time-consuming. The IRS estimates that an intelligence agent, on the average, spends a year investigating each case. Since it still remains for government attorneys to accept prosecution, for the judge or jury to convict, and for the judge to sentence, the full-time commitment in each fraud case is extensive and the outcome uncertain. Collection of taxes and interest must often be postponed until the trial[20] State tax department officials may believe that better resource allocation calls for a greater general audit effort rather than investment in half a dozen agents who spend their time in invesigations that at best average five or six convictions per year. However understandable, this attitude reflects a limited view of cost/benefit analysis. It does not take into account the ripple effects of each serious investigation on the associates and acquain-

[19]Memo from Roy E. Buchanan, Investigation Specialist, to Martin Huff, dated June 15, 1978, and provided to the author by Martin Huff, Executive Officer. The activities reported were accomplished by five field agents between June, 1968, and June, 1974. Thereafter, four trainees were assigned (three auditors and one tax representative) and became permanent field agents a year later. The two completed prosecutions of Franchise Tax Board employees illustrate another role frequently assigned to investigations staff—internal intelligence.

[20]Technically, the taxes and interest, sometimes with penalties, could be collected before the trial, but judges and jurors then appear prejudiced against convicting and sentencing. If the agency has collected, what more should be asked? The difficulties of successfully prosecuting criminal fraud tax cases result in many civil fraud settlements (in the IRS the intelligence division sends them back to the audit division). The taxpayer benefits from civil fraud charges because he avoids the possibility of a prison sentence and, perhaps more importantly, because he avoids general publicity. Neither the IRS nor the states provide for media knowledge unless the case goes to court. Australia is one nation that does publicize civil as well as criminal fraud cases.

tances of the taxpayer. The absence of news media coverage does not mean that individuals interviewed by tax agents will not talk. Moreover, each conviction helps to reassure honest taxpayers that the tax department does act against at least some of the dishonest.

With or without a special investigations unit, a number of problems plague the states in fraud and failure-to-file cases. Mobility and the multistate nature of many taxpayer activities frequently hamper state investigations. Over the years, the IRS has never officially offered data from its fraud investigations to the states. It has maintained that taxpayers would be less cooperative on federal income tax matters if they knew any disclosure would also be utilized by the state to assess fraud penalties. Friendly federal-state relations among field staff members have circumvented general policy in a number of states, just as states have provided information to federal agents making investigations. Although old, the following quotation can stand for recent experiences in several states, according to their tax department officials: "In Wisconsin we have an excellent relationship with the federal staff, and in one of the very most recent cases the federal bureau turned over to us its entire record of assessments and work papers so that we were able to make an assessment in a particularly reprehensible fraud case without the necessity of duplicating the work."[21]

Where a taxpayer fails to file, or his return is fraudulent, the income tax statutes of most states provide for assessment of tax and monetary penalties without a time limit. However, criminal prosecution may be restricted under the states' general statutes of limitations regarding misdemeanors or felonies. Until 1953, for example, Minnesota had a three-year statute of limitations for felonies. Now the statutes permit six and a half years for criminal prosecution of income tax evasion. California has a four-year statute of limitations for felonies. New York has a three year statute of limitations for felonies. Investigations must be completed and prosecutions begun within such time limits; otherwise only monetary assessments and penalties can be levied.

A further difficulty in obtaining prosecutions in fraud cases concerns the official prosecutor handling the case. Usually, state law requires that the tax department refer criminal prosecutions to the district attorney of the county in which the taxpayer resides. Local district attorneys, according to several tax administrators, frequently do not have the technical background and ability to prosecute fraud cases successfully. District attorneys may also hesitate to prosecute local citizens. The head of California's special investigations unit enters a demurrer as far as most *urban* California district attorneys are concerned. He finds them cooperative, knowledgeable, and frequently successful in prosecutions. New York law gives the attorney

[21] A. E. Wegner, "Preventing Tax Evasion in Wisconsin," in *Proceedings of the National Tax Association, 1946* (Sacramento, Calif.: National Tax Association, 1947), p. 130.

general concurrent jurisdiction with district attorneys in the prosecution of income tax violations. Except when a local district attorney has referred a possible tax violation case to the tax department, the attorney general's office handles all such prosecutions. In Oregon, the attorney general handles prosecutions. In Minnesota, the district attorney of Ramsey County (Saint Paul) has that responsibility. Tax fraud prosecutions involve highly specialized law, and there is a critical need for such knowledge if convictions are to be achieved.

Conclusions on Auditing

> A more intensive audit program would provide additional revenue immediately. Past experience in this and other jurisdictions has proved conclusively that the more intensive the administration of a tax, the higher the degree of voluntary compliance by taxpayers. . . . Inadequate auditing is grossly unfair to those taxpayers, from whatever level of income, who have reported their incomes and deductions in accord with the law. With the present high level of taxation, the equity consideration becomes increasingly important.[22]

This quarter-century-old comment states the case equally well today. Few individual and corporation audit programs meet reasonably satisfactory standards. Improvements that have occurred in the auditing of state tax returns have seldom kept pace with increases in the number of taxpayers or the growing complexity of returns. The conclusion remains that audit staffs, inadequate both in number and in competence, and inadequate planning of audit programs are the rule rather than the exception among the states.

Wage and salary withholding and probably quarterly estimates and payments (where required) by both corporations and individuals have aided tax administrators in their collections. Wage and salary withholding has reduced the number of personal income tax returns requiring formal audit to more manageable proportions. And computers, where fully utilized, have further enhanced the quality of preaudits and reduced the proportion of returns requiring full audit attention. Yet a statement made twenty years ago remains true, "No aspect of audit activities needs more attention than the techniques for selection of individual returns for office or field examination."[23] No tax department has the manpower to examine thoroughly every individual return; and in the case of the correct return, a thorough review represents lost effort. New York's adaptation of the IRS's Taxpayer Com-

[22]New York, *Temporary Commission on the Fiscal Affairs of Government: A Program for Continued Progress in Fiscal Management,* vol. 2 (Albany: Williams Press, February, 1955), p. 375.

[23]Clara Penniman and Walter W. Heller, *State Income Tax Administration* (Chicago: Public Administration Service, 1959), p. 196.

pliance Management Study serves as an aid in the audit selection process by identifying returns that are most likely to contain errors. A computer program based on these results enables New York to select those returns which currently are most likely to contain errors. California and several other states have developed computer selection devices based on past audit or preaudit findings from returns filed. Such programs aid but cannot be substituted for the quality selection programming that can follow full field examination of a properly drawn sample of returns. California's selection process is best suited for office auditing, while New York's program is especially useful in field audit selection. Perhaps both methods are needed. In both, the IRS's sharing of its DIF selection of taxpayers for audit would be a supplement.

The annual reports of state tax departments may regale the reader with some of the glories of the state or provide numerous statistics on the number and amount of income tax refunds or give a breakdown of taxpayer filing by geographic area, but they seldom reassure the public that the states are auditing a significant number of returns or are making substantial additional tax assessments. Annual reporting of the latter information might constitute the most persuasive budget data for governors, legislators, and citizens. If the data were accompanied by a statement of the proportion of returns audited, the information might compel attention. The frank statement in Colorado's 1976 annual report could be repeated for both individual and corporate auditing in most of the states: "We have scarcely begun an adequate corporate audit program. In fiscal 1975-76 the number of audits was equal to 1% of the number of corporations filing."[24]

More extensive and effective use of office resources on properly selected returns could allow field auditors to focus on their special role as strategic examiners of the books and records of taxpayers in agriculture, and professions, and business. Many of the states have so few field examiners capable of investigating and auditing that with limited office auditing, the taxpayer with other than wage and salary income may be able to rest in comparative peace during his income life regardless of deficiencies in his reporting. He need merely be consistent in reporting over the years to both the state and the IRS and also avoid the bad luck of having a federal audit come to the state's attention. It is true that he would face one other risk—at the time of his death, the value of his estate might appear too high to some inquisitive office auditor.

The multistate and multinational corporation is less susceptible than the individual taxpayer to critical auditing in most states. The values of IRS corporation auditing stop short of income allocation and apportionment, and corporations do not have estates. The author is not aware of any state tax official who believes that the state's corporation auditing program is

[24]Colorado, Department of Revenue, *Annual Report, 1976* (Denver, 1976), p. 16.

sufficient. For the majority of the states, the only answer lies in increasing the number and quality of corporation audits by the Multistate Tax Commission. Whether state tax departments and state legislatures will support this cooperative administrative venture better than they have developed individual state corporation auditing remains to be seen. California and Oregon alone cannot supply the sophisticated auditing needed, and few other states currently are giving the necessary leadership.

California, New York, Oregon, and Wisconsin continue to rank high on utilization of office resources, coverage and effectiveness of field audits, and ratio of technical audit staff to returns. Even these states, however, have not always kept up with the increasing volume and complexity of returns or with the need for more field audits.

The author's analysis has consistently shown that corporation auditing pays higher returns as a percentage of total collections than does individual auditing. Yet it would seem a strategic error to concentrate exclusively on one. Ratios of audit productivity to collections have different meanings for corporation and individual income taxes. The significantly larger revenues from individual over corporation income taxes in states having both a broad-based individual income tax and a corporation franchise or income tax reflect not only the different economic bases of the two taxes but also the ease of collection of the former through payroll withholding. Narrow cost-benefit analyses will fail to provide the assurance taxpayers need that the "other fellow"—whether law-abiding citizen, narcotics dealer, or corporation—is being audited at least occasionally and is paying his share of income taxes.

Chapter Nine

Intergovernmental Relations in State Income Tax Administration

A significant source of state income tax administrative strength lies in intergovernmental cooperation.[1] Most of the "pay dirt" comes from federal-state cooperation, and much of the following discussion outlines the practices and possibilities in this area over several decades. More recently, interstate cooperation has gained some ground, particularly through the experiment in multistate, joint tax auditing of corporations. Finally, the chapter will evaluate the states' pursuit of administrative goals through federal-state, interstate, and state-local information exchange and cooperation.

The American experiment with federalism dates from the adoption of the Constitution. Until the beginning of the twentieth century, there was virtual separation of actual tax sources used by the national government and the states. Property taxes dominated state-local revenue systems. Excises and customs dominated the national revenue system.[2] The original Constitution gave the national government the power to tax, and the Sixteenth Amendment (adopted in 1913) removed any doubt as to its authority to levy both individual and corporate income taxes. The two

[1]For some references on intergovernmental relations generally, as well as special references on taxation, see William Anderson, *The Nation and the States: Rivals or Partners?* (Minneapolis: University of Minnesota Press, 1955); and U.S., Advisory Commission on Intergovernmental Relations, *A Report to the President for Transmittal to the Congress* (Washington, D.C.: Government Printing Office, 1955). The numerous relevant tax reports of the Advisory Commission contain a fund of data and bibliographic references on the subject. A further major study of federal-state relations is Federation of Tax Administrators, *Federal-State Exchange of Tax Information, 1975* (Chicago: Federation of Tax Administrators, December, 1975); and U.S., Department of the Treasury, Comptroller General, *Better Management Needed in Exchanging Federal and State Tax Information: Report to the Joint Committee on Internal Revenue Taxation, Congress of the United States, GGD-78-23* (Washington, D.C.: General Accounting Office, May 22, 1978).

[2]The states are still barred constitutionally from the use of customs duties. A political barrier so far has barred the federal government from the use of the general sales tax employed by forty-five of the states and the District of Columbia.

world wars and the Great Depression pushed the country so deeply into duplication and overlapping of tax sources, however, that it is futile any more to speak of separation as a goal. Too many states, as well as cities and counties, now employ the income tax for anyone to consider restricting its use by them; and the national government depends on the income tax for the bulk of its revenues.

Complete separation of tax sources at one extreme or complete centralization of taxing at the other is neither politically realistic nor consistent with the maintenance of a vigorous and balanced federalism in a highly developed and interdependent economy. The national government in 1913 assuaged fears of income tax duplication or confiscatory taxation by providing in the national income tax for deduction of income and other state and local taxes.[3] Proposals in the 1930s and later for income tax credits floundered on the resistance of the non-income tax states to what they viewed as federal "coercion" to universalize the income tax. In the last twenty years, not only have more states adopted the income tax, but most have brought their tax base more into line with the federal base, used the federal base, or even used the federal tax and applied percentage rates (table 7). Such individual actions by a state to "simplify" income taxes for its citizens or increase administrative cooperation with the IRS have not, however, caused any state to go further and to accept the 1972 and 1976 congressional offers that the IRS be given the authority to collect income taxes for it.[4]

Federal-State Administrative Cooperation

Whereas federal deductibility of state income taxes and state adoption of the federal base are unilateral efforts, administrative cooperation requires actions by both national and state legislative bodies and executives plus joint efforts by the IRS and the state tax agency to achieve mutual benefits. In practice, cooperative federalism is often a complex activity that can be harmed or assisted by a number of individual actions either at the points of needed formal actions by the governments or at the grass roots level in the efforts of staff members in IRS service centers and district offices and in

[3] As others have noted, the deductibility of state income taxes provided the earliest form of revenue sharing by the national government. States, in effect, could levy income taxes somewhat higher than might have been politically or economically feasible without the federal deductibility. Taxpayers frequently overlook this virtue, though it is doubtful that they forget to take the deduction when filing a federal return.

[4] The State and Local Fiscal Assistance Act of 1972, public law 92-512, included such a provision, and it was repeated in the 1976 IRS Code, sec. 2116; see the discussion of "piggybacking" later in this chapter.

state central or district offices to cooperate graciously and fully. Despite actual and possible failures, administrative cooperation has steadily advanced in the income tax field. The federal government has opened and kept open its income tax returns and its audit reports to state tax administrators, and they, in turn, have made wide use of them in enforcing state income taxation. Arrangements for federal-state exchange of information had been well developed in most states on a continuing basis by 1970, and two states had utilized essentially full exchange as early as 1950. The flurry of criticism of the exchange as a violation of privacy in the mid-1970s was stemmed, and the revised 1976 IRS Code (sec. 6103) reinforced the exchange authority.[5]

The audit exchange has been supplemented in several ways: the IRS (1) makes its Individual Master File (IMF) tapes and withholding employer tapes available as a means for the states to monitor taxpayer filing and reporting and to aid states that have newly established income taxes; (2) permits access to its general computer to locate any taxpayer who has moved out of state; (3) shares to some degree its sophisticated audit selection processes to increase the efficiency and effectiveness of state audits. These and other exchange services have additional value because of the authority of the states to use individual social security numbers (sec. 6109 [d] of the IRS Code) or IRS employer numbers, which permit the necessary computer cross-checking. The possibility in 1975 and 1976 that the states would lose the authority to require social security numbers from taxpayers produced a state lobbying campaign sufficient to secure full reinstatement of state authority to require taxpayers to report their social security numbers on state tax returns.

No state can match the inherent and adduced resources of the federal government in income tax administration. Yet at least some of the states make a direct contribution to improving federal administration with the information their processing and audit activities disclose. Most states, with their own public information services, add to taxpayers' general awareness of the existence of income taxes. By joining inherently superior federal resources with increasingly effective state efforts, and by shortening the distance between two tax points for both taxpayer and administrator, federal-state cooperation serves the ends of economy and effectiveness in administration.[6]

[5]The 1978 report of the comptroller general (*Better Management Needed in Exchanging Federal and State Tax Information*) raised some of these issues again, and in at least three states—Minnesota, Utah, and Wisconsin—tax administrators found this distressing (ibid., pp. 32, 33).

[6]One proposal, without any apparent legislative backing at the moment, would recognize the administrative contribution of the states through some federal funding of state tax enforcement activities. Daniel G. Smith, "Benefits and Disadvantages of Federal Collection of State Individual Income Taxes" (Paper prepared for the Conference on Federal Income Tax Simplification, The American Law Institute and the American Bar Association, Warrenton, Va., January 4-7, 1978), pp. 44-45.

THE STATES' STAKE IN COOPERATION

Boundary lines handicap the state income tax administrator. Withholding, quarterly declarations, and state information-at-source requirements can at best reach only resident payers, domestic companies, and out-of-state corporations authorized to do business within the state. (A state may be able to induce over-the-border corporations to deduct withholding taxes from the salaries of the state's commuting residents if the corporation also does business in that state.) Many out-of-state payers of dividends, interest, rents, and royalties are outside the jurisdictional grasp of any given state. The in-state payer may be tempted to omit these payments from his state return. Nationwide jurisdiction gives the IRS the coverage the individual states lack. Access to taxpayer tapes, returns, and other information in the hands of the IRS provides the states with an independent check on payments from out-of-state payers to in-state payees.

A less tangible, important but not consistent, advantage which IRS administration enjoys as the result of its nationwide scope may be greater freedom from taxpayer influence and political pressures than is likely to be found in many of the states. Being farther from the ballot box than administrative personnel in states lacking merit-system protection, and even in some states with merit systems, federal officials may be in a better position to deal impersonally and impartially with taxpayers. It is an observable fact that taxpayers in most states respect, and perhaps fear, the federal administration more than they do the state. Congress provides more generously for the IRS than do the states, where taxpayers may more actively pressure legislators to be niggardly with administrative funds.[7] These factors restrict the effectiveness of many state tax administrators, and the comparative advantage of federal administration rises accordingly.

Entirely apart from the benefits that states derive from superior federal jurisdiction and resources, cooperation offers advantages of efficiency and convenience, which do not depend on the superiority of one agency over the other. By eliminating at least some duplication in auditing through an automatic exchange of audit results and some direct agreements on differing areas of the audit process, cooperation can bring about a more efficient allocation of resources and greater total coverage. It can also reduce taxpayer irritation, since one field examination suffices as the basis for two tax actions. Easier and less expensive compliance is an important part of the lure of cooperation.

HISTORICAL DEVELOPMENT

The Early Years

Congress first made explicit provision for state access to federal returns

[7]There is some evidence that Congress in its budget process regularly takes into account the fact that agencies such as the IRS have few, if any, lobbyists pressing for agency administrative funds.

in the Revenue Act of 1926.[8] Oral evidence in 1940 indicated that Massachusetts, at least, had sent men to Washington to examine returns before 1926. In general, the 1926 act provided that returns were to be made available to state officers on request of the governor of the state. The revenue acts of 1928 and 1932 essentially reiterated these provisions.[9] Although section 257 of the Revenue Act of 1926 had provided that a list of names and addresses of all federal income tax filers should be compiled and left open to inspection by state officials in each collection district, individual returns were not officially made available to state income tax officials until June, 1931, when an executive order of the president and regulations of the secretary of the treasury were issued persuant to the inspection provisions of the 1926 and 1928 acts.[10] At the same time, individual, joint, partnership, estate, and trust returns were open to any officer of any income tax state, provided the inspection was to be "solely for State Income Tax purposes."[11] A subsequent executive order and accompanying regulations (issued in December, 1932) broadened the earlier provisions to permit inspection of returns for taxes on income derived from intangible property.[12]

Information returns and other written statements filed with the commissioner to supplement or to become a part of tax returns were subjected to the same rules as the tax returns themselves. Authorized state officers could inspect returns either at the commissioner's office or in the offices of IRS agents or revenue collectors if these field officers had custody of the returns.

[8]Section 257 (a) of the Revenue Act of 1926 provided: "Returns upon which the tax has been determined by the Commissioner shall constitute public records; but, except as hereinafter provided in this section and section 1203, they shall be open to inspection only upon order of the President and under rules and regulations prescribed by the Secretary and approved by the President." Section 257 (c) of the same act provided: "The proper officers of any state may, upon request of the Governor thereof, have access to the returns of any corporation, or to an abstract thereof showing the name and income of the corporation, at such times and in such manner as the Secretary may prescribe." For further historical detail, see Clara Penniman and Walter W. Heller, *State Income Tax Administration* (Chicago: Public Administration Service, 1959), esp. pp. 217-34; Federation of Tax Administrators, *Federal-State Exchange of Tax Information, 1975;* and the appropriate footnotes in both references.

[9]Section 55 of the Revenue Act of 1928 and of the Revenue Act of 1932 provided: "Returns made under this title shall be open to inspection in the same manner, to the same extent, and subject to the same provisions of law, including penalties, as returns made under Title II of the Revenue Act of 1926."

[10]U.S., Department of the Treasury, decision 4317, approved June 9, 1931. This decision provided that the returns should be open to inspection "in the discretion of the Commissioner of Internal Revenue, and at such time and in such manner as the Commissioner may prescribe for the inspection, by an officer of any State having a law imposing an income tax upon the individual, upon written application signed by the Governor of such State under the seal of the State, designating the officer to make the inspection and showing that the inspection is solely for State Income Tax purposes."

[11]U.S., Department of the Treasury, decision 4359, issued December 13, 1932.

[12]The Costigan Amendment (public law 40, 74th Cong.) became section 55 (b) 2 of the Revenue Act of 1935.

For state income tax purposes at least, the Costigan Amendment of 1935 was little more than a gratuity.[13] Under the 1932 and subsequent acts, not only the commissioner but also collectors and revenue agents-in-charge could grant permission to state officials to inspect returns for income tax purposes. The permission was extended to all classes of income returns and material supplementary to them.[14] As an extension rather than an innovation, the Costigan Amendment made federal income tax returns filed after December 31, 1934, available to all state tax administrators rather than just to state income tax administrators. Neither this amendment nor subsequent legislation opened federal returns directly to local officials; only state officials for both state and local taxes have access to them.

As early as 1927, two income tax states requested and received transcripts of federal returns. But this action required the naming of the taxpayers whose returns were desired. It did not meet the states' need for a wholesale transfer of information on additional assessments arising out of audit and other enforcement activities. In 1935, Massachusetts attempted to solve this problem by paying federal employees for overtime work to make copies of federal audit adjustments. Further requests led the U.S. Treasury to set up a separate subsection in Washington to make transcripts of audit adjustments for all states requesting the service. The states reimbursed the Treasury for the approximate cost of the work.

The states were not limited to the audit transcript service. The Bureau of Internal Revenue filled numerous requests for photostatic copies of tax returns or supporting information throughout the 1930s and 1940s. Before 1940, all the income tax states except the Dakotas, South Carolina, and Vermont had requested the bureau to make photostatic copies of at least some tax returns. Some of the states making these requests also sent their own people to Washington to make hand transcripts or microfilms of returns, audit reports, or supporting papers. (There was no charge when a state sent its own staff.)

The decision to decentralize (beginning in 1948) the Bureau of Internal Revenue made access to returns easier for many state income tax offices.[15] Today, a federal district office is often located in the same city as the state tax agency. Federal and state employees may be personally acquainted, and one or more federal employees may have worked for the state tax

[13] Ibid.

[14] The statutory provision for inspection contained in the 1928 and 1932 acts was somewhat broadened in the 1934 act and was reenacted in the 1935 form in the 1936 and 1938 acts. The Revenue Act of 1934 duplicated the 1932 provision but added the following ". . . and all returns made under this Act shall constitute public records and shall be open to public examination and inspection to such extent as shall be authorized in rules and regulations promulgated by the President."

[15] Reorganization in 1952 included decentralization and eventually the name change to Internal Revenue Service. President Truman submitted the reorganization plan to Congress, which approved it. See Clara Penniman, "Reorganization and the Internal Revenue Service," *Public Administration Review* (Summer, 1961): 121-30.

agency or a state employee may have worked for the IRS.[16] Although the Washington office of the IRS has continued to define policies for national-state administrative relations, implementation of the policies rests almost exclusively with the district offices and service centers.

A joint conference of state and local representatives with U.S. Treasury officials to discuss intergovernmental tax problems and fiscal relations in 1949 recommended an exchange of information on audit plans and techniques between the national government and the income tax states. And in 1950, before full decentralization of the Bureau of Internal Revenue, the Federal-State Audit Information Exchange Program was initiated as an experiment in cooperative income tax administration.[17]

The first test of the information exchange program was authorized on February 6, 1950, for the states of North Carolina and Wisconsin. Actual exchange of information began in the spring and summer. Colorado, Kentucky, and Montana entered into cooperative agreements to participate in the experiment in 1951 and 1952. Minnesota made a cooperative agreement five years later. Montana discontinued its agreement in 1955. The other five states continued. Only the Wisconsin agreement initially covered exchange of information on corporate income tax audits.

The U.S. Treasury's 1952 *Coordination Study* described the program as follows:

> Under the procedure adopted for the two initial projects, the examining officers in the offices of collectors and revenue agents-in-charge prepare abstracts of audit information for each changed return showing a deficiency in tax.
>
> The abstracts are prepared in longhand by the examining officer at the time his report of examination is made and are attached to the face of the return. After the deficiencies have been listed for assessment, the abstract is detached and forwarded to the State tax authorities. The North Carolina and Wisconsin procedure with respect to the furnishing of abstracts is similar to the Federal practice.[18]

The program differed from the Washington or field office transcript service largely in timing, extent of detail, and in the reciprocal contribution of the states.

[16]Special promotion opportunities in a state, or early IRS retirement, or a personal decision not to move out of the state at the time of an IRS transfer may lure IRS personnel into state employment.

[17]The conference was held in Washington in April, 1949, at the initiation of the secretary of the treasury. The intertwined roots of the 1949 conference and the 1950 program decision can be traced out only in part. The report of the 1942 Committee on Intergovernmental Fiscal Relations, the 1947 and 1948 meetings of a joint conference of representatives of the Congress of the United States and the Governor's Conference, and numerous informal meetings such as those of the National Tax Association and the National Association of Tax Administrators probably all played important roles.

[18]U.S., Department of the Treasury, *Coordination Study* (Washington, D.C.: Government Printing Office, 1953), p. 39. A footnote following the first paragraph of the quotation states: In cases in which the 50 per cent fraud penalty is asserted, only the adjusted taxable income and the deficiency are shown on the abstract."

Minnesota's 1957 agreement differed slightly from the older federal-state arrangements in that it (1) required the state to make its own transcripts of federal office audits; (2) provided that some federal information be passed along to Minnesota in fraud cases; (3) provided, in effect, for the auditing of certain types of lower income tax returns *only* by Minnesota to avoid duplication of federal and state audit efforts; and (4) provided for joint decisions and use of federal- and state-punched cards.

The 1970s

Administrative cooperation expanded in a number of directions in the decades after the 1950s.[19] The exchange of audit information spread into all the states, cooperative auditing developed in several states, computers in the IRS and in state tax agencies made an exchange of tapes more valuable than the older taxpayer lists, and a centralized computer in Martinsburg, West Virginia, offered the means to check new addresses of delinquent taxpayers who had left a particular state. Table 34 lists the dates of the original agreements between the IRS and the states and the several services used by the states.

Agreements

In 1969, the IRS approved a new model coordination agreement for states wishing to cooperate through audit information exchange and provided for its adoption by states already cooperating. A third model agreement was written in 1975. Although all these agreements included provisions for confidentiality, the 1975 and amended 1976 agreements (reflecting the aftermath of Watergate) especially stressed more stringent safeguarding of returns than any earlier one had. In addition, the 1975 model agreeement for the first time provided for termination of the exchange by mutual agreement or by the IRS for any prohibited disclosure. This provision was repeated in the 1976 agreement.[20]

Under the federal-state audit information exchange agreements, the states receive revenue agent reports (RARs) from the IRS that summarize conclusions drawn from auditing taxpayer (both individual and corporation) returns. (In a few states, the tax agency's employees still go to IRS district offices and copy the revenue agent reports.) State agencies either immediately contact the taxpayer and advise him of any additional state income taxes due or file the federal audit adjustment notice for appropriate

[19] Federation of Tax Administrators, *Federal-State Exchange of Tax Information, 1975.* This is a good review of federal-state cooperation and its status in exchange of information at that time.

[20] In an address to the National Association of Tax Administrators on June 19, 1978, William E. Williams, Deputy Commissioner of the IRS, indicated that in addition to the general agreement on coordination, each state and the IRS would probably also reach an implementation agreement that would set forth those particular modifications or additions applicable "locally."

TABLE 34
Federal-State Exchange Agreements and State Use

State	Date of original agreement on information exchange[a]	Use of federal income tax return information		
		Audit adjustments	IMF tapes	Specific taxpayer returns
Alabama	11/24/70	x	x[b]	x
Alaska	9/5/67	x	x	x
Arizona	2/16/66	x	x[b]	x
Arkansas	5/22/63	x	x	x
California	1/5/61	x	x	x
Colorado	3/28/52	x	x[b]	
Connecticut[c]	7/29/70	x		x
Delaware	6/29/65	x	x	x
Florida[c]	9/17/63		x	x
Georgia	7/9/68	x	x	x
Hawaii	8/18/65	x		x
Idaho	2/31/64	x	x	x
Illinois	3/13/63	x	x	x
Indiana	10/31/61	x	x	x
Iowa	12/13/62	x	x	x
Kansas	7/5/60	x	x	x
Kentucky	7/16/51	x	x	x
Louisiana	3/26/71	x	x	x
Maine	8/19/64	x	x	x
Maryland	1/10/63	x	x	x
Massachusetts	12/10/63	x	x	x
Michigan	3/20/65	x	x	x
Minnesota	5/27/57	x	x[b]	x
Mississippi	8/11/66	x	x	x
Missouri	6/13/62	x	x	x
Montana	7/16/51	x	x	x
Nebraska	8/26/63	x	x[b]	x
New Hampshire[c]	5/13/64	x	x	x
New Jersey	9/27/66	x	x	x
New Mexico	12/13/63	x	x	x
New York	11/19/63	x	x	x
North Carolina	2/6/50	x		x
North Dakota	9/14/64	x	x	x
Ohio	8/21/61	x	x	x
Oklahoma	11/15/63	x	x	x
Oregon	12/14/61	x	x	x
Pennsylvania	4/19/65		x[d]	x
Rhode Island	3/30/70	x	x	x
South Carolina	8/24/64	x	x	x
Tennessee[c]	10/28/63	x	x	x
Utah	2/2/61	x	x	x
Vermont	6/4/65	x	x[b]	x
Virginia	6/21/63	x	x	x
West Virginia	10/25/62	x		x
Wisconsin	2/6/50	x	x	x

Sources: Column 1 taken from memo dated April 1, 1974, provided the author by the IRS Research Division. Columns 2, 3, and 4 adapted from table 1, p. 24, Federation of Tax Administrators, *Federal-State Exchange of Tax Information, 1975* (Chicago: Federation of Tax Administrators, December, 1975).

action when the taxpayer's file comes up for review. Immediately assessing additional taxes or instituting inquiries appears to be the more desirable course of action. Both the state, in making such assessments or inquiries, and the IRS, if acting on information supplied by a state, advise the taxpayer of the source of the assessment.

States with limited budgets depend upon IRS audit adjustment information, IMF tapes (discussed later), and withholding data for the collection and enforcement of individual and corporation income taxes. Mississippi reported that some 95% of its individual audit revenue was gained through the use of federal information.[21] For other states, these tools are important supplements to their own efforts. And a few states provide the IRS with valuable services in return for the help they receive. As shown in tables 35 and 36, state audit collections resulting from IRS revenue agent reports totaled $50,692,441 for individual income taxes and $56,227,841 for corporation income taxes in 1975. Additionally, the states gained $68,450,622 from use of IRS IMF tapes (table 35). Table 37's estimation of additional state recoveries of $182,077,434 in 1976 is based on 799,806 individual and 47,090 corporate audit reports plus IMF tapes and other information.[22] Since these statistics are not regularly gathered, we cannot make comparisons over time. The reader should also recognize that the value of the revenue agent reports depends not only on the richness of the state's tax base and its pursuit of taxpayers audited by the IRS but also upon the IRS's audit selection process, which may include a disproportionate number of audits in a particular state.

The IRS has never provided statistics on the value of its recoveries based on state audit information and apparently has never consistently maintained such data. Although even the best state tax administrations might concede that the IRS's greater resources pay off in more audit items for the states than they reciprocate, good state administrations can supply the IRS with a substantial number of audit findings. And with the higher federal rates,

[21] Federation of Tax Administrators, *Federal-State Exchange of Tax Information, 1975,* table 10, p. 62.

[22] Smith, "Benefits and Disadvantages of Federal Collection of State Individual Income Taxes," p. 36.

Note: Because this survey was made in 1975, it does not necessarily reflect current usage. The most probable difference is that at least one or two states have found it possible to use the federal resources more than they did in the past.

[a] It will be noted that several states made agreements before they had an income tax. The federal data can be used to administer other state taxes.

[b] These states report intermittent or minimal use in the past. Minnesota, Nebraska, and Vermont plan expanded use.

[c] These states do not have broad-based individual income taxes, but use federal tax return data in administering other taxes.

[d] Pennsylvania's use of federal tapes is limited to updating annual mailing list.

TABLE 35
Additional State Tax Collections from Federal Exchange—Individual Income Tax

State	IMF tapes[a]			RARs[a]		
	Latest year used	*No. of returns with additional tax*	*Additional taxes collected ($)*	*Latest year used*	*No. of returns with additional tax*	*Additional taxes collected ($)*
Alabama	1966	1,000[b]	100,000[b]	1974	3,259	488,000[b]
Arizona				1974	834	223,310
California	1973/74	67,000	40,100,202[c]	1973/74	46,843	16,348,046
Colorado	1973	11	40,446			
D.C.	1974/75	3,407	1,500,000[b]	1974/75	2,772	358,969[d]
Florida	1973		9,531,787[e]			
Georgia	1970	3,400	386,000	1974	7,889	1,251,986
Hawaii				1974/75	1,261[f]	358,725[f]
Idaho	1972	1,080[b]	144,850[b]	1972	3,120[b]	1,485,120[b]
Illinois	1971 & 1972	31,073[g]	1,637,179[g]	1974	12,000	315,000
Indiana	1972	89,000[b]	2,000,000[b]	1972	4,000[b]	350,000[b]
Iowa	1971	360	216,000	1973	3,475	637,000
Kansas	1970	1,580[h]	167,019[h]	1973	3,700[b]	457,832
Kentucky	1974/75		49,135	1974/75	3,019	682,028[d]
Louisiana	1973	26,000[b]	3,500,000[b]	1973	8,000	600,000[b]
Maine	1971/72		31,283	1974	1,704	97,249
Maryland	1971	1,873	562,746	1973	8,236	1,095,477
Massachusetts	1975		524,765	1975	7,338	2.892,116

Michigan	1971	4,064	878,914	1974	10,307	1,513,000
Minnesota				1974	9,872	2,139,188
Mississippi	1973	15,000[b]	750,000[b]	1973/74	656	199,220
Missouri				1974/75	2,305	217,000
Montana	1973	17,000	225,000[b]	1974	11,520	750,000
Nebraska				1974	4,500	767,100[d]
New Hampshire	1973	2,200[b]	150,000[b]			
New Jersey[i]				1973	200	4,542
New Mexico	1973	15,000	400,000	1973	975	169,944
New York	1973	20,161	3,400,000	1973	77,700	8,900,000
North Carolina				Current	21,241	2,462,832
North Dakota	1972	3,911	276,311	1973/74	652	138,312
Oklahoma	1973	20,000[b]	290,000			
Oregon	1972		42,863	1973	7,694	1,530,426
Rhode Island	1972	900[b]	225,000[b]	1973	797	37,118
South Carolina	1972	218		1974/75	987	523,679
Tennessee	1973	7,500[b]	550,000[b]			
Utah				1973	4,500[b]	700,000[b]
Vermont				1973/74	2,000	327,000
Virginia	1972	3,012	163,122	1974/75	6,577	1,750,167
Wisconsin	1972	1,500[b]	608,000[b]	1973/74	6,807	922,055
Total			68,450,622			50,692,441

Sources: Combined data from tables 2 and 5, pp. 27 and 36, Federation of Tax Administrators, *Federal-State Exchange of Tax Information, 1975* (Chicago: Federation of Tax Administrators, December, 1975).

[a] RAR = revenue agent report; data from state responses available at the time of publication.

[b] Estimated figure.

[c] Cash basis of taxes collected for the entire filing enforcement program. No separate collection figure available for IMF-matching-tape part of total program.

[d] Assessments.

[e] From Florida's intangible personal property tax.

[f] Individual income tax accounts for 90% of total; corporate, 10%.

[g] Information reported for 1971 and 1972 combined.

[h] Partial figure; does not include additional taxes paid to unit other than that responsible for IMF matching.

[i] Commuter tax only.

TABLE 36
Additional State Corporation Income Tax Collections from Use of Revenue Agent Report Audit Adjustments

State	*Latest year used*	*No. of RARs yielding additional taxes*	*Additional taxes collected ($)*
Alabama	1974	308	262,000
Arizona	1974/75	492	62,324
California	1973/74	2,346	17,501,643
D.C.	1974/75	19	12,251
Florida	1974/75	700	415,000
Georgia	1974	800	3,810,800
Iowa	1973	165	450,000
Kansas	1974	325	509,600
Kentucky	1974/75	670	529,014
Louisiana	1973	1,400	350,000[a]
Maine	1974	136	94,795
Massachusetts	1975	3,319	5,760,283
Michigan	1974	176	96,400
Minnesota	1974	314	862,892
Mississippi	1973/74	106	208,719
Montana	1974	281	273,577
Nebraska	1974	250	104,800
New Jersey	1973	1,200	1,982,110
New Mexico	1973	118	61,596
New York	1974	5,154	6,300,000
North Carolina	1974	1,393	2,693,877
Oregon	1974	464	343,315
Pennsylvania	Current	3,215	9,980,000
Rhode Island	1973	140[a]	81,000[a]
South Carolina	1974/75	303	436,086
Tennessee	1974/75	847	2,397,182
Utah	1973	400[a]	200,000[a]
Vermont	1973/74	111	148,577
Wisconsin	1973/74	748	300,000[a]
Total			56,227,841

Source: Federation of Tax Administrators, *Federal-State Exchange of Tax Information, 1975* (Chicago: Federation of Tax Administrators, December, 1975), table 7, p. 54.
Notes: Data taken from state responses available at the time of publication. RAR = revenue agent report.
[a]Estimated figure.

these should make a significant contribution if followed through as those states follow through on IRS notices. In a sample survey for the month of September, 1975, alone, Wisconsin estimated that the federal government derived $401,446 from 273 income tax abstracts it furnished the IRS. For a recent year, Wisconsin estimated that the IRS gained $4.5 million in tax revenues from its state audit adjustments.[23]

[23]Federation of Tax Administrators, *Federal-State Exchange of Tax Information, 1975*, pp. 51-52.

Cooperative Audits

The formal audit information exchange program broke some ground for dividing the audit responsibility between the IRS and the state tax agency. The Colorado and Minnesota agreements in the 1950s explicitly provided that the state would assume audit responsibility for the lower-income returns, whereas the IRS would audit only the larger-income returns in the state. Subsequently, many such understandings were reached with the states. In practice, these agreements further provided some state income tax agencies with the identification of returns selected under the IRS's DIF, or discriminant function, computer program that represent good audit prospects but that federal agents would not have time to audit. Although some ten states in recent years have officially or unofficially participated in the cooperative audit, New York's participation has been among the most successful. That state estimates that in five years the national government gained some $49 million from the state's efforts—$20 million from New York's substantiation audit of federal returns selected by the IRS and $29 million from cases selected by New York and given to the IRS.[24] In turn, in 1976 the IRS tagged 15,000 returns in its audit selection process for audit by New York State.

Most of the cooperative audit agreements spell out a division of audit responsibility based on income lines, but also stipulate that the IRS may provide audit return selection in accordance with its program. Occasionally the IRS undertakes cooperative special investigations. In Oregon during the early 1970s, the IRS undertook a special investigation and audit of commercial fishermen. Oregon auditors worked alongside IRS revenue agents. Where criminal fraud was suspected, the Oregon officials turned over all information to the IRS, since Oregon's tax statutes do not provide for criminal prosecution of tax fraud. If Oregon's statutes had provided for criminal prosecution, the state (in accordance with the federal-state exchange agreement) might have preferred to pursue its own fraud investigations and to withhold such information from the IRS until the disposition of charges. The IRS practices the same "lone ranger" efforts in fraud investigations. Nevertheless, there is behind-the-scenes collaboration, and the IRS has the benefit of the state's information in its investigation, as in this instance.

IMF and BMF Tapes

The most revolutionary change in income tax administration since World War II has been the development and expansion of computer applications in the tax field. Even the enormous change that came with the adoption of state withholding is partially dependent on the computer for its effectiveness. Once the IRS set up its first service center in Atlanta in the early

[24] Ibid., p. 51.

TABLE 37
State Estimates of Federal Tax Information Received during Calendar Year 1976

State	No. of taxpayer records received on IMF tapes	No. of IRS audit reports received		No. of federal tax returns identified by IRS for state audit	No. of copies of federal tax returns received	Other federal tax information received[a]	Estimated additional state taxes assessed as a result of using federal tax information ($)
		Individuals	Corporations				
Alabama	—[b]	9,666	898	—	457	Yes	833,000
Alaska	148,773	1,000	4	—	1	No	414,500
Arizona	828,780	18,656	265	—	10	Yes	1,565,701
Arkansas	693,774	3,000	360	—	368	Yes	1,172,800
California	8,477,454	216,000	8,000	—	900	Yes	45,839,772
Colorado	1,032,760	21,000	1,000	—	—	Yes	588,900
Connecticut	1,257,917	349	917	—	—	Yes	1,875,000
Delaware	230,263	2,500	150	—	25	No	787,000
D.C.	309,622	4,078	14	200	4,284	Yes	2,997,400
Florida	3,128,167	—	1,431	—	216,239	Yes	8,718,949
Georgia	1,759,553	9,115	397	—	250	Yes	5,264,660
Hawaii	345,444	4,000	480	—	12	Yes	420,466
Idaho	305,240	6,399	—[c]	—	2,000	Yes	391,999
Illinois	4,436,497	6,628[d]	—[e]	—	847[f]	Yes	3,814,247[d]
Indiana	1,999,208	10,000	1,500	—	20	Yes	1,849,702
Iowa	1,102,841	3,725	240	—	10	No	1,002,000
Kansas	—[b]	3,824	390	—	100	Yes	769,575
Kentucky	1,153,792	12,130	445	670	—	Yes	1,144,878
Louisiana	1,259,516	5,000	850	—	200	No	5,850,000
Maine	403,401	6,000	200	—	24	Yes	635,000
Maryland	1,620,935	7,200	—	—	7,250	No	1,943,228
Massachusetts	2,288,684	13,000	1,720	—	162	No	10,192,000
Michigan	3,319,749	28,611	639	—	379	Yes	6,094,102
Minnesota	—[b]	37,123	1,241	—	249	Yes	3,635,847
Mississippi	709,238	900	250	—	1,175	Yes	2,000,000

Missouri	1,766,180	17,100	1,416	—	50	No	2,252,441
Montana	290,827	4,987	166	—	200[f]	Yes	1,304,081
Nebraska	607,048	13,000	60	—	10	No	669,500
Nevada	—[b]	—	—	—	—	No	—
New Hampshire	335,215	1,382	257	—	30	Yes	447,947
New Jersey	2,895,873	—	300	—	50	Yes	250,000
New Mexico	417,745	1,120	100	—	20	Yes	699,000
New York	6,700,239	192,000	11,000	15,000	207,000	Yes	38,032,458
North Carolina	—[b]	19,670	1,015	—	1,541	Yes	4,258,665
North Dakota	244,242	2,200	140	—	100	Yes	386,000
Ohio	4,131,250	4,200	2,400	—	200	Yes	670,000
Oklahoma	976,103	70,000	1,000	—	72,000	Yes	1,350,000
Oregon	—[b]	4,328[g]	561[g]	—	100	Yes	1,161,720
Pennsylvania	4,533,875	—	3,944	—	15	Yes	7,225,958
Rhode Island	373,448	4,032	810	—	—	Yes	1,511,446
South Carolina	—[b]	769	186	—	—	Yes	924,274
South Dakota	—[b]	—	5	—	34	Yes	—
Tennessee	1,513,156	—	700	—	400	Yes	2,400,000
Texas	4,565,988	—	—	—	—	No	—
Utah	435,927	6,000	225	—	6,184	Yes	350,000
Vermont	178,535	3,764	100	—	—	Yes	593,218
Virginia	1,899,333	5,750	500	—	25	Yes	4,650,000
Washington	—[b]	—	—	—	10	Yes	—
West Virginia	609,826	600	—	—	12	No	290,000
Wisconsin	1,768,306	19,000	914	—	—	No	2,850,000
Wyoming	—[b]	—	—	—	6	Yes	—
Total	71,054,724	799,806	47,090	15,870	522,949		182,077,434

Source: U.S., Department of the Treasury, *Better Management Needed in Exchanging Federal and State Tax Information: Report to the Joint Committee on Internal Revenue Taxation, Congress of the United States, GGD-78-23* (Washington, D.C.: General Accounting Office, May 22, 1978), appendix 3, p. 44.

[a]Includes tax information on one or more of the following: estates, gifts, employers, exempt organizations, motor fuel, highway users, and others.

[b]State did not receive IMF tape in 1976.

[c]Unknown.

[d]For fiscal year 1976.

[e]Included in total for individuals.

[f]For July 1, 1976, to June 9, 1977.

[g]Represents number audited by state rather than number received.

1960s and the states purchased or rented equipment that could utilize IRS computer tapes, the states made substantial administrative gains. By 1967, the IRS had made its IMF tapes (name, address, taxpayer's and spouse's social security number, wages and salaries, adjusted gross income, deductions, interest income, taxable dividends, federal tax liability, audit adjustments, if any, and IRS coding as to whether return was selected for audit) available to any state tax department on request for a modest charge. Every income tax state has used these tapes on a regular, or at least an occasional, basis. In a 1975 survey, the Federation of Tax Administrators found that all income tax states except Minnesota, Nebraska, and Vermont regularly used the IMF tapes for some purposes (see table 34). Table 37 shows the number of taxpayer records received on IMF tapes by states in 1976. Of the income tax states, only Alabama, Kansas, Minnesota, North Carolina, Oregon and South Carolina did not buy the tapes that year.

Matching the IMF tape with a state's own master tape permits detection of nonfilers. Many states have then gone on to mechanize the inquiry and follow-up process for each federal taxpayer not shown on the state tape. (If the state tape lists a filer who is not on the federal tape, some states automatically, and other states occasionally, pass this information on to the IRS.) The next most common use of the federal tape by the states is to verify the taxpayer's statement of adjusted gross income with that reported on his federal return. Other verifications include filing status, amount of federal income tax, address, spouse's social security number, zip code, itemized deductions, interest and dividend payments. By matching social security numbers, any items on the IMF tape can be matched against items on the state tax department's master tape. Massachusetts, with its classified income tax, verifies dividends, interest, and capital gains.[25] A 1977 GAO study revealed that forty-one of the income tax states received data through IMF tapes on seventy-one million taxpayers and gained $38 million in additional tax assessments in 1976.[26] Any snapshot of this type tends to understate the value of the IMF tapes to the states since each additional taxpayer identified in this way will most likely continue to report and provide cumulative additional taxes that might otherwise have been missed.

The IRS now makes its Business Master File (BMF) tapes available to the states on request. The initial data on these tapes include the corporate taxpayer's identification number, the address of the taxpayer's principal place of business, and the location of the IRS district in which the return is filed. A survey in a few years should provide data on state use and the overall value of BMF tapes.

[25] Ibid., table 4, p. 32, indicates types of uses of IMF tapes by the states as of 1975. The study further indicates that thirty states had recovered some $70 million as a result of using IMF tapes (see table 35 above).

[26] Comptroller General, *Better Management Needed in Exchanging Federal and State Tax Information,* pp. 3 and 10.

An important flaw in the cooperative effort of the 1950s that has continued is the failure to follow through the initial experiment and subsequent efforts with adequate exchanges of information on results and face-to-face conferences for analysis and evaluation. After one or two meetings very early in the pilot project, the IRS in Washington failed to call further conferences until 1957. Since then the program has become largely one of routine exchange of specified audit information on tapes between the state tax department and the field office of the IRS. Despite the value of such local cooperation, it lacks the luster of Washington enthusiasm and official blessing. The comptroller general's 1978 report points to the problem.[27]

State Conformity with Federal Laws

Administrative cooperation has led to some solid achievements in strengthening income tax enforcement and improving administrative resources. Greater state conformity with federal laws and regulations has contributed to simpler administration and compliance and has smoothed the path to fuller administrative cooperation. Table 7 (chapter 2) examined the conformity of state individual income tax laws with the federal code, and table 26 (chapter 8) looked at state conformity at the corporation tax level in some detail.

History and significant recent activities indicate that we are moving toward automatic state conformity with federal income tax laws, especially with regard to the individual income tax, and even to the point of state "taxation by reference to" federal acts. State adoption of federal income tax statutes and regulations has taken five forms: (1) imposition of a state income tax in the form of a specified percentage of the federal tax; (2) adoption of the federal net taxable income, with minor adjustments, as the state tax base and application of state rates; (3) adoption of the federal adjusted gross income as the base for state adjustments; (4) state statutory direction to apply the federal income tax code in lieu of state action either on specific points or on all applicable points not covered by state law; (5) provisions in state regulations calling for use of federal regulations either in lieu of, or as a supplement to, the state regulations. As table 7 (chapter 2) indicates, states now have commonly adopted provisions that fall into categories (3), (4), and (5).

Full-scale taxation by reference to the federal income tax has a long, but checkered, history. In 1922, South Carolina enacted a tax on individuals and corporations at a rate amounting to a flat one-third of the federal income tax, and in 1929, Georgia enacted a similar tax. Both taxes withstood

[27] Ibid., pp. 26-28.

constitutional attacks in which it was alleged that automatic adoption of current and future federal statutes and regulations was an unconstitutional delegation of state legislative power to the U.S. Congress.[28] Yet both states speedily repealed their taxes-by-reference on the apparently paradoxical grounds of administrative difficulty. Such factors as limited and delayed access to federal income tax data, unsolved problems of interstate apportionment of income, budgetary uncertainties, and the loss of state initiative involved in dependence on congressional action were mentioned as reasons for repeal.

Later, New Mexico and Utah levied taxes expressed as a percentage of the federal liability. Utah, in 1951, and New Mexico, in 1953, adopted provisions giving lower-bracket taxpayers the *option* of computing their taxes as a percentage of the federal liability. Utah's provision was limited to taxpayers with incomes under $5,000. New Mexico gave taxpayers with adjusted gross incomes under $10,000 a choice between 4% of the federal tax or the usual New Mexico tax. But again, partly because of administrative complications and partly because of difficulties and defects in legislative drafting, both states gave up these options. Other states have followed. In 1978, Louisiana, Nebraska, Rhode Island, and Vermont determined their taxes as a percentage of the federal tax liability.

Congressional changes can have a disastrous effect, at least temporarily, on an individual state's revenues when the state taxes "by reference to" federal taxes—whether adjusted gross income, net taxable income, or a percentage of the federal tax. The state's reaction may be to revert to an earlier IRS code. Thus Alaska in 1974 applied a rate of 15% of the "total tax that would be payable for the same taxable year to the United States at the Federal tax rates in effect on December 31, 1961." Such "simplicity" becomes almost meaningless over a period of years, and in 1975, Alaska shifted to its own rates applied to federal "taxable income." But this does not necessarily fully solve the problem of revenue stability.

Less far-reaching than adoption-in-miniature of the entire federal income tax structure (including rates and exemptions) is state acceptance of the federal definition of adjusted gross income. Iowa, Kentucky, Montana, and Vermont were among the first states to use the federal adjusted gross income base in their individual income tax laws. The states then provided for a number of adjustments—notably, for interest on government securities, state tax deductions on federal returns, capital gains, taxation of dividends, and accelerated depreciation—before arriving at a minimum taxable income. Today twenty-seven states begin with federal adjusted gross income (see table 7). Corporate income taxes in thirty-three states are

[28] *Santee Mills etc.* v. *Query*, 122 S.C. 158, 115 S.E. 202 (1922); *Featherstone* v. *Norman*, 170 Ga. 370, 153 S.E. 58 (1930); *Head* v. *McKenney*, 6 S.E. 2d 405 (1939). These cases do not necessarily resolve the question of constitutionality in other states and under different circumstances.

based on the income computed for federal tax purposes, subject only to limited adjustments such as adding back the state income taxes deducted from the federal base, subtracting interest on federal obligations, etc. (table 26).

Conformity measures are far from a panacea for all state income tax ills. They do not eliminate such major problems as interstate apportionment of income and definitions of tax residence and situs. The basic problems of tax collection remain. Converting the tax entirely to a percentage of federal liability would radically recast the distribution of tax burdens in some states. With percentage taxation, the state is especially vulnerable to radical changes in revenue due to changes in federal law. (Since Nebraska determines its percentage each year, the problem is less critical there.) Even without a percentage the state may be vulnerable and attempt to solve the problem by tying the federal base to a particular year, but this adds future complexities for the taxpayer.

To the extent that state income tax provisions represent conscious legislative decisions to deviate from federal practices, they are part of the history of self-government, grass-roots initiative, and the "laboratory" function of state legislatures in the tax field. Conformity lessens state individuality and reduces the force of the claim for states' rights in defining income apportionment for multistate and foreign corporations. The easy appeals of taxpayer convenience and administrative simplicity frequently have not been balanced with these older values.

The Advisory Commission on Intergovernmental Relations—with its mixed representation of governors, members of Congress, officers of the federal executive branch, mayors, members of state legislatures, elected county officials, and the public—recommended in 1965 that the IRS assume responsibility for collecting and enforcing state income taxes. Provisions were included in the General Revenue Sharing Act of 1972 for states that wished to do so to turn over the administration of their income taxes (under specified conditions) to the IRS, which would then collect the states' taxes along with federal income taxes and turn back each state's share.[29]

[29]The author has not attempted to unravel the origins of the Advisory Commission's proposal to centralize income tax administration. Larry Woodruff, Chief of Staff of the Joint Revenue Committee (and later Assistant Secretary of the Treasury [Tax Policy]), is one who has been credited with the idea there.

At times there seems to be a substantial gulf in understanding between state tax administrators and the increasingly influential staff of congressional committees. Or perhaps in this instance governors, in states either without income taxes or with budget problems that seemed to make federal takeover an attractive idea, supported the proposal without much consultation back home. In any event, the more active state tax administrators have been working to discourage state piggybacking. John Shannon, Assistant Director, Advisory Commission on Intergovernmental Relations, recently expressed some misgivings of his own about federal collection of state income taxes. See John Shannon, "State Income Taxes: Living with Complexity," *National Tax Journal* 30 (September, 1977): 342, 343.

Neither the National Tax Association nor the National Association of Tax Administrators (NATA) supported the proposal. Moreover, IRS administrators were only lukewarm and did not develop the necessary rules and regulations to implement any takeover until September, 1977. The relevant NATA committee pointed up difficulties for the states in any turning over of responsibility for state income tax administration to the IRS—including (1) problems in state budgeting where late congressional changes in federal tax law affected state revenues; (2) a reduction in audit effectiveness of presently combined federal and state efforts unless the IRS received substantial additional appropriations; and (3) constraints on tax policies permitted the collaborating states.[30] The 1976 General Revenue Sharing Act repeated the earlier offer to the states and made it slightly more attractive, but so far no state has requested the Treasury and IRS to collect its income taxes.[31]

Federal-State Friction

The emphasis on successful administrative cooperation is appropriate, but friction also has occurred. At the same time that progress is made in federal-state tax administrative cooperation, some ground is lost through failure to discuss policies or contemplated administrative changes in advance. Some review of difficulties may help prevent future problems.

STATE ADOPTION OF WITHHOLDING

General Payroll Withholding

A tempest was raised in 1950 when Oregon and Vermont requested that state income taxes be withheld from the salaries of federal employees in their states—as all state governments had done for the federal government since the initiation of national withholding on wages and salaries in 1943. Oregon, which had been the first state to adopt a withholding law (1947), requested federal agencies to withhold, but the U.S. Comptroller General ruled that federal departments had no authority to spend any part of their

[30]Much more critical of the proposal is an NATA special committee report, "Federal Collection of State Individual Income Taxes" (Chicago, December, 1972). For a comprehensive discussion of the entire issue of piggybacking, see Otto G. Stols and George A. Purdy, "Federal Collection of State Individual Income Taxes," *Duke Law Journal,* 1977, no. 1. The article has an excellent bibliography on the whole area of federal-state cooperation. The authors conclude that "states having a high degree of existing conformity and a limited administrative staff which depends entirely or significantly on federal audit reports should find the system to be an attractive alternative" (p. 117). Again, philosophic federalism, or even practical politics, gets short shrift.

[31]The comptroller general's 1978 report (*Better Management Needed in Exchanging Federal and State Tax Information*) sees the prospect for state agreement to piggybacking as "dim" (pp. 22-23).

appropriations to comply with the state's request.[32] The annoyance of Oregon's tax administrators became an explosion in Vermont when national agencies refused that state's request for withholding under the 1951 Vermont Withholding Act. At the height of the latter controversy, an amused bystander said he expected the "gunboats to be called out on Lake Champlain!"

In 1952, Senator Flanders of Vermont introduced a bill in Congress to provide for payroll withholding of state taxes by federal administrators, and the U.S. Treasury and the Bureau of Internal Revenue (not yet renamed the IRS) strongly supported its passage. No one wanted a contest. With the president's signing of the bill on July 17, 1952, negotiations were undertaken by interested states. Federal departments began state withholding from federal employees' wages and salaries in Oregon and Vermont in January, 1953.[33]

States that have subsequently adopted withholding have had the cooperation of all appropriate federal payrolling agencies without fanfare. In a number of instances IRS staff members have directly assisted individual states, including Pennsylvania, where IRS staff prepared the withholding tables, and in California, where last-minute passage of a withholding measure in 1971 necessitated sending appropriate copies to Washington by air in order to obtain instructions for federal agencies in California. Many of the other states have asked for and received the IRS tape of withholding employers in their states.

Even though payroll withholding is no longer in contention, state complaints continue. In addition to the problem of servicemen (discussed below), tax administrators complain that federal agencies frequently neglect to make deposits on withholding taxes in accordance with state law. Claims for interest and penalty are, of course, disregarded. Federal agency reports may be casually identified, and annual summaries may be missing or incomplete. Although Maryland and Virginia suffer most from such federal staff agency carelessness or inattentiveness, almost every state experiences the problem.[34]

[32] *Tax Administrators News* 12 (February, 1948).

[33] In retrospect, the whole hassle might have been avoided if Senator Flanders or other sympathetic congressmen had been asked in 1947 to assure legitimacy of any state request for withholding. The states simply assumed that the federal agencies would accept their requests as they had accepted the earlier national request.

[34] Why do federal agencies not automatically prepare state reports when they prepare reports for the IRS? Of course, deposits for federal withholding income taxes are automatic without the need to write a check, etc. Apparently carelessness in paying state withholding taxes has been institutionalized (probably at quite a low level in the hierarchy) in some agencies. A Minnesota official complains that federal, state, and local government agencies are more casual in reporting and depositing than private industry as a whole. On the other hand, these funds presumably earn interest for some government, which is not necessarily true when private industry is careless. There is also a certain absoluteness about eventual collection from a government agency.

Military Withholding

A different type of withholding conflict between the states and the national government has simmered over several decades—that concerning the withholding of state income taxes by the military at its installations. The military was excluded from the 1952 requirement that federal agencies withhold state income taxes when a state adopts payroll withholding. From 1963 until OMB circular A-38 was released in 1975, it was assumed the military did have an obligation, which it more or less recognized, to submit wage information returns to the state of domicile of each individual, but the OMB circular withdrew this responsibility under its interpretation of the Privacy Act! The new uproar by the states that followed fairly well matched that of Vermont in the 1950s. The Department of Defense hastily agreed to provide the information again, but the states were not satisfied and eventually achieved congressional authorization for withholding.[35]

The Department of Defense had sought to avoid withholding state income taxes on the grounds of administrative cost and the problem of resolving the complex legal question of state of domicile of each member of the armed forces. For income tax purposes, was an individual member of the military a resident where he was stationed, where he enlisted or was drafted, or where he declared his home?[36] Even with the help of modern computers, the Department of Defense would have additional administrative problems if it had to withhold state as well as federal income taxes. On the other hand, as the pay of military personnel had increased over the years, the tax loss for the states also had increased. A federal study estimated that some $94 million had been lost and indicated that reporting was less than 50%.

In 1976, Congress responded to state pressures and approved state income tax withholding by the Department of Defense for military personnel under specified conditions. Individual states had to request income tax withholding in accordance with their own statutes and without discrimination toward military personnel. Military personnel would declare their state of domicile, normally the state from which they had enlisted. The states would take up any questions with the individual service person and in extreme cases would go to court. On July 1, 1977, the Department of Defense began payroll withholding for thirty-four requesting states and the District of Columbia.[37]

[35]U.S., Advisory Commission on Intergovernmental Relations, *State Taxation of Military Income and Store Sales* (Washington, D.C.: Government Printing Office, July 1976); see chap. 3 for a substantial history as well as analysis of the problem.

[36]Ibid., pp. 30-36. One of the complications in the whole domicile issue is not only the fact that nine states do not have broad personal income taxes, but that only nineteen of the income tax states fully tax all military pay. Five states do not tax military pay, and seventeen have varying rules. Some military personnel have developed a habit of choosing their domicile accordingly.

[37]The thirty-four states that requested Department of Defense withholding beginning July 1, 1977, were Alabama, Arizona, Arkansas, California, Colorado, Delaware, Georgia,

Treaty with the United Kingdom

Few things illustrate the world-wide interdependence of peoples today more clearly than the controversy that developed over a proposed tax treaty between the United States and the United Kingdom. The widespread development and expansion of multinational corporations has required complex decisions concerning the appropriate tax base for each nation. In our federal system these decisions have also affected the states. In 1974 and 1975, the secretary of state and the State Department negotiated a tax treaty with the United Kingdom that Presidents Ford and Carter supported for Senate ratification. The treaty cleared in 1978, but with an amendment that permits states to insist on a "unitary business" doctrine in arriving at tax liability (see chapter 8). California, New York, Oregon, and Alaska have used the unitary basis for some years (California for more than forty years with full clearance in court tests). Several other states use the unitary approach to at least some extent. Individual states, the National Association of Tax Administrators, and the Multistate Tax Commission all protested to Congress about the U.S.-U.K. treaty's provisions. California officials estimated that the unamended treaty could have cost the state $125 million.

Other states joined California in its opposition to the tax liability provision because the states are always concerned with anything that might limit different state tax decisions and because state tax officials generally viewed this as an example of national action that fails to consider the impact on the states—and national action taken without state consultation.[38]

INSUFFICIENT POLICY CONSULTATION

As indicated in the above case studies of "withholding" and of the tax treaty with the United Kingdom, much of the envy, fear, irritation, or concern of state tax officials is aimed not just at the IRS but at national government actions more generally. The specific targets of state wrath vary. Some of the fear and irritation stems from uncertainty regarding future congressional and presidential actions. Just as in state governments, few federal tax statutes remain fixed for long. Congressmen may propose change or "reform" in the IRS Code without looking into the possible effects of such action on state tax administration or state tax policy. The president may attempt to develop and implement domestic as well as foreign policies that affect at least some state tax policies. Any of the

---

Hawaii, Indiana, Iowa, Kansas, Kentucky, Louisiana, Maine, Maryland, Massachusetts, Minnesota, Mississippi, Missouri, Nebraska, New Jersey, New Mexico, New York, North Carolina, North Dakota, Ohio, Oklahoma, Oregon, Pennsylvania, Rhode Island, South Carolina, Utah, Virginia, and Wisconsin, plus the District of Columbia.

[38]On September 5, 1977, the *Washington Post* sec. A, p. 17 reported that California State Comptroller Kenneth Cory had told the Senate Foreign Relations Committee in July that "California first learned of the treaty through a routine press release." Such lack of concern about the implications of federal actions for the states is a constant source of irritation to state officials.

national executive agencies may take actions (e.g., the comptroller's original decision relative to agency withholding for the states) that are disadvantageous to the states. State concerns are never uppermost with national officials, and often these officials appear to give no thought to the possible implications of their actions for state tax policy and state tax administrators. When a state official learns of a decision only after it has been announced, he has no chance to be heard.

There *are* dividing lines—although they are not always obvious—between fundamental federal tax policy, where Congress and the national government must be supreme and over which the states can have no veto, and the many areas of tax policy in which appropriate consideration of state tax interests and of administrative implications does not undermine national tax sovereignty. State tax and revenue policies and the effectiveness of their administration are major elements in the integrity of federal membership for the states. The quality of both interstate and federal-state relations downgrades or reinforces federalism in the nation. Unnecessary interference or dictation by the national government may upset the always tenuous federal balance. In 1975 and 1976, the states were faced with a variety of threats from the national government to their tax policies or to their tax administrations. Late in 1974, as a result of the Watergate investigation, new congressional acts cast doubt on the continued ability of the states (1) to require or to use taxpayer social security numbers for identification and cross-checking purposes; (2) to continue the federal-state income tax information exchange; (3) and to secure wage information returns from the military for each state's citizens in service.

Congress eventually responds to most states' appeals for recognition of their needs.[39] Thus the 1976 IRS Code required the secretary of the treasury to enter into an agreement with a state requesting withholding of appropriate state income taxes from the pay of military personnel. Similar provisions apply to other federal employees. The 1976 IRS Code also assured the states of their right to use social security numbers on tax returns for purposes of identification and reinforced state-federal audit information exchange agreements. The settlement of the treaty with the United Kingdom met the states' demands, but the states predict continuing threats of adverse national action before state tax administrators are able to marshal their forces. And that feeds the states' distrust of the national government.

On the other hand, the states do not demonstrate great trust in each

[39]Or as Leon Rothenberg stated at the 1976 National Tax Association meeting, the states are likely to succeed in Congress "if state tax administrators communicate their views to their congressional delegations, together with the necessary research to demonstrate the soundness of the state's positions." National Tax Association-Tax Institute of America, *Proceedings of the Sixty-ninth Annual Conference, 1976* (Columbus, Ohio: National Tax Association-Tax Institute of America, 1976), p. 53.

other or great willingness to cooperate in fully effective ways. State officials appear to forget the number of times one or another state legislature (or state administrator) has acted independently to the detriment of a sister state or even occasionally to the inconvenience of the national government. The New Hampshire and New Jersey decisions to tax commuters, the unwillingness of the states to adopt a uniform definition of residence or domicile to insure against double taxation or tax avoidance, unilateral state actions to abrogate existing reciprocity agreements, special tax incentives to attract industry away from other states, or the failure of states to provide for appropriate exchange of administrative information to achieve better enforcement of state income tax laws may undermine federalism more than any federal tax intervention to date. Successful intergovernmental relations require cooperative interstate, as well as cooperative federal-state, relations.

Interstate Relations

Lack of vertical coordination between federal and state income taxation imposes additional costs on taxpayers and governments alike. Some of these costs are being removed; others are inescapable concomitants of fiscal federalism. Lack of horizontal coordination among the income tax states themselves also imposes substantial costs and may add the inequity of discriminatory double taxation or tax avoidance. The barriers to achievement of greater efficiency and equity through interstate cooperation lie partly in interstate competition and partly in inertia, neglect, provincialism, and inadequate appropriations.

Three main sources of difficulty in interstate income tax relations can be suggested: (1) the overlapping legal jurisdiction to tax both persons and business entities; (2) the diversity of income tax laws, their interpretation, and their application in practice to such matters as residence and multistate income; and (3) the operational limits that state boundary lines impose on tax enforcement efforts in the face of high population mobility. These factors promote taxpayer or administrative grievances of (1) inequity—taxpayers, expecially multistate businesses, may be subject to tax on the same income by more than one state or, of course, they may escape any tax; (2) excessive compliance costs—diversity of laws and regulations makes compliance complex and costly for multistate taxpayers and may require duplicate or multiple audits of the taxpayer's books and accounts; (3) tax avoidance—skillful deployment of income and manipulation of legal domicile may deprive a state of its fair share of tax liabilities and revenue (4) tax evasion—pursuit and prosecution of delinquent taxpayers across state lines is at best difficult and at worst impossible; and (5) unnecessary administrative costs—verifying taxable income and the state's allocable share of it for multistate and foreign corporations involves costly out-of-state auditing.

We have considered some of these interstate issues in earlier chapters, but I will attempt to highlight them here. A full discussion of the difficulties, grievances, and remedies would require a separate book.

OVERLAPPING JURISDICTION AND CONFLICTING APPORTIONMENT FORMULAS

Quite apart from inequities and high compliance costs, overlapping jurisdiction and diversity in rules for apportioning income pose vexing problems for tax administrators. Tax jurisdiction extends to income both at the taxpayer's legal domicile and at the situs or origin of the income. Both domicile and origin may be defined and interpreted differently in different states. Jurisdiction may attach to a corporation's place of incorporation; its principal place of business; its manufacturing, wholesaling, or retailing establishments; or even, as confirmed in 1959 by the *Northwestern States Portland Cement* case, to the site of solicitation of business by a foreign corporation engaged exclusively in interstate commerce.[40] (Congress subsequently limited the effect of this decision but has continued to debate imposing greater precision in state apportionment formulas.) Once jurisdiction to tax a given company's interstate business income has been established, the complexities of the apportionment formula take over. Not only do the components of the formula vary from state to state but the definitions of these components (especially the sales factor) vary widely; even when they are uniform there may be considerable latitude in the administrative interpretation and application of the definitions.

In sum, administrators and corporations in each state face a jungle of complexities through which they have to hack their individual paths, for they are unable to (a) turn to a single interpretation of a uniform law or (b) rely on some central interstate administrative agency to disentangle various state income tax claims on multistate businesses. Short of federal intervention, the main hope for improvement in this and other areas of interstate conflict lies in cooperative efforts stimulated and participated in by the tax administrators themselves. And this is a variant of traditional federalism.

Organization for Cooperation

The enforcement of substantial cooperation entails some giving up of decision-making by all states involved. It also requires agreement among

[40]Minnesota's jurisdiction to tax income deriving from sales in Minnesota under these circumstances was affirmed by the U.S. Supreme Court in *Northwestern States Portland Cement Company* v. *Minnesota,* 358 U.S. 450, February 24, 1959. In its opinion the court stated: "We conclude that net income from the interstate operations of a foreign corporation may be subjected to state taxation provided the levy is not discriminatory and is properly apportioned to local activities within the taxing state forming sufficient nexus to support the same."

state legislators, governors, and tax administrators. *At some point, full and significant interstate cooperation becomes equated with federal "intervention" or outside decision-making for the states.* Before that stage, however, the states could strengthen present administration by improving and extending the exchange of information to help resolve questions of legal residence, prosecute delinquent taxpayers for sister states, verify tax payments to other states, etc. Today joint efforts in auditing multistate corporations offer particular promise.

Voluntary Organizations

The framework for cooperation exists among state income tax administrators in organizations such as the National Association of Tax Administrators and the National Tax Association-Tax Institute of America. Annual meetings provide opportunities for discussion, committee work, resolutions and recommendations, and face-to-face negotiation. Publications by such associations provide further opportunities for exchange of ideas and experience. Both the National Association of Tax Administrators and the National Tax Association-Tax Institute of America have repeatedly appointed committees to deal with problems of interstate administrative concern.

The National Conference of Commissioners on Uniform State Laws drafted a Uniform Division of Income for Tax Purposes Act which has now been adopted by twenty-five states that levy corporation income or franchise taxes.[41] The proposal establishes a uniform three-factor formula of property, payrolls, and sales for apportioning interstate income. In the face of conflicting economic interests among the states, different attitudes toward business tax concessions, and differing convictions as to the "right" index of income, adoption of this uniform formula by all fifty states seems a long way off.

Interstate Compact

Since the mid-sixties, more than a dozen states have worked to achieve cooperative auditing of corporations. The Multistate Tax Commission, despite its slow start, may yet be the means of achieving genuine cooperation and improvement for some of the states. In 1966, in part as a result of congressional action following the U.S. Supreme Court's 1959 decision in *Northwestern States Portland Cement Company* v. *Minnesota,* a few state

[41] As of 1977, the following state legislatures had adopted UDITPA directly or through the Multistate Tax Commission: Alaska, Alabama, Arkansas, California, Colorado, Hawaii, Idaho, Illinois, Indiana, Kansas, Kentucky, Maine, Michigan, Montana, Nebraska, New Mexico, North Carolina, North Dakota, Oregon, Pennsylvania, and Utah. Oklahoma, South Carolina, Virginia, and West Virginia generally follow UDITPA but as of 1977 had not signed agreements. See tables 114 and 115 in U.S., Advisory Commission on Intergovernmental Relations, *Federal-State-Local Finances: Significant Features of Fiscal Federalism,* vol. 2, *Revenue and Debt* (Washington, D.C.: Government Printing Office, March, 1977), pp. 223 and 224.

legislatures agreed to form an interstate compact that would establish the commission and permit joint auditing of corporations for member-state tax purposes. By January 1, 1967, twelve states had joined the compact, which went into effect on August 4, 1967. By 1978, nineteen states, including fourteen with corporation income or franchise taxes, had adopted the compact. An additional twelve states—most of which have corporation income or franchise taxes—are associate members. Other states (and attitudes are generally determined by a state's tax administrators or business lobbyists, the latter having generally opposed the compact) have held off joining the compact either to see what the commission and its staff could accomplish or because they object to the concept.[42]

The Multistate Tax Commission, composed of representatives from the states that have entered into the compact, is the policy organization that also hires the executive director and broadly directs general administrative matters.[43] The executive director has a small staff. In addition to the headquarters in Boulder, staff are now located in regional offices in Chicago and New York. Auditing has been done by the commission's staff and by state auditors loaned by a few member states. The auditors have made some corporation assessments (see pp. 212-13) that member states might not otherwise have secured, but the refusal of several major corporations to permit examination of their records, together with the small staff available, has limited commission audit operations to date. In addition to providing some auditing, the commission has undertaken a program of auditor training for member-state examiners and has attempted to keep member states abreast of any major developments that would affect their corporation tax audits. Up until 1978, state contributions had to go largely to the battle in the courts for the right of the commission to engage in joint audits for several states.

[42] A leading opponent of the interstate compact has argued that "the states need to and are able to develop self-sufficient capabilities for managing their own tax affairs. . . . The vigor of each jurisdiction's enforcement program is proportional to the stamina each tax administrator brings to the task of acquiring and training a professional compliance staff." Abstracted from the covering letter of Daniel G. Smith, a top Wisconsin tax official, date April 17, 1975, which accompanied the paper, "An Appraisal of the Multistate Tax Compact and Commission by a Non-Member State (Wisconsin)," mimeographed (Madison, Wisconsin, April 14, 1975). Our federal system was built and perhaps has been maintained on just such views. Yet adjustments and compromises also have characterized our pragmatic federalism. The reality of corporation auditing today by many of the states whose legislators are unwilling to provide the necessary salary and travel appropriations would not bear close inspection. Even where state budgets are reasonably generous and the revenue department has historically had strong leadership, multistate and multinational corporations provide more and more difficult challenges to tax auditors. At some juncture it may become necessary to take a closer look at the costs of separate state corporation income tax laws and separate state administration (including the costs of equity and nonenforcement) and to consider whether state's rights values do or do not offset these costs.

[43] For a brief history of the origins of the Multistate Tax Commission, see George Kinnear, "The Multistate Tax Commission: A New Experiment in Intergovernmental Relations," *Canadian Tax Journal* 19 (March/April, 1971): 136-43.

Even though the commission has not yet shown continued, substantial audit productivity, it has had other successes. It has strengthened interstate agreement by developing regulations for interpreting the Uniform Division of Income for Tax Purposes Act. Eighteen member states have adopted these regulations and several others are in the process of doing so. Over the years, the commission has secured excellent national publicity in the *Wall Street Journal,* in national news weeklies, in the financial sections of leading newspapers, and occasionally in a front-page story in one or another national daily. With few exceptions, the tone of the stories suggests that they could have been written by the executive director of the commission. Any organization would be willing to pay well for such public relations.

Another success of the commission is one it might have been willing to do without. Major corporations viewed joint state audits as a threat by the states to secure more taxes, as an administrative nuisance, or as a violation of tax secrecy, although their legal argument took other grounds.[44] In any event, the commission ended up in a court fight over its right to conduct audits of corporation books in the name of member states for income or sales tax purposes. The commission won cases in state courts and in lower federal courts, but it also faced the highest court. When the U.S. Supreme Court handed down its decision in *U.S. Steel Corporation et al.* v. *Multistate Tax Commision, Eugene F. Corrigan et al.* (1978), the commission had cause to celebrate, but it now must prove its effectiveness in national auditing for its member states.[45] And member states will have to prove their good faith by making generous appropriations for audit staffing or long-term loans of their best corporation auditors. The commission's victory may also attract additional states to join in the compact.[46]

EXCHANGE OF INFORMATION

Exchange of available information among the states depends on the attitudes of administrators and the technical legal restrictions under which they have to work. Information on statutory provisions or general administrative practices is usually available for the asking. The staff of the Federation of Tax Administrators often acts as a clearinghouse for information desired by a particular state administrator and initiates many inquiries on matters known to be of mutual interest to the states.

Although the statutes of many states authorize tax administrators to make taxpayer return information available to other states, some do not.

[44]The legal argument turned on the compact clause of the U.S. Constitution. Did the compact require congressional approval? Did it pose a threat to the national government? By a vote of 7 to 2, the U.S. Supreme Court held that the compact was legal and was not a threat to national sovereignty.

[45]See Robert M. White, "The Constitutionality of the Multistate Tax Compact," *Vanderbilt Law Review* 29 (March, 1976): 453-69, for a predecision discussion of the issues.

[46]Victory in the Supreme Court has not ended all problems. Some corporations still drag their feet and put needless barriers in the paths of auditors.

Some states permit only limited exchanges or provide that tax information can be made available to other states only on the basis of full reciprocity. A number of states, including Minnesota, have refused full exchange with Wisconsin because Wisconsin had substantially open income tax files from 1923 until 1951 and still provides slightly more openness than other states.[47] Particular secrecy provisions, coupled with statutory exchange provisions, may make state administrators leery of violating their legislative directives. (The author knows of no instance in fact of a state exchanging information with Wisconsin or any other state and finding the information misused.) Some state statutes (e.g., Massachusetts, Missouri, and Utah) do not provide a basis for reciprocal exchange of detailed information with other income tax states. This is especially strange in view of the fact that all income tax states exchange information with the IRS.

Questions involving legal domicile or out-of-state income or tax payments occasion the most frequent informal exchanges. Did X file a return with state B for the year H? Did the return include Y income? Several state administrators indicated to the author that such questions are often raised with other states, and this is confirmed by the survey reported in chapter 4 (p. 117). Sometimes one administrator will call another state administrator about a situation in which his state is blocked from taxing when he suspects the other state has no information on the income that may be going untaxed.[48]

RECIPROCITY

All states with broad-based individual income taxes allow their own residents credit for taxes on income paid to another state. Five states, however, require reciprocity by the states that tax such nonresident income. Eleven states give credit for taxes paid by nonresidents in their states of residence.[49] The strangest reciprocity arrangement (and one that has been costly for Wisconsin) is the 1973 agreement between Minnesota and Wisconsin whereby each state's resident taxpayers file and pay taxes in the state where they live without regard to income earned in the other. Thereafter the two state tax departments calculate the portion of income earned by their residents in the other state. The taxes are then calculated and the net tax balance is paid to the creditor state.[50]

[47]To the annoyance of Wisconsin tax administrators, in the years before 1951 both IRS and Minnesota officials used Wisconsin's "open" tax returns to reinforce their administrative efforts without reciprocating.

[48]See Advisory Commission on Intergovernmental Relations, *Federal-State-Local Finances: Significant Features of Fiscal Federalism 1976-77,* vol. 2, tables 109 and 109a, pp. 206-8, for state provisions as to the definition of "resident" for tax purposes and reciprocity or credits for income taxes paid to other states.

[49]Ibid.

[50]Since Wisconsin taxpayers show a net tax due Minnesota, Wisconsin has paid several million dollars each year to Minnesota. Not only is such an agreement a costly administrative headache, but since Minnesota's effective tax rate is slightly higher than Wisconsin's, part of some Wisconsin taxpayers' taxes are being paid by the rest of the state's taxpayers.

TAX COLLECTION

Collection of unpaid income tax liabilities from taxpayers who have moved from the taxing state has long concerned administrators. Every matching of information-at-source with tax returns or of federal with state returns identifies debtor-taxpayers who have left the state. Wage and salary withholding have improved this situation but have not eliminated it. And withholding introduces the problem of the withholding agent who closes his business and moves on before remitting the taxes he has withheld.

Relying on an old doctrine of the English courts that was carried into the courts of this country in the early nineteenth century, state courts have either refused to get involved or have taken little interest in enforcing a sister state's tax laws.[51] Even some state reciprocity statutes have not significantly affected the courts or removed the barriers to interstate collection. No case of tax enforcement by a sister state has been considered by the U.S. Supreme Court, so the question of application of the full-faith-and-credit clause of the Constitution has not been resolved.

A *tax judgment* by state A will normally be enforced by state B. The problem occurs when state A must secure the initial judgment in state B after a delinquent taxpayer (together with all his property) has moved from state A, but before state A's tax department has established the taxpayer's income tax liability. The states appear to have found it inconvenient to sue for judgment in another state since their legal staff members may not be able to "practice law" in the second state or costs may be excessive for the taxes involved. And always there is the possibility that the other state's courts will not accept the originating state's law or interpretations.[52]

Some states have also found that without any legal action, but with the active cooperation of tax administrators in other states in supplying information and contacting taxpayers, it is possible to track down and collect from some delinquent taxpayers.[53] Yet some state administrators are hesitant to cooperate fully with other states in such collections on the grounds that such requests for assistance would only add to an already excessive administrative burden.

Wisconsin has developed a frequently effective action against delinquent taxpayers who have moved out of state but *into positions with corporations doing business in Wisconsin,* namely, a type of wage/salary garnishment.

[51] Robert A. Leflar, "Out-of-State Collection of State and Local Taxes," *Vanderbilt Law Review* 29 (March, 1976): 443-52. For a historical statement, see Federation of Tax Administrators, "Enforcement of Sister States' Claims," mimeographed (Chicago: Federation of Tax Administrators, July 1, 1950).

[52] Commerce Clearing House, *State Tax Guide* (Chicago: Commerce Clearing House, 1977), section 30 ("Collection of Out of State Taxes"). Several states have on occasion accepted other states' cases in their courts.

[53] As noted earlier, the IRS now has a search procedure which states may activate to locate a taxpayer who has moved out of state. This service is valuable, but unless the taxpayer voluntarily pays, actual collection depends on the willingness of the taxpayer's new state of residence to assist in enforcement.

Not wishing to tangle with the state unnecessarily, such corporations cooperate when they recognize the legitimacy of the claims against their employees.[54] California now has a similar statute.

State-Local Cooperation

Not all states have preempted the income tax within their borders. In some instances, as in Ohio, Pennsylvania, and Michigan, local governments passed income taxes under state constitutional or statutory authority before the states themselves adopted individual income taxes. In other instances, e.g., Delaware, Kentucky, Maryland, and Missouri, the state gave general authority to some or all of its local governments, even though it also used the income tax. And in still other states, e.g., New York, one local jurisdiction was given authority to adopt local income taxes.[55] Administrative arrangements also differ among the states. Initially, all local income taxes—often essentially payroll taxes—were administered by local governments. Where this is the situation, opportunities exist for local coordination and for exchange of information between the state and its local governments. Even with state/local withholding, however, some cracks always appear to develop that make clearances desirable. After administering its own income tax for ten years, New York City in 1976 turned over administration of its income tax to the New York State Department of Taxation and Finance. Maryland and Indiana have authorized local governments to levy a surcharge or an additional percentage to the state income tax which the state then collects from residents of those municipalities. In cases such as New York City and municipalities in Maryland and Indiana, full administrative responsibility rests with the state. New York City's experience, as well as other evidence, continues to suggest that the state is a more efficient collector than local governments in terms of comprehensiveness of enforcement and in terms of cost.

Conclusion

In the tax field, as in many others, the American states continue to be jealous of their prerogatives and reluctant to consider any intergovern-

[54]In 1977, however, a court in an employee's state of residence, Washington, was willing to sustain the employee's claim that Wisconsin had no jurisdiction to collect. Since the state of Washington has no income tax, this could have influenced the court in its decision, which thus would not necessarily serve as a precedent elsewhere .

[55]See U.S., Advisory Commission on Internal Revenue, *Local Revenue Diversification: Income, Sales Taxes, and User Charges* (Washington, D.C.: Government Printing Office, October, 1974), pp. 51-61. The Commerce Clearing House's *State Tax Handbook, 1978* (Chicago: Commerce Clearing House, 1978), p. 672, listed twenty-four cities with populations of over 125,000 that had local income taxes.

mental arrangements under which Congress might restrict their freedom of action. More progress has been made through informal cooperation, buttressed at times by federal or state statutes, in federal-state income tax relations than through all the proposals to date for tax supplements, credits, or takeover of administration. At the professional and technical levels, curiosity and enthusiasm for one's own kind have brought state and federal tax people together for discussion, exchange of information, and joint administrative efforts, even when presidents and governors, congressmen and state legislators, have remained at arm's length.

In the record of cooperative accomplishments, one finds that at one time or another and with varying degrees of intensity, every income tax state has availed itself of federal facilities in income taxation. Without exception, the author found that states making serious use of federal Individual Master File lists, transcripts, revenue agent reports, and related information realize some of their highest yields per unit of cost from such activity.

Turning to interstate relations, one is surprised to find that with all the state complaints against the IRS and the national government, the record of federal-state cooperation to date is better than that of interstate cooperation. The states show greatest unity in the face of possible national government action that would restrict the states, as in the case of the tax treaty with the United Kingdom, Defense Department withholding for state income taxes, or the threat of congressional definition of corporation income that would be taxable by the states. Informal exchanges of information occur on an ad hoc basis, and administrators who have become acquainted and respect each other may confer fairly often by telephone. Nevertheless, parochialism characterizes the majority of state tax administrators and perhaps even more state legislators and governors in designing tax legislation and carrying on tax administration to the competitive advantage of a particular state.

The Multistate Tax Commission stands out as an exception to the generally negative judgment of interstate administrative cooperation. Given a favorable U.S. Supreme Court decision, the states have an opportunity through the commission to prove the value of joint auditing efforts. Success requires resources and cooperation of a high order. Whether the Multistate Tax Commission can lead the way to interstate cooperation and the dramatic possibilities of a horizontal as well as vertical "federalism" is uncertain. At least another decade is needed for judgment.

Chapter Ten

The Future

As recently as 1972, the Advisory Commission on Intergovernmental Relations commented: "The personal income tax represents the last underutilized major revenue source for many states."[1] In that fiscal year the personal income tax produced 21.7% of state tax revenues in contrast to the general sales tax's 29.4%. In 1978, the personal income tax produced 25.7% of state tax revenues and the general sales tax 31.1%. Nevertheless, three states—Connecticut, New Hampshire, and Tennessee—still lack a broad-based personal income tax. Florida, Nevada, South Dakota, Texas, Washington, and Wyoming lack any form of personal income tax. And at least one-fourth of the states continue to tax at relatively low effective rates. What can be said of the future?

Increased Reliance on State Income Taxes

Despite the failure of a number of states to reach the Advisory Commission's goal of state dependence of at least 25% on the personal income tax, the record of the last two decades shows continued growth in the use of personal *and corporate* income taxes by the states. Twelve states have added income taxes (either individual or corporate) for the first time. Only five of the fifty states do not levy either one. Whereas both types of income taxes yielded only 17.5% of state tax revenue in 1957, they accounted for 34.3% in 1977 and 35.2% in 1978. For fiscal year 1978, the income tax (individual and corporate) ranked not only number one for state taxes generally but also as *the* top tax source for twenty-six states.[2] California, New York, Virginia, and many other states have varied their income tax rates as budget needs have shifted.

[1]U.S., Advisory Commission on Intergovernmental Relations, *Federal-State-Local Finances: Significant Features of Fiscal Federalism, 1971-72* (Washington, D.C.: Government Printing Office, 1972).

[2]Here, as elsewhere, the author has separated general sales taxes from other gross receipts and excise taxes.

Until the early sixties, supporters of the income tax had to recognize the depressing effect of recessions on the tax. The intervening years have produced few recessions strong enough to reduce critically the productivity of state income taxes. Instead, economic growth and inflation have dramatized the potential of even flat-rate or only mildly progressive income taxes. Concern for the potentially low yield of an income tax during depressions has shifted to concern for its high yield in periods of inflation and the consequent impact of progressive rates on middle-income families. Historically, memories can be short.

The increased productivity of the income tax has served well to match the growth in demand for state services. Throughout the sixties and most of the seventies, citizens have looked to state governments as well as the national government for a variety of programs. Whenever Congress has responded to calls for a range of social programs, educational aid, or environmental and transportation programs, much of its reaction has been in the form of intergovernmental grants that have required some expenditure by state governments. And state governments have initiated their own programs in all these areas. Taxes have climbed (whether through new taxes or growth) to meet the preference of citizens for increased governmental services.[3]

Additionally, all income tax states have used the tax for varied social purposes as well as for raising revenue. From the beginning, income tax deductions and credits have reflected legislative value judgments of the meaning of tax equity. Today's income tax statutes include provisions designed to serve immediate tax equity considerations and broader social purposes. Twenty-eight states have enacted some form of property tax credit for the elderly or for all low-income taxpayers; seven states have provided a sales tax credit to reduce the regressivity of that tax; and a majority of states have added a growing number and wide variety of deductions, credits, or income exemptions to meet changing views of social considerations. Such use of a major state tax reflects the view of many citizens that tax assistance or incentives offer a superior alternative to more governmental programs to assist individuals.[4]

[3]Following California's overwhelming adoption of Proposition 13, however, one might ask whether citizens have reached a limit in their demands on government or whether Proposition 13 merely represents a summer fluke that will soon pass. Clearly agreeing to reduce or limit taxes is much easier than agreeing on particular program expenditure limitations. If there can be no political agreement on the latter, taxes will not decrease.

[4]Although the author has reservations about the administrative difficulties of using the income tax for many such purposes, outstanding economists such as Charles L. Schulze, e.g., in his *The Public Use of Private Interest* (Washington, D.C.: The Brookings Institution, 1977), advocate the use of the federal tax system, and by implication state tax systems, to encourage action rather than more governmental regulation or programs where possible. As noted elsewhere, the Advisory Commission on Intergovernmental Relations has repeatedly advocated reducing the impact of both property and sales taxes in the states by means of credits against the income tax.

Administrative Effectiveness

In 1957, only nine states had adopted payroll withholding in an effort to achieve better income tax collection. Today all states except North Dakota have payroll withholding, although about a fourth of the states do not require quarterly declarations of nonwage income and current tax payments. Technology has aided tax administrators both through the greatly developed use of computers in processing, preauditing, and collection and through the new economy of the telephone, which has brought tax departments and taxpayers into increasingly direct communication. Closer federal-state ties through growing statutory uniformity and expanded information exchange between the IRS and the states have improved enforcement effectiveness. Millions of dollars are added to every state's treasury each year through IRS revenue agent reports, master tapes, and other services. Finally, the Multistate Tax Commission has slowly made its way as a joint state effort (although the majority of states are not active members) for improved auditing of corporations.

In 1959, it was concluded that income tax administration had improved over the previous decade, but that there were still "major deficiencies in available funds, in numbers and training of personnel, and in the intensity of audit and verification activities . . . in the majority of income tax states."[5] Twenty years later this author must repeat the same judgment. *Administration has improved, but the deficiencies remain.* The multiple improvements have not kept pace with the growing volume of taxpayers or the increasing complexities of enforcement. State legislators have called on tax departments to carry out more policies and greater volumes of enforcement activities than ever before. For example, California's Franchise Tax Board received 3,200,000 returns in 1957 and 9,600,000 returns in 1977. Moreover, the legislature added to the complexity of administration with a growing list of income exemptions and deductions, including a homestead credit administered by the board. Personnel climbed only from 931 to 2,100 regular employees.

To increases in the volume of returns must be added the fact that our society continues in flux. The environment of administration grows ever more complex. Just to maintain today's quality of tax compliance requires great flexibility and effort. Running to keep in place necessitates greater speed every year. To increase the level of compliance, states must show a substantial growth in resources, including that peculiarly limited commodity, managerial planning time. The States have not met the challenge.

What is worse is the fact that the above statements remain largely in the category of judgments. We do not know where we stand in effectiveness of enforcement. A quantitative assessment of the quality of income tax

[5] Clara Penniman and Walter W. Heller, *State Income Tax Administration* (Chicago: Public Administration Service, 1959), p. 259.

administration in the states either collectively or individually over time or at any given time remains outside our skills. The absence of independent measures of income by sector has discouraged state administrators from attempting the limited analysis the IRS has carried on from time to time to compare the gaps in income reported for taxes with the Commerce Department's estimates of sector income in the nation. Comparing the number of departmental employees, as above for California, with changes in the volume of returns between two points in time is a gross measure at best. We do not know the level of enforcement at the beginning or end. We do not know the full implications of the changing technology or the degree to which it adds manpower equivalents. We cannot account for changes in the tax law that may require more (or fewer) employees to stay in place. Perhaps the growth of state econometric models (if they do not build in figures from income tax returns) may provide the basic data on which gross-income reporting gaps can be established.

On the microlevel, only New York (through its taxpayer compliance management program) has sought to establish the types of taxpayers who are most likely to make errors in their returns. Such a program is an aid in audit selection but does not provide information on nonfilers or aggregate data on unreported income. Comparative state studies of administrative effectiveness require a foundation of at least one or more individual state studies. Realistically, this cannot occur until a state develops a model of its economy that does not rely on the state's revenue department for its data.

Needless to say, the author has formed impressions of the effectiveness of administration in different states based on characteristics of the different tax departments. Though qualitative in nature, these judgments rest on some objective comparisons of the income tax states in terms of basic tax statutes, available administrative tools, personnel management and standards, extent of coverage and auditing work, use of computers, and utilization of IRS enforcement information. California, New York, Oregon, and Wisconsin have most of the desired statutory provisions (although New York and Oregon do not provide for felony charges for fraud and Oregon still fails to require current declarations and payment of taxes on nonwage income); these states have quality personnel systems and provide (with the possible exception of New York) competitive pay scales for their auditors; and all four states have regularly used available matching information from the IRS. California, New York, and Wisconsin have special investigative units for pursuance of fraud cases. The budgetary resources of these three states appear to be relatively greater than those of most other states. All four states have active field audit operations, including out-of-state corporation audits, but even in these states, budgets have failed to keep up with increased costs and volumes. A 1% or smaller field audit of corporations must be judged inadequate.

Other states that probably rank in the upper quartile of administrative effectiveness include Alaska, Georgia, Massachusetts, Minnesota, Montana, and North Carolina. These states show relatively strong statutory administrative provisions. Minnesota has not utilized IRS resources as strongly as have the four leaders, nor does its field audit effort match theirs. For different reasons, Georgia, Massachusetts, Montana, and North Carolina do not meet the personnel standards of the leading states. Massachusetts is one of only three states that reduce their collections by allowing an offset to businesses that withhold for the state income tax. The volume of field audits is generally lower in all these states than in the leading states.

Given the degree of our ignorance in measuring tax enforcement effectiveness, the author hesitates to identify states that fall into the lowest quartile, although logic suggests that if there is a top quartile, there must be a bottom quartile. A review of tables 10, 11, 17, and 18 indicates that the statutes of Arkansas, Colorado, New Jersey, Ohio, Pennsylvania, Utah, and West Virginia omit several of the statutory tools deemed desirable. Missing are such provisions as quarterly declarations and current payment of taxes on nonwage income; low gross income return filing requirements; requirements to report IRS changes; or subpoena power for taxpayers or taxpayer records. None of these states has a strong merit personnel system. Tables 34, 35, 36, and 37 further indicate that most of these states do not regularly complement their own enforcement efforts by annually comparing tax filers with IRS tapes on federal filers or by making full use of audit reports available from the IRS. Only statutory changes in these states will assure the administrators adequate tools for carrying out their responsibilities. To these tools must be added greater budgetary resources to increase taxpayer equity and state revenues.

John F. Due has estimated that state sales tax administrators recover all but 1.0%-2.5% of sales taxes due; the percentage figure depends on the differing quality of administration in the individual states. The most parallel figure in income tax administration would be collection of income taxes withheld by businesses. Are the states losing 1.0%-2.5% of withholding taxes due? If reporting and delinquency are not carefully followed up, the figure is not improbable and represents millions of dollars in lost revenue.

In a special September 1979 report (*Estimates of Income Unreported on Individual Income Tax Returns,* Publication 1104), the IRS estimated a gap of 2%-3% between voluntary compliance and payroll withholding for the individual income tax. Overall voluntary compliance in the *legal* economy in 1976 approximated 91%-93%. Since the majority of state administrations appear to be less effective than the IRS, state individual income tax losses from the *legal* economy presumably run 10% or more.

The tentative identification of administrative leaders leaves out some states that may deserve praise today or at least tomorrow. But quantifying the states on the grounds of the age of the tax, the number of statutory administrative tools, the existence of a merit system, or the salary of the director or auditors (all important) does not touch on the utilization of tools, the reality of the merit system, etc. Neither does it account for the socioeconomic characteristics of the states or the traditions of voluntary compliance. Quantitative data that measured the proportion of income accounted for and the proportion of taxes collected would satisfy many questions that qualitative data only hint at.

Administration and Tax Policy

Does heavy reliance on the income tax as a source of revenue mean greater administrative effectiveness? According to a recent study, "the intensity of property tax use (effective rate . . .) was found to be significant in explaining assessment uniformity."[6] Establishing which states have heavily utilized income taxes over the years or adopted income taxes early and sales taxes late, etc., poses no problems. One can go even further by looking at state attitudes toward federal use of income taxes and combining this data with information on state utilization. By any of these measures (tables 1, 2, 3, 4, and 5), slightly more than one-fourth of the states stand out: Alaska, Delaware, Maryland, Massachusetts, Minnesota, Montana, New York, North Carolina, Oregon, Virginia, Vermont, and Wisconsin. The reader will immediately note that six of the eight states earlier suggested as ranking high in administrative effectiveness appear in this list of states that have historically utilized income taxes heavily. Today California has joined the states that place the income tax first in the tax dependence column. Michigan also is high on the list but added its income tax late and continues to rely more on sales taxes and its value-added tax (single business tax) on corporations. A precise ranking of the other high-user income tax states in terms of administration is beyond the skill of the author, but all would easily rank in the upper half in administrative effectiveness and quite possibly in the upper third.

Recommendations

ENFORCEMENT

Most income tax statutes could stand some tightening. Either they did not originally provide all the tools needed for effective administration or they have become dated in some respect. Legislators often give a green light to routine administrative enforcement proposals and in fact expect tax department officials to make recommendations that will aid implemen-

[6]John H. Bowman and John L. Mikesell, "Uniform Assessment of Property: Returns from Institutional Remedies," *National Tax Journal* 31 (June, 1978): 148.

tation. This is another of the myriad general concerns that time does not always allow top-level attention. Yet a statute closely paralleling the Uniform Personal Income Tax Statute proposed by the Advisory Commission on Intergovernmental Relations would improve the immediate tools of many state tax departments and would simplify the exchange of information among the states. Making deliberate tax evasion a felony rather than a misdemeanor would signal to at least some taxpayers that the state views tax fraud as seriously as it does other stealing from fellow citizens and as seriously as do the IRS and some neighboring states.

EQUITY

Some income tax policy changes would aid administrators. Overconcern for niceties can defeat equity in the real world as easily as a lack of concern for ability to pay in choosing a particular tax. Reducing the number of income exemptions and deductions alone would reduce the number of office or field verifications required.[7] Close conformity of state income tax policy in defining adjusted gross income, income exemptions, and deductions with the national law automatically provides one series of easy cross-checks for any state tax administrator. Unless a state appropriates the resources for unusually fine enforcement, leaving most income tax policy decisions up to Congress may promote effective administration and hence equity.

APPROPRIATIONS

Legislators and governors continue to take the narrow view of economy and fail to recognize that additional revenues can be gained from better funding of tax administration. With insufficient budget resources, administrators have not pushed the margins of enforcement activity to a point even remotely approaching a mere return of dollars invested. Every additional dollar invested in audit and compliance activities would return an additional $5, $10, or $20 in taxes. Higher appropriations would serve the ends of economy and equity.

BUDGETING

Despite the increased sophistication of budgeting over the last two decades, most administrators fail to utilize the budget as a tool for administrative planning, performance review, or for informing governors, legislators, and the public of the role and needs of the tax department. Not only may some administrators have little idea of the quality of their own

[7]One legislative test for each new proposed income exemption or deduction might be the data (singly or in the aggregate) available to the tax department for ascertaining the accuracy of the claim. The less public and less available the data, the less desirable the exception to current provisions. Even when data are easily available, however, the cost of checking remains a concern.

enforcement efforts but many may fear publicizing the current level. Yet careful cost/benefit analysis of specific project proposals could almost always be impressive. And the budget that established the reliability of past estimates would be even more convincing.

PERSONNEL

At a time when traditional civil service-merit systems are changing rapidly, only clichés and generalizations come to mind. The fact is that more than half the states have never selected their tax personnel on the basis of a full-scale merit system, and the changes that may be appropriate for a mature civil service may be totally inappropriate. No tax system can do well where a significant number of the employees owe their appointment to a political party or where the turnover of personnel prevents the development of loyalty or the institutional memory of an important number of career civil servants. Too much flexibility resulting from too frequent changes in personnel curses an agency as much as too much inflexibility in an agency controlled by administrators who have been there "forever." Each state and each tax department has the obligation to its taxpayers to find the proper mean between experience and inexperience, flexibility and inflexibility, long careers and turnover, and thereby to administer the tax laws of the state effectively.

ORGANIZATION

No single pattern of organization can be prescribed for the income tax function in all states. An organizational structure which facilitates administrative efforts in one state may thwart them in another. The trend away from tax-by-tax organization will probably contribute to administrative effectiveness to the degree that it combines common functions economically: mail rooms, processing, computer facilities, legal staffs, etc., probably have never justified separation on a tax-by-tax basis. The line function of collections also may need to be combined for most taxes as a convenience to taxpayers and as an economy measure for tax departments. Income tax auditing and fraud investigations may thrive better if separated to a degree. Although New York has recently reorganized on a functional basis after years of having essentially a tax-by-tax organization, its functional reorganization has not meant that each individual in the audit division must take on, for example, sales and income tax audits. Rather, auditors will continue to specialize within the new functional audit division.

FEDERAL-STATE COOPERATION

One of the least expensive ways to improve income tax administration in most states would call for full utilization of all presently available IRS compliance information. Either from lack of personnel or for other, less discernible reasons, the majority of states still do not consistently and fully use the IMF tapes for matching basic state return information with federal return information to assure both that taxpayers have filed a state return and that there are no discrepancies in income reported or in personal exemptions or deductions. If these tapes were matched and service center compliance information and revenue agent reports were followed through in audit assessments, the states could have essentially the same level of individual income tax enforcement as the national government.

INTERSTATE COOPERATION

Despite the subsequent development of a formal structure for joint state audits, much of what was said twenty years ago can be repeated verbatim today:

> Federal-state cooperation cannot meet problems relating to the states' more limited taxing jurisdiction. Here is an area for demonstration of the advantages of the much talked about interstate administrative cooperation. The development of joint audit programs for out-of-state corporate taxpayers offers the states some of their greatest opportunities for administrative savings, increased effectiveness, and improved public relations. Unfortunately, the wide disparity in quality of income tax administration among the states decreases the willingness of the leaders in administration to enter into any general program where their contribution is likely to exceed the proportionate contributions of others. Perhaps, however, the leading states should accept such a burden initially, as the federal government has in its relationships with many of the states. They are likely to find the differential returns to be, not the difference between gain and loss, but differences in the degree of gain.[8]

If the states that presently hold associate membership in the Multistate Tax Commission transferred to full membership, we would have a much better opportunity to test the above "hypothesis." Just as the majority of states have not exploited the opportunities for improving compliance by utilizing all the information made available by the IRS, neither have most states exploited opportunities to be of mutual assistance.

AUDITING

Extensive and efficient auditing is the only insurance policy of good income tax administration. After assuring themselves of the full advantages of cooperation with the IRS and fellow state administrators, each state still has a broad field in which to bring about audit improvements. In fact, only individual state audit improvements will assure the gathering of the fruits of federal-state and interstate cooperation. The best use of limited resources can be promoted by (a) carving out special areas of concentration where federal activity is not so intensive and then exchanging results with the IRS; (b) developing individual state taxpayer compliance programs that will identify and select returns for more intensive office review or field

[8]Penniman and Heller, *State Income Tax Administration*, p. 262.

audit; and (c) speeding up the audit cycle to reduce the lag between the filing and auditing of returns.

COLLECTIONS

Withholding has been a great aid in compliance and collection, but not all taxpayers pay all their taxes through withholding. And employers, as withholding agents, sometimes fail to deposit currently (or at all) the taxes collected. To maintain equity with wage and salary earners, tax departments have an obligation to continue to improve their effectiveness in collecting taxes not due under withholding, taxes withheld, and audit assessments. Each period of economic downturn shows an upturn in the unpaid taxes due the states. As in compliance efforts generally, greater success here would reduce the need for other revenues.

RESEARCH AND STATISTICAL ANALYSIS

1. Few states today fail to inform themselves or the public of the number of returns received, the gross and net taxable income reported, the amounts of deductions and exemptions claimed, and the amount of taxes paid. (Massachusetts is one of the few states that does not publish an annual or biennial report of the department that includes such data.) For policy legislation, it is often desirable that this information be broken down by certain major classes, including income size, income sources, family status, occupational areas, and (possibly) geographic sections of the state.

Few states follow California (and the IRS publishes somewhat similar data) in consistently publishing enforcement statistics that disclose the number of returns arithmetically checked, desk audited, checked with IRS, and field audited together with the additional assessments from each activity (the total, of course, being divided by the number of individual and corporation returns). There is no evidence that publication, even when the statistics suggest that only a small portion of returns have been fully audited, reduces voluntary compliance. Publication informs citizens and legislators and might help develop a lobby for greater effort.

2. Once the actual data—the *reality* of administration—become available, the next step is to develop the *reality* of the state's economy. How many returns should be filed? What amounts of gross and net taxable income (by tax brackets and family status) are we dealing with? Both policy and administrative planning would be illuminated by answers to these questions, but admittedly it is not an easy task. Agreement on standard classifications and definitions of data among the states and between the IRS and the states would be an important step, as would the development of a model of each state's economy.

Another approach to direct measurement of the gaps in income reporting that has occasionally been tried is periodic polling of taxpayers by interviewers entirely independent of the tax agencies. Such interviews would have to be conducted under conditions that rigidly protected interviewees from identification and disclosure of information. Our presently sophisticated knowledge of polling in many behavioral areas should make it possible for trained interviewers to overcome taxpayer resistance and to check, on a scientific sampling basis, the extent and classes of tax evasion.

3. Many special statistical studies can be devised to guide administrative efforts into the most productive channels. Several experiments in setting norms for various income and deduction relationships—gross-to-net income in various lines of business, deductions of various types at different levels of income, etc.—have proved to be useful aids in identifying returns for further investigation. The IRS's Taxpayer Compliance Management Program has proved highly useful, and New York is pleased with its own version of the plan. By making intensive field checks of a random sample of returns, the nature and dimensions of the underreporting problem in each state could be fairly sharply defined by occupational group, income sources, income level, and geographic area. However, such studies would not identify the nonfiler and probably would not be at a level to uncover the fraudulent filer. These cases would require other efforts.

Conclusion

Any established tax deserves administrative nurture. And taxes that provide more than one-third of all state taxes (and more than that in the user states, since five states employ neither corporate nor personal income taxes) demand special care and attention. Only in this way does government keep faith with *all* taxpayers.

The states have made significant advances in enforcing state income taxation over the last two decades, but other developments have at least partially offset these administrative improvements. Citizens will accept continued dependence on income taxes only if the states show no surcease in attention to equitable enforcement. Egalitarian progressive taxation policies remain only symbols unless there is adequate administrative follow-through.

Selected Bibliography

BOOKS AND MONOGRAPHS

Anderson, William. *The Nation and the States: Rivals or Partners?* Minneapolis: University of Minnesota Press, 1955.

Blakey, Roy G., and Blakey, Gladys C. *The Federal Income Tax.* New York: Longmans, Green, 1940.

The Book of the States, 1976-1977. Lexington, Ky.: The Council of State Governments, 1976.

The Book of the States, 1978-1979. Lexington, Ky.: The Council of State Governments, 1978.

Brandon, Robert M.; Rowe, Jonathan; and Stanton, Thomas H. *Tax Politics.* New York: Pantheon, 1976. The bibliographical note, pp. 272-81, is especially valuable, even though it mostly concerns national issues.

Chommie, John C. *The Internal Revenue Service.* New York: Praeger, 1970.

Chown, John F. *Taxation and Multinational Enterprise.* London: Longham, 1974.

Commerce Clearing House. *Professional Corporate Handbook.* Chicago: Commerce Clearing House, 1971.

_______. *State Tax Guide, 1977* (Chicago: Commerce Clearing House, 1977).

_______. *State Tax Handbook, 1978.* Chicago: Commerce Clearing House, October, 1978. Annual publication.

Diogenes. *The April Game.* Chicago: The Playboy Press, 1973.

Due, John F. *State and Local Sales Taxation.* Chicago: Public Administration Service, 1971.

Ecker-Racz, L. L. *The Politics and Economics of State-Local Finance.* Englewood Cliffs, N.J.: Prentice-Hall, 1970.

Edelman, Murray. *The Symbolic Uses of Politics.* Urbana: University of Illinois Press, 1967.

Epstein, Leon D. *Voters and Taxes.* Madison: University of Wisconsin Press, 1964.

Federation of Tax Administrators. *AFTA Bibliography on State Tax Administration, 1950-1977.* RR-74. Washington, D.C.: Federation of Tax Administrators, October, 1977.

_______. "Enforcement of Sister States' Claims." RM-293. Chicago: Federation of Tax Administrators, July 1, 1950. Mimeographed.

_______. "Federal Collection of State Individual Income Taxes." *Report of the Special Committee of NATA. RR-64.* Chicago: Federation of Tax Administrators, December, 1972.

———. *Federal-State Exchange of Tax Information, 1975.* RR-70. Chicago: Federation of Tax Administrators, December, 1975.

———. *State Income Tax Withholding and Declaration of Estimated Tax: Percentage of Collections, Percentage of Tax Returns, Volume of Refund Operations.* RR-45. Chicago: Federation of Tax Administrators, December, 1958.

———. *The Use of the Computer in Administration: Enforcement and Compliance of State Tax Laws.* RR-69. Chicago: Federation of Tax Administrators, July, 1975.

Galbraith, John Kenneth. *The Affluent Society.* Boston: Houghton Mifflin, 1958.

Golembiewski, Robert T., and Rabin, Jack, eds. *Public Budgeting and Finance: Readings in Theory and Practice.* 2nd ed. Itasca, Ill.: Peacock, 1975.

Howard, S. Kenneth. *Changing State Budgeting.* Lexington, Ky.: Council of State Governments, 1973.

Lee, Robert D., Jr., and Johnson, Ronald W. *Public Budgeting Systems.* Baltimore: University Park Press, 1973.

Maxwell, James A., and Aaronson, Richard J. *Financing State and Local Governments.* 3rd ed. Washington, D.C.: The Brookings Institution, 1977.

National Tax Association-Tax Institute of America. *Proceedings of the Sixty-ninth Annual Conference, 1976.* Columbus, Ohio: National Tax Association-Tax Institute of America, 1976. Annual publication containing some relevant papers each year.

Paul, Diane. *The Politics of the Property Tax.* Lexington, Mass.: D. C. Heath, Lexington Books, 1975.

Pechman, Joseph A., ed. *Comprehensive Income Taxation.* Washington, D.C.: The Brookings Institution, 1977.

Pechman, Joseph A., and Okner, Benjamin A. *Who Bears the Tax Burden?* Washington, D.C.: The Brookings Institution, 1974.

Peirce, Neal R. *The Megastates of America.* New York: W. W. Norton, 1972.

———. *The New England States.* New York: W. W. Norton, 1976.

Penniman, Clara, and Heller, Walter W. *State Income Tax Administration.* Chicago: Public Administration Service, 1959.

Phyrr, Peter A. *Zero-base Budgeting.* New York: Wiley, 1973.

Schick, Allen. *Budget Innovation in the States.* Washington, D.C.: The Brookings Institution, 1971.

Schulze, Charles L. *The Public Use of Private Interest.* Washington, D.C.: The Brookings Institution, 1977.

Steffens, Lincoln. *The Autobiography of Lincoln Steffens.* New York: Harcourt Brace, 1931.

Stocker, Frederick D. "The Rough Road to Tax Reform: The Ohio Experience." Working Papers in Public Policy, no. 1. Reproduced by the College of Administrative Science, The Ohio State University, March, 1972; originally prepared for the U.S. Advisory Commission on Intergovernmental Relations as part of the commission's presentation to the President's Commission on School Finance.

Surface, William R. *Inside Internal Revenue.* New York: Coward, McCann, 1967.

Surrey, Stanley S. "Automatic Data Processing and Tax Administration: The potentialities of ADP and Factors Involved in Its Adoption." In *Joint Tax Program: Problems of Tax Administration in Latin America* (1965), pp. 178-200, 200-208;

reprinted in Patrick L. Kelley and Oliver Oldman, *Readings on Income Tax Administration* (Mineola, N.Y.: The Foundation Press, 1973).

Wildavsky, Aaron. *The Politics of the Budgetary Process.* 3rd ed. Boston: Little, Brown, 1978.

GOVERNMENT DOCUMENTS AND PUBLICATIONS

Federal Documents

The Report of the President's Commission on Administrative Management. Washington, D.C.: Government Printing Office, 1937.

U.S., Advisory Commission on Intergovernmental Relations. *Changing Public Attitudes on Governments and Taxes, 1976.* ACIR Survey Report S-5. Washington, D.C.: Government Printing Office, July, 1976.

_______. *Changing Public Attitudes on Governments and Taxes, 1978.* Washington, D.C.: Government Printing Office, 1978.

_______. *Federal-State Coordination of Personal Income Taxes.* ACIR Report A-27. Washington, D.C.: Government Printing Office, 1965.

_______. *Federal-State-Local Finances: Significant Features of Fiscal Federalism, 1971-72.* Washington, D.C.: Government Printing Office, 1972.

_______. *Federal-State-Local Finances: Significant Features of Fiscal Federalism, 1973-74.* ACIR Report M-79. Washington, D.C.: Government Printing Office, February, 1974.

_______. *Federal-State-Local Finances: Significant Features of Fiscal Federalism, 1976-77.* Vol. 2: *Revenue and Debt.* ACIR Report M-110. Washington, D.C.: Government Printing Office, March, 1977.

_______. *Federal-State-Local Finances: Significant Features of Fiscal Federalism, 1978-79.* ACIR Report. Washington, D.C.: Government Printing Office, May, 1979.

_______. *Inflation and Federal and State Income Taxes.* ACIR Report A-63. Washington, D.C.: Government Printing Office, November, 1976.

_______. *Local Revenue Diversification: Income, Sales Taxes, and User Charges.* ACIR Report A-47. Washington, D.C.: Government Printing Office, October, 1974.

_______. *The Michigan Single Business Tax: A Different Approach to State Business Taxation.* ACIR Report M-114. Washington, D.C.: Government Printing Office, March, 1978.

_______. *A Report to the President for Transmittal to the Congress.* Washington, D.C.: Government Printing Office, 1955.

_______. *In Search of Balance: Canada's Intergovernmental Experience.* ACIR Report M-68. Washington, D.C.: Government Printing Office, September, 1971.

_______. *State-Local Finances and Suggested Legislation, 1971.* ACIR Report M-57. Washington, D.C.: Government Printing Office, December, 1972.

_______. *State Taxation of Military Income and Store Sales.* ACIR Report A-50. Washington, D.C.: Government Printing Office, July, 1976.

_______. *Understanding State and Local Cash Management.* ACIR Report M-112. Washington, D.C.: Government Printing Office, May, 1977.

U.S., Comptroller General. *Audit of Individual Income Tax Returns by the Internal*

Revenue Service, Department of the Treasury: Report to the Joint Committee on Internal Revenue Taxation, Congress of the United States, GGD-76-54. Washington, D.C.: General Accounting Office, December 2, 1976.

———. *Better Management Needed in Exchanging Federal and State Tax Information: Report to the Joint Committee on Internal Revenue Taxation, Congress of the United States, GGD-78-23.* Washington, D.C.: General Accounting Office, May 22, 1978.

———. *Collection of Taxpayers' Delinquent Accounts by the Internal Revenue Service, Department of the Treasury: Report to the Joint Committee on Internal Revenue Taxation, Congress of the United States, B-137762.* Washington, D.C.: General Accounting Office, August 9, 1973.

———. *How the Internal Revenue Service Selects Individual Tax Returns for Audit, Department of the Treasury: Report to the Joint Committee on Internal Revenue Taxation, Congress of the United States, GGD-76-55.* Washington, D.C.: General Accounting Office, November 5, 1976.

———. *Internal Revenue Service Assistance to Taxpayers in Filing Federal Income Tax Returns: Report to the Joint Committee on Internal Revenue Taxation, Congress of the United States, GGD-76-49.* Washington, D.C.: General Accounting Office, April 1, 1976.

———. *IRS Can Improve Its Program to Collect Taxes Withheld by Employers: Report to the Joint Committee on Internal Revenue Taxation, Congress of the United States, GGD-78-14.* Washington, D.C.: General Accounting Office, February 21, 1978.

———. *No Apparent Need to Regulate Commercial Preparers of Income Tax Returns: Report to the Joint Committee on Internal Revenue Taxation, Congress of the United States, GGD-65-8.* Washington, D.C.: General Accounting Office, December 8, 1975.

———. *A Proposed Automated Tax Administration System for Internal Revenue Service—An Evaluation of Costs and Benefits: Report to the Joint Committee on Internal Revenue Taxation, Congress of the United States, LCD-76-114.* Washington, D.C.: General Accounting Office, November 23, 1976.

———. *Repetitive IRS Audits of Taxpayers Are Justified: Report to the Joint Committee on Internal Revenue Taxation, Congress of the United States, GGD-77-74.* Washington, D.C.: General Accounting Office, November 18, 1977.

———. *Safeguarding Taxpayer Information—An Evaluation of the Proposed Computerized Tax Administration System, Department of the Treasury, Internal Revenue Service: Report to the Joint Committee on Internal Revenue Taxation, Congress of the United States, LCD-76-115.* Washington, D.C.: General Accounting Office, January 17, 1977.

———. *Use of Jeopardy and Termination Assessments by the Internal Revenue Service, Department of the Treasury: Report to the Joint Committee on Internal Revenue Taxation, Congress of the United States, GGD-76-14.* Washington, D.C.: General Accounting Office, July 16, 1976.

U.S., Congress, House of Representatives, Committee on Ways and Means, Subcommittee on Oversight. *Collection of Delinquent Taxes: A Report of the Steering Committee for the Internal Revenue Service Project of the Administrative Conference of the United States, 1976.* 94th Cong., 2nd sess., 1976.

_______. *Collection of Delinquent Taxes by Internal Revenue Service: Hearings, April 27-August 5, 1976.* 94th Cong., 2nd Sess., 1976.

_______. *I.R.S. Audit Procedures: Hearing, December 14, 1976.* 94th Cong., 2nd Sess., 1976.

U.S., Congress, Senate, Committee on Finance. *Federal, State, and Local Government Fiscal Relations.* 78th Cong., 1st sess., June 23, 1943, Doc. 69.

U.S., Department of Commerce, Bureau of the Census. *Compendium of Government Finances in 1947: State Finances, 1947,* no. 2. Washington, D.,C.: Government Printing Office, 1948.

_______. *Compendium of Government Finances in 1957: State Finances, 1957,* no. 2. Washington, D.C.: Government Printing Office, 1958.

_______. *Historical Statistics of the United States, Colonial Times to 1970.* Bicentennial ed., pt. 2. Washington, D.C.: Government Printing Office, 1975.

_______. *State Government Finances in 1967,* no. 1. Washington, D.C.: Government Printing Office, 1968.

_______. *State Government Finances in 1971* (and subsequent annual reports through 1977). Washington, D.C.: Government Printing Office, 1972-78.

_______. *State Government Tax Collections in 1978.* Ser. GF-78, no. 1. Washington, D.C.: Government Printing Office, 1979.

U.S., Department of Housing and Urban Development, Office of Policy Development and Research. *Property Tax Relief Programs for the Elderly: A Compendium Report.* HUD-PDR-153-2. Prepared by Abt Associates, Inc., Cambridge, Mass., April, 1975.

U.S., Department of Housing and Urban Development, Office of Policy Research and Planning. *Property Tax Relief Programs for the Elderly: An Evaluation.* HUD-PDR-153-1. Prepared by Abt Associates, Inc., Cambridge, Mass., May, 1976.

U.S., Department of the Treasury, Commissioner of Internal Revenue. *Annual Report, 1977.* Washington, D.C.: Government Printing Office, 1977.

State Documents

For more detailed information, the reader is referred to the income tax statutes for each state, the published rules and regulations for the income tax in each state, the annual or biennial budgets of the income tax states, and the annual reports of the Multistate Tax Commission (Boulder, Colo.).

Listed below are most of the available annual/biennial reports of the state tax departments. Some states, e.g., Massachusetts, do not publish such reports. All reports are published from a few months to a year or two after the reporting period.

Alaska, Department of Revenue. *Treasury Report.* Issued annually.

_______. *Revenue News: An Annual Supplement.*

Arizona, Department of Revenue. *Annual Report, 1975/76* and earlier. Phoenix.

California, Franchise Tax Board. *Annual Report, 1976* and earlier. Sacramento.

_______. *Operations Report, 1976/77* and earlier. Sacramento.

Colorado, Department of Revenue. *Annual Report, 1976* Denver.

Delaware, Department of Finance, Devision of Revenue. *Annual Report, 1975 Fiscal Year.* Dover.

District of Columbia, Tax Revision Commission. *Financing an Urban Government.* Washington, D.C.: University of the District of Columbia, 1978. Special Report.

Georgia, Department of Revenue. *Statistical Report, 1976.* Atlanta.

Hawaii, Department of Taxation. *Annual Report, 1975/76.* Honolulu.

Idaho, Division of Department of Revenue and Taxation. *Thirty-second Annual Report of State Tax Commission, Division of Department of Revenue and Taxation, 1976.* Boise.

Illinois, Department of Revenue. *Report to Taxpayers, Fiscal 1976.* Springfield.

Iowa. *Annual Statistical Report.* Des Moines. 1975 individual income tax returns filed in 1976.

———. *Corporation Income Tax Report.* Des Moines. 1976 returns.

Kansas, Department of Revenue. *Annual Report, 1976* and earlier. Topeka.

Kentucky. *Annual Report* ("Forty Years of Tax Administration, 1936-1976"). Frankfort, 1976.

Louisiana, Department of Revenue and Taxation. *Thirty-sixth Annual Report, 1975/76.* Baton Rouge.

Maryland, Comptroller of the Treasury, Income Tax Division. *Summary Report.* Annapolis. Individual income tax returns, 1975.

———. *Condensed Annual Report, 1976* and earlier. Annapolis. The 1974 typed report includes a brief history.

Massachusetts. Occasional publications of general laws and rules and regulations. Boston.

Michigan, Department of the Treasury. *Report of the State Treasurer, 1975/76.* Lansing.

———. *Annual Report of the Commissioner of Revenue.* Lansing.

Minnesota, Department of Revenue. *Biennial Report, 1976/77* and earlier. Saint Paul.

———. *The Minnesota State and Local Tax System.* State and Local Tax Bulletin no. 1, 1974. Saint Paul.

Mississippi. *Service Bulletin, 1975/76.* Jackson.

Missouri, Department of Revenue and State Treasurer. *Annual Combined Financial Report, 1975/76.* Jefferson City.

Montana. *Report of the State Department of Revenue, 1976.* Helena. Biennial report.

Nebraska, Department of Revenue. *Annual Report, 1976* and earlier. Lincoln.

———. *Tax Form Guide, 1976.* Lincoln.

New Jersey, Department of the Treasury, Division of Taxation. *Annual Report, 1976 Fiscal Year.* Trenton.

New Mexico. *Annual Report, 1975/76.* Santa Fe.

New York, Department of Taxation and Finance. *Annual Report.* Albany.

New York, Governor. *Annual Budget Message, 1977/78.* Albany.

North Carolina, Department of Revenue, Tax Research Division. *Biennial Report, 1976.* Raleigh.

North Dakota. *Thirty-second Biennial Report of the Tax Commissioner, 1973-75.* Bismarck.

Ohio, Department of Taxation. *Annual Report, 1976.* Columbus.

Oklahoma, Tax Commission. *Fiscal Year 1976 Annual Report.* Oklahoma City.

Oregon, Department of Revenue. *Biennial Report, 1974-76* and earlier. Salem.

_______. *Personal Income and Corporation Income and Excise Tax Laws and Administration Rules, 1974.* Salem.

_______. *Analysis of Oregon's Personal Income Tax Returns for 1972.* Salem.

_______. *Fifty-three Years of Property Tax Relief in Oregon.* Salem.

Pennsylvania, Department of Revenue. *Taxable Income by County, Size, Income Type, and Poverty Income, 1976.* Harrisburg.

South Carolina, Tax Commission. *Sixty-third Annual Report, 1977* and earlier. Columbia.

Utah, State Tax Commission. *Twenty-third Biennial Report, 1974-76.* Salt Lake City.

Vermont, Department of Taxes. *Biennial Report of the Commissioner of Taxes, 1976.* Montpelier.

Virginia, Department of Taxation. *Annual Report, 1975/76.* Richmond.

West Virginia, Tax Commissioner. *Thirty-sixth Biennial Report, 1976.* Charleston.

Wisconsin, Department of Revenue. *Biennial Report, 1977* and earlier. Madison.

ARTICLES

Allphin, Robert. "The Illinois Federal-State Tape Match Program." In *Revenue Administration, Proceedings of the Forty-third Annual Meeting of the National Association of Tax Administrators,* pp. 83-84. Chicago: Federation of Tax Administrators, 1975.

Back, Kenneth. "Upgrading Non-federal Tax Administration." *Tax Executive* 25 (July, 1973): 303-14.

Baldwin, Claude D. "Federal-State Tax Relationships in 1975." In *Revenue Administration, Proceedings of the Forty-third Annual Meeting of the National Association of Tax Administrators,* pp. 53-57. Chicago: Federation of Tax Administrators, 1975.

Blackman, John A. "What Are the State and Local Tax Administrators Doing?" *National Tax Journal* 27 (September, 1974): 419-25.

Boetsch, Frederick P. "Interstate Cooperative Audits." In *Revenue Administration, Proceedings of the Forty-second Annual Meeting of the National Association of Tax Administrators,* pp. 78-80. Chicago: Federation of Tax Administrators, 1974.

Bowman, John H. "Federal Restrictions on State Taxation of Military Pay: Are They Justified?" *National Tax Journal* 29 (June, 1976): 131-42.

Brannon, Gerard M., and Morss, Elliott R. "The Tax Allowance for Dependents: Deductions versus Credits." *National Tax Journal* 26 (December, 1973): 599-609.

Cahoon, C. R. "Consolidated Annual Wage Reporting for Federal Income Tax and Social Security Tax and State Income Tax and Unemployment Tax Purposes." In *Revenue Administration, Proceedings of the Forty-first Annual Meeting of the National Association of Tax Administrators,* pp. 18-19. Chicago: Federation of Tax Administrators, 1973.

Capataides, Peter. "Reducing Corporation Income Tax Delinquency: The Pennsylvania Program." In *Revenue Administration, Proceedings of the Forty-third Annual Meeting of the National Association of Tax Administrators,* pp. 75-76. Chicago: Federation of Tax Administrators, 1975.

Carley, William M. "Evasion Abroad: Americans Use Schemes in Growing Number of Countries to Avoid Paying U.S. Taxes." *Wall Street Journal,* February 6, 1974.

Clarke, Owen L. "A Report on the U.S. Senate Subcommittee on Financial Depositories." In *Revenue Administration, Proceedings of the Forty-fourth Annual Meeting of the National Association of Tax Administrators,* pp. 11-15. Chicago: Federation of Tax Administrators, 1976.

———. "Review and Status Report on Interstate Taxation Bills Pending in Congress." In *Revenue Administration, Proceedings of the Forty-first Annual Meeting of the National Association of Tax Administrators,* pp. 5-9. Chicago: Federation of Tax Administrators, 1973.

Conlon, Charles F. "Interstate Taxation Bills and Proposals—A Review." In *Revenue Administration, Proceedings of the Thirty-eighth Annual Meeting of the National Association of Tax Administrators,* pp. 13-21. Chicago: Federation of Tax Administrators, 1970.

DeLooze, Theodore W. "Developments in State Taxation of Multistate and Multinational Corporations." In *Revenue Administration, Proceedings of the Forty-fourth Annual Meeting of the National Association of Tax Administrators,* pp. 66-78. Chicago: Federation of Tax Administrators, 1976.

DeYoung, Jack E. "Collection of Delinquent Taxes by Employer Withholding." In *Revenue Administration, Proceedings of the Forty-fourth Annual Meeting of the National Association of Tax Administrators,* pp. 49-50. Chicago: Federation of Tax Administrators, 1976.

———. "Use of Unemployment Compensation Data to Discover Nonfilers." In *Revenue Administration, Proceedings of the Forty-fourth Annual Meeting of the National Association of Tax Administrators,* pp. 50-51. Chicago: Federation of Tax Administrators, 1976.

———. "Wisconsin Tax Appeals: Administrative and Judicial Handling of Cases." In *Revenue Administration, Proceedings of the Forty-second Annual Meeting of the National Association of Tax Administrators,* pp. 15-20. Chicago: Federation of Tax Administrators, 1974.

"Exchange of Information between the I.R.S. and States Means Efficient Tax Collection." *Taxation for Accountants* 11 (July, 1973): 40-43.

Farioletti, Marius. "Tax Administration Funding and Fiscal Policy." *National Tax Journal* 26 (March, 1973): 1-16.

Forst, W. H. "The Role of the State Tax Administrator." In National Tax Association, *Proceedings of the National Tax Association, Sixty-fifth Annual Conference on Taxation,* pp. 128-32. Columbus, Ohio: National Tax Association, 1973.

Fruits, Stanley C. "Enforcement of State Tax Claims Based on Federal Assessments." In *Revenue Administration, Proceedings of the Thirty-eighth Annual Meeting of the National Association of Tax Administrators,* pp. 74-77. Chicago: Federation of Tax Administrators, 1970.

Glaser, Sidney. "Improvement of Taxpayer Public Relations," In *Revenue Administration, Proceedings of the Forty-second Annual Meeting of the National*

Association of Tax Administrators, pp. 118-19. Chicago: Federation of Tax Administrators, 1974.

_______. "New Developments in the Use of Phone Power in Tax Administration." In *Revenue Administration, Proceedings of the Forty-fourth Annual Meeting of the National Association of Tax Administrators,* pp. 48-49. Chicago: Federation of Tax Administrators, 1976.

Goodman, Ernest P. "Applications of the Unitary Principle to Multinational Corporations." In *Revenue Administration, Proceedings of the Forty-third Annual Meeting of the National Association of Tax Administrators,* pp. 73-75. Chicago: Federation of Tax Administrators, 1975.

Gronouski, John A. "The Zip Code Program." In *Revenue Administration, Proceedings of the Thirty-third Annual Meeting of the National Association of Tax Administrators,* pp. 2-4. Chicago: Federation of Tax Administrators, 1965.

Huff, Martin. "State Tax Aspects of the United States-United Kingdom Tax Treaty and the Special Task Force Study of Foreign Source Income." In *Revenue Administration, Proceedings of the Forty-fourth Annual Meeting of the National Association of Tax Administrators,* pp. 8-11. Chicago: Federation of Tax Administrators, 1976.

James, Mildred. "Use of EDP in Processing Individual Income Taxes." In *Revenue Administration, Proceedings of the Forty-fourth Annual Meeting of the National Association of Tax Administrators,* pp. 97-104. Chicago: Federation of Tax Administrators, 1976.

Kennedy, James H. "Experience with Collective Bargaining: Operating with a Labor Union." In *Revenue Administrations, Proceedings of the Thirty-ninth Annual Meeting of the National Association of Tax Administrators,* pp. 39-40. Chicago: Federation of Tax Administrators, 1971.

Kinnear, George. "The Multistate Tax Commission: A New Experiment in Intergovernmental Relations." *Canadian Tax Journal* 19 (March/April, 1971): 136-43.

Kosydar, Robert J. "A Simplified Personal Income Tax Form." In *Revenue Administration, Proceedings of the Forty-first Annual Meeting of the National Association of Tax Administrators,* pp. 48-49. Chicago: Federation of Tax Administrators, 1973.

Kosydar, Robert J., and Bowman, John H. "Modernization of State Tax Systems: The Ohio Experience." *National Tax Journal* 25 (September, 1972): 379-90.

Lindstrom, Thure A., Jr. "Exemption and Deduction Problems—Non-resident Taxpayers." In *Revenue Administration, Proceedings of the Thirty-ninth Annual Meeting of the National Association of Tax Administrators,* pp. 60-62. Chicago: Federation of Tax Administrators, 1971.

McReynolds, Neil L. "Communicating with the Public." In *Revenue Administration, Proceedings of the Thirty-ninth Annual Meeting of the National Association of Tax Administrators,* pp. 23-25. Chicago: Federation of Tax Administrators, 1971.

Mahin, George E. "Internal Audit and Fraud Units." In *Revenue Administration, Proceedings of the Thirty-eighth Annual Meeting of the National Association of Tax Administrators,* pp. 30-32. Chicago: Federation of Tax Administrators, 1970.

Melvin, Robert R. "Computerizing State Tax Administration in Georgia." In

Revenue Administration, Proceedings of the Forty-fourth Annual Meeting of the National Association of Tax Administrators, pp. 41-44. Chicago: Federation of Tax Administrators, 1976.

Metaxas, Nicholas L. "Data Elements Needed for IRS Tape Programs on Corporation Returns." In *Revenue Administration, Proceedings of the Thirty-ninth Annual Meeting of the National Association of Tax Administrators,* pp. 85-87. Chicago: Federation of Tax Administrators, 1971.

_______, chairman. "Report of the Committee on IRS Business Master File Data." In *Revenue Administration, Proceedings of the Forty-first Annual Meeting of the National Association of Tax Administrators,* pp. 99-101. Chicago: Federation of Tax Administrators, 1973.

Mikesell, John L. "Administration and the Public Revenue System: A View of Tax Administration." *Public Administration Review* 34 (November/December, 1974): 615-24.

Milbourne, Robert H. "Econometric Forecasting in Wisconsin: Personal Income Tax Collections." In National Association of Tax Administrators, *Conference on Revenue Estimating,* pp. 19-32. Chicago: Federation of Tax Administrators, 1976.

Mitchel, Philip H. "Use of Federal and Other State Laws to Prosecute Violators of Illinois Revenue Laws." In *Revenue Administration, Proceedings of the Fortieth Annual Meeting of the National Association of Tax Administrators,* pp. 36-37. Chicago: Federation of Tax Administrators, 1972.

Morgan, James R. "Tax Department Reorganization." In *Revenue Administration, Proceedings of the Thirty-seventh Annual Meeting of the National Association of Tax Administrators,* pp. 15-17. Chicago: Federation of Tax Administrators, 1969.

Osganian, George. "Computerizing State Tax Administration in Massachusetts." In *Revenue Administration, Proceedings of the Forty-fourth Annual Meeting of the National Association of Tax Administrators,* pp. 38-41. Chicago: Federation of Tax Administrators, 1976.

Peters, William E. "An Experience in the Functional Integration of Tax Administration." In *Revenue Administration, Proceedings of the Forty-fourth Annual Meeting of the National Association of Tax Administrators,* pp. 47-48. Chicago: Federation of Tax Administrators, 1976.

_______. "The Nebraska Package XN." In *Revenue Administration, Proceedings of the Forty-third Annual Meeting of the National Association of Tax Administrators,* pp. 49-50. Chicago: Federation of Tax Administrators, 1975.

Pionkowski, J. T. "Processing Individual Income Tax Returns: Wisconsin." Paper read at the National Association of Tax Administrators' *Seminar on Management Problems in State Tax Administration,* Bloomington, Minn., 1977.

Pond, Chester B. "Estimating Revenue and Refunds under a New Withholding Plan." In National Association of Tax Administrators, *Conference on Revenue Estimating,* pp. 51-54. Chicago: Federation of Tax Administrators, 1960.

Reiss, A. Gerald. "Federal Prosecution of Mail Fraud Involving False State Tax Returns." In *Revenue Administration, Proceedings of the Forty-second Annual Meeting of the National Association of Tax Administrators,* pp. 32-33. Chicago: Federation of Tax Administrators, 1974.

_______. "Organizing a Special Investigations Bureau." In *Revenue Administration,*

Proceedings of the Forty-third Annual Meeting of the National Association of Tax Administrators, pp. 47-48. Chicago: Federation of Tax Administrators, 1975.

Roberts, Carlisle B. "Judicial Disposition of Tax Appeals: Report on an Experiment." In *Revenue Administration, Proceedings of the Forty-second Annual Meeting of the National Association of Tax Administrators,* pp. 13-15. Chicago: Federation of Tax Administrators, 1974.

Rothenberg, Leon. "A New Look at State Finances: Tax Reductions and Restructured Tax Systems." *National Tax Journal* 27 (June, 1974): 175-83.

Roy, H. J. H., "Audit Selection to Obtain the Greatest Net Revenue." In *Revenue Administration, Proceedings of the Thirty-eighth Annual Meeting of the National Association of Tax Administrators,* pp. 72-74. Chicago: Federation of Tax Administrators, 1970.

Simmons, Al, chairman. "Report on Management Systems Section's Survey of States' BMG Tape Needs." In *Revenue Administration, Proceedings of the Forty-fourth Annual Meeting of the National Association of Tax Administrators,* pp. 92-93. Chicago: Federation of Tax Administrators, 1976.

Smith, Daniel G. "Computer Programs for Control of Delinquency." In *Revenue Administration, Proceedings of the Forty-second Annual Meeting of the National Association of Tax Administrators,* pp. 33-36. Chicago: Federation of Tax Administrators, 1974.

———, chairman. "Report of the Committee on State-Federal Legislative and Administrative Matters." In *Revenue Administration, Proceedings of the Forty-third Annual Meeting of the National Association of Tax Administrators,* pp. 32-33. Chicago: Federation of Tax Administrators, 1975.

Smith, William H. "Automation in Tax Administration." *Law and Contemporary Problems* 34 (Autumn, 1969): 751-68.

Smith, William M. "Reciprocal Interstate Enforcement of Tax Claims." In *Revenue Administration, Proceedings of the Thirty-second Annual Meeting of the National Association of Tax Administrators,* pp. 90-92. Chicago: Federation of Tax Administrators, 1964.

———. "Reciprocal Interstate Enforcement of Tax Claims." In *Revenue Administration, Proceedings of the Thirty-fifth Annual Meeting of the National Association of Tax Administrators,* pp. 94-96. Chicago: Federation of Tax Administrators, 1967.

Southard, Arthur L., Jr. "Use of Terminals in Income Tax Auditing." In *Revenue Administration, Proceedings of the Thirty-eighth Annual Meeting of the National Association of Tax Administrators,* pp. 82-84. Chicago: Federation of Tax Administrators, 1970.

Spellman, Henry A. "A Computerized System for Tracking Taxpayer Inquiries and Correspondence." In *Revenue Administration, Proceedings of the Forty-fourth Annual Meeting of the National Association of Tax Administrators,* pp. 90-92. Chicago: Federation of Tax Administrators, 1976.

Thompson, Earl G. "Disclosure and the Tax Reform Act of 1976." *National Tax Journal* 29 (December, 1976): 391-97.

Throwerer, Randolph W., "I.R.S. Regulations and Rulings: Their Contribution to Improved Tax Administration in the United States." *National Public Accountant* 15 (August, 1970): 8-11.

Tully, James H., Jr. "Innovations in Administration and Policy." In *Revenue Ad-*

ministration, Proceedings of the Forty-fourth Annual Meeting of the National Association of Tax Administrators, pp. 45-47. Chicago: Federation of Tax Administrators, 1976.

Vecchio, Ralph. "Use of a Weighted Sales Factor in Apportioning Corporate Income." In *Revenue Administration, Proceedings of the Forty-fourth Annual Meeting of the National Association of Tax Administrators,* pp. 78-80. Chicago: Federation of Tax Administrators, 1976.

Watt, Graham W. "The Application of Recent Training Developments to State Tax Administration." In *Revenue Administration, Proceedings of the Forty-fourth Annual Meeting of the National Association of Tax Administrators,* pp. 32-36. Chicago: Federation of Tax Administrators, 1976.

Williams, William E. "Improving the Climate in Federal-State Tax Relations." In *Revenue Administration, Proceedings of the Forty-second Annual Meeting of the National Association of Tax Administrators,* pp. 1-4. Chicago: Federation of Tax Administrators, 1974.

Index

Page numbers for charts and tables are in italics

Library of Congress Cataloging in Publication Data

Penniman, Clara.
State income taxation.

Bibliography: pp. 275-86.
Includes index.
1. Income tax—United States—States. 2. Tax administration and procedure—United States—States. I. Title.

HJ4655.A1P43 353.9'3'724 79-20081
ISBN 0-8018-2290-4